# Halsbury's Laws of England
# Centenary Essays
# 2007

*Edited by*
Simon Hetherington
Publisher, Halsbury's Laws of England

LexisNexis®
Butterworths

Members of the LexisNexis Group worldwide

| | |
|---|---|
| United Kingdom | LexisNexis Butterworths, a Division of Reed Elsevier (UK) Ltd, Halsbury House, 35 Chancery Lane, LONDON, WC2A 1EL, and London House, 20–22 East London Street, EDINBURGH EH7 4BQ |
| Argentina | LexisNexis Argentina, BUENOS AIRES |
| Australia | LexisNexis Butterworths, CHATSWOOD, New South Wales |
| Austria | LexisNexis Verlag ARD Orac GmbH & Co KG, VIENNA |
| Benelux | LexisNexis Benelux, AMSTERDAM |
| Canada | LexisNexis Canada, MARKHAM, Ontario |
| Chile | LexisNexis Chile Ltda, SANTIAGO |
| China | LexisNexis China, BEIJING and SHANGHAI |
| France | LexisNexis SA, PARIS |
| Germany | LexisNexis Deutschland GmbH, MUNSTER |
| Hong Kong | LexisNexis Hong Kong, HONG KONG |
| India | LexisNexis India, NEW DELHI |
| Italy | Giuffrè Editore, MILAN |
| Japan | LexisNexis Japan, TOKYO |
| Malaysia | Malayan Law Journal Sdn Bhd, KUALA LUMPUR |
| Mexico | LexisNexis Mexico, MEXICO |
| New Zealand | LexisNexis NZ Ltd, WELLINGTON |
| Poland | Wydawnictwo Prawnicze LexisNexis Sp, WARSAW |
| Singapore | LexisNexis Singapore, SINGAPORE |
| South Africa | LexisNexis Butterworths, DURBAN |
| USA | LexisNexis, DAYTON, Ohio |

© Reed Elsevier (UK) Ltd 2007
Published by LexisNexis Butterworths

A CIP Catalogue record for this book is available from the British Library.

Printed and bound in Great Britain by William Clowes Ltd, Beccles, Suffolk.

ISBN for this volume
ISBN 13: 9781 405 733 915

ISBN 978-1-4057-3391-5

9 781405 733915

Visit LexisNexis Butterworths at www.lexisnexis.co.uk

# FOREWORD

## LORD CHANCELLOR AND SECRETARY OF STATE FOR JUSTICE

## RT HON JACK STRAW MP

As the ink dried on the first copy of *Halsbury's Laws of England*, I doubt that the Editor-in-Chief would have thought that one hundred years later a commemorative edition of essays celebrating the success of his vision would be published. Let alone with a foreword written by the first Lord Chancellor to sit in the House of Commons. It is hard to imagine which would have caused the greater surprise.

As a fellow bencher in the Inner Temple and the holder of the office that has played such a big part, not only in Lord Halsbury's life but in the success of *Halsbury's Laws of England*, it is an honour for me to be able to acknowledge the impact and influence his legacy has had on generations of lawyers.

Lord Halsbury was a uniquely gifted individual. His grasp of legal principles and his pre-eminent mastery in applying them ensured that *Halsbury's Laws of England* quickly became the authoritative guide to all English law. It enshrines the constitutional principle of the rule of law and acts as a constant reminder to all of the poetic words of Thomas Fuller: "To every subject of this land, however powerful, be ye never so high, the law is above you."

Such is the significance of *Halsbury's Laws of England* that since the first edition four Lord Chancellors have taken on the role of Editor-in-Chief, overseeing the publication of three substantively new editions. It is tribute to the quality of this work that *Halsbury's Laws of England* has gone from strength to strength, gaining in size and stature. *Halsbury's* is now available in a variety of formats, is regularly updated and having embraced the electronic age is accessible online from anywhere in the world.

For practitioner and student alike, *Halsbury's* has become an invaluable resource. Its presence in law libraries right across the globe has played a significant role in helping our legal system achieve its status of universal recognition and international admiration. It has been a powerful advocate for a legal system which has been so influential in the development of common law across the world. A system in which the rule of law remains a resolute and immoveable bedrock.

*Halsbury's Laws of England* has been a very welcome part of the English legal system's fabric since 1907. It is my hope that it continues to inform many future generations.

Rt Hon Jack Straw MP
Lord Chancellor
September 2007

# PREFACE

## THE RIGHT SIDE OF HALSBURY

### THE PUBLISHERS' PERSPECTIVE

*Introducing Halsbury*

Where else to start, in presenting any thoughts connected with the centenary of *Halsbury's Laws of England*, but at the beginning of the beginning? By which is meant not the conception of the encyclopaedia – which is the subject of the far abler account by Lord Mackay which opens this collection – but the opening pages of the first volume: Lord Halsbury's introduction to the First Edition.

It is a piece which bespeaks erudition, intended to impress the reader perhaps a little with the learning of its author but no doubt much more with the intellectual weight of the work it introduces. We have deemed it entirely appropriate to reproduce it in these pages, and it is hereby commended to you. Nonetheless, it is also a piece very much of its time. Lord Halsbury flavoured his foreword with a sprinkling of ancient Greek, a liberal serving of Latin and plenty of reference to thinkers in the classical traditions. And it was not an affectation for him to do so; his words read as if he expected them to be routinely understood by his readership. Is it then a reasonable inference that Lord Halsbury took for granted that the lawyers reading his foreword would have received an education grounded in the classics? If such is the case, would he have been right in believing that?

So far as the latter question is concerned, it is plausible to suggest that formal education at the beginning of the twentieth century – at least among those likely to aim at a profession – would still have drawn upon the classical tradition. One is speaking here of a great deal more than the understanding necessary to work with the Latin tags and maxims which have been terms of art in the law for centuries. After all, if a legal *concept* is comprehensible, it hardly matters whether the name of that concept is in English or Latin. However, it may as well be remarked at this point how strong a movement there has been in recent years to remove Latin from the law. The principal justification for this is of course the demystification of the law; *quaere* whether such demystification is necessary as much for the benefit of the profession as for that of the public.

But to return to the question: it seems at least fair to postulate that Lord Halsbury's introduction to the first volume was either aimed at the readership he believed it would have, or intended to impress upon the work the stamp of scholarship, to which he believed that lawyers should aspire. The *gravitas* he leant to that volume by his foreword, and to the whole work by his whole self, undoubtedly added several pounds to the weight of authority of the encyclopaedia. It has been a challenge to the encyclopaedia ever since to maintain that weight – albeit on a different diet.

It is no longer the case that the typical lawyer – if there is such a creature – in the late twentieth or early twenty-first century has had a classical education. Perhaps this is to be deplored but I do not do so here. The fact is that the academic options available in our schools and universities, and the variety of educational histories which successive generations of lawyers bring with them, are wider than ever. It follows that the proportion of those to whom the classics are familiar territory is correspondingly smaller. So to keep its reputation as a work of weight and authority – as *Halsbury's Laws* has done – something else must be happening; the regard that lawyers continue to have for Halsbury must be engaged by some means other than the quantity of classical reference. Doubtless this can be partly set down to history: a reputation can feed itself, after all, but without substance it is a bubble reputation, and for a bubble to grow for 100 years tests credulity.

Lord Halsbury's introduction will bear a little more scrutiny. In one place he suggests – rather hopefully, I feel:

> "Happily the general view of our present lawyers is more in harmony with Cicero's advocacy of clearness and simplicity than appears to have been the case with the lawyers of Cicero's time."

Opinion may be divided on this. Opinion may also be divided on whether it is desirable that the language of the law should be clear and simple. There are many who feel, for sound reason, that simplicity is not the business of the law or lawyers, if precision is thereby dulled.

In another place Lord Halsbury suggests that:

> "it may well be doubted whether any code, call it a digest or anything else, can come up to the digest recommended by the Commission of 1866."

I beg to differ. That Commission, according to Lord Halsbury:

> "recommended a digest, which they defined as a condensed summary of the law as it exists arranged in systematic order under proper titles and sub-divisions, and divided into definite statements or propositions, which should be supported by references to the sources of the law whence they were severally derived, and might be illustrated by citations of the principal instances in which the rules stated have been discussed or applied."

This precisely describes *Halsbury's Laws*, to this day. Lord Halsbury continues:

> "It has occurred to some minds that an attempt might be made by private enterprise to carry out in its main outlines the scheme which was recommended in the report of the Commission appointed in 1866, and such an attempt has been made in this work."

I would offer two comments on this. First, that if (as Lord Halsbury also states) the initial "attempt" was a collection of treatises brought together, the encyclopaedia has evolved into a more integrated work over the century of its existence. Through its indexing and cross-referencing it is designed to be considered as a single work, the full extent of which is accessible whatever one's point of entry. Secondly, I would argue that, with the backdrop of the quasi-constitution that we have in England and Wales, it is more or less impossible for the digest conceived by the Commission to be produced from within the organs of state; in other words, that *only* by private enterprise could the end be attained. Private enterprise has certainly achieved the result, and in so doing *Halsbury's Laws* has achieved a remarkable status: it is a commercial undertaking which has become part of the establishment – long before privatisation, deregulation, contracting-out and Next Steps Agencies became a usual manner of government.

It is in this connection, as much as in the scholarship which Lord Halsbury presented and as much as in the powerful intellects marshalled over the decades to write and edit the encyclopaedia, that we find a specific reason for the longevity of *Halsbury's Laws*. It does for the establishment what the establishment ought to do for itself, by putting the law in one place, by accommodating the expansion of law very nearly as quickly as Parliament and the courts have generated it, by maintaining and improving the accessibility of the vast quantities of information, and by remaining comprehensive. This is a major factor in explaining the regard in which *Halsbury's Laws* is held and why the reputation is more than a bubble.

Where, perhaps, Lord Halsbury's introduction is a little disappointing to the modern reader is in not explaining more fully the reasons that the attempts to expound the law had been unsuccessful up to that time. Perhaps he felt that simply pointing out the diversity of sources and volume of material was enough to deal with any issue of the sort, but even if that were sufficient reason then to refuse the question, it is not so now. The answer, I believe, is peculiarly tied up with the question of the constitution of the United Kingdom. One suspects that a Parliamentary reluctance to digest the existing law has much to do with a deeper reluctance to go down the road of total codification, which in turn might be felt to be tantamount – or on the way – to setting down a written constitution. This is not the place for that debate (which continues to exercise minds, even within these pages) and in any case it is as much a political as a jurisprudential question. But there has always been some uncertainty as to what might be lost in reducing the constitution to writing, or indeed whether anything other than revolution or new independence can ever really occasion a new constitutional basis for government. Constitutional reform in the United Kingdom has never been root and branch; rather it rebuilds or replaces the institutions, piece by piece, and then not always successfully. One is tempted to observe, with the mildest measure of mischief, that being in government is not a guarantee of comprehension of the constitution. Joshua Rozenberg's remarks on the reforms of 2003 serve to make the point.

*The Centenary Collection*

In considering the various and many ways in which the centenary of *Halsbury's Laws* might be marked, there has been some concern to identify a common theme that would, for instance, unite the pieces in this collection. The prevailing opinion has been that to do so would run counter to the principle of this or any encyclopaedia. An encyclopaedia is comprehensive and diverse, not selective: to choose and follow a theme would be to oppose that principle. If anything, our theme should be the absence of a theme: hence the wide range of the pieces in this volume. Yet it is possible to discern two threads linking these essays, and further to see a clear connection to the encyclopaedia itself; happily, neither of these interferes with my notion of what the encyclopaedia should represent. The common elements concern access to the law and the operation of right, described separately below but clearly closely connected.

*Access to the law*

By "access to the law" I do not mean, as some would like, *free* access to the law; rather the forging of a link between the making of law and being governed by it, which is the business, ultimately, of lawyers and law publishers alike. So in these pages can be found some observations which touch explicitly on this area and others where the connection is beneath the surface but undeniably there.

Where it is explicitly referred to, free access to the law is generally held by the authors of these pieces either as an end desirable in itself or as a fact, though in the latter case usually with the accompanying observation that the access to materials without more, is at least unhelpful and quite possibly dangerous, if one does not have the skill to navigate and interpret them. From direct knowledge it can be related that *Halsbury's Laws* is used by members of the public in libraries and community centres, and to that extent those people are freely accessing its contents. But that is something different. *Halsbury's Laws* is not the law. It may be regarded as authoritative; it may be an essential path to understanding some elements of the law; but it is both more and less than the law itself. More, in the sense that it has the added value of the expert in organising the materials of the law and in showing what the law, from all its sources, requires of any person in any circumstances; less, in that Halsbury does not have the force of law. It is not a statute; it is not a binding decision of a superior court, though it may be the means of discerning what that binding decision may be.

**Professor Niall Whitty**, among many other accomplishments, is General Editor of *The Stair Memorial Encyclopaedia of the Laws of Scotland* (which he describes as a "sibling" of *Halsbury's Laws* – jealously and rightly protecting the perception of Scots law as an equal and independent system). His account of that encyclopaedia is a most valuable one, but just as interesting is his analysis of the classification of law. One must evidently acknowledge the major differences between English and Scots law: the latter is rooted in the institutional tradition; legislation emanating from Westminster varies in both substance and detail in application to Scotland; and since 1998 there is now a Scottish Parliament with a developing power to take the law on a diverging path. And in so acknowledging one must further recognise that any given method of classifying the law may not suit two systems equally well. The debate which Professor Whitty joins in his article describes the competing arguments in favour of classification of the law by institutional principles and classification by alphabetical organisation. It is as you would expect a scholarly debate (a fact of which Lord Halsbury would have no doubt approved), but at a simplistic level it is about access to the law. A taxonomy which does not promote or enable such access is of little value.

The bizarre juxtaposition of subject areas in *Halsbury's Laws* is highlighted by some of the fiercest critics of an alphabetical taxonomy (noted neutrally by Professor Whitty). In this writer's view such examples are an easy target. No doubt they do offend against the jurisprudential aesthetic of an institutional or conceptual arrangement of law, but such an arrangement (again in the writer's view) is an objective of limited value. In the first place the legal issues faced by practitioner and public alike do not fall conveniently into conceptual holes; and in the second place, in seeking to understand the relationships between concepts, there is a danger of seeing too much wood and too few trees. Details as well as concepts are important: individual and corporate behaviour is affected as much by the rules, as by the rule, of law. Alphabetical classification has the prime virtue of giving access to those rules using the basic building blocks of acquiring and understanding information.

I do not here reject the structuring, development and teaching of legal thought along lines variously described as "systematic", "conceptual" or (especially) "institutional", whether the legal system in question is (Scotland) or is not (England and Wales) so constructed. However, as a means of presenting the entirety of the law, its appropriateness can be questioned.

**Professor Timothy Jones** holds the Chair of Public Law at the University of Swansea, and is a powerful voice on questions of Welsh government and devolution. He traces the nice distinction between the extent of law, and the effect of law, which is at the crux of the mechanism by which devolution for Wales has been pursued without requiring constitutional redefinition. One result of that mechanism is that there is no need for the application of conflict of laws arrangements between England on the one hand and Wales on the other, which is not the position in regard to Scotland. Whether that remains the position indefinitely is less certain: the vehicle of devolution appears to have considerable momentum, and some distance yet to travel. The required use of the Welsh language in legislation is on the increase; crucially, the powers of the Welsh Assembly Government and the National Assembly for Wales extend now beyond the enactment of law, to the enactment of law in pursuit of their own policy. Thus by the most conspicuous means, access to the law – from influencing its creation to knowing and understanding its effect – has been massively boosted for an entire nation.

**Daniel Greenberg** is Parliamentary Counsel and an authority in the field of legislative drafting: who better to give us an insight into the business of making law? He shows clearly how much there is to be said on the subject; indeed one is tempted to wonder about the amount of paper and Parliamentary time that is given over to the discussion not of law but of how to make it. *Halsbury's Laws* itself has an entire title *Statutes:* over 230 pages devoted to the nature, creation, authority, operation, interpretation and commencement of statute law; other specialist texts are much longer. And all this comes before one gets to the law that is thereby created. Put another way, it might seem that we spend a great deal of time governing the business of government; the exercise of precisely circumscribing the legislative process can sometimes fog, rather than clarify, the legal issues affecting what we do.

Naturally, if Parliament chooses to legislate more (a fact that is hardly likely to dismay a publisher), the manner in which it does so needs to be more carefully watched. Mr Greenberg explains this question instructively, in the context of an account of the increasingly complex legislative environment regulating our every move, and of the evolving methods of Parliamentary scrutiny. These latter undoubtedly amount to a serious democratic advance – or at least to a serious protection against a backwards slide – in promoting access to the law-making process. Either by the route of elected representatives scrutinising legislation in committee, or in the increased opportunity to present evidence to such committees, the room to influence the legislative procedure is widened.

In one strand, Mr Greenberg concludes that an up to date database of legislation in its current state is highly desirable. Whether to lawyer or layman, this is not a contentious position. He shows us loyally the progress being made in the government's own Statute Law Database, refers us to its hard copy precursors and acknowledges that such a tool can be had from commercial sources. Where one might go further is to assert that the commercial sources – especially *Halsbury's Statutes* in print and *Legislation Direct* and subsequently *LexisNexis Butterworths'* legislation service online – have for a long time met this need, and done so with far greater efficiency than successive governments have yet managed. This chimes with the suggestion made earlier – that private enterprise is better placed to meet some civic needs in this sphere. For it is plain, and agreed everywhere, that this is a need, and it is an easy inference to draw that the extraordinary and high success of Butterworths' major works owes much to Stanley Bond's perception of that need, and to his ability to translate it into a market. It is possibly contentious to assert the superiority, even preferability, of the private sector's delivery of primary legal information; it is uncomfortably close to the debate as to the privatisation or nationalisation of public services. But I would make the distinction, as far as *Halsbury's Statutes* is concerned, that a person is not forced to a single source of information: both private and public sources are available – the former is simply better. So far as *Halsbury's Laws* is concerned there has been no public sector equivalent.

It is very appropriate that we have the thoughts of **Joshua Rozenberg** on the role that the media have in connecting the governors with the governed. Well-known as both legal correspondent with the BBC and legal editor of the Daily Telegraph, Mr Rozenberg shows how legal questions can and should be explained in an intelligent and accessible way; what the compromises of detail are which a journalist can make in giving an explanation that is both true and interesting; and how sometimes it can go wrong. It is a particularly difficult task to bridge the gap between law and layman: on the one hand is the principle that everyone should have full access to an understanding of the law that affects them, and on the other is the practical truth that much of the law can actually only be understood by lawyers (and not necessarily all of them). The recognition that there is such a gap, and that it is desirable to bridge it where possible, is – or at least should be – a unifying force in the legal community, embracing publishers, practitioners and the media.

Common law, specifically the doctrine of precedent which allows common law to be enshrined as part of our legal framework, is discussed by **Lord Neuberger of Abbotsbury**. Access to the law is not simply about the capacity to find legal materials nor about the rights of fairness and representation which are constitutionally so important. More subtly, it is about access to the *proper understanding* of the law. That proper understanding depends to a great degree upon the clarity and accuracy both of judicial decisions and of the ways in which those decisions are recorded and handed on. Thus law reporting has played a highly – perhaps unduly – influential part in the development of the common law, especially in less recent history. The selection of cases, and in some instances the selection of points from a case, to report will clearly have affected the materials on which subsequent decisions are based. More recently, however, an avalanche of unfiltered decisions now available online has in one sense had the effect that there are no unreported decisions any more.

Lord Neuberger points out the value to our common law system of those many instances where more than one judgment is delivered in a case (though it would be unfair not to mention that he goes on to point out the disadvantages too). To paraphrase him, there is benefit in exploring all the various paths of reasoning which may be opened by a prospective change in the law. But this is not the effect; the result of the multi-judgment decision of the Court of Appeal or House of Lords is that to follow the development of the law one cannot move chronologically from case to case – which is to say from decision to decision – but is forced to track lines of thought from judgment to judgment. If, as Lord Neuberger says, the headnote of a report is a key feature of the researcher's equipment, then it is surely desirable that the judgments which support a decision are capable of being reasonably reduced to the context of a headnote. The more that the reasoning is expounded by two or more judges in a single case, the less, surely, can that desirable outcome be achieved.

Another crucial aspect of access to the law is the subject of a piece by **Professor Michael Zander**, in his wide-ranging survey of the many contentious issues related to the process, efficacy and desirability of trial by jury. Professor Zander tackles the various defects commonly alleged to exist in the jury system under English law. The highly sensitive questions raised by the ethnic composition of a jury – whether it is adequately representative of the population and, separately, whether it affects the verdict – are clearly the most conspicuous of these. In recent times the further issues of overturning an acquittal returned by a jury, and trying offences of serious fraud without a jury, have made the general news rather than vexing only the legal community.

One reason that this part of the legal system is so readily reported must surely be that the subject (or citizen, if one's view of the constitution accords with that of Lord Lester) regards with jealousy his or her final control of sanction-based law. This is because the principle of trial by jury reduces the law to a human condition, warts and all. Its weakness – the dependency, in the last analysis, on a highly variable and multi-layered organism – is also its strength. The view which, as if with a shrug of the shoulders, seems to say "this system will have to do, if there is nothing better" could be more positively (but no less accurately) expressed by omitting all but the last four words. Though it may creak a bit, there is more right in the principle of jury trial than there is wrong with its operation. Access to the law coincides here with access to justice and Professor Zander's final remarks, concerning the jury's right to deliver a verdict in defiance of the law, underline the point.

*The Illusion of Inclusion* is the deceptively gentle title of a piece by **Baroness Helena Kennedy QC**, which is anything but a comfortable read. Characteristically forthright and articulate, she argues powerfully that women have been, and are still, failed by a system built with a male perspective. She is clear in her view that inclusion is not an end to be pursued if it means that women must adapt to that perspective. And she reasons cogently that that perspective operates with deleterious effect both upon the advance of women in the legal professions and upon the treatment of women who have recourse to law as defendants or (especially) victims. It is possible to reach from Baroness Kennedy's reasoning the view that, even were the composition of the judiciary reflective of the number of women entering the professions, *institutionally* the law is not equipped to reflect the needs of the modern society or to take a sufficient lead in effecting necessary change. Here then is a yet wider view to be taken of access to the law, which encompasses the need to ensure full access to participation in making and administering law and to the full protection of the law.

In lighter vein, **His Honour Judge Robert Winstanley** has given us an entertaining account of his route through his practice of law as a solicitor to his eventual appointment to the circuit bench, and beyond. But there are important messages here too. If access to the law is in part about connecting the law with those subject to it, then a sure way is make the points of contact clear and comprehensible. Judge Winstanley makes (and embodies) the case for wider representation of the solicitors' profession in the judiciary and he shows us how, throughout his experiences in a variety of judicial capacities, the preparation is thorough and relevant. This ought to give great encouragement to those who fear – however misguidedly – that the law and its functionaries are distant, mysterious or unapproachable. Moreover, Judge Winstanley highlights for us another important development: the growing transparency in the mechanisms for judicial appointment.

If there is a subject area in respect of which the need for access to the law is both greatest, and least fulfilled, it is surely IT law. An excellent piece by **Professor Steve Saxby** and **Caroline Wilson** takes us through a number of the many legal issues which have arisen in the wake of technological advance, in particular refuting convincingly the suggestion that IT law is not really law. On a purely human level, dependence on IT is almost frightening: how many of us truly understand the technologies in play in catering for the most basic needs? The speed of communications development is simply bewildering to some, but almost all have wit enough to realise that the reach that IT has into our lives is extensive indeed. Such pervasion is a characteristic of the law, and as Professor Saxby and Ms Wilson indicate, IT law is "pervasive of law itself".

## The Operation of Right

An alternative unity to this collection can be found in what might be described as seeking the operation of right. Terence Rattigan's play *The Winslow Boy* rests for the resolution of the drama on the presentation of a Petition of Right. "Let right be done"; not justice obtained, nor the law upheld, but right done. This is an attractive notion and rings true across the whole range of legal discussion. Much debate, at every stage in the law-making process, is aimed at achieving the *right* result. After the making of a law, whether by Parliament or the court, much commentary is directed at whether the *right* result has been achieved and at whether safeguards are needed to ensure that it does not then go wrong, or more wrong.

It is generally acknowledged that strict application of legal rules is not in the least a guarantee of right; as Lord Halsbury suggested in his introduction, what have become referred to as "legal technicalities" and "loopholes" have been complained of since Cicero's time. The wrong that can be perpetrated in the name of the law is the basis of more than one crime novel or courtroom drama, leading a hero to pursue the nobler course. Hence Sherlock Holmes in *The Abbey Grange*:

> "'Once or twice in my career I feel that I have done more real harm by my discovery of the criminal than ever he had done by his crime. I have learned

caution now, and I had rather play tricks with the law of England than with my own conscience.'"

Not perhaps an approach likely to find judicial favour; nor, in *The Blue Carbuncle*:

"'I suppose that I am commuting a felony, but it is just possible that I am saving a soul.'"

In the real (if less heroic) world, the whole of equity took root in judicial unease with the results of following the law. These days, of course, equity is as much law as the common law which it grew up to give relief from, and it is ironic that iniquity can quite plausibly be reached by the equitable path. So in order to maintain the pursuit of right, the case law of the land continues to develop (under the fiction that it is revealed rather than new); statutes are written, rewritten and repealed; the legislature and the judiciary, though they may frequently lock horns, continue to steer each other towards their several views of what is the right course.

**Professor Jeremy Horder**, in his essay on the criminal liability of organisations, cites a number of cases which are precisely in point, such as the impossibility of bringing companies to account in certain notorious tragedies, notably the *Herald of Free Enterprise* disaster. The Corporate Manslaughter and Corporate Homicide Act 2007 is specific proof that the law had to be changed because its existing state was simply not right. At a fundamental level this could be felt to be so and the eventual legislative response, after exploring various models of corporate criminal culpability, has been the passing of this important Act. Though its effects are yet to be seen, the development of the sentencing guidelines around the Act will, as Professor Horder shows, be important and will surely bear out the point made above about government and judiciary steering each other along the right path.

In a marvellously lucid essay, **Lord Lester of Herne Hill** presents with relentless logic the case for a rights-based and written constitution; and he gives form to the connection, which one had felt instinctively was there, between that case and the serious issues raised by the concept of Britishness in the twenty-first century. He makes his points coherently, graciously tracing his path through previous editions of *Halsbury's Laws*, and it is difficult to see where there is room to argue. And yet, if the question were not one with two sides it would have been settled decades ago. As it is, one may wonder, for example, whether in fact the interpretative debate has merely underlined that "Convention rights" are, after all, only as strong as they are drafted; and whether the undoubted liberalisation of individual behaviour which has accompanied greater concern for the rights has been altogether a good thing. What emerges, perhaps not surprisingly in light of a century or more of consideration of the question, is that the most significant advances in promoting the rights of the individual have been achieved from within existing constitutional arrangements, not by dismantling them. The many examples which Lord Lester gives of working written constitutions relate to forms of governance devised *de novo*, following revolution (France and the United States) or independence (India and Australia). It is at least a possibility, in the mature democracy of the United Kingdom, that a written constitution could not achieve the "sanctity" – to borrow Lord Lester's term – which would be required for it to underpin the system. It is, moreover, quite plausible to doubt whether written constitutions have in practice absolutely guaranteed the rights they seek to uphold: whether the cause of liberty and justice for all is actually promoted more by the possible rigidity of a constitution committed to paper or the ethereal quality of one committed to convention.

It is a concern to those who believe the present constitution to be flawed, that the supremacy of Parliament is illusory and really means the supremacy of the executive. But there are enough examples of Parliament holding the executive to account, of its refusing to bend to the executive's will, for that concern to be at least debatable and for the point to be reasonably made that the executive tempers its activities according to the likely response of Parliament.

The executive, and public authorities generally, are also held to account by the courts. **Michael Supperstone QC** and **Joanne Clement**, in a survey of the development of judicial review, show how it has emerged from the mixed assortment of rules which form the *corpus* of administrative law, to become the strongest of controls over the use of power. Time and again it has been used to curb state excess and the state has accepted that control to the extent that legislation regularly requires tribunals to apply principles of judicial review to matters before them. Judicial review is a most important piece in the search for right, and it is interesting that in having the powers to strike down statutory instruments and to declare legislation to be incompatible with the Human Rights Act 1998, there is in effect a power of judicial review of legislation itself. But paradoxically the case for a written rights-based constitution is thereby both strengthened and weakened. Strengthened, in that judicial review shows up clearly the shortcomings of protection against misuse of power; weakened, because it has supplied the remedy itself, in a way which is arguably more flexible and penetrating than a written framework could be. However, it must be acknowledged that when the judiciary itself, at its highest level (as in *YL v Birmingham City Council*, referred to by Mr Supperstone and Ms Clement), inclines towards a narrow view of protected human rights, it is not easy to see what further recourse there is.

"Right" is an issue when it comes to the conflict of laws, which **Sir Peter North** has discussed in his survey of a century of developments in this area. If we accept for the moment the premise that the law and legal commentators seek the doing of right, we must come quickly to realise that what is right is a social and moral question as much as a legal one, meaning different things to different people and subject to a broad array of historical and cultural influences. Much of the conspicuous development in private international law is to do with the growth of international commerce, as Sir Peter shows; but in the fields of consumer and (especially) family law, the growth of multi-cultural societies and the increasing exposure of individuals to international social regimes and pressures, have made it more likely that different views of the right course will collide. This is obviously true, for example, in the matter of validity of marriage, where the law recognises the validity of forms of marriage which are compatible with polygamy, but not a marriage which is itself polygamous. There is no single answer that is right for everyone; indeed, ascertaining the right course may well be impossible, and Sir Peter shows us at least two instances of questions which remain unresolved even after a century of debate.

From the conflict of laws to the law of conflict, and the difficult problem of striking the balance between discipline and efficiency in the armed forces on the one hand and the treatment of those who come under military jurisdiction on the other. Concentrating on the circumstances of British forces operating in Northern Ireland, Afghanistan and Iraq, **Professor Peter Rowe** examines the way in which the development of human rights jurisprudence has affected the enforcement of discipline and law as administered in a military context. The fairness of courts-martial (especially in relation to the independence of the board) and summary disposition; determining who is subject to military jurisdiction – such as dependants, prisoners and others – in addition to serving members of the armed forces; the review of decisions of courts-martial: all these have been considered at length by domestic appellate courts, the institutions and organs of human rights law in Europe and the United Kingdom Parliament. Professor Rowe shows us the course of the debate, which at its heart has been about how far the law (domestic or other) should reach into the business of making war. To return to the theme of what is right, this is an instance where the answer may rest on a basis not shared by any other circumstances. It is suggested above that the question of what is right is a social and moral one; in the military context there would be those (presumably members of what Professor Rowe calls the "military club") who say it should be predominantly – perhaps exclusively – one of expediency.

By contrast, the social and moral dimensions are unambiguously to the fore in **Professor Kenyon Mason's** study of the "reproductive torts" of wrongful pregnancy (or conception), wrongful birth and wrongful life. As elsewhere, the greatest dilemma is in the fact that the right result varies according to the person. For a long time the birth of a child disclosed no cause of action because it could not be considered a harm. For some this is still the case. For others, an unwanted pregnancy, for example, and the concomitant burden of bringing up a child can be considered such an interference with the enjoyment and comfort of life that if the steps taken to avoid it were unsuccessful due to the negligence of another, then there should be redress for that negligence. This field demonstrates more than most the lengths that the law will go to in order to see that right is done, or least harm inflicted, and the contortions of established legal principles which occur along the way.

**Michael Beloff QC** and **Rupert Beloff** have written an absorbing piece on the reach of the law onto the field of play. They examine first the justiciability of decisions reached by umpires, referees and sports' governing bodies; secondly the principles which come into play when conduct seems to attract criminal process; and thirdly the liability of players and others in damages for negligence in or around the sporting arena. In few circumstances does the human need for right present such difficulty as in sport. Few issues excite such passion on the part of both onlookers and participants as a crucial penalty (or lbw) decision. Now that more and more sports have a lucrative professional side to them, and those that have been professional for a while are huge global industries, it seems somehow more important than ever that fairness and right be observed. But if the benchmark of behaviour used to be "the spirit of the game", that benchmark is somewhat obscured by the interests at stake. However, with the laws of various games being apparently more strictly enforced – witness the firmer stand being taken against banned substances in athletics – and the general law being brought into play a little, one still has the sense that the right result (in all senses) is still the objective.

To complete the collection are the texts of addresses given by the Chairman of the Bar Council, **Geoffrey Vos QC**, and the President of the Law Society, **Andrew Holroyd OBE**, to an invited audience at the Café Royal on 27 September 2007. From the perspectives of the professions they represent, their thoughts on the practice of law over the previous century, its condition now and its likely future direction could hardly have been more timely. At the time of writing, contemplated reform of legal practice, in the shape of the Legal Services Bill, is set to have a profound impact on much more than the livelihoods of lawyers. The cost of attaining the (ostensibly) worthwhile object of widening choice and improving access for those in need of the law is one that needs to be weighed carefully. What some see as the widening of choice, and others as fragmentation, risks under either name losing the cohesion of a system in which access to expertise and specialism are of the essence. Whatever the future, *Halsbury's Laws* reflects that cohesion and will continue to do so.

*The Publisher's Perspective*

Each piece in this book is written by an expert, with the single and deliberate exception of the one you are reading now. The exception is deliberate because there is a place in the law for the generalist and it is hard to think of anything more generalist than an encyclopaedia. Indeed the argument is in danger of confounding itself by concluding that editing and publishing *Halsbury's Laws* makes a speciality out of generalism.

In grander moments the Halsbury publishing team considers itself the guardian of generalism. We have a naturally high regard for expertise, but it is a cautious regard. With authors and consultants who are experts and specialists in the practice or theory of law in their various fields, the encyclopaedia could easily have become a work comprehensible only to themselves or others of the same stamp. It is for the editors to ensure that this does not happen. An expert is very often also an enthusiast for a particular subject; the editors have to guard against undue weighting in favour of that subject. Further, it is quite frequently true that the more expert a person is, the narrower the field of their expertise; the publishing team ensures that *Halsbury's Laws* covers everything, neutrally and objectively, from the most commercially compelling to the most esoteric and abstruse of subject areas – just so long as they form part of the corpus of law. Though much of the work and the research behind it is scholarly, and though a great many of the contributors and consultants have held academic posts, *Halsbury's Laws* is a work not of scholarship but of record.

The challenge is to harness the expertise and avoid the specialism, and thereby to ensure that the generalist purpose of the work is achieved. If this happens successfully, then to adopt an analogy which might be more fittingly used by Michael Beloff, Halsbury levels the playing field. Happily, what then transpires on that field is outside our remit.

There must be acknowledged a great debt to a great number of people for the initial and continued success of *Halsbury's Laws of England*.

The many authors, consultants, advisory editors and members of editorial boards to the four editions (and the reissue programme of the fourth edition) are the foundation of the work's reputation. Whether one-off or repeat contributors, their participation in the encyclopaedia is a necessary part of its strength. The Publishers wish to express gratitude to all, and their names are recorded in the first Appendix to this book.

A host of people has formed the in-house editorial and publishing backbone of *Halsbury's Laws*. The service of a number of them can be measured in many years, and for some in decades. Theirs have been the perpetual tasks of ensuring cohesion in the editing and presentation of the work, accuracy at every level of detail, comprehensive coverage across the sources and areas of law, and updating the work in the many formats that have been devised. We are grateful to each of them too and their names appear in the second Appendix.

For the preparation of this book I am particularly grateful to Clare Blanchard, Tanja Clarke and Kate Pamphilon.

It also appropriate to acknowledge the debt we owe to the various printers from whose presses and binderies the published volumes, supplements and other parts of *Halsbury's Laws* have emerged. Particular mention needs to be made of William Clowes & Sons, printers of the first volume in 1907, of the majority of the volumes since, and fittingly of this volume.

Finally, our Editors-in-Chief, who have provided great authority and wisdom, and whose names appear on the following page. All have contributed greatly to the encyclopaedia, but we wish to record particular thanks to the present incumbent, Lord Mackay of Clashfern.

Simon Hetherington
Publisher, *Halsbury's Laws of England*
October 2007

# EDITORS-IN-CHIEF OF HALSBURY'S LAWS OF ENGLAND

## 1st Edition (1907–1917)

The Rt Hon the Earl of Halsbury

Lord High Chancellor of Great Britain 1885–86, 1886–92, 1895–1905

## 2nd Edition (1931–1942)

The Rt Hon the Viscount Hailsham

Lord High Chancellor of Great Britain 1928–29, 1935–38

## 3rd Edition (1952–1964)

The Rt Hon the Viscount Simonds

Lord High Chancellor of Great Britain 1951–54

## 4th Edition (1973–1985)

and

## 4th Edition Reissue (1988–2008)

(1973–1996)

The Rt Hon the Lord Hailsham of St Marylebone

Lord High Chancellor of Great Britain 1970–74, 1979–1987

(1997 to date)

The Rt Hon the Lord Mackay of Clashfern

Lord High Chancellor of Great Britain 1987–1997

# LORD HALSBURY'S INTRODUCTION TO THE FIRST EDITION

———

AN ideal code has been contemplated by many law reformers in which every case which could possibly occur should be provided for, and the determination of it be simply effected by reference to the code—a code so universal in its application that no difficulty could be found, but the solution of every legal problem would be at once disclosed. A very small experience, however, of the infinite variety of the incidents of human life will convince us that such an ideal code is an impossibility, and that the utmost that can be done is to establish some principles by reference to which a question may be decided; but even then the principles must be stated so generally that their very generality may work injustice if rigidly adhered to. Hence Aristotle's idea of the ἐπιεικές and the ἐπανόρθωμα νόμου ᾗ ἐλλείπει διὰ τὸ καθόλου.

The necessity of some regulations to enable human creatures to live as an associated body has produced and reproduced the same cycle of events in the various countries of the world. This necessity has developed forms of government, and systems of laws and written rules would seem to be an essential element, though tradition attributes to Lycurgus that his laws were only spoken, and hence have been called ῥῆτραι.

Laws and forms of government grow imperceptibly at first until the necessities of an advancing civilisation compel the reduction of what has been tribal custom or individual genius into a systematic development of the principles of justice. The same causes have produced the same results; and in every country it has been found that the system of providing for each necessity as it arises, without reference to any principle which governs the whole, has over and over again produced confusion and contradiction. Jeremy Bentham considers a code of laws to be like a vast forest: the more it is divided, the better it is known. He says—"To render a code of laws complete it is necessary to know all the parts which should be comprised in it. It is necessary to know what they are in themselves and what they are in relation to one another. This is accomplished when taking the body of the laws in their entirety; they may be divided into two parts in such manner that everything which belongs to the integral body may be found comprised in the one or the other part, yet nothing shall at the same time be found in both parts."

It may well be doubted whether Bentham's division of the law into two parts of what he is pleased to call "the integral body" is defensible either in theory or practice. The analogy of any integral body is a false one. Of the human body it may be true that you do not find the same complete organ in two different parts—you do not find a toe in the head—but there are veins in both. So, in a code, there might be rules applicable to one class of subjects which nevertheless would extend to others, as in our own law there are rules which are applicable to both real and personal, civil and criminal, jurisprudence.

But no State begins with a regular system of law. A code is a want developed by progressive and unscientific legislation; and the political relations of the citizens to each other give a form and tone to the laws which may ultimately produce confusion and contradiction. *Justitiae fruendae causâ reges olim constituti sunt;* but whatever the form of government may be, the desire to have justice, and to know what the State considers justice, is essential to civilisation.

The code of laws of the Twelve Tables at Rome was the result of a commission to Athens, at least in respect of ten of them, and the work, as Mommsen says, was a political compromise between the popular and the aristocratic parties. Livy tells us that the laws of the Twelve Tables formed the foundation of all the Roman law, but Livy's own description of the "heap of laws accumulated one upon the other" shows what must have been in his time the confusion, and therein the uncertainty, of the law. When one considers the power of every prætor in turn having jurisdiction to dictate by published rules what rules of justice he would observe during his tenure of office, and that these were not binding on his successor, it is not wonderful that the Roman law required the labours of such men as Gaius, Papinian, Paul, Ulpian, Modestinus, and Tribonian, to make it intelligible or fit for practical life. Lawyers who advised and judges who decided had a resource which a modern digestor or compiler does not possess: the sovereign power of the Emperor, which could enact that an opinion should become the law, rendered the task of the law reformer a very different one from what it is in our own day.

The alteration of existing law and the process of merely stating what the law is are two very different functions, and the confusion between the two has marred many an effort to get a clear and intelligible code. Mr. Gladstone once said in the House of Commons that you should first get a comprehensive account of what the law is before you commence amending it; and a great many law reformers have failed because they have not observed the necessity of this preliminary inquiry.

It is somewhat singular to observe that Cicero, in treating of the law as administered in his own day, complained of the mode in which the simplicity and clearness which he attributed to the Roman law were obscured in administering justice. He says that the laws themselves were clear enough, so far that you might duly distinguish on what principle every legal case depended, and it would be easy for every one possessed of a moderate share of intelligence to find the rights of a question; whatever new case should arise, he would know how to refer the points of debate to their proper section. "But unhappily our lawyers," he adds, "prefer, for the sake of raising objections, and in order to show that they may be, or appear to be, more knowing than they are, raise difficult points; and our lawyers, I say, do divide the legal doctrine, which is essentially simple, into an infinite variety of technical distinctions." The *nimia subtilitas* of which Cicero complains has had its day in our own country, and even in our own time. Happily the general view of our present lawyers is more in harmony with Cicero's advocacy of clearness and simplicity than appears to have been the case with the lawyers of Cicero's time.

It is, perhaps, interesting to observe the identity of the process which, at divers times and in different countries, has exhibited itself, when the carelessly aggregated "heaps of laws" have been found so cumbrous and confused that nations have sought to get rid of the confusion resulting therefrom. Frederick the Great, like Cicero, complained of the lawyers; and his code was, as he said himself, intended to get rid of them. The

Code Napoleon, imperfect as it was and is still alleged to be, was, nevertheless, an immense boon when compared to the confused system of jurisprudence, if jurisprudence it can be called, which prevailed over France. The provinces, differing in their historical origin, in their traditions, and in their constitutions, had no system of law common to them all; and rights differed, not only in different provinces, but even in respect of different persons. The proclamation of 1789 of equality of rights paved the way for a code which should be applicable to all persons alike, and in every part of France.

It is not necessary to insist upon the hundred and eighty customs which were more or less observed in France and in divers parts of it. It was manifest that when the equality of rights was proclaimed the whole system would have to be put in the hands of some authority calculated to bring it out of chaos into something like a reasonable adaptation to the wants of human life. Cambacérès made three attempts, each of them differing from the other, to produce this result, but in vain; and Napoleon himself intervened at last, and, indeed, has more claim to be treated as the author of the code than Justinian has to that which goes under his name.

M. Portalis, one of Napoleon's commissioners, was alive to the impossibility, already pointed out, of making a code so universal in its application that it would not require to be expounded. He says: "We have guarded against the dangerous ambition of wishing to regulate and to foresee everything. The wants of society are so varied that it is impossible for the legislator to provide for every case or every emergency. We know that never, or scarcely ever in any case, can a text of law be enacted so fair and precise that good sense and equity will alone suffice to decide it. A new question springs up: Then how is it to be decided? To this question it is replied that the office of the law is to fix by enlarged rules the general maxims of right and wrong, to establish firm principles fruitful in consequences, and not to descend to the detail of all questions which may arise upon each particular topic. It is for magistrates under Government, penetrated by the general spirit of the law, to direct this application."

Mr. Best, speaking of the expositions of the code, complains that they had already, in his time, run to a considerable length. That of Locré in thirty-one volumes, that of Toullier and Troplong in nearly fifty volumes, and, on the Civil Code, those of Pailliet and Teulet and of the Bulletin des Lois, bid fair to rival our own statute book in bulk. "France," he said, "may well tremble for the future."

With us a commission was issued in November, 1866, to the following distinguished persons: Lord Cranworth; Sir Hugh Cairns, afterwards Earl Cairns; Lord Westbury; Sir James Wilde, afterwards Lord Penzance; Robert Lowe, afterwards Lord Sherbrooke; Sir William Page Wood, afterwards Lord Hatherley; Sir George Bowyer; Sir Roundell Palmer, afterwards Earl of Selborne; Sir John Shaw-Lefevre; Sir Thomas Erskine May, afterwards Lord Farnborough; Mr. Daniel, Q.C.; Henry Thring, afterwards Lord Thring; and Sir Francis Reilly. The commission was to inquire into the exposition of a digest of the law and the best means of accomplishing the object, and other ways of exhibiting in a compendious and classical form the law as embodied in judicial decisions.

After pointing out that the law of England, as they understood it, comprised the whole civil law, in whatever Courts administered, the criminal law, the law relating to the constitution, the jurisdiction, and procedure of the Courts, including the law of evidence and constitutional law, the commissioners proceeded to point out the extent and variety of the sources from which the existing law is to be ascertained. Speaking of the bulk of the statutes and the amount of judicial decisions, they calculated that the judicial decisions were included in thirteen hundred volumes, exclusive of a hundred and fifty volumes of Irish reports, and they calculated the number of cases at a hundred thousand. They recommended a digest, which they defined as a condensed summary of the law as it exists arranged in systematic order under proper titles and sub-divisions, and divided into definite statements or propositions, which should be supported by references to the sources of the law whence they were severally derived, and might be illustrated by citations of the principal instances in which the rules stated have been discussed or applied.

The commission sat and took some evidence; but it is very remarkable that they made no allusion in their first report, the only one that ever appeared, to the exhaustive and complete Index to the Statutes, and the edition of them down to the reign of Queen Anne, which was prepared by very distinguished commissioners in answer to addresses of the House of Commons. Both the index and the edition of the statutes are a marvellous exhibition of painstaking labour and profound learning. The various volumes when published were deposited in the Parliament Office, and received this inscription: "This book is to be perpetually preserved in, and for the use of, the Parliament Office."

It may be truly said that so great a monument of learning, both legal and archæological, is hardly to be found elsewhere; and it is most unfortunate that the edition of the statutes does not go beyond the reign of Anne, and does not, indeed, reach the end of that reign. Mr. Raithby's index goes down nearly to the period of his own death in 1826, but many indices have been completed and continued since his time. Nevertheless, both for design and execution, Mr. Raithby's index deserves to be remembered.

The commission, after the publication of its first report on May 13, 1867, appears to have died out. It propounded various treatises to be sent in as specimens of the Digest contemplated; but some litigation ensued with Mr. Macleod, one of the writers selected, and no more has been heard of that commission since its first report; but if ever the experiment could have been successfully accomplished, it would have been when such a body of commissioners was selected to try it.

A less ambitious, but very useful, course has been pursued in taking specific subjects and consolidating various statutes in relation to that subject. The Sale of Goods Act, the Interpretation Act, the Partnership Act, the Bills of Exchange Act, and the Marine Insurance Act, are examples of how useful such a course may be, but no amount of human ingenuity will ever make a code that will not require exposition.

An ancient philosopher thought he could make the law clear by a preparatory account of what it was intended to effect; but modern ideas rather point to plain enactment and desire to omit preambles altogether. Bacon undoubtedly favours the modern view that law should commence with enactment. He says: "Neque nobis prologi legum, qui inepti olim habiti sunt, et leges introducunt disputantes non jubentes, utique placerent, si priscos mores ferre possemus. Sed prologi isti legum plerumque (ut nunc sunt tempora) necessario adhibentur, non tam ad explicationem legis, quam instar suasionis ad perferendam legem in comitiis; et rursus ad satisfaciendum populo. Quantum fieri potest tamen, prologi evitentur, et lex incipiat a jussione." It may be that Bacon had in his mind what another judge expressly said: that the preamble might act as the "key" of the statute to explain its object, and thereby elucidate its meaning; otherwise he would not have added the qualification "quantum fieri potest." The difference was between the speculative Greek philosopher and the practical lawyer and man of the world, but the controversy whether the laws should *incipere a jussione* or whether they should have an expository, though not perhaps a hortatory, preamble is not settled yet. At all events, the function of one who is entitled to alter or make the law is very different from that of one who is only intrusted with the duty of making an index to it, however wide may be the system upon which the index may be made. The various attempts to state what laws are have occasionally slipped into apparently authoritative expositions of law by the digestor himself; and that profound lawyer, Mr. Austin, points out what he describes as the enormous fault of Justinian's Code, considered as a *code*, that it is a compilation of statutes and judicial decisions, a heterogeneous mass of subjects having no other relation than that they are all of them imperial constitutions, that is to say, statutes and other orders emanating from the emperors directly, and not emanating directly from subordinate legislatures or tribunals. While it may be true to say that no one case can necessarily decide another case under different circumstances and between different persons, the principle of law or justice may be severable from the difference of circumstances or persons, and may establish a rule applicable to both, and it may well be contended that a selection of cases in which some one principle of law is argued will illustrate more cogently the real solution of a legal problem than any amount of technical or abstract reasoning.

The great difficulty, of course, is to state the law as it is without giving such an authority to the mode of its statement as to make itself equivalent to a statute. This is what Bentham apprehended. He says the legislator in the code which he is recommending should direct that the text of the law should be the standard of the law. In judging whether a given case falls within the law, the text ought to be kept principally in view, the examples which may be given being designed only to explain, not to restrain, the purport of the law. No commentary should be written on this code with a view of pointing out the sense thereof; and men should be required to pay no regard to this comment, neither should it be raised in any Court of justice in any manner whatsoever, either by express words or by any circuitous designations whatsoever. A passage appears to be obscure; let it be cleared up rather by alteration than by comment; retrench, add, substitute, as much as you will, but never explain. By the latter certainty will generally, perspicuity and brevity will always, suffer. The more words there are, the more words are there about which doubts may be entertained.

The Commission on the criminal law shared the fate of its predecessor. It is still a valuable compilation to be referred to as an authoritative exposition of the views of the very learned lawyers who composed it, but of no authority in a court of law. The truth is that the difficulty is inherent in the subject treated of, and it may well be doubted whether any code, call it a digest or anything else, can come up to the digest recommended by the Commission of 1866.

It has occurred to some minds that an attempt might be made by private enterprise to carry out in its main outlines the scheme which was recommended in the report of the Commission appointed in 1866, and such an attempt has been made in this work. Different treatises upon various divisions of the law, and by different authors, have been brought together, so that a selected body of writers may expound their several topics, and at the same time refer to such authoritative decisions and enactments as support the propositions which they lay down. A similar system was devised by the late Lord Acton in respect of history, and is being successfully carried out.

The result is not a mere encyclopædia, it is not a mere collection of cases, but a number of treatises composed by learned lawyers, supported by the decisions of the great judges who have from time to time adorned the English Bench; and it is hoped that when finished the work will furnish a complete statement of the Laws of England.

HALSBURY.

# HALSBURY'S LAWS OF ENGLAND: 100 YEARS OLD, YESTERDAY

## AN ADDRESS BY THE RT HON THE LORD MACKAY OF CLASHFERN[1]
## 15TH NOVEMBER 2007

In the later part of last century a very general feeling grew up among legal practitioners in England that the criminal law, particularly the law of offences against the person, had for far too long depended for its statutory base on legislation then over 100 years old and that the modernisation of this law provided an ideal opportunity for codification of the criminal law. This sentiment was taken up by the Law Commission and in 1985 it published a *Report on the Codification of the Criminal Law* (HC Paper 270). This was followed four years later by the Commission's proposals for a criminal code contained in two substantial volumes. By this time I had become Lord Chancellor and I felt very supportive of the idea, having heard a number of eloquent lectures in support of it. However, there were many difficulties.

In the nature of a code it is a complete entity with all its parts interdependent, the precise formulation at any point dependent on a balance in the whole code. In our system for enacting legislation, members of the legislature may propose an amendment to a particular provision which is judged on its own merits, and if it is accepted consequential amendments to other provisions may be enacted without much discussion, but there is little opportunity to assess an individual amendment against the background of a huge text such as would be contained in a code.

A criminal code would involve legislating in the whole field of criminal law. There are many areas of the criminal law in which very different views are held and therefore when put before Parliament are likely to stimulate lively discussion which is likely to be prolonged. In the 1980s one of these was the question of the mandatory life sentence for murder, and a criminal code with any claim to be a complete code would involve a provision dealing with that matter. If the government held a particular view on such a matter, proposing a code would give a unique opportunity to opponents of the government view to air their opposition and possibly to carry the day. A government would not be in a hurry to create such an opportunity.

Legislation for a criminal code would be a major Bill, and require a great deal of Parliamentary time. Lawyers, particularly, would wish to discuss it fully – and the lawyers in Parliament do not have a great reputation for succinctness.

The Home Office was at that time the department responsible for legislation dealing with the criminal law. Accordingly it was necessary to have the Home Secretary take the initiative in promoting legislation for a criminal code.

In the light of considerations such as these, and after discussion with the Law Commission, a proposal emerged to consider enacting such a code in parts. Because of the age of the legislation concerning offences against the person, it was decided that the Commission should work up proposals for starting the legislation for such a code with this part of the law; and in 1993 the Commission produced a report *Legislating the Criminal Code: Offences against the Person and General Principles* (Cmd 2370). What was then

---

1  Lord High Chancellor of Great Britain 1987–1997. Editor-in-Chief of *Halsbury's Laws of England*, from 1997.

proposed was a great deal more modest than seeking to legislate the whole code, and thus greatly reduced the problems I have mentioned; and so I certainly hoped we might make progress.

However, the Home Office had more pressing matters on its mind. Mandatory sentences for certain crimes; and the need for clear statutory provisions governing disclosure in criminal cases in preparation for a trial. The latter had produced important judgments in the courts, and parties needed to know where they stood, otherwise the whole trial process might be undermined. Again, the Royal Commission on Criminal Justice had produced proposals which were accepted by the government, and required legislation. Issues such as these were continually arising. The years were passing; May 1997 came and my opportunity to have any influence in these matters from the Lord Chancellor's office passed away. Since then, some small part of the codification of the criminal law has come to fruition in the shape of the Sexual Offences Act 2003.

But the idea for a codification of the laws of England was not new in the second half of the twentieth century. In November 1866 a Commission with very distinguished members was set up to inquire into the exposition of a digest of the law and the best means of accomplishing this object, and other ways of exhibiting in a comprehensive form the law as embodied in judicial decisions.

The Commissioners understood the law of England to contain the whole civil law, in whatever courts administered, the criminal law, the law relating to the constitution, the jurisdiction and precedence of the courts, including the law of evidence, and they pointed out the variety of sources from which the existing law was to be ascertained. They calculated that the judicial decisions were contained in 1,300 volumes, excluding 150 volumes of trial reports, and that the number of cases was 100,000. The Commission:

> "recommended a digest, which they defined as a condensed summary of the law as it exists arranged in systematic order under proper titles and sub-divisions, and divided into definite statements or propositions, which should be supported by references to the sources of the law whence they were severally derived, and might be illustrated by citations of the principal instances in which the rules stated have been discussed or applied."

The Commission, for all its great distinction, died out, and Lord Halsbury commented "if ever the experiment could have been successfully accomplished. It would have been when such a body of commissioners was selected to try it".

When a public initiative of this kind in the hands of most distinguished lawyers foundered it fell to a private citizen, but a very remarkable man, to take up the challenge.

Stanley Shaw Bond was born at Wimbledon on 8 July 1877, the second son of Charles Bond, joint proprietor with his brother Richard of Shaw and Sons, the local government stationers, printers and publishers. On 8th January 1895 the proprietor of the family law publishing business of Butterworth & Co, founded in 1818, died. The Bonds bought the business on 25 June 1895. Stanley was put into the business to conduct it from day to day. After launching in 1902 a 20 volume Encyclopaedia of Forms and Precedents, Stanley embarked on an even more ambitious project: The Laws of England.

He was a man with a great creative talent, which he was able to bring to a practical result by building up loyal and industrious teams of editors (salaried and freelance) and salesmen. He knew that if his proposed work on the laws of England was to succeed he must secure the services of a top lawyer to lead the project. In those days the Lord Chancellor was regarded as at the pinnacle of the legal profession in England, and Bond decided to try and retain him. When he had all his plans well laid he approached Lord Halsbury and asked him to become Editor-in-Chief.

I let Bond himself take up the story.

"I determined to invite the Lord Chancellor to be Editor in Chief and I obtained an interview with him. He was obviously interested but said he must have time to think it over. I waited for a while and then hearing nothing, I made enquiries to find, to my consternation, that Lord Halsbury had gone on holiday to Nice. As I needed to start as soon as possible, I took myself to Nice and finally ran Lord Halsbury to earth in an hotel.

I accosted him in the foyer and in surprised tones he said, 'Hello Bond, what are you doing here?' I replied, 'I've come for my answer, my Lord.' 'But I'm on holiday,' Halsbury replied. 'I'm sorry, my Lord,' I said, 'but I must have a reply one way or the other.' 'Well, Bond,' he said, 'I admire you for your cheek ... and, yes, I'll do it. Only, Bond, the labourer is worthy of his hire ... eh?' 'Name your fee, my Lord,' I replied. He named it and it was a stiff one. I pulled out my cheque book and wrote him a cheque for the lot. 'Done, my Lord,' I said."

The first volume was published on 14 November 1907. It was not immediately successful. After a few volumes the work was running at a loss, but despite the pleas of his friends and relatives to stop before he was ruined, Bond determined to hang on a little longer. He described the turning point: "You could say that one night I went to bed facing blue ruin and awoke the next morning to find myself a wealthy man."

The work was completed in 1917 and consisted of 28 volumes and three volumes of Tables of Cases and Index.

In the closing words of his introduction to the First Edition, Lord Halsbury described the work thus:

"The result is not a mere encyclopaedia, it is not a mere collection of cases, but a number of treatises composed by learned lawyers, supported by the decisions of the great judges who have from time to time adorned the English bench; and it is hoped that when finished the work will furnish a complete statement of the Laws of England."

The situation for lawyers in the pre-Halsbury era has been thus described (Law Journal: 15 November 1957):

"at that time their libraries comprised law reports and individual text books, but no legal encyclopaedias, apart from 'Forms and Precedents' of which publication had just begun. The solicitor faced with a legal problem of any magnitude at all was by circumstances compelled to send the papers to counsel who, in turn, had no alternative but to study the multitude of available text books and browse among the reports and statutes."

Every legal problem, in fact, involved a great deal of complex research. The description went on:

"with the publication of Halsbury all this was changed. As the volumes appeared, one by one, on the solicitor's shelves he found that he had now a key to the whole breadth of the law within the confines of a single work. Each proposition of law was digested and recorded, the authorities collected, and indices and cross-references supplied. A question which had hitherto involved hours of patient research on the part of counsel could now be answered in very much shorter time at the solicitor's desk. Even in the case of involved points incapable of positive answer it became possible to start the necessary research armed with a list of authorities and pointers."

In general the work was well received. Slightly less successful was a compact version printed on thin paper intended – and advertised – as a resource for the travelling lawyer to which he might refer while on the train. These days a laptop is quite sufficient.

In 1915 the Daily Chronicle published a paragraph headed "Lord Haldane bans Lords Halsbury's book". The Lord Chancellor had referred to the rule against citing a work by a living author as conclusive authority on a point of law, and stated that in that sense *Halsbury's Laws of England* was "not to be cited here again". The newspaper omitted the rest of Lord Haldane's remarks, namely that it "was edited by a distinguished living author, and that several eminent legal authors had written in it, and that the admirable statements in it might be read by counsel as part of their argument".

In his preface to the Second Edition, written in 1931, Viscount Hailsham said of *Halsbury's Laws*:

> "The work possesses many of the best attributes of a code yet, since it is not a binding authority, it has escaped the endless embroidery of commentary and explanation with their resulting obscurity which is the normal fate of a code."

The Third Edition was published with a preface by Viscount Simonds, the then Lord Chancellor, written in 1952, and the fourth with a preface by Lord Hailsham of St Marylebone, written in 1972.

The size of *Halsbury's Laws* has increased markedly, and the Fourth Edition is still being published with re-issues of volumes whose contents have been overtaken by the need for revision. In 2008, the work will begin rolling into a Fifth Edition, which we can be sure will maintain the traditions and standards of all the editions up to now, and make it as apt a resource at the beginning of the twenty-first century as it was at the beginning of the twentieth.

The impact of the Halsbury name was such that, from an early stage, Stanley Bond made great capital out of it in launching *Halsbury's Statutes* in 1929. In the 1950s *Halsbury's Statutory Instruments* commenced. Both of these titles, though younger than *Halsbury's Laws*, remain reputable resources in their own right.

*Halsbury's Laws of England*, although originally a publication specially designed for one country, was soon being exported to other parts of what was formerly the British Empire, and is now the Commonwealth. In more recent times it has been the model for encyclopaedias of ten countries, most of which carry the Halsbury name, and the number is likely to increase further.

The Law Journal of 15 November 1957 contained an article on Fifty Years of Halsbury. It concludes thus:

> "upon this anniversary one looks instinctively forward to Halsbury's centenary. What will Halsbury be like in the year 2007? What form will it take: paperback, magnetic tape or micro-card? What new titles will it contain: Atomic Power and Transport? Robots and Automation? Rockets and Space Navigation? What law will be administered and practised by our grandchildren and great grandchildren? One thing is certain at least: Halsbury's Laws of England, which has survived and adapted itself to fifty tempestuous years of upheaval and change, will still be there to assist and guide them."

This is certainly justified by our meeting today. I hope I have shown that the climate today is no more favourable to a code than it was in 1907.

As a past Lord Chancellor I look back. To look forward I am happy to pass the baton to my distinguished friend Richard Susskind. In the meantime I content myself with the thought that *Halsbury's Laws of England* continues to enjoy the reputation and quality spoken of by its earlier Editors-in-Chief. This is due to the high standards of contributors, of the editors of the various titles, of the editorial and administrative staff of the publishers, and of the Publisher, Simon Hetherington.

I am greatly honoured to be its Editor-in-Chief in this centenary year.

# Table of Contents

## Centenary Essays*

# CITIZENSHIP AND THE CONSTITUTION

## ANTHONY LESTER[1]

"To produce Utopian theories of government is especially the part of a
Frenchman; to disbelieve in them is especially the part of an Englishman."

Anthony Trollope *North America* (1862) Vol II Ch 9[2]

"A map of the world that does not include Utopia is not worth even glancing
at, for it leaves out the one country at which Humanity is always landing. And
when Humanity lands there, it looks out, and seeing a better country, sets sail.
Progress is the realisation of Utopias."

Oscar Wilde *The Soul of Man under Socialism* (1891)

## INTRODUCTORY

Hardinge Giffard, the first Earl of Halsbury and founding father of the legal encyclopaedia
we know as *"Halsbury's Laws"*, served for ten years as Lord Chancellor in the
Conservative administrations of Disraeli, Salisbury and Balfour. He lost office when
the 1905 election brought Campbell-Bannerman's Liberal government to power. Two
years later, in 1907, Butterworths published Halsbury's first volume, whose centenary is
marked by the present collection of essays.

In 1909, Professor WS Holdsworth's work on constitutional law was published in
vols 6 and 7. Holdsworth was also responsible, together with another distinguished
scholar, F H Lawson, for the section on constitutional law in the second edition, published
in 1932. Lawson, by then Professor of Comparative Law at Oxford University, was a joint
editor of the constitutional law section in the third edition, published in 1954, and, as
Emeritus Professor, of the fourth edition, published in 1974.

The narrative changed little in these four editions, despite the momentous political and
social changes which occurred during the period they spanned. This was because nothing
changed in the conventional legal orthodoxy about the British constitution.

Much of the work done by these eminent jurists has become outdated, but it remains of
more than antiquarian interest. Their description of the status of "British subjects", of the
relationship between the individual and the state, and of the concept of "rights" and
"liberties", is relevant to the current political debate about "British identity", citizenship,
"multiculturalism", a "British Bill of Rights", and whether there is now a need for a written
constitution.

## LORD HALSBURY'S DESIGN

*Halsbury's Laws* was described by its Victorian begetter as containing "a complete
statement of the Laws of England". In his introduction, Halsbury explained his hostility to

---

1  Lord Lester of Herne Hill QC is a barrister practising at Blackstone Chambers and a Liberal
   Democrat life peer. He is currently independent adviser to the Minister of Justice on aspects of
   constitutional reform. He was joint editor of *Halsbury's Laws* (4th edn) vol 4(2) (Reissue) section on
   *British Nationality, Immigration and Race Relations*, and of vol 8(2) (Reissue) on *Constitutional
   Law and Human Rights*.
2  Cited by Professor Sir David Edward QC, also of Blackstone Chambers, in European Essay
   No 34 *Thinking about Constitutions* (2005). The author is indebted to him and to Khatun
   Sapnara, of Coram Chambers, for their valuable comments on a draft of this essay.

the codifying of English law on the lines of the Code of Justinian or the Institutes of Gaius. He expressed his conviction that the law should be stated "as it is without giving such an authority to the mode of its statement as to make itself equivalent to a statute". The work was not intended to express critical opinions about the state of the law, or to place the law within a political or social context. The aim of Halsbury's grand design was to provide an accurate and complete digest of the law contained in English common law and legislation.

The work was to be confined to the "laws of England"; and so Scots law, but not Northern Ireland law[3], was excluded, even in the sections on "constitutional law". The topic of "the Constitution", as described in *Halsbury's Laws* and so earnestly discussed by Victorian parliamentarians in Anthony Trollope's Palliser novels, was what Walter Bagehot had famously described as "The *English* Constitution". Viscount Stair had published his "Institutions of the Law of Scotland" in 1681, but it was only in 1987, that Butterworths – the publishers of *Halsbury's Laws* – also published the *Stair Memorial Encyclopaedia*, a comprehensive statement of Scots law.

And it was only in 1997, as part of the reissue of the fourth edition of *Halsbury's Laws*, that the section on what was now described not as "Constitutional Law" but as "Constitutional Law and Human Rights" included both English and Scots law, as well as the human rights and fundamental freedoms protected by the European Convention on Human Rights, previously covered as part of Foreign Relations Law[4]. The bringing of Scotland into *Halsbury's Laws* description of the "British" rather than "English" constitution happened on the eve of the devolution by the Westminster Parliament of wide constitutional powers to a Scottish Parliament and Executive, in the Scotland Act 1998.

## THE TANGLED HISTORY OF "BRITISH" CITIZENSHIP

Our confused contemporary understanding of what is meant by "British" identity is attributable in large part to our imperial history and its effects, and to the lack of a coherent concept of British citizenship, or of the rights and duties inherent in citizenship, in post-imperial Britain. The British citizen travelling abroad has to make a conscious decision in explaining to immigration authorities the country to which he or she belongs: whether it be England, or Scotland, or Wales, or Northern Ireland, or the United Kingdom, or a combination of these identities.

Halsbury's first volume included a section on "Aliens", explaining that "An alien is, at common law, a subject of a foreign state who has not been born within the allegiance of the Crown". Those who were not aliens but British were not citizens of the British state but "British subjects" born within the allegiance of the Crown, subject to rule by royal prerogative, by the common law, and under laws enacted by the sovereign Parliament of Westminster. That feudal concept of subjection to the Crown continues to influence the relationship between the governors and the governed.

The first volume summarised the provisions of the Aliens Act 1905 enacted two years earlier. True to Halsbury's design, it did not make value judgments about that measure or place it within its political context. In fact, the 1905 Act was highly controversial, having been designed by the Balfour government to appease a wave of virulent anti-semitism in this country by restricting the immigration of Jewish refugees escaping persecution in Tsarist Russia.

Further xenophobia and war hysteria led to the Aliens Restriction Act 1914, which was hurried through all its parliamentary stages in a single August day after war was declared[5].

---

3   The various constitutional and political changes in Northern Ireland are beyond the scope of this essay.
4   The present author shares responsibility for that work and is grateful to the publishers for supporting this radical departure from the previous treatment of the subject.

During the same year, 1914, the British Nationality and Status of Aliens Act proclaimed that everyone born within the allegiance of the Crown in any part of the Empire was a natural-born British subject. This so-called "common code" had been intended to confer equality of citizenship throughout the Empire, but in practice the situation was somewhat different. Those of the overseas dominions which pursued discriminatory population policies consented to the "common code" only on the understanding that they might continue to enforce those policies under another guise – that of immigration control. The result was that the "common status" of British subjects did not connote any substantive equality in relation to the right to enter or settle in any particular part of British territory. The idea of a common code of imperial citizenship remained a dream.

Despite resistance to the imperial "common code", Attlee's government attempted to preserve it in an attenuated form in the British Nationality Act 1948. They did so in the vain hope that Commonwealth countries, with their own nationality and citizenship laws, would eventually introduce an interlocking and harmonious system of local laws under which Commonwealth citizens would enjoy equal rights and privileges. And so the first of two confusing legal concepts was inserted into the 1948 Act: Commonwealth citizenship. It was defined in a way which defied comprehension. Every person who was a citizen of any Commonwealth country had, by virtue of that citizenship, "the status of a British subject"; any person having that status "may be known either as a British subject or as a Commonwealth citizen", and "the expression 'British subject' and the expression 'Commonwealth citizen' shall have the same meaning".

In other words, citizens of independent Commonwealth countries, like Australia, Canada and India, and those of British dependencies like Hong Kong, were all alike "British subjects" or "Commonwealth citizens". This had as little practical effect under the 1948 Act as it did under the 1914 Act. As before, the old dominions continued to pursue discriminatory population policies based on ethnicity against Commonwealth citizens, and the vision of a common Commonwealth citizenship was not translated into a harmonious system of citizenship laws.

The ghost of the 1914 legislation, which continued to haunt the 1948 Act, did however have considerable practical significance for the United Kingdom. Before the passage of the Commonwealth Immigrants Act 1962, Commonwealth citizens were entitled freely to travel to this country and to settle here. Once here, they enjoyed equal rights with United Kingdom citizens and could acquire United Kingdom citizenship automatically by registering after a period of residence. The very inter-changeability of the expressions "British subject" and "Commonwealth citizen" and the use of the word "British" to describe a citizen of an independent Commonwealth country, confused Parliament and the public about the real meaning of British citizenship. To add to the confusion, citizens of the Republic of Ireland were treated as if they were British subjects; as if they were not aliens and the Republic of Ireland was not a foreign country.

The other bewildering concept introduced by the 1948 Act was that of citizenship of the United Kingdom and colonies. Instead of defining two separate citizenships, one for the

---

5   It enabled Orders in Council to be made imposing much more severe controls over all aliens in times of war, imminent national danger or great emergency. After the war, however, it was continued and extended by the Aliens Restriction (Amendment) Act 1919, which also repealed the 1905 Act. It was renewed annually until superseded by the Immigration Act 1971. In addition, the Defence of the Realm Act was passed on 8 August 1914, giving the government wide-ranging powers during the war period. The legislation gave the government executive powers to suppress published criticism, imprison without trial and to commandeer economic resources, including land, for the war effort. The British public were also constrained from various everyday activities such as flying kites or burning bonfires.

United Kingdom itself and a more temporary citizenship for British colonies before their attainment of full independence, the 1948 Act merged the two into a single citizenship. Confusion was bound to result from the fact that our citizenship law did not reflect the genuine links between the citizens of the United Kingdom and the United Kingdom itself, or the citizens of a dependency and the dependency itself.

The combined effect of these "portmanteau" concepts was to weaken the positive content and value of the very notion of citizenship of this country. Because the law did not reflect the genuine link between the citizen and the State, it was easy to transpose the fact that some citizens were undoubtedly closely linked to Britain by birth, descent, marriage or residence here, into the conclusion that other citizens were "non-belongers" because they lacked those connections. And, since the vast majority of those citizens of the United Kingdom and colonies who did not have those connections were non-white, the absence of such connections could be used as a device to discriminate against them on the grounds of their colour or ethnicity.

## THE *EAST AFRICAN ASIANS*' CASE: A CAUTIONARY TALE[6]

Under the Commonwealth Immigrants Act 1962, immigration control was applied for the first time not to aliens but to "Commonwealth citizens". In broad terms, the only persons to whom the 1962 Act did not apply were those who were born in Britain, or citizens of the United Kingdom and colonies holding a United Kingdom passport issued by the United Kingdom government, as distinct from the government of a dependency.

The citizens of the United Kingdom and colonies of asian descent who were resident in Kenya and Uganda, in common with other colonial United Kingdom citizens, lost their right of entry to Britain by this means, since they were United Kingdom citizens by virtue of their colonial connection, and were entitled only to colonial United Kingdom passports. However, they still had the right to live in colonial Kenya and Uganda.

At this time, the British government was engaged in constitutional talks about the coming independence of the East African dependencies. One of the problems which concerned the British government was the future well-being of the European and Asian minorities, especially in Kenya in the aftermath of the Mau Mau uprising. The government decided to permit the asian minority to retain their United Kingdom citizenship after Kenya and Uganda became independent, restoring to them the right to enter the United Kingdom free of immigration control. But the British Asians had to choose, either to apply within two years for local citizenship and renounce their citizenship of the United Kingdom and colonies, or else to retain their United Kingdom citizenship and thereby their right of entry into the United Kingdom. In this crucial respect the British Asians were treated less favourably on racial grounds than the European minority in East Africa who were permitted to re-acquire their United Kingdom citizenship and their right of entry in the event that they had renounced those rights in order to become citizens of other Commonwealth countries.

In reliance on their rights as United Kingdom passport holders, the vast majority of British Asians in Kenya and Uganda retained their citizenship of this country during the two years when they could have opted for local citizenship. They thereby lost their right to live in East Africa. But they had a new positive attribute of citizenship – the right to a United Kingdom passport issued by the United Kingdom government and thus of entry into Britain. That made, or should have made them "belongers" if the word had any meaning other than as a reference to their colour or ethnic origins. A genuine link had been created between them and their country of citizenship; the British government intended to confer

---

6  *East African Asians v UK* (1973) 3 EHRR 76, EComHR.

full citizenship on them; and they in turn altered their position by relying on the genuineness of their link with their only country of citizenship.

In 1967, because of the policy of "Africanisation", at that time especially in Kenya, the British Asians began in increasing numbers to exercise their right as United Kingdom passport holders to come to Britain. A campaign was led by Enoch Powell and Duncan Sandys to deprive them of their right of entry. The government responded by driving another Commonwealth Immigrants Bill through Parliament as an emergency measure in three days and nights, in February 1968.

Thenceforth, a United Kingdom passport holder could enter Britain only if he, or at least one of his parents or grandparents, was born, naturalised, adopted or registered as a United Kingdom citizen *in the United Kingdom itself*. Upon its face the 1968 Act was merely applying a familiar set of qualifications for the acquisition of United Kingdom citizenship to our immigration law, but the real purpose of this measure was to deprive the British Asians of their right of entry because of their colour or ethnicity.

In the result, the vast majority of British Asians were unable to leave Kenya and Uganda because, according to the government, they had no substantial connection with this country. Many had been deprived of their livelihood under the local law, and they and their families were rendered destitute. Some tried to enter this country without Home Office vouchers. Regarded as queue-jumpers, they were shuttle-cocked around the world, or detained for weeks or even months in prison in this country. Others were stranded in Europe or India. In all these respects they were treated less favourably than their fellow United Kingdom citizens of European origin, and indeed second generation Australians, Canadians and New Zealanders who were "partials" because one of their parents was British-born. They were also treated less favourably than Irish citizens who were neither United Kingdom citizens nor Commonwealth-born. Because of their skin colour and ethnicity, they had become refugees and second-class citizens without status.

In the absence of effective British judicial remedies challenging the compatibility of the measure with the European Convention on Human Rights, the only recourse open to these dispossessed British Asians was to complain to the European Commission of Human Rights. The Commission upheld their complaint and concluded that publicly to single out a group for differential treatment constituted a special affront to human dignity, and that as British citizens the applicants had been subjected by Parliament to degrading treatment in breach of art 3 of the Convention. The government accepted the Commission's verdict and made administrative changes to its policy.

If a similar unsightly measure were to be enacted today, there would be a limited remedy available under the Human Rights Act 1998, in that a British court could declare the measure to be incompatible with Convention rights. However, unlike the courts of most other European and Commonwealth countries, and unlike the position under directly effective European Community law, a British court could not strike down the offending statute but would have to leave it to the political branches of government to decide whether to amend the legislation or leave the victims to their remedies on the international plane before the European Court of Human Rights.

The *East Africans'* case illustrated the unsatisfactory concept of British citizenship and the lack of effective domestic remedies for violations of human rights and fundamental freedoms. To pave the way to exclude the Hong Kong Chinese from being able to enter and settle in the United Kingdom when sovereignty was transferred to the People's Republic of China, the 1981 British Nationality Act created a distinction between British citizens and citizens of the remaining dependent territories. It created the separate categories of "British" citizenship, "British overseas territories" citizenship, and "British overseas" citizenship; but it did not tamper with the concept of Commonwealth citizenship or seek to codify the rights and duties of British citizens. The subsequent cascade of immigration legislation has not contributed to popular understanding of the meaning and attributes of citizenship.

## CONSTITUTIONAL ORTHODOXY

Among the Victorian theorists, Walter Bagehot famously separated what he called the "dignified parts" of the "English Constitution" that "excite and preserve the reverence of the population" and the "effective parts" by which it "in fact works and rules". The cornerstone of the system was the absolute and unfettered sovereignty of the national legislature. AV Dicey's "Introduction to the Study of the Law of the Constitution" attempted to reduce the tangled undergrowth of medieval, monarchical, and parliamentary prerogatives to a series of lucid constitutional theorems about the royal prerogative, parliamentary sovereignty, and the rule of law, and, like his Benthamite predecessors, to demonstrate the superiority of our unwritten flexible arrangements over the rigid written constitutions of continental Europe and the United States.

Dicey gloried in the unrestricted legislative sovereignty of the imperial Parliament of Westminster: in his words, "the one fundamental dogma of English constitutional laws is the absolute legislative sovereignty or despotism of the King in Parliament". For Dicey, as for Bentham, the concept of "natural rights" was nonsense, and the idea of "natural and imprescriptible" rights "nonsense on stilts"[7].

There are important English sources of the concept of fundamental, or "natural", rights, including Milton, Locke and Paine. However, for the past two centuries, the prevailing constitutional ideology, influenced by Burke, Bentham, Austin, Dicey and Sir Ivor Jennings, has treated British citizens as subjects of the Crown without benefit of positive and fundamental constitutional rights giving legal protection to the individual against the public authorities of the state. What were known as "the liberties of the subject" were residual and negative in their nature – the individual's freedom to do what he or she likes, unless forbidden by the common law or by statute.

The idea of "fundamental rights" and of a "fundamental" constitutional law, taking precedence over ordinary laws, became eclipsed at the end of the seventeenth century by the concept of absolute parliamentary sovereignty. In the early part of that century, the judges had struggled not only for independence from the Executive but also for the right to withhold effect from laws they regarded as unconscionable, or contrary to a higher fundamental and immutable natural law. They won their struggle for independence against the Crown's claim to rule by prerogative, but the price paid by the common lawyers for their alliance with Parliament against the divine right of kings was that the common law could be changed by Parliament as it pleased. The "glorious bloodless" revolution was won by Parliament, and, although the Bill of Rights of 1688–89 and the Act of Settlement of 1700 recognised some important personal rights and liberties, the terms of the constitutional settlement were mainly concerned with protecting the rights and liberties of Parliament. The alliance of Parliament and the common lawyers ensured that the supremacy of the law would mean the supremacy of Parliament; or, in reality, the supremacy of the central government in Parliament.

According to traditional, post-seventeenth century English political and legal theory, therefore, since the King or Queen-in-Parliament is sovereign, in practice, the Executive-in-

---

7   However, it is noteworthy that Dicey's passionate opposition to Home Rule for Ireland, and his enthusiasm for the Unionist cause, led him to turn his back on his two fundamental principles: parliamentary sovereignty and the rule of law. In 1913, Dicey contended that if Asquith's Home Rule Bill were enacted by Parliament, it would have no constitutional justification as a law; and he also argued that it would be justifiable for the Ulster Unionists to resort to rebellion, if necessary, to prevent Irish Home Rule.

Parliament, the "subject" cannot possess fundamental rights such as are guaranteed to the citizen by written constitutions. There are no British rights that are fundamental in the sense that they enjoy special constitutional protection against Parliament. The liberties of the subject are merely implications to be derived from two principles. The first principle is that we may say or do as we please, provided that we do not transgress the substantive law or the legal rights of others. The second principle is that public authorities, including the Crown, may do only what they are authorised to do by some other rule, including the royal prerogative, or by statute.

Again, according to the traditional English theory, the role of the independent judiciary is essential in maintaining the common law principles of the rule of law, but the courts are subordinate to the Executive-in-Parliament, not as an equal and co-ordinate branch of government. Judges are in Francis Bacon's phrase, "lions under the Throne". The task of law-making is the exclusive province of Parliament. It would be undemocratic for the non-elected judiciary to act as lawmakers. It would also be inappropriate because judges are ill-equipped by their training and professional experience to make law. It would be undesirable for judges to become involved in controversial issues of policy, because their decisions would make them more vulnerable to public criticism in the political arena. The judges' constitutional task is faithfully and strictly to interpret the will of Parliament, expressed in detailed legislation, to be read according to its so-called "plain meaning", and to declare the common law when it is incomplete or obscure. If either the textual analysis of the words of a statute or the courts' interpretation of the common law has undesirable consequences, the matter must be corrected by the legislature and not by the courts. The ancient prerogative writs, including the writ of habeas corpus, were available to curb abuses of public powers, but they could be overridden by legislation.

Once more according to this traditional English political and legal theory, the surest and most effective safeguards of what we now term "human rights" are not the rigid legalisms and paper guarantees of written constitutions, but the benevolent exercise of administrative discretion by civil servants acting as guardians of the public interest, accountable through their political masters to the legislature and to the people. Effective safeguards against the misuse of public powers were not so much enforceable legal safeguards but constitutional conventions: the sense of fair play of ministers and the professional integrity of civil servants in exercising their broad delegated public powers; the vigilance of Her Majesty's Opposition and of individual members of Parliament; the influence of a free and vigorous press and a well-informed public opinion; and the periodic opportunity of changing the government through free and secret elections.

The best conditions for the working of the system were those of Victorian society: a society self-conscious in its homogeneity and insularity, that overshadowed its professed ideals of tolerance and fair play, a society rejoicing in its abundant wealth, the fruits of early industrialisation and exploitation of a vast empire; a society of *laissez-faire*, in which the protection of property and contract rights was the dominant concern of the courts; a society administered at home and abroad by a new breed of Platonic guardians, permanent, well-paid civil servants educated in the classics and recruited on merit; a society whose imperial Parliament was not subjected to the pressures of highly organised political parties, a mass electorate, and mass communications, as well as the centrifugal forces of nationalism and self-determination.

In such an age it was natural to extol the virtues of an omnipotent Parliament working in partnership with an independent judiciary to uphold fair play and the supremacy of the rule of law. According to this view, the British people have no need for written constitutions, fundamental rights or new-fangled notions of citizenship. Parliament makes the rules flexibly as and when necessary, leaving the Executive to exercise wide prerogative and statutory powers.

It is this traditional constitutional orthodoxy that was expressed repeatedly in each of the four editions of *Halsbury's Laws*. One of its great virtues is that it reminds us that a culture of liberty is more significant than formal legal rights. One of its great defects is legal positivism and ethical aimlessness in interpreting and applying the law – the notion, which persisted throughout the first half of the twentieth century, that whatever is laid down in a legal rule is a "law" and that it must be interpreted strictly according to its letter, irrespective of issues of ethics or public policy. Another great defect is that the legal remedies for the abuse of public powers were weak or non-existent.

Although the rights-based ideology was rejected by successive generations of governors of the United Kingdom and the British Empire, it was a potent force across the rest of the world. American and French concepts of human rights and judicial review shaped the rise of constitutionalism in Europe and elsewhere. The conquests of Napoleon's armies spread throughout the European continent not only the Code Civil, but also the public philosophy and public law of the United States and France. The Declaration of the Rights of Man and of the Citizen expressed a commitment to the principles of political liberty and equality before the law as natural and inalienable rights of the individual which became the template for liberal constitutions throughout Europe, after 1848. These ideas were eventually to spread to other continents in the wake of the decline of Europe's empires.

By the mid-twentieth century, when the third edition of the title of *Halsbury's Laws* on Constitutional Law was published, there were three countries – the United States, India and Ireland – with legal systems based on the common law, each giving constitutional protection to human rights. Australia's written constitution contained a couple of fundamental rights to property and religious freedom. Canada was governed under the British North America Act, but without expressly guaranteed fundamental rights. New Zealand had the same flexible and unwritten system as the British did. By 1974, when the fourth edition of that title was published, British law-makers had used the European Convention on Human Rights as the model for the written constitutions of newly independent Commonwealth countries in Africa and the Caribbean. The Convention was exported in this way, but it was not imported into United Kingdom law.

## THE CHANGING BRITISH ZEITGEIST

From the mid-1960s, political events in the United Kingdom occurred that were to have a profound effect in altering conventional attitudes towards the role of law and the judicial process in protecting human rights. They included the creation of the Law Commissions in 1966, the enactment in 1968, 1975 and 1976 of anti-discrimination legislation containing positive civil rights, and accession in 1972 to the European Community. The Law Commission for England and Wales, under the leadership of its first chairman, Lord Scarman, paved the way for the procedural reforms to English judicial review made in 1977, at a time when a new generation of judges were fashioning a modern system of administrative law giving greater protection against the misuse of public powers by public authorities, and adopting a purposive rather than a literal interpretation of the law. Membership of the European Community added a further level of legal protection for equality and other human rights.

Another political event which was to have a profound, if unforeseen, effect was the Wilson government's acceptance in January 1966 of the right of petition to the European Commission of Human Rights and the jurisdiction of the European Court of Human Rights in British cases. This gave British lawyers an important opportunity to obtain redress for their clients under the Convention for want of effective remedies within the United Kingdom.

Acceptance of the right of petition resulted in many significant and far-reaching cases in which the United Kingdom was found by the European Commission and Court of

Human Rights to have breached Convention rights. Convention rights were also frequently invoked in proceedings before English courts, before it was brought home by the 1998 Act; and the courts gradually became willing to have regard to the unincorporated Convention and its case law as sources of principles or standards of public policy, influenced by the cases in which United Kingdom law and practice had been held by the Strasbourg Court to have violated Convention rights. English courts did so where a statute was ambiguous; or where the common law was developing or uncertain; or as a source of legal public policy; or when determining the manner in which judicial powers were to be exercised.

However, at common law, Convention rights could not be directly invoked to determine whether administrative discretion, exercised under broad statutory powers, unnecessarily interfered with those rights, or had been disproportionate to the decision-maker's aims. This is because a statute conferring broad discretionary powers was regarded as unambiguous, and the Convention as irrelevant, in ascertaining the purpose of the statute. Rigidly adhering to the dualist concept of public international law, according to which treaty provisions do not become part of the law of the land unless incorporated by Act of Parliament, the Law Lords decided that, for the courts to have required ministers to comply with the Convention in performing their public functions would have involved a breach of the constitutional separation of powers between the judiciary and the legislative and executive branches of government. According to this view, it was impermissible for them to give direct effect to Convention rights and obligations when Parliament had failed to do so. There was, therefore, a significant gap in the domestic protection of Convention rights which could be filled only by legislation.

In 1974, Scarman had given his great authority, in his Hamlyn Lectures – *English Law – The New Dimension*, to the campaign to make Convention rights directly enforceable as part of a new constitutional settlement. In 1976, the Home Secretary, Roy Jenkins, published a Home Office discussion document on the subject, and revealed his personal support for incorporation. In 1977, the Northern Ireland Standing Advisory Commission on Human Rights published a report recommending incorporation, as did a Lords Select Committee in the following year. *Charter* 88, created in November 1988, became a political movement supporting constitutional reforms. In the eighties and nineties, a series of Private Members' Bills were introduced and debated in both Houses of Parliament. In 1991, two organisations, Liberty and the *Institute of Public Policy Research* ("the IPPR"), published separate proposals for bills of rights, modelled in part on the Convention. The IPPR went further and produced a draft written constitution for the United Kingdom.

In March 1993, the Leader of the Labour Party, John Smith, gave a lecture entitled "A Citizen's Democracy", under the IPPR's auspices, calling for "a new constitutional settlement, a new deal between the people and the state that puts the citizen centre stage". The lecture marked a political watershed. One measure of reform which he proposed was incorporation of Convention rights. In September 1993, Smith's statement of policy was expressed in the Labour Party's "*A new agenda for democracy: Labour's proposals for constitutional reform*". The 1993 Labour Party conference adopted a policy supporting a two-stage process: the first included the incorporation of the Convention; the second stage was for a Labour government to set up an all-party commission to consider and draft a home-grown bill of rights.

When Smith died suddenly in May 1994, the new Labour leader, Tony Blair, inherited the policy on constitutional reform. In December 1996, the shadow Home Secretary, Jack Straw, published Labour's consultation paper, "*Bringing Rights Home*", setting out the case for incorporation and proposals for the way this should be done.

In March 1997, the Labour and Liberal Democrat Joint Consultative Committee on Constitutional Reform, co-chaired by Robin Cook and Robert Maclennan, published their report. Their foreword proclaimed that:

"The objectives of the British Constitution should be to secure a government that is democratic and a society that is open and free. Democratic government should ensure that those who hold power in the name of the people are accountable to the collective wishes and interests of the people. Each individual citizen should have equal rights and responsibilities in an open society where the aim is to guarantee civil liberty, social cohesion and economic opportunity."

The *Cook-Maclennan* report contained proposals for bringing Convention rights home and for freedom of information legislation, as well as to bring power closer to the people by devolving power in Scotland, Wales, the English regions, and London. It also proposed reviewing the electoral systems and reforming both Houses of Parliament.

## THE NEW HALSBURY

It was with the probability that a Labour government would soon be returned to power, committed to an ambitious programme of constitutional reform, that the reissue of *Halsbury's Laws* title on Constitutional Law was published, in 1996, with the addition of sections on human rights and on Scotland. As already mentioned, the reissue marked a radical departure from previous work. It recognised[8] that the task of defining our constitutional law is peculiarly difficult because of the absence of a written constitution for the United Kingdom as the sole or supreme source of legal authority for all public action, whether executive, legislative or judicial. It noted that the task is made even more difficult because of the United Kingdom's membership of the European Community which has had "a profound effect on the traditional English constitutional principles and rules, including the doctrine of parliamentary sovereignty, the royal prerogative, the functions of the judiciary, and the concept of citizenship". In addition, it observed, a modern restatement of English constitutional law has to take account of the increasing influence of the Convention on rights, duties, and remedies which in other European states are protected by written constitutions and enforceable Bills of Rights.

The critique continued in the following terms, for which the present author takes responsibility:

"The United Kingdom is unusual in that it lacks a comprehensive constitutional charter which establishes and gives limited powers to the institutions of government; confers and protects the civil and political rights of citizens; may be repealed or amended only in accordance with special procedural requirements; and enjoys particular sanctity ...

United Kingdom constitutional law is an incomplete system, consisting of piecemeal legislation, ancient common law doctrines, and constitutional conventions which are binding in a political rather than in a legal sense. The United Kingdom constitution lacks the coherence of comprehensive written constitutions.

The boundaries of English constitutional law have never been satisfactorily defined, partly because there is no constitutional document possessing an extraordinary sanctity or legally protected status, partly because the constitutional rules are susceptible to change by more or less formal means, partly because many of the rules are not justiciable, and partly because the differences between public law and private law are not clear.

---

8   Volume 8(2) (Reissue) para 1.

Nor is there any clear distinction between state bodies and others in the United Kingdom ...

There have, especially over the past two decades, been criticisms of many aspects of British government; and many proposals for constitutional change."

## THE CHANGING CONSTITUTION

As soon as it won power in May 1997 the New Labour government introduced a far-reaching programme of constitutional reform, including:

- creating a Scottish Parliament, a Northern Ireland Assembly, a Welsh Assembly, and a Greater London Authority, devolving legislative and executive powers from Whitehall;
- removing the right of most hereditary peers to be members of the House of Lords;
- giving direct effect to Convention rights via the 1998 Act;
- creating a right to freedom of information about public authorities;
- abolishing the role of the Lord Chancellor so that the holder of the office is no longer head of the judiciary or Speaker of the House of Lords;
- creating a new, free-standing Supreme Court, separating the highest appeal court from Parliament and removing the Law Lords from the legislature; establishing an independent Judicial Appointments Commission to select candidates for judicial office; and
- establishing the independence of the Bank of England, allowing interest rate decisions to be made free of active political involvement.

## THE HUMAN RIGHTS ACT 1998

For present purposes, the 1998 Act is the most significant of these changes. It is a well-drafted and subtle measure, expressed in the open-textured language appropriate to a constitutional charter. It declares basic rights and freedoms inherent in our common humanity, and the ethical values of a modern democratic society governed under the rule of law – a society in which individual and minority rights must be protected against the tyranny of majorities and the abuse of public powers, especially where excessive means are used to pursue legitimate ends. The Act provides an ethical framework to guide law-makers, judges, and individual men and women. Its language contains studied and necessary ambiguities giving the courts leeway in developing and applying its concepts to changing social needs and values without usurping executive or legislative powers. It respects the jurisprudence of the European Court of Human Rights but it does not fetter the ability of British courts to develop a home-grown jurisprudence that suits our own system of government and law. Convention case law gives guidance but does not hobble the progressive development of British law.

The 1998 Act does not challenge the doctrine of parliamentary supremacy by empowering the courts to strike down acts of Parliament. Instead it uses the device of judicial declarations of incompatibility where it is impossible to read and give effect to statutes in harmony with Convention rights. That compromise enables the executive and legislative branches to choose an appropriate remedy for the injustice identified by the courts; and, if they fail to do so, it provides an incentive for the Strasbourg Court to give or require effective redress.

Although the 1998 Act respects the legislative supremacy of Parliament, it is no ordinary law. It enables the courts to breathe new life into fossilized archaic statutes by applying the dynamic values and standards prescribed by the 1998 Act. It speaks both to old statutes and to new statutes. In the absence of a clear and unequivocal legislative intention to the contrary, the rights it declares and protects must, where possible, prevail over latent or apparent inconsistencies in future as well as existing legislation.

The Act commands public bodies and officials to exercise their powers in accordance with Convention rights, including the principles of legal certainty and proportionality. Where they fail to do so, victims have a claim of right for breach of the statutory duty to exercise public functions in a way that is compatible with Convention rights; and the courts are empowered to fashion effective remedies.

For good constitutional reasons, based on the democratic imperative and the separation of powers, the courts must and do take care not to act in place of the legislative or executive branches, or to reach decisions for which they lack sufficient authority or expertise. Equally, the independent, politically neutral and impartial judiciary has a duty to protect fundamental rights.

The Act envisages that the courts will strive by a process of constitutional interpretation familiar in other common law jurisdictions to find at least implied safeguards of human rights in legislation and to give a restrictive meaning to broadly delegated public powers where they interfere excessively with basic rights and freedoms.

The Act also envisages that the courts will interpret and apply the common law compatibly with Convention rights, reconciling the demands of legal certainty with the need to provide effective legal remedies for breaches by those endowed with public powers. It adds strength to the traditional role of our courts in developing the common law and equity to suit contemporary conditions of life. In that way it allows the courts to play a complementary role in reforming the law. Convention law is to be approached through and not around statute law and common law.

The 1998 Act does not depend only on the judiciary to secure and protect human rights, nor does it create a government of unelected judges. It is holistic in its organising principles, engaging the responsibility of all three branches of government to act in a way compatible with fundamental civil and political rights. It is based on a mature theory of the nature of parliamentary democracy and the role of the judiciary. The notion of parliamentary government which it reflects is neither a metaphysical dogma nor a rigid mechanical rule. It is a flexible notion rooted in the political reality of the sharing of power needed in meeting the changing needs of a complex post-industrial society.

The 1998 Act is also an essential element in the constitutional re-settlement of the different nations and regions, limiting the powers of the devolved institutions by applying common standards of protection of human rights – a species of what in other countries would be federal constitutional law. It ensures that our basic rights do not alter according to the particular part of the United Kingdom in which we live or work, or according to whether we are or are not British citizens.

During its passage, the Human Rights Bill was opposed by the Conservative front bench and by right-wing sections of the media. It was and remains a target of the tabloids which fear that it will result in legal restraints on their intrusions on personal privacy. They continue to attack the 1998 Act, wrongly claiming that it is a charter of rights for criminals, terrorists and bogus asylum-seekers, and that it enables unelected British judges to frustrate the will of the majority and to undermine the effectiveness of necessary state powers.

Most regrettably, Prime Minister Blair and other senior ministers added their own attacks, and threatened to cut down the protection given by the 1998 Act. The fact that they were members of the very government responsible for the Act undermined the legitimacy of it, and has been damaging to the protection of human rights and to the rule of law.

## THE GOVERNANCE OF BRITAIN: FURTHER CONSTITUTIONAL CHANGE?

In July 2007, Gordon Brown's new administration published a Green Paper entitled *The Governance of Britain* (Cm 7170)[9]. In their foreword, the Prime Minister and the Secretary for Justice and Lord Chancellor, Jack Straw, explained their wish to build on the constitutional changes made by New Labour:

> "[W]e want to go further. We want to forge a new relationship between government and the citizen, and begin the journey towards a new constitutional settlement – a settlement that entrusts Parliament and the people with more power.
>
> The proposals in this Green Paper seek to address two fundamental questions: how should we hold power accountable, and how should we uphold and enhance the rights and responsibilities of the citizen."

The Green Paper describes the government's vision and proposals for constitutional renewal, but it does not seek to set out a final blueprint for a new constitutional settlement. It is only "the first step in a national conversation" in which people throughout the country will participate to strengthen democracy[10]. That national conversation will involve the other political parties, each of which is developing policy in this area.

Almost alone in the democratic world, we British have no written constitution protecting our basic civil and political rights. We have no constitutional charter defining the scope of the powers of the legislative, executive and judicial branches of government. Where Parliament remains passive, the government, clothed in ancient monarchical authority, exercises unbridled prerogative powers – to wage war, to make binding treaties, to control the civil service, to appoint public officers of state, and to issue or withhold passports.

Ever since the American and French Revolutions, British political leaders have rejected the idea of entrenching fundamental rights in a written constitution. Dicey's "dogma" of parliamentary supremacy has meant executive domination based on a highly centralised system of unitary government, with ineffective checks and balances protecting individual rights and the status and prerogatives of each level of government. It is essential that the courts are able and willing to ensure that our governors do not act lawlessly or use their powers to excess, but the courts are subordinate to an Executive-dominated parliament – lions under the throne – and their independence can be undermined by political interference. Both the 1998 Act and the Constitutional Reform Act 2005 are capable of being repealed by a future government with a controlling majority in the House of Commons. The fundamental question is whether we should bridle the powers of the Executive and strengthen human rights, democracy and the rule of law by means of a new constitutional settlement which allocates public powers to each level of government – central and devolved, including local government – and protects their status and prerogatives.

---

9  In the wake of Gordon Brown's statement that "The role of Attorney General, which combines legal and ministerial functions, needs to change", the government also published a consultation paper on the role of the Attorney General.

10 In August 2007, the SNP administration published a White Paper entitled *Choosing Scotland's Future: A National Conversation*, proposing either enhanced devolution or complete independence for Scotland, and including a Scottish Referendum Bill. Before its launch, the Scottish Labour, Conservative and Liberal Democrat party leaders issued a joint statement setting out their opposition to the SNP administration's plans.

There are many other important and difficult questions that need to be considered, for example:

- are there distinctively "British" values of liberty and equality under law?
- do we need to strengthen the legal protection of human rights, for example, by recasting the 1998 Act as a British bill of rights and responsibilities?
- how should we protect economic, social and cultural rights?
- what does it mean to be a British citizen in our plural society?
- how do we express British core constitutional values and explain them to new citizens and young people?
- what is and what should be the institutional relationship between the three branches of British government?
- what should be their institutional relationship with Europe?
- should a new constitutional settlement guarantee the powers and prerogatives of the devolved institutions of government, including regional and local government?
- what are and should be the functions of the two Houses of Parliament and their relationship with each other and with the devolved legislative and executive institutions of government?
- how should members of each House of Parliament be chosen?
- should the Scottish devolution settlement be changed by giving wider powers to the Scottish Parliament and government, or by creating a federal framework, or should Scotland become a sovereign, independent state?
- what are the respective benefits and burdens of our present mainly unwritten constitutional arrangements and of a more written constitution of the kind which exists in other common law countries?
- given public distrust in government and low voting turnout, would further constitutional reform help to regain public trust and confidence and reinvigorate the political system?
- should we engage the people in discussion and dialogue about British values and government, as part of a process leading to a written constitution?
- could such a constitution be developed by act of Parliament without the need to entrench it by means of a new settlement endorsed by the people?
- would it be appropriate and necessary to obtain not only parliamentary approval but also popular consent by means of a referendum?
- what about the Northern Ireland constitutional questions?

## CITIZENSHIP AND NATIONAL IDENTITY

One important theme explored in the Green Paper on *The Governance of Britain* is the relationship between citizenship and national identity. The Green Paper explains that:

> "181. Identity is important because it shapes people's sense of self. Some components of our identity are given to us and are matters of fact. But others are the subject of at least a degree of choice: faith, political affiliations, occupation, for some, nationality. Yet even those elements that are 'chosen' are not the result of a completely free choice. The influence of identity of family, geography, education, ethnic background and origin, and how we are perceived by others, is huge.
>
> 182. Each of us possesses multiple identities because we identify ourselves in different ways, depending on the factors that matter most to us. Factors such as gender, race, ethnicity, age, disability, class and faith are shared with some and different from others. But in addition there is a national identity that we

can all hold in common: the overarching factor – British citizenship – that brings the nation together.

183. We can look to history to help us to define citizenship. We can learn much from countries that have a more clearly defined sense of citizenship, and what goes with it; notably from the United States, Canada, Australia and South Africa, and from those parts of Western Europe which have had to develop the idea of citizenship to survive as nations or, indeed, simply to be nations …

185. … [T]here is common ground between British citizens, and many cultural traits and traditions that we can all recognise as distinctively British. The government believes that a clearer definition of citizenship would give people a better sense of their British identity in a globalised world. British citizenship – and the rights and responsibilities that accompany it – need to be valued and meaningful, not only for recent arrivals looking to become British but also for British people themselves."

This discussion about citizenship and national identity, involving all of the main political parties, springs from concerns about the consequences of a withdrawal of some of our fellow citizens into divisive and alienating separatist identities, whether a politicised ethnic identity, as among some Scottish nationalists, or a politicised religious identity, as among Islamicists with foreign radical encouragement and support.

It is 40 years since Roy Jenkins made a public statement of his attitude as Home Secretary towards racial discrimination and the problems of integration. He explained that he did not think that "we need in this country a 'melting pot', which will turn everybody out in a common mould, as one of a series of carbon copies of someone's misplaced vision of the stereotyped Englishman". Jenkins defined integration:

"… not as a flattening process of assimilation but as equal opportunity, accompanied by cultural diversity, in an atmosphere of mutual tolerance. This is the goal. We may fall a little short of its full attainment, as have other communities both in the past and in the present. But if we are to maintain any sort of world reputation for civilised living and social cohesion, we must get far nearer to its achievement than is the case today."

Forty years ago, the problem of integration was defined in terms of ethnicity and migrant culture, and of solutions involved combating racial discrimination and prejudice among the "host" community. The landmark study of British race relations by EJB Rose, Nicholas Deakin, and Mark Abrams, published in 1970, was entitled, significantly, "Colour and Citizenship". Religious identity was perceived mainly in the context of Northern Ireland, and Northern Irish problems were regarded as having scant relevance to the problems of racial integration in Britain. Only the problems of sex discrimination were tackled by similar legislation on both sides of the Irish Sea.

Forty years ago, Irish and Scottish nationalism were recognised as creating potential risks to the unity of the British state, but the problems associated with the arrival and settlement of migrants from South Asia were analysed in terms of racial discrimination and disadvantage and the need to respect cultural and linguistic differences rather than a need to promote "British" values and a "British" national identity that is greater than the sum of its parts.

Until relatively recently, no one involved in developing legal and other strategies to combat prejudice and discrimination foresaw that a new form of politico-religious sectarianism might become a new phenomenon on this side of the Irish Sea, or that a small but vocal minority of second generation British Muslims would define themselves and their political aims in terms that reject the values of Britain's liberal, secular democratic society. Many opinion-formers and decision-takers concentrated on promoting multiculturalism and diversity without tackling economic neglect and the creation of separate and segregated minority communities. There was also a failure to introduce effective measures to deal with oppression among elements within Britain's new minorities – the mistreatment of girls and women, the forcing of children and young adults into "marriages" against their will and the carrying out of so-called "honour-killings" if they defy the wishes of their parents and community leaders.

This is the context in which right-wing, xenophobic organisations, such as the BNP, seek to whip up group hatred, using anti-Muslim propaganda as a surrogate for racist hostility to British Asians. They are helped by terrorist outrages committed in Britain in the name of a politically distorted version of Islam, as well as by the militant rhetoric of fundamentalist clerics, recruited from abroad, preaching their own brand of hatred against Jews and other non-Muslims, and using the Iraq war and the situation in Israel/Palestine to justify the slaughter of the innocent.

These problems are not unique to this country. They are global in nature and need to be tackled with enlightened and courageous leadership and support both from public authorities and from within majority Muslim communities. The goal is the ancient concept of unity in diversity – the precondition of civilised living.

Constitutional reform is, of course, not a panacea. But a British statement of values setting out the ideas and principles that bind us together as a nation, together with a coherent definition of the rights and obligations of British citizenship, would achieve a stronger sense of what it means to be British today. There would appear to be broad support for such measures across and beyond the main political parties.

A century after the publication of Halsbury's first volume, we have begun the journey towards a new constitutional settlement. It should not take a further century to complete that journey.

# JUDICIAL REVIEW: A CITIZEN'S REMEDY

## MICHAEL SUPPERSTONE QC AND JOANNE CLEMENT[1]

"... the court ... has the constitutional role and duty of ensuring that the rights of citizens are not abused by the unlawful exercise of executive power."[2]

## INTRODUCTION

In 1971, Lord Reid noted the absence of a "developed system of administrative law" in this country, observing that until fairly recently, it was not needed[3]. Indeed, it was not until the Fourth Edition of *Halsbury's Laws of England*, published in 1973, that a new title "Administrative Law" was produced, edited by Professors S de Smith, B A Hepple and D GT Williams. It was noted that the "increasing importance of the judicial control of executive actions" had led to the introduction of a separate section in the Administrative Law title.

Judicial review describes the process by which the courts exercise a supervisory jurisdiction over the activities of public authorities in the field of public law. It is the process by which the courts control the exercise by public authorities of their powers. During the 1980s in particular, a new mood pervaded the courts and many landmark judicial review decisions were delivered during this time. In *R v IRC, ex p National Federation of Self-Employed and Small Businesses Ltd*[4], Lord Diplock described the progress towards a "comprehensive system of administrative law" that he regarded as having been the greatest achievement of the English courts in his judicial lifetime. The circumstances in which the courts have been prepared to intervene to provide relief for unlawful administrative action have expanded in spectacular fashion[5] since the first Administrative Law title in *Halsbury's Laws*. Indeed, matters have developed to such an extent that the Fifth Edition of *Halsbury's Laws*, to be published in 2008, for the first time will contain a Judicial Review title separate from an Administrative Law title.

The most important public law statute in recent years, which has had a significant effect on judicial review proceedings, is the Human Rights Act 1998. The 1998 Act provides that it is unlawful for a public authority to act in a way which is incompatible with certain of the rights contained in the European Convention on Human Rights[6]. An individual who claims that a public authority has acted in a way which breaches his Convention rights can bring a claim, and judicial review is most often the medium for such a claim. The 1998 Act also introduced an "interpretative obligation", requiring all legislation, so far as possible, to be "read and given effect" in a way that is compatible with Convention rights[7]. If it is not possible to do so, the High Court or higher courts may declare that provisions of primary legislation are incompatible with Convention rights[8].

---

1   Barristers, 11 KBW, 11 King's Bench Walk, Temple, London EC4Y 7EQ.
2   *R v Ministry of Defence, ex p Smith* [1996] QB 517 at 556, [1996] 1 All ER 257 at 264 per Sir Thomas Bingham MR (as he then was).
3   *Breen v Amalgamated Engineering Union* [1971] 2 QB 175 at 189, [1971] 1 All ER 1148 at 1153.
4   [1982] AC 617, [1981] 2 All ER 93.
5   De Smith, Woolf and Jowell *Judicial Review of Administrative Action* (5th edn, 1995) para 1-001. See generally Supperstone, Goudie and Walker *Judicial Review* (3rd edn, 2005) ch 5; and Wade and Forsyth *Administrative Law* (9th edn, 2004) ch 17.
6   Human Rights Act 1998 s 6.
7   *Ibid* s 3(1).
8   *Ibid* s 4.

Claims for declarations of incompatibility are frequently included in claims for judicial review[9].

This essay outlines the major changes that have occurred in judicial review claims over the last 25 years. There has been a wide expansion in the type of decisions that are amenable to judicial review, and the courts have reduced the "zone of immunity" formerly surrounding a great deal of administrative action. The standard of review applicable in judicial review claims has also undergone a significant change, particularly with an increasing focus on proportionality as a criterion for determining the lawfulness of the exercise of discretionary powers under the 1998 Act and in EU law. This essay also outlines developments in other grounds for judicial review, such as substantive legitimate expectation and material error of fact. We highlight the increasingly liberal standing rules and the rise in public interest litigation, alongside the reduced focus on the rule of procedural exclusivity based on *O'Reilly v Mackman*[10]. Finally, important changes to judicial review procedure and the introduction of the Civil Procedure Rules (CPR) Pt 54 are also summarised.

## WHAT MAY BE JUDICIALLY REVIEWED?

The notion that judicial review is confined to jurisdictional error and error of law on the face of the record has been seriously eroded, if not destroyed. In the past, the courts were troubled with the question of whether every error of law amounted to a jurisdictional error which the court was entitled to correct on judicial review, or whether erroneous decisions within jurisdiction were beyond challenge. However, the distinction between errors within and errors without jurisdiction should be regarded as having passed into history. The general approach is now to regard almost every error of law by a public body as being amenable to judicial review[11].

As we note above, in recent years, the range of decisions that are amenable to judicial review has greatly widened. Judicial review is available against a public body in a public law matter. A claim for judicial review can be brought against an inferior court or tribunal or any person or body performing public duties or functions.

A public body deriving its powers from statute has always been amenable to judicial review. Powers derived from the royal prerogative were traditionally treated differently; judicial control was limited to inquiring into the existence and the extent of the prerogative powers, and whether the power had been superseded or limited by statute. The courts could not review the manner of the exercise of the power in the way that they could if the power was statutory[12]. However, in *Council of Civil Service Unions v Minister for the Civil Service*[13] ("*GCHQ*"), the House of Lords confirmed that powers derived from the prerogative are public law powers and that their exercise is in principle amenable to judicial review. The only limitation on judicial review concerned the justiciability of the issue. It is the subject matter of the power, and suitability for review in a particular case, that is determinative[14]. In recent years, the courts have been prepared to review the residual powers of the Home Secretary in the immigration field[15], the refusal

---

9   Another important constitutional change relates to devolution in each of Northern Ireland, Scotland and Wales; however, a detailed examination of devolution is beyond the scope of this essay. The other major source of challenge to legislation or the actions of public bodies derives from European Union law, and is also beyond the scope of this work.

10   [1983] 2 AC 237, [1982] 3 All ER 1124, HL.

11   *Anisminic Ltd v Foreign Compensation Commission* [1969] 2 AC 147, [1969] 1 All ER 208; *R v Hull University Visitor, ex p Page* [1993] AC 682, [1993] 1 All ER 97; *R v Bedwellty Justices, ex p Williams* [1997] AC 225, [1996] 3 All ER 737.

12   *Attorney General v De Keyser's Royal Hotel Ltd* [1920] AC 508, [1920] All ER Rep 80, HL.

13   [1985] AC 374, [1984] 3 All ER 935, HL.

to issue a passport[16], and the refusal by the Home Secretary to recommend a posthumous pardon for a man hanged for murder[17]. However, certain areas falling within the royal prerogative remain immune from review. Treaty making and/or breaking[18], the conduct of foreign affairs and the deployment of the armed forces are still "forbidden areas" for the courts[19]. Moreover, national security decisions which, before the mid-1980s, were off-limits have in recent years regularly been considered by the courts[20].

In addition, powers which are not derived from statute or the prerogative may also involve a sufficiently "public" element to render the exercise of those powers amenable to judicial review. Since the late 1980s, the "source" of the power has not been the only test for determining whether a particular body is susceptible to judicial review. The nature of the function will be important and bodies performing public duties or exercising powers that could be characterised as "public" may be subject to judicial review even though its powers are not statutory or prerogative. In Datafin[21], the courts held that the Panel on Take-overs and Mergers was susceptible to judicial review, even though it had no statutory underpinning at all, because of the quasi-governmental functions it performed in the public interest. Important factors considered by the courts in determining whether a body is performing public functions are whether the body exercises extensive or monopolistic powers in carrying out the function in question; whether, but for the existence of the body, the government would itself have intervened to regulate the activity in question; and whether there is an element of "statutory recognition" of the body, even though there is no specific authority for the power under review. Judicial review is not, however, available in relation to bodies whose sole source of power over individuals derives solely from contract. The courts have consistently held that judicial review is not available against purely religious bodies[22] or bodies regulating horseracing[23], football[24] or travel agents[25], as there is no suggestion that those bodies were part of a system of government regulation of those activities or that the government would regulate the activities if those bodies did not exist.

The courts have also held that judicial review is only available as against public bodies in relation to their public functions. It is not available to enforce purely private law rights against public bodies. Judicial review is not usually available in respect of decisions made

---

14  See eg R (on the application of Abbasi) v Secretary of State for Foreign and Commonwealth Affairs [2002] EWCA Civ 1598 at [85], [2003] 3 LRC 297 at [85].

15  R v Secretary of State for the Home Dept, ex p Beedassee [1989] COD 525.

16  R v Secretary of State for Foreign and Commonwealth Affairs, ex p Everett [1989] QB 811, [1989] 1 All ER 655, CA.

17  R v Secretary of State for the Home Dept, ex p Bentley [1994] QB 349, [1993] 4 All ER 442, DC.

18  Maclaine Watson & Co Ltd v International Tin Council [1990] 2 AC 418 at 499–500, [1989] 3 All ER 523 at 544–545, HL. See also A-G v Nissan [1970] AC 179, [1969] 1 All ER 629, HL; Blackburn v A-G [1971] 2 All ER 1380 at 1382, [1971] 1 WLR 1037 at 1040, CA (challenge to the Treaty of Rome); R v Secretary of State for Foreign and Commonwealth Affairs, ex p Rees-Mogg [1994] QB 552, [1994] 1 All ER 457, DC, (challenge to the decision to ratify the Maastricht Treaty); Lewis v A-G for Jamaica [2001] 2 AC 50 at 77, [2000] 5 LRC 253 at 273 (confirming that treaty-making and declaring war are areas in which the exercise of the prerogative are beyond review).

19  See Abbasi [2003] 3 LRC 297 at [106(iii)], note 14 above; R (on the application of Al Rawi) v Secretary of State for Foreign and Commonwealth Affairs [2006] EWCA Civ 1279, [2007] 2 WLR 1219, [2007] 2 LRC 499; R (on the application of Campaign for Nuclear Disarmament) v Prime Minister [2002] EWHC 2777 (Admin), [2003] 3 LRC 335.

20  See below at the text to notes 42–44.

21  R v Panel on Take-overs and Mergers, ex p Datafin plc [1987] QB 815, [1987] 1 All ER 564, CA.

22  R v Chief Rabbi of the United Hebrew Congregation of Great Britain and the Commonwealth, ex p Wachman [1993] 2 All ER 249, [1992] 1 WLR 1036.

by an employer during disciplinary proceedings[26]. Nor is it available in relation to the exercise of a public body's private rights to dispose of and manage its assets, and/or enter into contracts, unless an additional public law element is shown (such as bad faith or power being exercised for an improper purpose). To this extent, then, even public bodies have private lives.

A more recent conundrum for administrative law has been the increased use by public bodies of contractual arrangements to discharge their functions. Legislation may permit a public body either to discharge certain obligations and functions itself or to enter into contractual arrangements with a private sector body under which that private body does so. If the public body performs the function, it will be subject to judicial review proceedings. Is the private body stepping into the shoes of the public body also subject to judicial review? At common law, the courts have generally answered this question in the negative, unless there are some additional features to make the activities of an ordinary private sector provider sufficiently public to be amenable to judicial review. In *R v Servite Houses, ex p Goldsmith*[27], a local authority had a statutory duty to provide residential accommodation for the elderly, and entered into contractual arrangements with a private sector company to provide this service. The High Court held that the private sector provider was not amenable to judicial review at the behest of the residents, who had no contractual relationship with the private sector company. There was no sufficient statutory underpinning to the private sector company's activities, as the statutory provisions in question did not impose any obligations on the private sector body, but merely conferred authority on the local authority to enter into the contractual relationship with the private sector provider[28]. However, a private sector body will be discharging public functions where it has been created or established by the public body, and subsequently assumes the responsibilities previously carried out by the public body, and continues to receive assistance from the public body (such as finance and facilities): see *R (Beer t/a Hammer Trout Farm) v Hampshire Farmers' Market Limited*[29].

The courts have very recently been grappling with the difficult question of how the 1998 Act applies to such private sector bodies[30]. Under the 1998 Act, "core" public authorities, which are wholly "public" in nature, have to act compatibly with the Convention in everything they do[31]. However, a "public authority" also includes other

---

23 *R v Jockey Club, ex p RAM Racecourses Ltd* [1993] 2 All ER 225, DC; *R v Disciplinary Committee of the Jockey Club, ex p His Highness the Aga Khan* [1993] 2 All ER 853, [1993] 1 WLR 909, CA. Moreover, a private body could not turn itself into a public body, or turn a private function into a public function, by creating an appeal board: *R (on the application of Mullins) v Appeal Board of the Jockey Club* [2005] EWHC 2197 (Admin), (2005) Times, 24 October.

24 *R v Football Association, ex p Football League Ltd* [1993] 2 All ER 833.

25 *R v Association of British Travel Agents, ex p Sunspell Ltd (t/a as Superlative Travel Ltd)* [2001] ACD 88.

26 *R v East Berkshire Health Authority, ex p Walsh* [1985] QB 152; *R (on the application of Arthurworrey) v Haringey LBC* [2002] ICR 279; *R (on the application of Tucker) v Director General of National Crime Squad* [2003] EWCA Civ 57, [2003] ICR 599, [2003] IRLR 439.

27 [2001] LGR 55.

28 See also *R (on the application of Heather) v Leonard Cheshire Foundation* [2002] EWCA Civ 366, [2002] 2 All ER 936.

29 [2003] EWCA Civ 1056, [2004] 1 WLR 233, [2003] All ER (D) 356 (Jul).

30 *Poplar Housing and Regeneration Community Association Ltd v Donoghue* [2001] EWCA Civ 595, [2002] QB 48, [2001] 4 All ER 604; *R (on the application of Heather) v Leonard Cheshire Foundation* [2002] EWCA Civ 366, [2002] 2 All ER 936; *YL v Birmingham City Council* [2007] UKHL 27, [2007] 3 All ER 957, [2007] 3 WLR 112.

31 1998 Act s 6(1).

bodies, whose functions are "of a public nature". Such public authorities have to act compatibly with the Convention, unless the nature of the particular act complained of is private[32]. The most recent judgment of the House of Lords on this issue, *YL v Birmingham City Council*, takes a restrictive approach to the issue. By a bare majority, their Lordships held that a private company, in providing care and accommodation under contract with the local authority, on a commercial basis and without any subsidy from public funds, was not carrying out an inherently public function and fell outside the ambit of the 1998 Act s 6(3). It is respectfully submitted that the minority opinion of Lord Bingham of Cornhill and Baroness Hale of Richmond is to be preferred and better accords with the intention of Parliament in enacting s 6(3), (5). The majority placed an undue reliance on the contractual nature of the power of the private sector company, instead of focusing on the similarity of the activities being carried out by the local authority, in cases of direct provision, and the private sector company, where services have been contracted out. When the statute directs attention to "functions " of a "public nature", it is remarkable that a private sector body, providing services which had previously been provided by the state for many years, and which formed part of "core" governmental activities carried out for the benefit of the public, does not fall within the definition in the 1998 Act. It remains to be seen whether the House of Lords will re-visit this question in future years so as to revitalise this aspect of the 1998 Act.

## GROUNDS OF CHALLENGE

The first Administrative Law title of *Halsbury's Laws* pre-dates Lord Diplock's classic restatement, in the *GCHQ* case[33], of the three potential grounds for judicial review of administrative action, namely: illegality, irrationality and procedural impropriety. "Illegality" includes unlawful delegation, fettering of discretion, failing to have regard to relevant considerations and having regard to irrelevant considerations and acting in bad faith or for an improper purpose. (As considered below, the 1998 Act s 6(1) has now added a significant new element, namely incompatibility with Convention rights. In considering whether there has been a breach of Convention rights, the principle of proportionality frequently comes into play.)

"Irrationality" refers to *Wednesbury* unreasonableness, as being a "decision which is so outrageous in its defiance of logic or of accepted moral standards that no sensible person who had applied his mind to the question to be decided could have arrived at it"[34]. It is a trite observation that under *Wednesbury,* the court does not embark upon a merits based review, and is not concerned with what it regards as the appropriate decision; instead the court embarks on an exercise of whether sensible decision-makers, properly directed in law and properly applying their minds to the matter, could have reached the same conclusion.

"Procedural impropriety" has a wide meaning and covers many different aspects of procedural fairness. The requirements of fairness are not fixed, and the content of the duty to act fairly depends on the circumstances and the nature of the decision to be made[35]. In recent years, two particular aspects of natural justice or the duty to act fairly have been developed by the courts. First, there has been an expansion in the areas in which a body is under a statutory duty to give reasons for its decisions, which must then satisfy a minimum standard of clarity and explanatory force. While there is as yet no general duty at common

---

32  *Ibid* s 6(3)(b), (5).
33  Ie *Council of Civil Service Unions v Minister for the Civil Service* [1985] AC 374 at 410, [1984] 3 All ER 935 at 950–951, HL.
34  See [1985] AC 374 at 41], [1984] 3 All ER 935 at 951, HL, referring to *Associated Provincial Picture Houses Ltd v Wednesbury Corpn* [1947] 2 All ER 680, [1948] 1 KB 223.
35  See, for example, *Roberts v Parole Board* [2005] UKHL 45, [2005] 2 AC 738, [2006] 1 All ER 39.

law to give reasons for a decision, in a substantial number of decisions a duty to provide reasons has been found to exist on the particular facts of the case, having regard to the nature of the interest concerned and the impact of the decision on that interest[36]. Secondly, there have been numerous cases clarifying the test for apparent bias, both at common law and under the Convention art 6(1). The question is whether the fair-minded and informed observer, having considered the facts, would conclude that there was a real possibility that the decision-maker was biased[37]. The "fair-minded and informed observer" will adopt a balanced approach and be neither complacent nor unduly sensitive or suspicious[38].

## STANDARD OF REVIEW

In addition to the expansion in the type of decisions that are amenable to judicial review, there has also been a dramatic change in the standard of review adopted by the courts. The language of *Wednesbury* is pitched at a very high standard[39]. However, the courts have recognised that *Wednesbury* is a flexible concept, well able to accommodate a broad or narrow degree of latitude, depending on the subject matter of the claim and the statutory context.

In general, the greater the policy content of the decision, and the more remote the subject matter of a decision from ordinary judicial experience, the more hesitant the court will be in holding a decision to be unreasonable. Scrutiny of administrative action will be less intense where the exercise of a discretion involves the allocation of resources[40] or considerations of policy, or where the decision is subject to political controls[41].

Courts have traditionally been reluctant to intervene in situations of emergency or where issues of national security are involved, which were seen as prime areas of responsibility for the Secretary of State, who is best placed to judge what national security requires[42]. However, even in this area, courts in recent years have shown a greater willingness in principle to intervene, holding that attempts to invoke national security unsupported by evidence did not preclude judicial intervention[43]. More fundamentally, in December 2004, the House of Lords found that the exercise of the power to derogate from the Convention in times of war or other public emergency threatening the life of the nation is subject to review[44], although great weight was to be given to the political assessment made by the Executive and Parliament. The House of Lords concluded that provisions in primary and secondary legislation conferring the power to detain without trial foreigners

---

36 See, for example, *R v Secretary of State for the Home Dept, ex p Doody* [1994] 1 AC 531, [1993] 3 All ER 92.

37 *Porter v Magill* [2001] UKHL 67 at [103], [2002] 2 AC 357 at [103], [2002] 1 All ER 465 at [103].

38 *Lawal v Northern Spirit Ltd* [2003] UKHL 35, [2004] 1 All ER 187.

39 See the *GCHQ* case at note 13 above; see also the language of Lord Greene MR in *Wednesbury* itself: "... so absurd that no sensible person could ever dream that it lay within the powers of the authority."

40 See *R v Cambridge Health Authority, ex p B* [1995] 2 All ER 129, [1995] 1 WLR 898.

41 See *Nottinghamshire CC v Secretary of State for the Environment* [1986] AC 240, [1986] 1 All ER 199, HL; *R v Secretary of State for the Environment, ex p Hammersmith and Fulham LBC* [1991] 1 AC 521, [1990] 3 All ER 589.

42 See *R v Secretary of State for the Home Dept, ex p Cheblak* [1991] 2 All ER 319, [1991] 1 WLR 890, CA; *Secretary of State for the Home Dept v Rehman* [2001] UKHL 47, [2003] 1 AC 153, [2002] 1 All ER 122.

43 See *R v Secretary of State for the Home Dept, ex p Ruddock* [1987] 2 All ER 518, [1987] 1 WLR 1482.

44 See *A v Secretary of State for the Home Dept* [2004] UKHL 56, [2005] 2 AC 68, [2005] 3 All ER 169.

who were "suspected international terrorists" did not rationally address the threat to security, constituted a disproportionate response and were not strictly required by the exigencies of the situation. Accordingly, the secondary legislation was quashed and the primary legislation declared incompatible with the Convention. This recent decision demonstrates that even in the context of national security – traditionally a hands-off area – the courts have discerned a responsibility to ensure ministerial compliance with the rule of law.

Further, even prior to the 1998 Act, the courts had developed a sophisticated framework for reviewing the reasonableness of decisions where human rights questions arose. The "anxious scrutiny" or "heightened scrutiny" in *R v Ministry of Defence, ex p Smith*[45] was to the effect that the more substantial the interference with human rights, the more the court will require by way of justification before it is satisfied that the decision is reasonable. Fundamental human rights are guarded by the common law with particular care[46].

The court's role in a claim under the 1998 Act for breach of a Convention right is more exacting. Even when modified by "anxious scrutiny" in human rights cases, *Wednesbury* set too high a threshold for national courts to be able to enter into issues of judgment that arose under the Convention[47]. The principle of proportionality is frequently invoked under the Convention, is applied by the European Court of Human Rights and is therefore taken into account in England and Wales by the 1998 Act s 2(1).

The proportionality test was endorsed by the House of Lords in *R (on the application of Daly) v Secretary of State for the Home Dept*, adopting the three-stage test set out in *de Freitas v Permanent Secretary of Ministry of Agriculture, Fisheries, Lands and Housing*[48]. The first question is to ask whether the legislative objective is sufficiently important to justify limiting a fundamental right. Secondly, are the measures designed to meet the legislative objective rationally connected to it? Thirdly, are the means used to impair the right or freedom no more than is necessary to accomplish the objective? Proportionality does not mean "that there has been a shift to merits review" under which the courts can substitute their own judgment for that of the decision-maker. However, the doctrine of proportionality may require the reviewing court to assess the balance which the decision-maker has struck, and not merely to enquire whether it is within the range of rational or reasonable decisions. The proportionality test may also go further than traditional *Wednesbury* review in that it will require attention to be directed to the relative weight accorded to interests and considerations[49]. The intensity of review is greater than that available under *Wednesbury*. The court must itself objectively determine whether the decision under challenge was proportionate[50].

While giving more power to the courts to intervene, proportionality does not alter the respective roles of judges and primary decision-makers. The European Court of Human Rights developed the well-known "margin of appreciation" doctrine, recognising that national authorities may be best placed to determine what measures are suitable or necessary in the circumstances in their own countries. Similarly, domestic law has recognised a "discretionary area of judgment" whereby the courts acknowledge that there

---

45  [1996] QB 517, [1996] 1 All ER 257.
46  See, in addition, the principle of legality set out by Lord Hoffmann in *R v Secretary of State for the Home Dept, ex p Simms* [2000] 2 AC 115, [1999] 3 All ER 400, [1999] 3 WLR 328.
47  Applications 33985/96 and 33986/96 *Smith v UK* (1999) 29 EHRR 493, ECtHR.
48  [1999] 1 AC 69.
49  *R (on the application of Daly) v Secretary of State for the Home Dept* [2001] UKHL 26 at [27], [2001] 2 AC 532 at [27], [2001] 3 All ER 433 at [27] per Lord Steyn.
50  See, for example, *R (on the application of Begum) v Governors of Denbigh High School* [2006] UKHL 15, [2007] 1 AC 100, [2006] 2 All ER 487.

is an area of judgment within which the courts will defer, on democratic grounds, to the considered opinion of the primary decision-maker, as the Legislature or Executive are, in some circumstances, better placed to evaluate and decide. The scope of the discretionary area of judgment will depend on the nature of the rights in issue. The courts are more willing to recognise such an area of judgment where the Convention itself requires a balance to be struck, and where the issues involve questions of social or economic policy as opposed to rights of high constitutional importance or are of a kind where the courts are especially well placed to assess the need for protection[51]. Thus the intensity of review, even in cases under the 1998 Act, is still dependent on the subject matter at hand. As Lord Steyn observed in *Daly,* "in law, context is everything".

While the proportionality principle is applied in relation to claims under the 1998 Act, and also in cases involving EU law, domestic administrative law has not, to date, extended the categories of review to include a free-standing principle of proportionality[52]. Lord Slynn of Hadley and Lord Cooke of Thorndon[53], among others, have called for the proportionality principle to be recognised in domestic administrative law. The Court of Appeal in R (*on the application of Association of British Civilian Internees: Far East Region*) *v Secretary of State for Defence* ("*ABCIFER*")[54] appeared to sympathise with these views, but recognised that it was not for that court "to perform the burial rites" for *Wednesbury*. The House of Lords has not yet taken up the Court of Appeal's invitation to replace reasonableness with proportionality as the criterion for common law review, and indeed, refused leave to appeal in *ABCIFER*.

## THE HUMAN RIGHTS ACT 1998

The United Kingdom government ratified the European Convention on Human Rights in March 1951. As an international treaty, the rights guaranteed by the Convention were not enforceable as a matter of domestic law. The courts were only entitled to apply the Convention where (a) legislation was ambiguous and a Convention-compliant interpretation was possible; and (b) the common law was developing and the court was able to develop the law in a manner that was Convention-compliant[55]. The 1998 Act was enacted on 9 November 1998 and came into force on 2 October 2000. No measure of law reform has had "such wide and profound effects on administrative law as has the 1998 Act"[56].

The purpose of the 1998 Act was to "give further effect" to the rights and freedoms guaranteed by the Convention. The term "Convention rights" is defined in s 1(1) as meaning the rights and freedoms set out in the Convention arts 2–12, 14, together with certain Protocols, as read with arts 16–18. In deciding questions about Convention rights, the 1998 Act s 2 requires all courts and tribunals to take into account decisions of the European Court of Human Rights.

Three particular aspects of the 1998 Act have had significant effects on judicial review proceedings. First, the 1998 Act introduces an extremely strong "interpretative obligation". By s 3, all legislation, both primary and secondary, whenever enacted, must be "read and given effect in a way which is compatible with the Convention rights", "so far as it is possible

51  *R v DPP, ex p Kebilene* [2000] 2 AC 326 at 380, 381, [1999] 4 All ER 801 at 843–844, HL; *M v Secretary of State for Work and Pensions* [2006] UKHL 11 at [137], [138], [2006] 2 AC 91 at [137], [138], [2006] 4 All ER 929 at [137], [138].
52  *R v Secretary of State for the Home Dept, ex p Brind* [1991] 1 AC 696, [1991] 1 All ER 720, HL.
53  *R* (*on the application of Alconbury Developments Ltd*) *v Secretary of State for the Environment, Transport and the Regions* [2001] UKHL 23, [2003] 2 AC 295, [2001] 2 All ER 929; *Daly,* see note 49 above.
54  [2003] EWCA Civ 473, [2003] QB 1397, [2003] All ER (D) 43 (Apr).
55  M Hunt *Using Human Rights Law in English Courts* (1997).
56  Wade and Forsyth *Administrative Law* (9th edn, 2004) p 174.

to do so". Where a Convention-compatible interpretation is not possible, the High Court or above has a discretion to make a declaration of incompatibility under the 1998 Act s 4. This preserves the traditional sovereignty of Parliament, in that the courts cannot strike down a provision in primary legislation that is incompatible with Convention rights. A declaration of incompatibility affords no practical relief to a claimant, but it may lead to an amendment of the law by means of a remedial order under the 1998 Act s 10. The House of Lords has held that the s 3 interpretative obligation is the "prime remedial remedy" under the 1998 Act, and that resort to a declaration of incompatibility must be an exceptional course. The interpretative obligation applies regardless of whether the legislation in question is ambiguous, and does not depend on the precise language used in the statute[57]. The courts are even prepared to read words into a statute in order to ensure compatibility with Convention rights[58]. This goes far beyond any common law principle of statutory interpretation. The outer limits of the interpretative obligation are still being explored by the courts. In *Ghaidan*, it was stated that the courts cannot adopt a meaning under the 1998 Act s 3 "inconsistent with a fundamental feature of the legislation" and that words cannot be read in "that are inconsistent with the scheme of the legislation or with its essential principles"[59].

Secondly, the 1998 Act imposes a duty on all public authorities to act in a way which is compatible with Convention rights. The nature of a "public authority" is discussed above. Section 6(1) has added a "significant new element to the existing grounds on which administrative action may be held ultra vires"[60]. For a public authority to act incompatibly with a Convention right, in breach of 1998 Act s 6(1), is now an additional ground for judicial review, to be added to Lord Diplock's threefold classification in the *GCHQ* case (above).

Thirdly, the 1998 Act makes provision for damages to be paid for breach of Convention rights. Outside the 1998 Act, the Administrative Court may order damages to be paid in judicial review proceedings, although a claim for judicial review may not seek damages alone[61]. However, damages are not payable at common law simply because a decision is shown to be ultra vires; for a claim for damages to succeed, the claimant must show that the defendant's conduct amounts to a tort. Under the 1998 Act s 8(1), any court or tribunal which finds that an act of a public authority has been unlawful, ie in breach of s 6(1), may award damages to the victim if it considers that such a remedy would be just and appropriate. In considering the question of damages, the courts must take into account the principles applied by the European Court of Human Rights under the Convention art 41, awarding damages where this is "necessary to afford just satisfaction". The leading case in this field is now that of *R (on the application of Greenfield) v Secretary of State for the Home Dept*[62]. The House of Lords recognised that the focus of the Convention was the protection of human rights rather than the award of compensation, and that frequently the European Court of Human Rights would treat the finding of a violation as itself affording just satisfaction to the injured party, particularly in relation to a violation of art 6. Even where awards are made, the amounts are likely to be modest. The 1998 Act is not a tort statute, and national courts should not apply a domestic scale of damages. The aim of the 1998 Act was to make it easier for claimants to obtain remedies to which they were entitled under the Convention, not to give them a better remedy. National courts should follow the approach of the European

57  *Ghaidan v Godin-Mendoza* [2004] UKHL 80, [2004] 2 AC 557, [2004] 3 All ER 411.
58  By analogy with decisions in European Community law: *Pickstone v Freemans plc* [1989] AC 66, [1987] 3 All ER 756, CA; and *Litster v Forth Dry Dock* [1990] 1 AC 546, [1989] 1 All ER 1134, HL.
59  *Ghaidan* [2004] 2 AC 557 at [121], [2004] 3 All ER 411 at [121].
60  Supperstone, Goudie and Walker *Judicial Review* (3rd edn, 2005) at para 4.12.1.
61  Supreme Court Act 1981 s 31(4); CPR 54.3(2).
62  [2005] UKHL 14, [2005] 2 All ER 240, [2005] 1 WLR 673.

Court of Human Rights in assessing what is fair and equitable in the individual case. These awards should not aim to be significantly more or less generous than the awards made in Strasbourg. If other relief is sought in addition to damages, the claim should be brought by way of judicial review in the Administrative Court. Otherwise, alternative procedures should be used, including alternative dispute resolution, to keep the costs down.

## LEGITIMATE EXPECTATION

Other grounds of judicial review have been developed by the courts. It has been recognised that an unequivocal representation or a previous course of conduct by a public authority may give rise to a legitimate expectation. In this field, the law seeks to establish a balance between the importance of preserving a public body's freedom lawfully to exercise discretionary statutory powers without restraint, and the desirability of the body in question honouring its statements of policy and intention. The doctrine of legitimate expectation is the means by which the courts seek to resolve this conflict.

A legitimate expectation may give rise to procedural rights, such as the right to be consulted before a decision is taken or a right to make representations[63]. The existence of such expectations may be a relevant consideration which a decision-maker must take into account. Recently, the courts have extended this doctrine still further, to recognise "substantive" legitimate expectations. In exceptional circumstances, the legitimate expectation may give rise to a right to enjoy a substantive benefit which it would be unfair and an abuse of power to frustrate[64]. This will arise where a promise is made to an individual or small group. The court will then consider whether to resile from that promise would be so unfair that to take a new and different course would amount to an abuse of power. Any legitimate expectation which may have arisen will be defeasible if there is some overriding public interest. While not beyond doubt in the authorities, it appears that reliance, which may be relevant in most cases, is not essential to a legitimate expectation claim. Three practical questions thus arise in legitimate expectation cases. First, to what has the public authority committed itself? Secondly, has the public authority acted unlawfully in relation to this commitment? And thirdly, what should the court do in light of the expectation generated?[65]

The courts have relied on two important factors to avoid the risk of fettering the exercise of discretion by decision-makers, who must not be prevented from changing their policies. First, as in the *Wednesbury* analysis, the more the decision challenged lies in the "macro-political" field, the less intrusive will be the court's supervision. Further, in this field, an abuse of power is less likely to be found, since changes of policy, fuelled by broad conceptions of the public interest, may more readily be accepted as taking precedence over the interests of groups which enjoyed expectations generated by an earlier policy. The courts are unable to intervene to a greater extent "without themselves donning the garb of policy-maker, which they cannot wear"[66].

---

63 *R v Lord Chancellor, ex p Law Society* (1994) 6 Admin LR 333, CA; *A-G of Hong Kong v Ng Yuen Shiu* [1983] 2 AC 629, [1983] 2 All ER 346, PC.

64 *R v North and East Devon Health Authority, ex p Coughlan* [2001] QB 213, [2000] 3 All ER 850, CA.

65 *R (on the application of Bibi) v Newham LBC* [2001] EWCA Civ 607, [2002] 1 WLR 237, [2003] All ER (D) 218 (Jun).

66 *R v Secretary of State for Education, ex p Begbie* [2000] 1 WLR 1115, [1999] All ER (D) 983. See also, for a recent example, *R (on the application of Legal Remedy UK Ltd) v Secretary of State for Health* [2007] EWHC 1252 (Admin), (2007) 96 BMLR 191, Goldring J rejecting the challenge to the modified-MTAS regime for recruiting junior doctors, holding that as a judge, he was not equipped to decide issues of policy requiring expertise on the running of the NHS and the training of doctors.

Secondly, even if a court finds that the claimant has a legitimate expectation, it will not order the public authority to honour that promise where to do so would be to assume the powers of the Executive. If the court does find an abuse of power, it may ask the decision-maker to take the legitimate expectation properly into account in the decision-making process[67].

The courts are still developing the law governing legitimate expectations. In recent time, Laws LJ embarked on a reformulation of the theoretical underpinnings of substantive legitimate expectation, noting that where a public authority had issued a promise or adopted a practice that represented how it proposed to act in a given area, the law required the promise to be honoured unless there was a good reason not to do so. The principle behind that proposition was explained as being one of good administration, such that public bodies ought to deal in a straightforward and consistent manner with the public. That standard might only be departed from where to do so was the public body's legal duty or was otherwise a proportionate response having regard to the legitimate aim pursued by the public body in the public interest[68]. It remains to be seen whether this analysis will be widely accepted by the courts.

The courts have developed a doctrine of substantive unfairness amounting to an abuse of power. In *R v IRC, ex p Unilever plc*[69], the court found that the Revenue had engaged in an extremely precise and focussed course of conduct which engendered very specific expectations on the part of the taxpayer claimant. The court treated it as a case of conspicuous unfairness, tantamount to irrationality, in failing to follow the same established practice in relation to permitting tax rebate claims to be made in a particular way, so that the claims were defeated at very substantial cost to the public purse.

While the first *Halsbury's Laws* Administrative Law title identifies the doctrine of waiver and estoppel in administrative law, much less emphasis is now being placed upon these private law concepts in this field. In recent years, Lord Hoffmann has stated that in this area, "public law has already absorbed whatever is useful from the moral values which underlie the private law concept of estoppel and the time has come for it to stand upon its own two feet"[70]. Estoppel had been applied in earlier cases as an attempt to achieve justice at a time when the concepts of legitimate expectation and abuse of power had scarcely made their appearance in public law. Now that those concepts are recognised, there is no longer a place for the private law doctrine of estoppel in public law[71].

The courts have also considered whether judicial review is available to quash a decision on the ground that it was based on a material error of fact. The general principle is that questions of fact are determined by the courts where they go to the decision-maker's jurisdiction and by the decision-maker in other cases. The Court of Appeal has now held in *E v Secretary of State for the Home Dept*[72] that mistake of fact giving rise to unfairness is a separate head of challenge on an appeal on a point of law.

---

67 *Bibi*, see note 65 above.
68 See *Nadarajah v Secretary of State for the Home Dept* [2005] EWCA Civ 1363, [2005] All ER (D) 283 (Nov).
69 [1996] STC 681, 68 TC 205, CA.
70 *R v East Sussex CC, ex p Reprotech (Pebsham) Ltd* [2002] UKHL 8, [2002] 4 All ER 58, [2003] 1 WLR 348.
71 *South Bucks DC v Flanagan* [2002] EWCA Civ 690, [2002] 1 WLR 2601, [2002] All ER (D) 248 (May).
72 [2004] EWCA Civ 49, [2004] QB 1044, [2004] LGR 463.

## PROCEDURAL EXCLUSIVITY

The seminal decision of the House of Lords in 1982 in *O'Reilly v Mackman*[73] established that, as a general rule, public law issues must be brought by way of judicial review and cannot be brought by way of an ordinary claim. Two well-known exceptions were recognised by Lord Diplock, namely where the invalidity of a decision arises as a collateral issue in a claim for an infringement of a right under private law, and where none of the parties object to the use of the ordinary action. The rationale for the procedural exclusivity rule is that public authorities are entitled to the protections incorporated into the judicial review procedure, such as the need to obtain permission to bring a judicial review claim, and the short time limit for applying for judicial review, which protections do not exist in ordinary proceedings. The dichotomy established by *O'Reilly v Mackman* led to a large amount of litigation seeking to establish the distinction between "public law" and "private law" proceedings and whether claims had been brought in the right forum. Such satellite litigation, which did not focus on the legal merits of the claims, was the subject of much judicial criticism[74].

In recent years, the courts have been less willing to allow claims to be struck out on the purely procedural ground that they should not have been brought by an ordinary claim and should have been brought by way of judicial review, and the need for flexibility has been emphasised. In *Roy v Kensington and Chelsea Family Practitioner Committee*[75], the House of Lords left open the proper scope of the exclusivity rule. We suggest that the better approach is that the rule in *O'Reilly v Mackman* should be focussed on ensuring that questions raising solely public law issues are determined through judicial review proceedings and in accordance with CPR Pt 54. An individual who therefore sought to establish that there had been a breach of a principle of public law but was also seeking to vindicate a private law right would be free either to bring a claim for judicial review or to proceed by an ordinary claim[76]. The procedural exclusivity rule has not been applied in civil cases where the individual seeks to establish private law rights which cannot be determined without an examination of the validity of a public law decision[77]. Further, in criminal matters, the courts have emphasised the desirability of individuals being able to raise public law issues as a defence in criminal courts as it may be easier and cheaper for them to do so than to institute separate judicial review proceedings: see *Boddington v British Transport Police*[78]. The courts now also have the power under the CPR to transfer claims out of Pt 54 (CPR 54.20) or into Pt 54 if the claim has been commenced in the wrong way (CPR 30.5). Recent cases on procedural exclusivity are relatively rare, and it is to be hoped that the rule in *O'Reilly v Mackman* has now "crept unsung from the scene"[79].

---

73  See note 10 above.
74  See, for example, *Davy v Spelthorne BC* [1984] AC 262, [1983] 3 All ER 278, HL; *Mercury Communications Ltd v Director General of Telecommunications* [1996] 1 All ER 575, [1996] 1 WLR 48, HL; *British Steel plc v Customs and Excise Comrs* [1997] 2 All ER 366, CA; *Rye (Dennis) Pension Fund Trustees v Sheffield City Council* [1997] 4 All ER 747, [1998] 1 WLR 840, CA.
75  [1992] 1 AC 624, [1992] 1 All ER 805, HL.
76  C Lewis *Judicial Remedies in Public Law* (3rd edn, 2004) para 3–017.
77  See *Roy v Kensington and Chelsea Family Practitioner Committee* at note 75 above; *Steed v Secretary of State for the Home Dept* [2000] 3 All ER 226, [2000] 1 WLR 1169, HL; *Clark v University of Lincolnshire and Humberside* [2000] 3 All ER 752, [2000] 1 WLR 1988, CA.
78  [1999] 2 AC 143, [1998] 2 All ER 203, HL.
79  Wade and Forsyth *Administrative Law* (9th edn, 2004) p 678.

## WHO MAY BRING PROCEEDINGS – STANDING TO SUE

A claimant must demonstrate that he has standing to apply for judicial review. Administrative law traditionally contained a number of restrictive rules about standing. However, as governmental powers and duties have increased, and as public interest has gained prominence at the expense of private right, there has been an increasingly liberal approach to standing on the part of the courts over recent years[80].

The two groups of remedies, the prerogative remedies on the one hand, and declarations and injunctions on the other, were originally governed by different rules as to standing, and there were also differences between the different prerogative orders. The 1977 procedural reforms introduced the application for judicial review, governed by a new ord 53 of the Rules of the Supreme Court. Whichever form of relief was sought, the applicant required the leave of the court in order to proceed. Order 53(7) provided that the court should not grant leave unless it considered that the applicant had a "sufficient interest" in the matter to which the application related. This formula was subsequently repeated in the 1981 Act s 31(3). While ord 53 has been revoked by the CPR, CPR Pt 54 does not deal with standing to bring a claim for judicial review, and the 1981 Act s 31(3) remains in force.

The courts now adopt a two-stage approach to standing: see *IRC v National Federation of Self-Employed and Small Businesses Ltd*[81]. At the permission stage, the court is primarily concerned to exclude hopeless cases where the claimant truly has no interest in the proceedings and is no more than a "meddlesome busybody"[82]. At the full hearing, the sufficiency of the claimant's interest will be assessed against the full legal and factual background to the claim.

The courts now recognise that individuals ought to be able to bring a genuine and serious issue of public law before the courts. Individuals will have standing not only if they are directly affected by the decision[83] but also if they are purporting to act in the public interest. Lord Diplock's "public spirited tax-payer"[84] may be allowed to seek judicial review where there is a serious issue of public importance which the court considers should be examined. For example, a citizen who had sincere concern for constitutional issues was allowed to challenge the lawfulness of ratification of the Treaty of European Union[85] and a journalist had standing to seek a declaration that a policy of non-disclosure of the names of magistrates was unlawful[86]. The court will not accord an individual standing if there is evidence that he is acting out of ill-will or for some other improper purpose, even if there is a public interest in challenging the decision in question[87].

---

80 *R v Secretary of State for Foreign and Commonwealth Affairs, ex p World Development Movement Ltd* [1995] 1 All ER 611, [1995] 1 WLR 386, DC.

81 See note 4 above.

82 *R v Monopolies and Mergers Commission, ex p Argyll Group plc* [1986] 2 All ER 257 at 266, [1986] 1 WLR 763 at 774, CA, per Lord Donaldson MR.

83 Ie it affects their legal rights, or raises legitimate expectations, or is a refusal to confer some discretionary benefit on them, or the individual will be financially affected by the outcome of the case, or had an entitlement to make representations or objections during the course of the decision-making process.

84 *R v IRC, ex p National Federation of Self-Employed and Small Businesses Ltd* [1982] AC 617 at 619, [1981] 2 All ER 93 at 96, HL.

85 *R v Secretary of State for Foreign and Commonwealth Affairs, ex p Rees Mogg* [1994] QB 552, [1994] 1 All ER 457, DC.

86 *R v Felixstowe Justices, ex p Leigh* [1987] QB 582, [1987] 1 All ER 551, DC.

87 *R (on the application of Feakins) v Secretary of State for the Environment, Food and Rural Affairs* [2003] EWCA Civ 1546, [2004] 1 WLR 1761, [2003] All ER (D) 39 (Nov), although on the facts of the particular case, the Court of Appeal accepted that the claimant had standing.

There has been an increased willingness to acknowledge that representative bodies or public interest groups acting on behalf of their members or the wider public interest should have standing to seek judicial review. Groups acting in a representative capacity have standing to bring claims on behalf of their members[88]. Following the *Rose Theatre* case[89], the courts have also taken an expansive approach to the standing of public interest groups set up to represent particular interests or to campaign on a particular issue. In two well-known cases, the courts have accepted that Greenpeace has standing in respect of environmental issues[90] and that the World Development Movement Ltd had standing to challenge the lawfulness of the grant of overseas aid[91]. In both cases, the international reputation and expertise of the public interest group was an important factor, together with the importance of the issue in question. Public bodies, including local authorities, may also have standing to challenge the decision of another public body.

There is, however, a special test for standing in judicial review claims that are based on the 1998 Act s 6(1). A person who claims that a public authority has acted in a way made unlawful by s 6(1) may only bring proceedings if he or she is, or would be, a "victim" of the unlawful act[92]. Similarly, in judicial review proceedings, the claimant is to be taken to have a sufficient interest in relation to the unlawful act only if he or she is, or would be, a victim of that act[93]. The test as to whether a person is a victim is the same test as applied by the European Court of Human Rights under the Convention art 34. In general, a person is a "victim" if he or she is directly affected by the impugned measure. Therefore, pressure groups or campaigning organisations acting in the wider public interest will not be entitled to bring a claim for judicial review based on the 1998 Act s 6(1)[94].

A further development in response to the increase in public interest litigation is the protective costs order. An unsuccessful claimant will normally be ordered to pay the defendant's costs. The "ordinary" costs rules may have a chilling effect on judicial review claims, and claims may never be brought if the potential claimant can neither obtain legal aid nor afford to run the risk of an adverse costs order. The solution found by the courts is to make a protective costs order – that is, an order that a claimant is not liable to pay the costs of a successful defendant or that his liability is restricted to a particular amount, even if the claimant is ultimately unsuccessful at the hearing[95]. The courts have confirmed that they have jurisdiction to make such orders, but will only make them in exceptional circumstances. They will not generally do so unless (i) the public law challenges raised are ones of general public importance; (ii) the public interest requires that those issues should be resolved; (iii) the claimant has no private interest in the outcome of the case; (iv) it is fair and just to make the order having regard to the financial resources of the claimant and the defendant and to the amount of costs that were likely to be involved; and (v) the claimant

---

88 *ABCIFER*, see note 54 above.

89 *R v Secretary of State for Environment, ex p Rose Theatre Trust Co* [1990] 1 QB 504, [1990] 1 All ER 754.

90 *R v Her Majesty's Inspectorate of Pollution, ex p Greenpeace Ltd (No 2)* [1994] 4 All ER 329.

91 *Ex p World Development Movement Ltd*, see note 80 above.

92 1998 Act s 7(1).

93 *Ibid* s 7(3).

94 Pressure or campaigning groups may wish to fund a direct victim. Additionally, a claimant with standing at common law can rely on other aspects of the 1998 Act (such as the interpretative obligation in s 3 and the declaration of incompatibility in s 4) regardless of whether the "victim" test is satisfied.

95 *R (on the application of Corner House Research) v Secretary of State for Trade and Industry* [2005] EWCA Civ 192, [2005] 4 All ER 1, [2005] 1 WLR 2600; *R v Lord Chancellor, ex p Child Poverty Action Group* [1998] 2 All ER 155, [1999] 1 WLR 347.

would probably discontinue proceedings and would be acting reasonably in doing so if such an order were refused[96]. At present, the "no private interest" requirement is viewed as unduly restricting the availability of protective costs orders[97], and it remains to be seen how the rules will develop in the future.

There has been an increase in recent years in the number of bodies granted permission by the courts to intervene in judicial review proceedings. Ministers are frequently granted permission to intervene in cases, as are public interest groups such as Liberty, Amnesty and the United Nations High Commissioner for Refugees (UNHCR).

In terms of judicial review procedure, CPR Pt 54 and its accompanying *Practice Direction* recently replaced the Ord 53 procedure. A specialist Administrative Court has been established[98]. The Latin names for the prerogative writs have been replaced with English names, the orders now being referred to as mandatory, prohibiting and quashing orders. The CPR makes provision for a Pre-Action Protocol letter, requires the production of an acknowledgement of service on behalf of the defendant and lays down a detailed timetable for the serving of evidence etc. Provision is also made for interim remedies and urgent applications.

The courts have also taken a more flexible approach to disclosure in judicial review claims. While disclosure would not ordinarily be necessary for disposing of the predominantly legal issues, it is no longer the rule that disclosure will only be ordered where the decision-maker's affidavit can be shown to be materially inaccurate or misleading. In *Tweed v Parades Commission for Northern Ireland*[99], the House of Lords held that a flexible, less prescriptive approach should be taken, and the need for disclosure should be judged on the facts of the individual case. Disclosure will be particularly important when the proportionality of a decision is in issue, as this will necessarily be fact-specific.

CONCLUSION

There continues to be a steady stream of judicial review claims in the Administrative Court, which shows no sign of abating. The Court of Appeal and the House of Lords are dealing with a large number of public law matters, with almost a third of appeals concerning administrative and human rights law[100]. Major changes have occurred in judicial review over the last 25 years. As Lord Woolf observed in his 1989 Hamlyn Lectures, the amendment to RSC Ord 53, which took effect in 1980, provided "the highway for the dramatic progress in administrative law that has taken place" since then[101]. The modern procedure of judicial review "has encouraged judges to develop their power to intervene to combat abuse of power in a way that they would not have done otherwise"[102]. The 1998 Act has had a significant impact on judicial review, particularly in relation to the intensity of the review carried out by the courts and the increasing focus on proportionality.

---

96   *Corner House*, see note 95 above.
97   See, for example, *R (on the application of Goodson) v Bedfordshire and Luton Coroner* [2005] EWCA Civ 1172, [2006] ACD 6, [2005] All ER (D) 122 (Oct), where the Court of Appeal noted that a personal litigant who had sufficient standing to apply for judicial review would normally have a private interest in the outcome of the case. The only exceptions appear to be for pressure groups or "a public spirited individual" in relation to a matter in which he has no direct personal interest separate from that of the population as a whole.
98   With effect from 2 October 2000, the Crown Office has been known as the Administrative Court, which is within the Queen's Bench Division of the High Court.
99   [2006] UKHL 53, [2007] 1 AC 650, [2007] 2 All ER 273.
100  Judicial Statistics Annual Report 2005.
101  "*Protection of the Public – A New Challenge*" The Hamlyn Lectures 41st Series (1989) p 7.
102  *Ibid.*

Landmark decisions, such as *Daly*[103] and *A v Secretary of State for the Home Dept*[104] have clarified the relationship between the courts and the executive. These are exciting times for public law and one can look ahead with optimism for the future development of an already healthy and thriving "citizen's remedy" to control executive action.

---

103  See note 49 above.
104  [2004] UKHL 56, [2005] 2 AC 68, [2005] 3 All ER 169.

# THE ILLUSION OF INCLUSION: WOMEN 100 YEARS ON

## BARONESS HELENA KENNEDY QC

When *Halsbury's Laws* was first published one hundred years ago women played no part in law's creation. They did not sit on the bench nor in Parliament, nor were there female commentators on the law in the universities. Until 1919 it was not possible for women in the United Kingdom to become solicitors, barristers or magistrates, let alone judges. Even after women had broken into teaching and medicine, the Law Society and the Inns of Court steadfastly resisted the entrance of women into the legal professions. Margaret Hall was barred from taking the entrance examination to the Scottish Society of Law Agents in 1900. Bertha Cave was excluded from Gray's Inn in 1903. Repeated applications by women to join the Law Society or the Inns were refused. It was only persistence and repeated challenge to the institutions that eventually overcame the spurious claim that women's brains made them unsuited to the law or to politics.

The advance of women has been slow. The first women to become King's Counsel were Rose Heilbron and Helena Normanton in 1949. The first woman to be appointed a county court judge was Elizabeth Lane in 1962; she was promoted to the High Court ten years later to become the first female amongst the men. That same year, 1972, Rose Heilbron was appointed as a judge at the Old Bailey. Since then a slow drift of women has made it on to the benches of the higher courts. The recognition that confidence in the legal system by the public required a more balanced judiciary has had its impact. It has also been acknowledged that if law is made exclusively by men it is not surprising that the perspective of the law will be male.

In 1992, after 20 years' practice at the Bar, I wrote a book about the law called *Eve Was Framed*. After the publication of the first edition, I took part in many debates about women and the criminal justice system. Elderly judges were paraded through television studios to take issue with my claim that the system frequently failed women. They would all insist that justice was blind; the gender of an accused was of no consequence and, if anything, being female worked in her favour. To reassure me that he was not a misogynist one judge told me that he had voted for women to be allowed to join the Kennel Club!

In the years that have followed a lot has happened. There is now greater awareness of the ways in which discrimination works. The institutions have been forced into reforms. Women are more visible in the courts and the legal establishment talks a good talk on domestic and sexual violence. It is tempting to swallow the claim that we have moved into a post-feminist era; the battles having been won, the picture is completely changed, and women have the world at their feet. Any attempts to document the continuing problems facing women or the entrenched attitudes which persist elicit a dismissive insistence that gender bias has been addressed and remaining pockets of resistance are few.

However, re-reading *Eve Was Framed* in 2003 in preparation for a new edition I realised that while a lot had happened not enough had changed. With the increased numbers of young women in the law schools and the legal profession, with a growing number of women receiving appointments to the bench, we can be seduced into premature conclusions that the systemic problems have been solved and it is now just a question of more women working their way through the profession. The illusion of inclusion can deny the reality that professional structures still do not adequately accommodate the reality of women's lives; the conjuring trick done with numbers can disguise the fact that certain attitudes to women remain unchanged and that women coming before the courts still encounter myths and stereotypes which disfigure the legal process. Yes, as the 1970s Virginia Slims cigarette advert used to say, "we've come a long way, baby" but the journey is as yet unfinished.

Over fifty per cent of students in law schools are female. They come out with great degrees and are hugely talented women. The competition for places in professional practice is now so fierce that many use their degrees to go into other activities, but for those determined to enter legal practice, the majority is steered towards public service law, by which I mean fields largely funded out of legal aid. Two women for every one man now apply for a place in sets of chambers doing publicly-funded work. The same is happening with traineeships in legal aid solicitors' practices. Men make career choices much more related to money and prestige and head for the high-rewarding areas of practice, but women find their place doing poor folks' law. Women invariably do the ill-rewarded work in all walks of life and what ensues is a lowering of the esteem of that professional activity. I have always worked as a legal aid lawyer myself and without regret but I mind that women are denied the choices that are open to so many of their male colleagues because doors are not oiled for them.

The lawyer's reward gradient between the litigant who is legally aided and the one who is privately funded is huge. When governments justify taking the scythe to legal aid they summon up for the public the notion of the fat cat lawyer, a bloated male barrister dining out on public funds, when in fact those who will suffer will largely be committed young women (who work tirelessly for little reward) and their clients.

There is public trumpeting every time a woman is made a senior judge and private harrumphing that she is probably not up to it. The pace is slow and explained by the insistence that only the best will do – as though mediocre men have never adjudicated, and women still do not have what it takes. It is as though evolution might sort out our deficiencies, like fish growing feet. There is still insufficient recognition that the merit principle has to be examined to ensure that it is underpinned by criteria which also value the particular skills and experience women could bring to the role. As Dame Brenda Hale, our only woman judge in the House of Lords, has said, we need "to forge a new picture of a judge who does not fit the traditional model but is still recognisably a judge"[1].

The failure is that we still do not take sufficient account of the ways that women's experience is different from that of men, whether as practitioners or as women forced to use the law as victims of crime or as defendants. Women of my generation have to take some of the blame because in all our talk of equality we crowded out some important arguments about difference. The reason was our own sensitivity to difference; it had been used so successfully to exclude women from public life – our psychological wiring was considered inappropriate for the logical requirements of legal decision making or medicine or governing and our feminine vulnerability was used to explain why we should be kept in the domestic arena. We were so cagey about special pleading that we started out by arguing simply for fair treatment. We argued for equality as "equal treatment" not realising the *cul-de-sac* this would create. Equalisation has almost invariably been towards a male norm. The public standards already in place were assumed to be valid so instead of our attempting to order the world differently, women have been expected to shape up, whether as lawyers or as women before the courts.

There are still too many in the law who believe that the law is an objective set of rules, that law is neutral. The point of *Eve Was Framed* was to show that this claim of neutrality was bogus. Law was male because it was made by men and only when law making was reconsidered could law become just. But reforming the law with some legislative changes and the appointment of a few women will not resolve the deeply embedded problems with

---

1   "Equality and the Judiciary: Why Should We Want More Women Judges?" [2001] Pubic Law 489 at p 498.

the law. There has to be a serious acknowledgment that legal cultures are premised on notions which are themselves excluding rather than including.

When women of my generation began to turn the spotlight on the treatment of women by law and in the law, we argued for law reform. But what has become increasingly clear is that law reform of itself is not the answer. Law is often part of the problem. We argued for equality, but of course treating as equal those who are unequal does not produce equality. We have to start talking about *substantive* equality, which acknowledges the historic imbalances between men and women in our society, rather than formal equality. Real equality means treating "as equals" while taking account of the context of our lives.

I had a perfect example recently when, in the spirit of equality, some very decent liberal peers supported a reactionary call to provide men in rape cases with the cover of anonymity. The call came in response to a small number of high profile cases where celebrities had to undergo tabloid hysteria and public humiliation only to have cases of a sexual nature dropped before charging. The police should never have released the names of the men to the press in the first place but leaks of this sort can create a "nice little earner" for errant police officers. Instead of insisting that names should not be published until after charging, "good for the goose, good for the gander" arguments were made. The undertow of the arguments questioned the rationale for protecting the identity of women complainants who could be malicious liars. In fact, the provision of anonymity was introduced to help women to come forward after rape because it was recognised that the shame of the experience had such serious implications for women. The slow lifting of the taboo around rape has meant that some women waive the protection and speak publicly about their horrifying experience, but for many women it is still such a source of humiliation and degradation that public attention would be the final straw. In some communities exposure will affect the safety of women and their prospects as wives and mothers; rape is still such a source of dishonour it may even lead to family rejection.

There is no doubt that men wrongly accused suffer too, but openness as a principle is in the public interest. Crime is not a private matter. The rape of women concerns us all and should not be swept under the carpet any more than any other crime. An accusation of murder, if unsubstantiated, also has terrible consequences for the accused but public notice of alleged wrongdoing is a crucial element of a democracy, where openness of the process prevents abuse by the authorities. The police have also been able to clear up serial rapes because the publication of a man's name can encourage other women to come forward. Adam Carruthers, a Scots policeman, was convicted of two rapes in May 2001 but it transpired that as many as 20 women had made complaints against him over the years, ranging from indecent exposure to rape. One woman was raped by him several times. A case had been dropped in 1998 by the Dumfries and Galloway Police for whom he worked. In 1993 a Channel 4 programme *Dispatches: Getting Away with Rape* also exposed the case of a man who was tried seven separate times for rape, each time getting away with it because the connections were not made between the cases. After Richard Baker, a disc jockey, was convicted in 1999 of multiple rapes, many more women came forward to describe convincingly how they too had been preyed upon. In another case the House of Lords ruled in 2000 that it was permissible for the Crown to call four women who had made allegations against the defendant in the past to support the rape charge on which he was then standing trial[2].

A time may come when women who seek justice after being raped will not feel they are the ones on trial and our cultures may evolve so that women who are violated are not themselves blamed but until those anomalies are resolved a differential in treatment is justified. It is worth noting that the very same people who argued "difference" to keep

---

2   *R v Z* [2002] 2 AC 483, [2000] 3 All ER 385.

women in their box, hate its invocation when it is a remedy for disadvantage. Suddenly equality is the by-word.

Rape is the perfect example of the inadequacy of legal reform to challenge the more immutable forces operating in the law: all the changes designed to secure justice for women who have been raped – from removal of the corroboration requirement to restrictions on the right to cross-examine – have amounted to little. The conviction rate for rape in Britain is still the lowest for all serious crime, and despite increased reporting the convictions are falling. Over the past decade the number of reported rapes has doubled but only 7 per cent of complaints ever lead to conviction. Sometimes it is as low as 5·8 per cent[3]; in Scotland the conviction rate is only 4 per cent. Very few rape cases proceed to court because a huge number are withdrawn. This is often because women cannot face the legal process. Despite all the efforts to improve the system, the stumbling block is that the woman knows that cross-examination will expose her to all the double standards that confront women and it will be her word against his. Women know that it is difficult to secure a conviction; they make their own calculations as to whether they are prepared to go through with it. Of the cases which do proceed to trial the conviction rate in rape is 41 per cent when the general conviction rate for crime across the board is 73 per cent. The reason for law reform's failure is because rape is the ultimate buffer; it is where the law crashes up against the rawest display of the continuing power imbalance between men and women.

The mythologies around rape are still present although members of the judiciary are much more circumspect about making the kind of public utterances which they did with frequency right up to the mid-1990s. The cases which used to hit the news are legendary, and I have commented on them in *Eve was Framed*, from which the examples below are taken[4]: the guardsman who walked free after his conviction because of his fine service record, although his victim's vagina was torn by the rings on his hand; the woman who was "contributorily negligent" because she was walking alone at night; and so on. It was often in their unguarded moments when passing sentence that judges disclosed their prejudices. I remember blanching early on in my practice when I heard Sir Melford Stevenson, a judge who was extravagant in doling out long sentences, being generous to a rape defendant because, he said, the girl was "asking for it". She had been hitch-hiking, a far more serious offence in his Lordship's view. The rape was described as "an anaemic affair as rapes go", as though something a bit more colourful might be expected from a red-blooded rapist. The sentence was suspended. Some of the most notorious cases gave rise to extensive criticism of the particular judges involved. In 1987, Jupp J passed a suspended sentence on a man who twice raped his ex-wife, explaining that this was "a rare sort of rape. It is not like someone being jumped in the street. This is within the family and does not impinge on the public". The late Leonard J, in the Ealing Vicarage rape case in 1987, passed sentences of five years and three years on the defendants because the victim had apparently made a "remarkable recovery". Lucky defendants! They had repeatedly raped the victim at knifepoint, forced her to have oral sex, and penetrated her anally with the handle of a knife. Any recovery was no thanks to them. (Since the trial the young woman has courageously written and spoken publicly about her experience, and was deeply critical of the judge.) In 1986 two paratroopers had their sentences of 18 months reduced because their victim was "dissolute and sexually depraved". In July 1991 Alliot J gave a rapist a three-year jail sentence, although the recommended minimum for someone found guilty of the offence is five years, because his victim was a "common prostitute" and a "whore". In passing sentence he explained, "While every woman is entitled to complain about being violated,

---

3   646 HL Official Report (5th series) col 1098 (31 March 2003).
4   See also Philip NS Rumney "Progress at a Price: the Construction of Non-Stranger Rape in the *Milberry* Sentencing Guidelines" (2003) 66 Mod LR 870, and the other articles there mentioned.

someone who for years has flaunted their body and sold it cannot complain as loudly as someone who has not". As late as 1983 in his *Textbook of Criminal Law*, Professor Glanville Williams asserted the relevance of the fact that women frequently enjoy fantasies of rape. He cited as his authority Helene Deutsch's *The psychology of women: a psychoanalytic interpretation* (published 45 years before) and Paul H Gebhard's *Sex offenders: an analysis of types* (published 25 years before). He included no contemporary references and seemed to take no account of the possibility that a woman might enjoy a private fantasy where she is in control, whilst not welcoming the reality

Women's organisations from Townswomen's Guilds to church groups, from the Women's Institute to student unions increased the volume of their discontent with the law. The arrival of over 100 women on the Labour benches after the 1997 election undoubtedly shifted the debate. These women MPs, in coalition with women in other parties, have fought hard to place women's issues on the agenda and, despite attack and accusations of political correctness, they have instigated legal reform, pushed for better systems to deal with domestic violence and championed the case for a change in parent leave and the work/life balance. Unfortunately successive Home Secretaries have recognised the value to be drawn from women's support and have harnessed women's issues to their own regressive programmes on law and order. We should have realised the downside when legislation introduced to deal with stalking was used to curb picketing. Women's requests that magistrates should be able to exclude men who batter their partners from the family home on a *prima facie* case, and imprison them for breach of the order, has given birth to the Anti-social Behaviour Order (ASBO), which is now used extensively and often in alarming ways. There are concerns that young people who could have been diverted from crime are acquiring criminal records and experience of prison too readily because of ASBOs. Women's pleas that men whose lawyers insidiously cross-examine rape complainants about their sexual history should have their own previous convictions or history placed before the courts has now led to a generalised legal change to disclose the convictions of an accused even in theft cases. Women's campaigns for a power of arrest to be attached to common assault was designed to deal with domestic violence – to give women in the absence of their partner the opportunity to seek help and advice before violence escalated and to stop the police dismissing a "domestic" unless there was blood on the walls. Instead of confining it to domestic violence, all common assault now carries a power of arrest for the first time ever and we can be sure it will be used most actively against boys on street corners.

The hijacking of women's movement campaigns for attacks on civil liberties is now commonplace. More justice for women cannot be bought at the price of less justice for men. Lowering standards to improve conviction rates and introducing increased police powers always end up affecting women too because their use becomes generalised. With the best of intentions law officers of the Crown began appealing the sentences passed on men convicted of manslaughter of their wives because they thought them too lenient. The argument was that infidelity by a wife or an announcement that she is leaving the home should not be a justification or mitigation in the contemporary world for outbursts of rage. That is right; but arguing for increased sentences at that time simply fed into the current clamour for increased punishment generally. The outcome has been the ratcheting up of sentences across the board for domestic killing so that women who were receiving appropriate, compassionate sentences are now less likely to walk free from the court, even when they have killed after being battered for years. The law of unintended consequences is not one that is on the statute books.

The lesson for all of us is that improving justice requires careful strategies. The law is undoubtedly an instrument of change but it can be a blunt instrument when the context in which it operates is not fully understood. Law does not exist within a vacuum.

Understanding and acknowledging the cultural, physical and societal disadvantages women experience is crucial to doing justice, but sometimes even women are oblivious to those effects. Women who have never themselves experienced such obstacles are just as inured as any man to their meaning. I have a successful woman colleague at the Bar, whom I like enormously, who is very dismissive of arguments about "a woman's perspective". She has little truck with women's complaints of sexual harassment because she thinks young professional women are not tough enough to be in the law if they cannot deal with unwelcome overtures. Her education and upbringing have inducted her into seeing the world from the perspective of men and no experience to date has provided the electric awakening shock. Paradoxically, some men instinctively recognise gender and race disparities, even if they are far outside their personal experience, and are the most effective advocates of dynamic shifts in legal custom and practice.

Domestic violence is an area where the law is still being dragged into the real world. The argument that violence against women is an abuse of their human rights is now being understood, but there is an increasingly vocal claim of equivalency – that women also hit men, that men are abused by women but tell no one out of shame. We are being asked to believe that battered men are suffering in silence just as battered women once did. While there are no doubt such cases they do not reflect the norm, and they distract us from the really serious problems which blight women's lives and make equality impossible. At public meetings, the police and officials often talk about "people" who experience domestic violence, using language which disguises the reality that in our society it is women who are most often battered, women who are killed by their partners at a rate of two a week, women and their children who are all slain by a vengeful partner who then turns the gun on himself, girl children who are disproportionately the victims when we read of cruelty and neglect leading to death. According to the Home Office statistics at least a quarter of all violent crime is domestic violence, and it is perpetrated against women[5]. The refusal to acknowledge the gendered nature of violence is a continuing problem.

In the last decade a number of high-profile miscarriages of justice have reminded us that women still face special kinds of risk within the system. In 2003, three criminal cases involving the prosecution of mothers for causing the deaths of their babies created public consternation. Sally Clark and Angela Cannings were both convicted of murder and sentenced to life imprisonment, before being finally released by the Court of Appeal[6]. Trupti Patel's case was a miscarriage of justice waiting to happen, had the courts not become alert to the potential problem of expert testimony in cases involving the deaths of babies. The common feature in these trials was a mother who had suffered the loss of more than one infant. The repetition of sudden deaths without explanation raised suspicion amongst professionals and, in the absence of any eye-witness evidence of harmful conduct, the police investigations relied upon medical expertise, particularly that of paediatricians and pathologists. The courts were provided with the spectacle of professional men of high standing condemning mothers who had suffered the terrible trauma of losing their children on evidence of a highly questionable kind, often buttressed by spurious judgements about the appropriateness of the woman's response to her loss. The assumption was that the babies had been suffocated when in fact pointers in other directions were overlooked. Ninety per cent of babies who die unexpectedly do so from natural causes and in some families genetic factors may explain more than one infant death, but the presumption of innocence was ignored and hawkish beliefs about the propensity of certain mothers to kill

---

5    *Safety and Justice: The Government's Proposals on Domestic Violence* (Cm 5847) (Home Office, 2003) Foreword.

6    *R v Clark* [2003] EWCA Crim 1220, [2003] 2 FCR 447. *R v Cannings* [2004] EWCA Crim 1, [2004] 1 All ER 725.

their babies took hold. All the old stereotypes about appropriate behaviour for women and traditional mothering permeated the courts, and it was as though we had learned nothing in the last decade. Travesty was added to tragedy for these women and they will never recover.

In 2004, after the conviction of Ian Huntley for the Soham murders, an inquiry[7] was launched into the police failure to keep records of numerous previous complaints against him of rape and underage sex with girls, all of which had been dropped by police. Huntley had applied for a job as a school caretaker at the school attended by the two young girls he subsequently murdered. A security check revealed no relevant history because the police in Humberside had destroyed the records. They claimed unconvincingly that this had been done to comply with the Data Protection Act 1998. On that basis no police intelligence on suspects would ever be kept. The reality was that police took the sexual complaints with a pinch of salt. They claimed the underage sex was not prosecuted because the girls consented – which is not actually a defence. One of the alleged rapes had not been pursued because the police were able to show from CCTV footage that the alleged victim had danced closely with Huntley before the sexual encounter in an alley. Consent to any intimacy is still consent to all in the minds of some police officers.

In characterising the law's shortcomings I am aware that powerful cultural forces are at work. It is claimed that the law only reflects public attitudes which are prejudicial to women. However, we are entitled to expect more. The law transmits powerful messages, which construct and underpin our social relations. It is important that those messages do not reinforce stereotypical images of womanhood and femininity or indorse notions of masculinity which are detrimental to women and indeed negative for men. Judges say to me that one minute I want equality for women, yet the next minute I want the law to treat them differently. All I am really asking is that the law should be capable of transcending difference by first acknowledging it. The Supreme Courts in Canada, Australia and South Africa all now accept that formal equality is not good enough. Ameliorative or substantive equality requires courts in those jurisdictions to take account of the ways that women or other groups in society have endured discrimination.

The law regulates our social relations. In doing so it issues messages which resonate throughout society. Those messages are internalised, which is why the law is so important. The law can never be completely out of step with public feeling or it will be held in contempt; but it should be capable of taking a lead in reshaping attitudes to violence, in challenging sexual double standards and in addressing gender disparities. This two-step which the law has to perform, of leading public opinion yet also reflecting it, is a difficult manoeuvre, but what does not work is for the law to lag behind public concerns or to dismiss their value.

Women up and down the country still feel that the law does not address their concerns. The perception that the courts are simply out of touch with the reality of people's lives poses a serious threat to justice. When the legal system fails, or is seen to fail, in the fulfilment of its practical function, society reaps the consequences. "But the law cannot be subject to fashion" is the judicial refrain. No one would dispute this, but it can become an excuse for atrophy and blinkered vision. Real and generous shifts in attitudes are required to maintain confidence in the law.

The ritual and mystique of court procedure is itself out of date. A recurrent theme, heard from prisoners and witnesses alike when talking about their courtroom experiences, is the terror of the witness box, the intimidation of the procedure, made undoubtedly worse by the paraphernalia of wigs and gowns and a language which obfuscates rather than illuminates. Some people feel they are unable to give a good account of themselves because of disadvantage in the face of articulate middle-class lawyers. Self-consciousness then interferes with their ability to recollect events accurately. They are often unsure of the

---

7   The Bichard Inquiry Report (2004) HC 653.

questions asked, but answer them as best they can because they do not want to be told off. That process makes many defendants and victims, particularly women, feel like children again, undoubtedly because they often are treated as children.

The criminal trial is a terrifying process. Those who are most affected by it, the victims and defendants, are those who are most alienated by the ambience and the procedures.

The courtroom mysticism is not unintentional: the participants are supposed to feel in awe of the process for its magic to work. But for many it brings back some of the nightmares of childhood. For the witness or defendant it means having the focus of attention turning on them in an environment which is comfortable only to a small class of people. It means speaking aloud in front of everyone. It means being scrutinised and perhaps being found wanting.

The number of jurors who cannot read the oath is often cited as a sign of our illiterate times; in fact the problem is more likely the difficulty of enunciating the words in public. The performance is the inhibitor. In an important trial with racial overtones the Crown asked for one of the few black jurors to be "stood by" (released from service) because of his difficulty with reading; it was later discovered that he had no problem at all but was terrorised by the process. The *faux pas* had in the meantime wiped out confidence in the prosecution team, whose insensitivity was seen as an example of biased white justice.

Many people have misapprehensions about how the courts work. Schooled on American films, they do not realise that our system is different. They also fail to appreciate the degree of dramatic licence which operates. To the victim of a crime, for example, it comes as a shock that the person they see as conducting "their" case almost never sits down and has a chat with them. Because the victim in a case is a witness the code of professional conduct in relation to witnesses comes into force, which means the prosecuting lawyer cannot speak to them about their evidence. Prosecuting counsel is counsel for the state. Defence barristers are also prohibited from talking directly to witnesses other than experts. Indeed, defence counsel should only really talk to his or her client in the presence of a solicitor. (There is some flexibility about the rules in lower courts.)

Obviously prosecutors could introduce themselves to witnesses, and many counsel for the Crown are now doing this, but there are still a large number of practitioners who feel that their impartiality should not be impugned. They do not want to run the risk of allegations that they said something inappropriate or tried to coach a witness, so the violated woman or child is left bewildered as to who is who amongst the bigwigs.

Even expert witnesses at times complain of their treatment as either patronising or dismissive. Psychiatrists, psychologists and sociologists have a particularly rough ride. They come like lambs to the slaughter if their reports are full of references to "cycles of deprivation" or "cognitive dissonance". We have our own arcane language in the courtroom and we do not want anyone else's creeping in.

Blame for the lack of confidence in the law cannot be placed at the door of judges or any one group of people. Nor is there any conspiracy afoot. It is the nature of the beast, and the attitudes which support the survival of the *status quo*, that need reassessment. Justice can be compromised because people who are caught up in an already flawed legal process are often judged on grounds which have nothing whatsoever to do with the facts of the case. Those who are most susceptible are the young and the working class, the immigrant, Muslim, Irish, black, homosexual or female. It is often the way with discriminatory practice that its victims know full well what is happening whilst those who perpetrate it are oblivious.

Creating a legal framework which is truly equitable means a real overhaul of our legal thinking. The institution itself has to change. Only then will the law be just.

# THE UNITED KINGDOM ARMED FORCES: THE ADVANCE OF HUMAN RIGHTS

## PETER ROWE[1]

To some the term "human rights" may seem out of place when discussing the work of the armed forces, an organisation designed to apply lethal force in pursuit of the objectives set by the state. In the United Kingdom the term was hardly spoken of in this context until the "troubles" in Northern Ireland began in 1969 and then only in relation to military operations there. It has now carried its influence, largely as a result of the Human Rights Act 1998, to many fields of public activities previously unvisited. The armed forces have been no exception. This chapter will consider the influence of the European Convention on Human Rights (the Convention for the Protection of Human Rights and Fundamental Freedoms 1950, Rome, 4 November 1950; TS 71 (1953); Cmnd 8969) on the disciplinary processes of the armed forces and in respect of their conduct of military operations in Northern Ireland, Afghanistan and Iraq. It will then attempt to draw some conclusions from its influence on the workings of this unique institution.

## SERVICE DISCIPLINE

29 July 1990 was to turn out to be a very significant day both in the life of Lance Sergeant Alexander Findlay and for the whole system of military justice in the United Kingdom. On that day and following a "heavy drinking session", Lance Sergeant Findlay "held members of his own unit at pistol point and threatened to kill himself and some of his colleagues". He fired the pistol twice, without aiming at anyone, surrendered the weapon and was arrested. At his subsequent court-martial he was sentenced to two years' imprisonment, reduced to the rank of guardsman and dismissed from the army.

Since Findlay had pleaded guilty to serious charges[2] at his court-martial he would have expected some reasonably severe punishment. It is doubtful whether he would have expected the sentence of two years' imprisonment (as compared with military detention), reduction in rank to guardsman and dismissal with its concomitant loss of pension rights[3]. He had no opportunity open to him to appeal to the Courts-Martial Appeal Court and so he sought, within the limits of the military justice process and at the High Court[4], to challenge the sentence imposed on him. This course was not successful and Findlay was eventually transferred to a civilian prison in December 1991[5].

---

1   Barrister, Professor of Law, University of Lancaster.
2   These were offences against the criminal law of threatening to kill and common assault and a military offence of conduct to the prejudice of good order and military discipline, Army Act 1955 ss 70 and 69 respectively.
3   He estimated his total loss of income as a result of the conviction to be £440,200 made up by loss of earnings in the Army and loss of pension rights, see *Findlay v UK* (1997) 24 EHRR 221 (para 82).
4   *R v General Court Martial (Regents Park Barracks), ex p Findlay* (14 December 1992, unreported). See also J Mackenzie, acting on behalf of Findlay, who discusses this application, (1995) 145 NLJ 1624. At the time there was no right to appeal against sentence alone to the Courts Martial Appeal Court.
5   Although the events which formed the subject of the charges took place in July 1990 his court-martial did not start until over a year later.

If the officers, who formed the board for his court-martial, had been more lenient in the sentence imposed it is interesting to speculate whether Findlay would have set in motion events which would see the most radical reform of the military justice system in modern times. The officers concerned could not have known, when in their retiring room, what would be the consequences of their decision[6]. Nor could they have anticipated that some three months later a decision of the Supreme Court of Canada[7] would lead English lawyers, on behalf of their clients, to challenge the structure of the British court-martial system which had convicted them[8].

An application was made on behalf of Findlay to the European Commission of Human Rights in 1993 which decided in February 1995 that it was admissible on the ground that the "applicant's complaints under [art 6(1)] of the Convention raise serious and complex issues of fact and law which require determination on their merits"[9]. The government had mounted a stout defence of the court-martial system and had argued that Findlay's application was manifestly ill-founded or, in the alternative, that it did not disclose a breach of the Convention. Shortly afterwards it appears to have decided that the cause was lost. Courts-martial would have to be reformed, preferably before the case reached the European Court of Human Rights ("ECtHR"). It was able to achieve this by bringing forward an Armed Forces Bill, which gained royal assent on 24 July 1996, two months before the hearing by the court. The government subsequently argued at the hearing that "it did not contest the Commission's conclusions but asked the Court to take note of the changes to the court-martial system to be effected by the Armed Forces Act 1996 which ... more than satisfactorily met the Commission's concerns"[10].

The end result of all the proceedings brought on behalf of Alexander Findlay was that his conviction stood but he would have the satisfaction of knowing that he had been tried by a court-martial which objectively had not given the appearance of independence and impartiality as required by art 6 of the Convention[11]. The consequence of this protracted legal action was to cause many senior soldiers, former Chiefs of the Defence Staff and

---

6   At that time the judge advocate was not a member of the court-martial for sentencing decisions. See generally, R Beddard "The Right to a Fair Trial in the Services" [1998] 23 European Law Review Human Rights Survey HR49; (1997) 68 BYIL 433; A Lyon "After Findlay: A Consideration of Some Aspects of the Military Justice System" [1988] Crim LR 109; Judge Rant QC "The Real Issue of Findlay" (1997) 147 NLJ 405. In his evidence to the Select Committee on the Armed Forces Bill 1995–96 and thus prior to the changes brought about by the 1996 Act, Judge Rant QC (the then Judge Advocate General) referred to the "perception of independence [in courts-martial]" and added "the reality of it I would argue exists already", (HC Paper 143) Q 347.

7   R v Genereaux (1992) 88 DLR (4th) 110.

8   For at least one lawyer active in this field see the memorandum by Gilbert Blades to the House of Commons Select Committee on the Armed Forces Bill 1995–96 (HC Paper 143) p 168. For another see J Mackenzie "Who's afraid of the big bad judge" (2000) 150 NLJ 638 at p 639 who concluded that "in around 1992, I came to the conclusion that the existence of the military criminal jurisdiction was not in the interests of ... the efficiency of the armed forces".

9   Application no 22107/93.

10  Findlay v UK [1997] ECHR 22107/93 (para 60). For the court's comment on this see (1997) 24 EHRR 221 (para 67). The relevant parts of the 1996 Act came into force on 1 April 1997.

11  Ibid, para 80. See also the concurring opinion of Judge de Meyer. The court had "no jurisdiction to quash convictions pronounced by national courts" (see at para 88). Even if it had it was "impossible to speculate as to what might have occurred had there been no breach of the Convention", ibid. Compare the view taken by the Courts Martial Appeal Court, R v Dundon [2004] EWCA Crim 621 at [16], [2004] All ER (D) 364 (Mar) at [16]; R v Dudley [2005] EWCA Crim 719 at [9], [2005] All ER (D) 122 (Apr) at [9]; R v Stow [2005] EWCA Crim 1157 at [40], [2005] All ER (D) 132 (May) at [40].

government ministers to spend a great deal of time defending unsuccessfully the system by which he had been tried. He had also paved the way for a number of other convicted servicemen and women to bring their cases to the court based on the same issue[12].

From 1955 the Army and Air Force Acts were to be renewed every five years with the Royal Navy (governed by the Naval Discipline Act 1957) joining this process in 1971. The agreed procedure was for the relevant Bill to be submitted to a House of Commons *ad hoc* select committee with power to examine witnesses. The decision in February 1995 of the European Commission in the *Findlay* case fell at the right time for the government to bring forward its *Findlay* reforms to the House of Commons Select Committee on the Armed Forces Bill 1995–96, which began its sittings in January 1996.

The Armed Forces Bill contained clauses which would both abolish the power of a senior service officer to confirm the decisions of a court-martial, and permit appeals from a court-martial to a civilian court, the Courts-Martial Appeal Court, on sentence alone. The procedure of reviewing the decisions of a court-martial was also to be amended. A new prosecuting authority, independent of the chain of command, was established and courts-martial would be convened by court administration officers. The judge advocate would, thenceforth, be a member of the court and be able to vote on sentence, but not on the finding. In relation to summary proceedings a right was given to the serviceman or woman to elect trial by court-martial but only after the person conducting the summary proceedings had found the charge to be proved.

There was relatively little discussion of the ECtHR during the deliberations of the select committee, which heard from ministry officials that they believed the "measures [as described above] will put the matter beyond doubt"[13]. The committee, with a degree of prescience, was not so sure and concluded that that "obviously ... remains to be seen"[14].

Although the United Kingdom had been a party to the European Convention on Human Rights since 1953[15] there had been no references to the Convention in the three preceding select committee reports in 1990–91, 1985–86 or 1975–76[16]. The incorporation of the 1998 Act into English law was to lead, however, to a much greater shining of a light into the effect of the Convention on the United Kingdom's armed forces.

Parliament had been informed by the Lord Chancellor that incorporation of the Convention into English law "pose[d] no threat to the effectiveness of the Armed Forces"[17] and that "we do not see a case for exempting the Armed Forces from the terms of the Bill"[18]. The argument that the armed forces should be exempted from the Convention and from the 1998 Act had been a long-running one. The French government had paved the way when in 1974 it had entered a reservation to the Convention to the effect that arts 5 and 6 "shall not hinder the application of the provisions governing the system of discipline in the armed forces"[19]. This precedent would be invoked on a number of occasions, particularly from the moment the Armed Forces Discipline Bill was introduced in the House

---

12  See, for example, *Mills v UK* [2001] ECHR 35685/97; *Wilkinson v UK* App no 31145/96 (6 February 2001, unreported); *Moore v UK* App no 36529/97 (2 March 1999, unreported); *Cable v UK* App no 24436/94 (1999) Times, 11 March; *Coyne v UK* App no 25942/94 (1997) Times, 24 October.

13  *Special Report from the Select Committee on the Armed Forces Bill* (HC Paper 143 (1995–96)) para 12 referring to Q 395.

14  *Ibid.*

15  When it entered into force, although the United Kingdom had ratified it in 1951.

16  Respectively HC Paper 179; HC Paper 170; HC Paper 179.

17  585 HL Official Report (5th series) col 768 (5 February 1998). He also stated that the "Secretary of State for Defence takes the view that the [Human Rights Bill] raises no issues which are special to the Armed Forces", *ibid.*

18  *Ibid*, col 767.

of Lords on 18 November 1999. It came outside the normal quinquennial sequence of Armed Forces Bills with their special select committee procedure. This was due to the fact that the 1998 Act was to come into force in 2000 and it seemed clear to the Ministry of Defence that further challenges, particularly to the system of summary disposal and to detention prior to conviction, would be successful[20].

The Bill was met by a largely hostile reaction from former Chiefs of the Defence Staff and from what has been called the "military club"[21] of members of the House of Lords. This was, perhaps, not surprising. They could be forgiven for thinking that the 1996 Act had cured the problems highlighted by the ECtHR in the *Findlay* case. The new Bill now purported to introduce more changes and not merely "lawyer's law" ones but ones which would, in their view, affect adversely military discipline and the role of the commanding officer. To add to their ire the court had decided in *Smith v UK*[22] only a month earlier that the policy of dismissing homosexual members of the armed forces breached their rights to a private life. This particular decision gains significance from the fact that in May 1996 the House of Commons decided to uphold the longstanding position that "homosexuality [was] incompatible with military service"[23]. By its decision three years later the court had, effectively, overturned a decision of the House of Commons and had, it was argued, decided on an issue relating to the composition of the United Kingdom's armed forces.

To the "military club" the Bill struck at the hallowed principle that the commanding officer (CO) was the lynch pin of military discipline. The power contained in it to permit soldiers to appeal the decisions of their COs by way of summary disposal of charges to a summary appeal court presided over by a judge advocate and comprising of two military officers would, it was argued, "not only undermine [the powers of a CO] and create tensions but also mean that the soldiers, sailors and airmen will suffer"[24]. The reason given for coming to this conclusion was that instead of taking a defaulting serviceman through this new process "commanders will not in fact hear such cases [since it] will become too complicated, so they will not bother"[25]. Even if the new procedure was to be followed the 14-day period in which the soldier could appeal his CO's decision would lead, it was suggested, to "his mates, his wife and his wider family ... [telling] him that he has been unfairly treated, should not take his medicine and should explore the appeal process"[26] and it would lead to the rise of the "barrack-room lawyer"[27]. Moreover, it was argued that the power given to an accused at the start of the summary disposal process by his CO to elect a court-martial instead was argued to be sufficient to cure the fact that the CO could not be considered to be an "independent and impartial tribunal"[28].

---

19  Reservations in one form or another in respect of their respective armed forces have also been made by Armenia, Azerbaijan, the Czech Republic, Moldova, Portugal, Russia, Slovakia, Spain, and Ukraine.

20  See, for example, the decisions in *Hood v UK* (1999) 29 EHRR 365; *Jordan v UK* (2001) 11 BHRC 1. See generally, *Fourth Report of the Select Committee on Defence* (HC Paper 253 (1999–2000)) and for the government's view on the possibility of following the French example, para 5.

21  607 HL Official Report (5th series) col 692 (29 November 1999).

22  (2000) 29 EHRR 493; (2001) 31 EHRR 620 and see *Lustig-Prean v UK* (2000) 29 EHRR 548.

23  277 HC Official Report (6th series) cols 510–511 (9 May 1996).

24  607 HL Official Report (5th series) col 685 (29 November 1999), Lord Inge (a former Chief of the Defence Staff).

25  *Ibid* Lord Inge. Compare the view of the Ministry of Defence in the *Fourth Report of the Select Committee on Defence* (see note 20 above) at para 19.

26  344 HC Official Report (6th series) col 1168 (17 February 2000),

27  344 HC Official Report (6th series) col 1197 (17 February 2000).

The arguments put forward by those who argued against the Bill (and indeed against most of the changes brought about through the influence of the court) were premised on the principle that military discipline should be consistent as between times of peace and of war[29]. Indeed, this has been the governing principle since the development of the modern law relating to the armed forces. It was therefore to be expected that opponents of the Bill would concentrate on its effects during wartime.

In order to ensure that art 5 of the Convention (which deals with deprivation of liberty) was complied with the Bill provided for a civilian judge advocate to make decisions about the custody of a soldier, against whom charges were being considered or pending a court-martial, since his CO could not be considered to be a "competent court" nor a "judge or other officer authorised by law to exercise judicial power". How, it was argued, would the requirement for a civilian judge advocate to make decisions about the custody of a soldier work where a "unit [was] trapped behind enemy lines or just very isolated"[30]. Whilst the proposed video links to a judge advocate might provide a means of communication in such circumstances it was doubted whether this would be effective in practice[31].

Given the dissatisfaction with the Bill by the "military club" in the House of Lords and by some members of Parliament it was, perhaps, not surprising to see that a proposal was made to decline to give the Bill a second reading. The reasons given for such a move were that "[the Bill] adds unnecessary administrative burdens and costs to Her Majesty's Forces, proposes hasty and impractical solutions to the administration of military law for forces on active service, [and] transfers to civilians powers which rightly lie with the chain of command"[32].

Despite arguments to the contrary the Bill was duly passed without significant amendment. The "military club" in particular were left to draw some satisfaction from the statement of the minister that the changes proposed in the Bill would "provide copper-bottom protection to the Armed Forces ... against legal challenges in courts and tribunals in this country. For that reason, the Armed Forces may have to learn to live with it, albeit reluctantly"[33].

This "copper-bottom protection" turned out to be no such thing. Further challenges to the military justice system continued to be made before the courts. Following the Armed Forces Act 2001 (which made only minimal changes as a result of the influence of the Convention) the next opportunity to amend the military legal system through primary legislation would not, in accordance with the quinquennial cycle, present itself until 2006.

---

28  For the first successful challenge to the status of a CO as "a judge or other officer authorised by law to exercise judicial power" under art 5(3) see *Hood v UK* (1999) 29 EHRR 365. For the suggestion that the right to elect court-martial was sufficient without any need for the Summary Appeal Court see 607 HL Official Report (5th series) col 687 (29 November 1999). This view is not supported by the jurisprudence of the court, which has been concerned about whether a right to waive a trial by court-martial and thus to accept a summary disposal by a soldier's CO can, in practical terms, amount to an effective waiver, *Thompson v UK* (2005) 40 EHRR 114; *Bell v UK* App no 41534/98 (16 January 2007). The High Court has taken the view that it can as a "matter of general principle", *Baines v Army Prosecuting Authority* [2005] EWHC 1399 (Admin) at [65].

29  The term "war" is used here to refer to situations of armed conflict, whether of an international or of a non-international character, and any other military operations involving the potential involvement of an "enemy" (as defined in the Armed Forces Act 2006 s 374). At the time of writing the 2006 Act has not been brought fully into force.

30  607 HL Official Report (5th series) 693 (29 November 1999), Earl Attlee (who, at the time, was a serving TA officer).

31  *Ibid.*

32  344 HC Official Report (6th series) col 1132 (17 February 2000).

33  607 HL Official Report (5th series) col 677 (29 November 1999), Lord Bramall.

In the meantime two further and separate challenges to court-martial procedures were made, both of which resulted in the quite unprecedented suspension of such trials for a short period.

The first of these was *Morris v UK*[34] in which the court found that the military officers (other than the permanent president) who were members of an army court-martial could not be compared with a civilian jury since they "remained subject to army discipline reports and there was no statutory or other bar to their being made subject to external army influence when sitting on the case"[35]. The consequence was that the "risk of pressure being brought to bear on the relatively junior serving officers who sat on the applicant's court-martial" could not be excluded[36]. In addition, the power given to a senior military officer by the then Army Act 1955 to review a decision of a court-martial was held to be inconsistent with the "the very notion of a 'tribunal'"[37]. With the 1998 Act in force, which prohibited a public authority from acting in a way incompatible with the Convention[38], the result of *Morris v UK*, decided on 26 February 2002, was a suspension of army and RAF courts-martial[39].

The suspension was relatively short-lived in respect of the junior military members of the court-martial[40]. Courts-martial had been resumed by the time of the House of Lords decision in *R v Spear*[41] in July 2002 which decided that the safeguards relating to those members of the court-martial were "such as effectively to protect the accused against the risk that they might be subject to 'external Army influence', as ... the European Court would have appreciated had the position been more fully explained [in *Morris v UK*]"[42]. It also concluded that the review procedures were not inconsistent with art 6 of the Convention, since they could only benefit an accused, and the review procedure was then re-activated[43].

Subsequently, in *Cooper v UK*[44] the Grand Chamber of the ECtHR departed from the earlier decision of the court in *Morris v UK* finding that, on the facts, there were sufficient

---

34 (2002) 34 EHRR 1253. The court (para 61) noted that the "changes introduced by the 1996 Act have gone a long way to meeting its concerns in the Findlay case".

35 *Ibid*, para 72.

36 *Ibid*.

37 *Ibid*, para 73.

38 Section 6. Whilst primary legislation set out the composition of a court-martial it did not deal with the issues raised by the decision in *Morris v UK* relating to the risk of the appearance of a lack of impartiality of the members of an army court-martial. Compare the position with review in the 1955 Act s 113 (the relevant provision at the time) which gave a statutory basis for review of the finding and sentence imposed by a court-martial. For a comment on the link between the *Findlay* and the *Morris* cases on the issue of administrative review of decisions of courts-martial see J Mackenzie "Courts-martial – what happens now?" (2002) 152 NLJ 422 and for further criticism of this process, see P Camp "Courts-martial an independent and impartial tribunal?" (1998) 148 NLJ 1156 at p 1157.

39 Lord Bach, for the government, stated in a written answer that "Army and Royal Air Force courts martial scheduled for the near future are being postponed", 632 HL Official Report (5th series) written answers col 69 (12 March 2002). Army courts-martial were resumed on 3 April 2002 and those for the RAF on 23 April, see 633 HL Official Report (5th series) col 527 (11 April 2002). In *R v Spear; R v Saunby* [2002] UKHL 31, [2003] 1 AC 734, [2002] 3 All ER 1074, Lord Rodger of Earlsferry stated (at [29]) that "the Government did not request that the case [*Morris v UK*] should be referred to the Grand Chamber".

40 See letter from Tim Lawson-Cruttenden (2002) 52 NLJ 565, 12 April 2002.

41 See note 39 above.

42 *Ibid*, Lord Bingham of Cornhill (at [12]).

43 See the Minister of State for Defence, 387 HC Official Report (6th series) col 4 (18 June 2002).

safeguards in place to guarantee the impartiality of the junior members of the court-martial[45].

The Royal Naval court-martial, which exhibited significant differences from its army and RAF counterparts, also came under sustained attack and in *Grieves v UK*[46] the court decided that the use of a uniformed naval officer (who was also a lawyer) as judge advocate in a court-martial deprived the court-martial of "one of the most significant guarantees of independence enjoyed by the other services' courts-martial" where civilians are employed in the role[47]. The immediate consequence was the laying before both Houses of Parliament within a month of a remedial order to amend the Naval Discipline Act 1957 in order to give effect to the judgment[48]. The longer term consequence was to make the call for the uniformity of discipline systems across all three services irresistible. This was one of the main reforms contained in the 2006 Act.

The trial of civilians before British courts-martial has a long history[49]. In modern times it could be exercised in respect of civilians employed by or accompanying the army when it was on active service[50] or where, overseas, certain categories of civilians came within the limits of the command of a CO. The reasons given for subjecting civilians to military jurisdiction were that this process enabled civilians with some connection to the armed forces to be tried by a British court rather than by the courts of the territory concerned[51] and it enabled the civilian to be dealt with abroad rather than having to be repatriated to the United Kingdom (where the courts may or not have jurisdiction in respect of a crime committed overseas). The justifications for assuming such jurisdiction abroad were argued to be to the advantage of the civilian, assuming he had been charged with a crime.

Most civilians subject to service law tend to be members of the families of servicemen/women serving abroad and who are living with them, or to be civilian employees or contractors working directly for the armed forces abroad. They can, therefore, be contrasted with civilians subjected to military jurisdiction in their home state.

---

44 (2004) 39 EHRR 171. It was able to rely extensively on the judgments of the House of Lords in *R v Spear* (see note 39 above), an advantage generated by the 1998 Act, see 651 HL Official Report (5th series) col 210 (8 July 2003). The ECtHR is, of course, able to challenge (see para 45) the reasoning employed by the House of Lords sitting in its judicial capacity, *Martin v UK* App no 40426/98 (24 October 2006, unreported), referring to *R v Martin* [1998] AC 917, [1998] 1 All ER 193.

45 (2004) 39 EHRR 171 (paras 123–126). It also decided that the role of the reviewing authority was not contrary to art 6, see paras 130–133. Note that the 2006 Act abolishes the power of review except for summary findings and punishment, see s 152 and compare s 273.

46 (2004) 39 EHRR 2. Compare *R v Skuse* [2002] EWCA Crim 991 at [54].

47 (2004) 39 EHRR 2 (para 89). For the effect that this decision had on other cases subsequently brought before the Courts Martial Appeal Court, see note 11 above.

48 See Naval Discipline Act 1957 (Remedial) Order 2004, SI 2004/66; *Ninth Report of the Joint Committee on Human Rights* (*Naval Discipline Act 1957 (Remedial) Order 2004*) (HL Paper 59, HC Paper 477 (2003–04)).

49 See *Manual of Military Law* (1977) Part I, Civilian Supplement, pp 1–7 and generally, G Borrie "Courts-Martial, Civilians and Civil Liberties" (1969) 32 MLR 35.

50 The position in the army is given by way of example. This condition, contained in the 1955 Act s 209, was removed by the 2006 Act s 370, Sch 15. "Active service" had been defined in the 1955 Act s 224.

51 These courts are the standing civilian court and the court-martial. Potential conflicts of jurisdiction with the receiving state will normally be resolved by a status of forces agreement or a memorandum of understanding. They may provide that United Kingdom jurisdiction is exclusive or that it is concurrent with the local courts. These arguments were made by the United Kingdom at the hearing in *Martin v UK* App no 40426/98 (24 October 2006, unreported) (para 37) and see the *Select Committee on the Armed Forces Bill* (HC Paper 143 (1995–96)) Qs 401–407.

Human rights bodies have been generally unforgiving where a state subjects civilians to military courts[52]. Their views should, however, be treated with a degree of caution since they are primarily concerned with military courts displacing civilian ones within the jurisdiction and not with such courts establishing jurisdiction over their civilian nationals abroad where the alternative is a foreign jurisdiction.

The only case to reach the ECtHR of a civilian being tried by a British military court was *Martin v UK*[53] in which the son of a soldier serving in Germany had been convicted of murder by a court-martial sitting there. This was an unusual case since the courts in England also had jurisdiction over this offence. The effect of his trial by court-martial rather than in the Crown Court was that he was tried by a board comprising five army officers and two civilians rather than by a jury.

The court concluded that "the power of military criminal justice should not extend to civilians unless there are compelling reasons justifying such a situation, and if so only on a clear and foreseeable legal basis"[54]. Unlike in *Martin v UK* the vast majority of civilians subjected to military jurisdiction abroad by the 2006 Act who commit an offence against the law of England and Wales will do so where the courts in England and Wales will have no jurisdiction. Here the choice of jurisdiction will be a British military court or the courts of the host state. To respond to the ECtHR the composition of a court-martial trying a civilian has been altered to permit it to be composed solely of civilians[55].

## HUMAN RIGHTS AND MILITARY OPERATIONS

It was, perhaps, not surprising to see invocation of the Convention in respect of the British Army's actions in Northern Ireland, since these operations occurred within the territory of the United Kingdom (to which the Convention applied). In this context, one of the earliest cases brought before the court was in fact brought by another state party to the Convention, the Republic of Ireland[56].

In times of civil unrest the Convention is normally a one-sided process, available to those who are acting against government security forces, since only a state party to the Convention (and not a non-state actor) can be a respondent. In this respect it can be contrasted with

---

52  See generally, JM Henckaerts and L Doswald-Beck *Customary International Humanitarian Law* (2005) vol 1, pp 356–357; P Rowe *The Impact of Human Rights Law on Armed Forces* (2006) Ch 4.

53  See note 44 above. In England Martin's appeal had been disallowed, *R v Martin* [1998] AC 917, [1998] 1 All ER 193.

54  *Martin v UK* App no 40426/98 (24 October 2006, unreported) (para 44). The court concluded that there had been a breach of art 6 on the same basis as that which applied to *Findlay v UK* and other cases based on its reasoning and it was therefore unnecessary to decide whether there were sufficiently compelling reasons in this particular case for the invocation of military jurisdiction. This would not have been an easy question to resolve since it had been argued before the House of Lords that his trial by court-martial rather than by a court in England was an abuse of process. Compare, however, the facts in *Ergin v Turkey* App no 47533/99 (4 May 2006, unreported).

55  The Armed Forces (Alignment of Service Discipline Acts) Order 2007, SI 2007/1859. For an explanation of this as a response to the *Martin v UK* judgment, see 693 HL Official Report (5th series) cols 298, 303 (20 June 2007). Given this requirement to show "compelling reasons" in relation to each trial of a civilian the ECtHR is unlikely to accept that trial before the courts of one state member of the Council of Europe is "better" than before the courts of another. *Quaere* where the receiving state is a non-member state and jurisdiction is concurrent.

56  *Ireland v UK* (1978) 2 EHRR 25, which also noted that the United Kingdom had previously forbidden use of the "five interrogation techniques" (para 241). See also *Farrell v UK* (1983) 5 EHRR 466; *Stewart v UK* (1984) 7 EHRR 453.

criminal proceedings to which all individuals, government forces and "rebels" alike, operating within the territory may be liable.

The threshold beyond which there is a breach of the right to life, as provided by art 2 of the Convention, is not dissimilar to the standard of "reasonable force in the circumstances" set by the criminal law[57]. Thus, a soldier who killed a suspected gunman through the use of reasonable force in the circumstances which applied to him may find that his actions are not culpable within the criminal law or his military law[58].

So far it is unlikely that military lawyers would have been too concerned about the Convention. At least *Ireland v UK* had confirmed the boundaries as to what was on the wrong side of the line in respect of the separate constituents of art 3[59]. Those soldiers who infringed the criminal law by using force other than to the degree permitted could expect to be tried by the civilian courts. There were, however, two particular problems for the army arising out of the operations in Northern Ireland which were probably not anticipated.

The first related to those who planned a particular operation, but who did not themselves use, or order, any degree of force against "suspected terrorists". Their actions (or inactions) could cause the United Kingdom to be in breach of art 2 because of their failure to provide other opportunities to enable the suspected gunman to be arrested, rather than being shot dead[60]. Whilst such individuals may well be outside the scope of the criminal law their role in ensuring as far as possible the right to life even of those who seek to kill civilians during armed operations was given considerable importance by the court.

The second problem was more intractable simply because the law had to strike a balance between the army being accountable for its actions and a situation being created where a soldier was fearful of using force when the circumstances clearly warranted it. The court had earlier established a duty on the part of the state to conduct an independent investigation into the circumstances surrounding the death of an individual following the use of force by state agents[61]. Two particular issues arose from this. First, could the army carry out an independent investigation of shootings by its own soldiers and secondly, when would an incident require to be investigated under art 2 of the Convention? In Northern Ireland, unlike in Iraq or in Afghanistan, the civilian police could investigate and thereby provide independence from the army. Like modern armed operations in Iraq or in Afghanistan those incidents which showed a possibility that the rules of engagement (in Northern Ireland the "yellow card") had been flouted would be most likely to be fully investigated by the service police independently of the chain of command.

Once military operations involving the British army re-commenced after Northern Ireland operations had been scaled down they were to do so in Afghanistan and, subsequently, in Iraq. The practical issue then became whether the Convention applied at all to the actions of British armed forces operating in territory outside the range of the Council of Europe states. No one had seriously thought of it applying at the time during the Falklands conflict[62] or in the Gulf War 1990–91. The issue of its extra-territorial effect had been tested in respect of the bombing of a TV station in Belgrade in 1999 in *Bankovic v Belgium*[63]. The Grand Chamber held that the victims of the bombing raid were not

---

57  See *McCann v UK* (1996) 21 EHRR 97.
58  In Northern Ireland the soldier was guided by the "yellow card" which indicated when, within the law, force could be used. This card has also been referred to as setting out his rules of engagement, see *ibid*, para 136.
59  For a detailed critical assessment of the view of the majority of the court on the meaning of art 3 see the separate opinion of Judge Sir Gerald Fitzmaurice, paras 13–36 and for a wider view of the definition of "torture", the separate opinion of Judge Evrigenis. See also note 73 below.
60  *McCann v UK* (para 213), see note 57 above; *Anik v Turkey* App no 63758/00 (5 June 2007, unreported) (para 63).
61  *McCann v UK* (para 161), *Anik v Turkey* (para 72), *ibid*.

"within the jurisdiction"[64] of a Convention state since the Convention operates in an "essentially regional context and notably in the legal space (espace juridique) of the contracting states. The FRY [Federal Republic of Yugoslavia] clearly does not fall within this legal space. The Convention was not designed to be applied throughout the world, even in respect of the conduct of contracting states"[65].

This seemed to be a pretty clear position. The ECtHR had, however, made earlier decisions which had recognised a limited extra-territorial application of the Convention[66]. It was not surprising therefore to see arguments presented before the High Court in London that (at least some) Convention rights were owed by the United Kingdom to Iraqi citizens who claimed to be victims of actions committed in Iraq by members of the British army.

There was one main obstacle for the claimants to overcome, although this came in two forms. The first was whether the 1998 Act had incorporated art 1 of the Convention, since it did not appear on the face of the Act and the second was, assuming that it did, were each of the claimants "within the jurisdiction" of the United Kingdom when the acts of British soldiers affected them? The House of Lords in R (on the application of Al-Skeini) v Secretary of State for Defence[67] held that Bankovic v Belgium had envisaged very limited extra-territorial jurisdiction but that this was wide enough to include one of the defendants (Mr Mousa) who had been killed while in the custody of British soldiers in a military detention facility in Basra. None of the other defendants, some of whom had been shot by British soldiers in the streets, came within the jurisdiction of the United Kingdom and, in consequence could not take advantage of the 1998 Act.

The significance of Al-Skeini was in denying the reach of the Convention to the activities of British forces otherwise than where they were in direct control of an individual, as they were in the case of Mr Mousa[68]. (Providing compensation, in an appropriate case, to those killed or injured by British soldiers at home[69] or abroad[70] was not new.) Had the House decided that those who had been shot by British soldiers in the streets were within the

---

62  In *Ibanez v UK* App no 58692/00 (Admissibility Decision) (19 July 2000, unreported) the court held that the applicants, who complained about the sinking of the *General Belgrano* by the Royal Navy in 1982, were out of time to pursue their application. The Convention applied to the Falkland Islands (and to Gibraltar, in the *McCann* case) since the United Kingdom had made such a declaration under art 56.

63  (2001) 11 BHRC 435.

64  Article 1.

65  *Bankovic v Belgium* (para 80).

66  *Ibid*, paras 71, 73, 81. There have also been subsequent decisions such as *Issa v Turkey* (2005) 17 BHRC 473; *Ocalan v Turkey* (2005) 18 BHRC 293. For an excellent analysis see Lord Rodger of Earlsferry in R (on the application of Al-Skeini) v Secretary of State for Defence [2007] UKHL 26 at [65]–[83], [2007] 3 WLR 33 at [65]–[83], [2007] 3 All ER 685 at [65]–[83].

67  See note 66 above. Lord Bingham of Cornhill dissented on the ground that, in his view, the 1998 Act had no extra-territorial effect.

68  The case of Mr Mousa was agreed by the parties and thus the exact requirements for extra-territorial reach were not fully explored. Compare Lord Rodger of Earlsferry (at [61]) (with whom Baroness Hale of Richmond and Lord Carswell agreed) with Lord Brown of Eaton-under-Heywood (at [132]). See also the view of the Divisional Court [2004] EWHC 2911 at [287], [2005] 2 WLR 1401 at [287] and compare it with that of Brooke LJ in the Court of Appeal [2005] EWCA Civ 1609 at [109], [2007] QB 140 at [109] and Sedley LJ at [183]. It was not sufficient that the United Kingdom was in occupation of that part of Iraq where the events took place. In one passage of the *Bankovic v Belgium* judgment (para 70) it was suggested that this extra-territorial jurisdiction could occur where a state was in occupation of territory but this passage was, in the view of the House of Lords in *Al-Skeini* (see note 66 above) not consistent with the limited grounds which formed the decision in the case. See, in particular, Lord Brown of Eaton-under-Heywood (at [129]).

jurisdiction of the United Kingdom, an independent investigation under art 2 of the Convention would have to be carried out in all cases even if there had been no complaint by relatives.

Despite the ruling in *Al-Skeini* a soldier remains personally accountable for his actions. In keeping with the English criminal law he may be subject to criminal proceedings (either before a court-martial or in an English court)[71] where he has used any degree of force which is in excess of that which the criminal law permits. In practice, he can expect an investigation to be carried out by the army authorities if there is evidence that he has not complied with his rules of engagement[72] or if some other breach of the criminal law, such as the use of torture against those detained is shown[73].

The Convention will not therefore apply to military operations during the course of an international armed conflict where British armed forces are fighting on the territory of a non-Council of Europe state (such as Iraq or Afghanistan) since there can be no question of enemy soldiers coming "within the jurisdiction" of the United Kingdom during the course of such military operations. Should enemy soldiers be captured by British forces they will be entitled to the protection of the Geneva Convention Relative to the Treatment of Prisoners of War 1949 (Geneva, 12 August 1949; TS 39 (1958); Cmnd 550) and the 1998 Act[74]. It is, however, unlikely that the latter adds any liabilities to soldiers since the accountability of the soldier for any ill-treatment of a prisoner of war is contained in English law and, as a result, in his service law. What the Act will enable an ill-treated prisoner of war (or his family, should he be killed) to do is to bring an action in the High Court in London seeking satisfaction[75] for alleged breach of his Convention rights. It is difficult to see the "military club" becoming concerned about this.

## CONCLUSIONS

The place of discipline, essential to some degree or other in any organisation, as a predominant factor in the working of the armed forces can be justified since their *raison d'être* is to act as a disciplined body during time of armed conflict. Discipline and the ability to enforce it at the appropriate level are the main safeguards for others against the potential and lethal force available to members of the armed forces[76]. The United Kingdom's armed

---

69 See for example, *Farrell v Secretary of State for Defence* [1980] 1 WLR 172, [1980] 1 All ER 166; *Doherty v Ministry of Defence* (1981) 44 MLR 466; *Ireland v UK* (para 143), see note 56 above.
70 See *Bici v Ministry of Defence* [2004] EWHC 786 (QB), [2004] All ER (D) 137 (Apr).
71 For the relationship between these two jurisdictions see the statement by the Attorney General concerning the military and civilian court proceedings against Trooper Williams, see 678 HL Official Report (5th series) col 1292 (16 February 2006); 675 HL Official Report (5th series) written answers col 111 (10 November 2005). The 2006 Act seeks to prevent such a situation re-occurring by denying the power of a CO to dismiss a charge. This is the effect of s 113.
72 See *R (on the application of Al-Skeini) v Secretary of State for Defence* [2005] EWCA Civ 1609 at [23]–[31], [2007] QB 140 at [23]–[31] per Brooke LJ.
73 Section 134 of the Criminal Justice Act 1988 is based on the United Nations Convention against Torture and Other Cruel, Inhuman or Degrading Treatment or Punishment 1984 (New York, 10 December 1984; TS 107 (1991); Cm 1775) art 1; the International Criminal Court Act 2001 ss 50, 51 and the elements of crimes relating to the Statute of the International Criminal Court (Rome, 17 July 1998) art 8.2(a)(ii), 8.2(c)(i), (ii).
74 At least when they are held within a prisoner of war facility run by British authorities but possibly not during the transit stage. See also note 68 above.
75 Alternatively, or in addition, a claim may be made for judicial review to challenge a decision not to conduct an independent investigation into the death of the prisoner of war.
76 See also the comments of Lord Bingham of Cornhill in *R v Spear* [2003] 1 AC 734 at [3], [2002] 3 All ER 1074 at [3].

forces, unlike those of some other states, are actually deployed to situations of armed conflict on a regular basis and so their "battle-readiness" is not mere rhetoric. A number are killed in the service of their country. It is perfectly understandable therefore to fear that the concept of human rights, quite properly applied to civilian public organisations, might cause damaging effects to a *sui generis* organisation, the armed forces.

In pursuit of this fear there has been considerable criticism of the ECtHR in certain quarters in Parliament, although it relates almost entirely to its judgments affecting service discipline. The reality of its judgments has been affected, it has been suggested, by the fact that the judges have "not served in a crowded mess in a ship or in a cramped army bivouac"[77] and "kno[w] nothing about the national interests at stake in a military operation"[78]. They have been described as a "so-called 'Court'"[79] and a "bunch of foreign judges in some continental city"[80] who have "overrul[ed] the will of this sovereign Parliament"[81]. Their decision in *Hood v UK* (discussed above) was stated to be "insulting"[82]. Within the normal realm of the legal criticism of court decisions the description of the court's decision in *McCann v UK* (also discussed above) as "a most unfortunate judgment"[83] seems hardly worthy of inclusion in this paragraph.

It should not be thought that all decisions of the ECtHR affecting the United Kingdom's armed forces attract disdain. Those who have seen the court in a negative light might well have been tempted to applaud its judgment in *McBride v UK*[84] where the decision by the army to permit two of its soldiers, previously convicted of murder and sentenced to life imprisonment, to re-join their units after six years in prison was upheld.

One of the reasons for the generally negative way in which the various reforms to the military legal system have been brought about, following the series of incidents set in motion by Lance Sergeant Findlay, has been the issue of who has been in control of this reform. Had the government conducted a full investigation into the compatibility of all its procedures with the Convention at an early stage many of the difficulties subsequently encountered might not have arisen. What actually happened was that the government was placed in the position of being forced to make changes following each particular decision. Understandable though this was, control of the pace and nature of reform passed, in effect, to those lawyers representing former service clients before the court[85].

The result was that the government felt able to assure[86] Parliament during the passage of each successive Armed Forces Bill that the problem had been solved, only for another to appear shortly afterwards. Indeed, the Joint Committee on Human Rights concluded that it was "unfortunate that the Ministry of Defence waited for the adverse finding in *Grieves*

---

77  342 HC Official Report (6th series) col 298 (12 January 2000) discussing the decision in *Smith v UK* (see note 22 above).

78  461 HC Official Report (6th series) col 1584 (21 June 2007).

79  568 HL Official Report (5th series) col 1225 (29 January 1996).

80  342 HC Official Report (6th series) col 299 (12 January 2000).

81  277 HC Official Report (6th series) col 520 (9 May 1996).

82  607 HL Official Report (5th series) col 673 (29 November 1999).

83  568 HL Official Report (5th series) col 1226 (29 January 1996).

84  Application no 1396/06 (9 May 2006, unreported).

85  685 HL Official Report (5th series) col 278 (11 October 2006). Most of the judgments of the ECtHR have involved applicants who had been sentenced to dismissal (or who have been administratively dismissed) from the relevant service rather than an individual challenging the compatibility of his court-martial proceedings whilst still a serving member. Compare *Bell v UK* (see note 28 above).

86  See the "copper-bottom" guarantee (see note 33 above) and the fact that, following the 1998 Act s 19, a certificate is required to be inserted in a Bill prior to its second reading to the effect that it complies with Convention rights.

before making the changes necessary to bring the Royal Navy's court martial system into line with those of the other two armed services in respect of this particular issue of compliance. In our view", it concluded, "a more dynamic approach to giving effect to previous adverse decisions of the European Court of Human Rights"[87] would have led it to foresee that this decision was likely.

How can the effect of all these reforms be assessed and, in particular, did the negative predictions of the "military club", no doubt genuinely felt at the time, come about? It must be the case that those who ought properly to have been tried by court-martial by the system in existence prior to the "Findlay reforms" would now also be tried by court-martial. It is difficult to show that the results of the trials would be any different before and after these reforms. This is, perhaps, not surprising, since the underlying basis of all the ECtHR's decisions relating to trial by court-martial has been the risk of a *perception* of a lack of independence from the chain of command of each of the key participants in the court and not any *actual* lack of independence. The court-martial system may be more expensive to administer now than previously but this can hardly be set in the scales against the desirability of ensuring soldiers secure a fair trial by the standards agreed by all state members (including the United Kingdom) of the Council of Europe.

The enforcement of discipline by a CO gets closer to the core activities of the unit concerned. Summary hearings are intended to be speedy without the formal procedures operating at a court-martial. They are many times more numerous than court-martial trials and, in consequence, their potential effect on discipline will be that much greater. A summary system which operated more through the dictates of the ECtHR rather than through the need to enforce discipline effectively in the armed forces could lead directly to a compromised discipline system. No evidence has been presented to Parliament to show that any such effect has come about[88].

Since 2001 the United Kingdom armed forces have been tested in battle in Afghanistan and in Iraq. Could it seriously be argued that the decisions of the ECtHR have had any damaging effect on the discipline shown by individual members, or the military efficiency during those military operations, of the armed forces[89]?

---

87 *Ninth Report of the Joint Committee on Human Rights* (HL Paper 59, HC Paper 477 (2003–2004)), para 23.

88 The opportunity to do so would have been given by the passage of the Armed Forces Bills of 2001 and 2006 and during the course of the annual continuation orders of these Acts. In particular, see the comments of Sir Michael Boyce (then) Chief of the Defence Staff to the Select Committee on the Armed Forces Bill 2000–01 (HC Paper 154-II) Q 1006. Compare his view (as Lord Boyce) that "The Armed Forces are under legal siege", 673 HL Official Report (5th series) col 1236 (14 July 2005).

89 A similar point was made by Lord Grocott, 633 HL Official Report (5th series) col 527 (11 April 2002) and by Lord Drayson, 673 HL Official Report (5th series) col 1263 (14 July 2005).

# THE VOLUME AND COMPLEXITY OF UNITED KINGDOM LEGISLATION TODAY

## DANIEL GREENBERG[1]

### THE PROBLEM

When Chief Baron Pollock solemnly declared "Everyone is bound to know the law"[2] one wonders if it was one of those occasions on which a judge, finding an attempt at humour greeted with unsmiling deference, feels compelled to behave as though the pronouncement was intended to be taken seriously: it would not be the only legal maxim that one suspects may have been created in this way. Even in 1862, the idea that ordinary citizens could reasonably be expected to have actual knowledge of all the law that applied to them was risible. In some ways, more so than today, if the number of laws was far smaller than it is now, so too was the likelihood of most citizens having reasonable access to the text of legislation.

Be that as it may, one of the few rules of law that almost everyone does know is that ignorance of the vast remainder is no excuse for failure to comply[3]. But a system of law is just and effective only if people know at least in outline by what laws they are bound, are readily able to discover an authoritative text of those laws, and can properly understand the text once obtained. Although those are trite enough conditions precedent for the rule of law[4], there is room to question whether the legal systems of the United Kingdom today satisfy them to a sufficient degree[5]. For a number of reasons and in a number of ways, our substantive law is so voluminous and complicated that no citizen could really be expected to know more than a fraction of the law that applies to him or her, despite the fact that in

---

1 Of Lincoln's Inn, Barrister; Parliamentary Counsel. The views of the author do not necessarily represent the views of the government. I am very grateful to Saira Salimi and Catherine Lister for comments on drafts.

2 *Cooper v Simmons* (1862) 7 H & N 707.

3 In its normal form the doctrine is represented as *ignorantia juris non excusat* – 1 Co 177. But it should be noted that traditional expositions of this principle do not have it as a duty to know everything, but as a duty to understand properly what is known. "The subjects of this country are bound to construe rightly the statute law of the land; it is not competent to them to aver in a court of justice that they have mistaken the law; it is a plea which no court of justice is at liberty to receive." – *The Charlotta* (1814) 1 Dods Adm 387 at 392 per Sir William Scott. It is much easier to accept the idea that people cannot be excused for misunderstanding a law – the possibilities for wilful evasion being only too obvious, if the state had to prove the lack of a genuine misunderstanding – than the idea that people are expected to be aware of laws which they could have had no real opportunity to discover. Hence the dictum of Goddard LJ in *Bowmaker v Tabor* [1941] 2 KB 1 at 5, [1941] 2 All ER 72 at 75 – "It is entirely fallacious to say that everyone is presumed to know the law ... 'The rule is, that ignorance of the law shall not excuse a man, or relieve him from the consequences of a crime, or from liability upon a contract'."

4 They form, for example, the basis of the agreement between the three major political parties of the reasons of principle why retrospective legislation is proper only in exceptional circumstances – see Hansard (HL Debates) (Compensation Bill 2006–07), 19 July 2006, cols 1317–1319.

5 See, for example, the following statement dated 27 October 2005 found under the heading *Your Right to Know* on the website www.yrtk.org.uk: "In the UK, although the public funds the courts and public representatives pass laws, the public do not have free access to the law. We are deemed to know the law, and yet nowhere can the common man or woman freely access the updated laws of the UK."

the course of almost every enterprise in which a person is involved during a normal day, from driving a car on the road to using a computer at home, he or she becomes insensibly bound by a large number of laws failure to comply with which could result in financial liability or loss of liberty.

This article examines the nature of the problem and explores some actual and potential partial solutions.

## INCREASE IN THE VOLUME OF LEGISLATION

Whatever perceptions people may have, recent decades have not shown a marked increase in the annual number of Acts of Parliament. If comparison is made with past centuries there is an increase, although not a big one; but over the last 40 years or so the trend shows, if anything, a decrease in the number of Acts[6]. But despite this, the popular perception of an enormous and constantly accelerating increase in the number of laws is fully justified by the facts, for a number of distinct reasons.

First, if Acts are not more numerous they are certainly longer. The average number of pages of the annual statute book has increased steadily since about 1900, multiplying by a factor of more than five and with a particularly sharp rate of increase since the 1950s[7]. And pages are a much more accurate reflection of the statute book than the number of Acts: the increase in the number of pages tells a tale not only of portmanteau Acts[8], combining a number of measures that might once have been legislated separately, but also of an increasing level of technical detail; and it is the level of detail which is very often determinative of the degree to which citizens find statutes intruding into and interfering with their daily occupations.

Secondly, not content with increasing the degree to which primary legislation controls people's lives, successive governments have also provided for an increasing degree of regulation through secondary legislation, the rate of increase far exceeding that for primary legislation[9]. Although not a new development, it is relatively recent in terms of English legal history: a perceived sudden expansion of the range of delegated powers caused the establishment of the Donoughmore Committee in 1929[10] which found[11]:

> "We doubt ... whether Parliament itself has fully realised how extensive the practice of delegation has become, or the extent to which it has surrendered its own functions in the process, or how easily the practice might be abused."

---

6  *Acts & Statutory Instruments: Volume of UK legislation 1950 to 2006*, House of Commons Library Standard Note: SN/SG/2911, 5 February 2007. Some other figures referred to in this article are gratefully adopted from that Note.

7  Some key figures are: 1911–430; 1921–420; 1931–280; 1940–370; 1950–720; 1955–540; 1960–850; 1965–1,340; 1970–1,110; 1975–2,060; 1980–2,110; 1985–2,380; 1990–2,390; 2000–3,865; 2005–2,712.

8  "This is a Home Office portmanteau Bill. It deals with the important issue of establishing the Serious Organised Crime Agency, and then a whole series of other issues only tangentially related, if at all, to the main purpose." – Hansard (HL Debates) (Serious Organised Crime and Police Bill 2004–05), 14 March 2005, Lord Harris of Haringey. Note also that the Health and Social Care Bill is described by the government as a portmanteau Bill in *The Governance of Britain – The Government's Draft Legislative Programme* (Cm 7175).

9  In the early decades of the twentieth century the annual page count for statutory instruments ranged between one and two thousand – itself a dramatic increase compared to earlier times – while in the last decade of that century and the first years of the present century 10,000 pages or more has been a common annual count.

10 The Committee on Ministers' Powers, the report of which was published in April 1932 (Cmd 4060).

11 *Ibid* para 4.

Thirdly, the last few years have seen the introduction of a new form of subordinate legislation[12], laws made in accordance with legislative power delegated by the Westminster Parliament to the Scottish Parliament, the Northern Ireland Assembly and the National Assembly for Wales. And in addition to the increase in laws directly imposed by or by virtue of United Kingdom Acts and statutory instruments, the citizen of the United Kingdom is today increasingly affected by an enormous quantity and complexity of legislation emanating from the institutions of the European Communities[13], as well as by a number of other international conventions and instruments passed under them, all of which are incorporated in general terms into our law[14].

The primary reason for the increase in the volume of legislation is, of course, simply the increasing level of detail at which the government wishes to legislate, or is obliged to legislate in order to comply with international obligations entered into by the United Kingdom; and the primary reasons for that are the increasing complexity of modern life, both national and international, and the increasing industry of efforts by individuals and corporations to avoid the effects of legislation. In the case of tax law, in particular, so long as there exists a multimillion pound industry constantly examining each new fiscal rule for the express purpose of devising ways of avoiding or minimising its application, it is inevitable that each rule will spawn a large number of subsidiary rules designed to protect the efficacy of the first[15].

The increasing volume of legislation and the suggestion that, in particular, an accumulation of legislative detail can have an undesirably constraining effect on industry, has led to a number of projects designed to reduce or at least contain the increase in volume. Consolidation Bills, prepared within the Law Commissions[16], have been used for decades as a method of replacing a complicated set of much amended Acts on a particular topic with a single coherent Act. More recently, a series of three Acts have conferred gradually widening powers on the executive to make orders for the purpose of, in effect, reducing the regulatory burden on industry and others[17]. None of these systems is presently used in a manner or to an extent which is likely to have a significant effect on the accelerating increase in the overall legislative burden on the citizen: indeed each of them has some potential for increasing that burden, since they require the citizen to become familiar with

---

12 Even where in the form of "Measures" or "Acts", laws of a devolved legislature are clearly subordinate and not primary, because they owe their continuing authority to the Act of the Westminster Parliament which established these legislatures and continues to confer authority on their legislative activities.

13 As a result of their incorporation in general terms into the law of the United Kingdom by the European Communities Act 1972.

14 The most obvious being the European Convention on Human Rights; but there are many other examples of importance in particular, often highly technical areas. See, for examples: the Carriage of Goods by Road Act 1965 s 1 (Convention to have force of law); the Arbitration (International Investment Disputes) Act 1966 s 4 (status, immunities and privileges conferred by the Convention); the Civil Jurisdiction and Judgments Act 1982 s 2 (the Brussels Conventions to have the force of law); the Administration of Justice Act 1982 s 27 (form of an international will); the Contracts (Applicable Law) Act 1990 s 2 (Conventions to have force of law); and the Merchant Shipping Act 1995 s 183 (carriage of passengers and luggage by sea: scheduled convention to have force of law).

15 The possibilities and limitations of general purpose anti-avoidance drafting are discussed below.

16 That being an express statutory task of each of the Law Commissions – see the Law Commissions Act 1965, s 3(1)(d) and the Justice (Northern Ireland) Act 2002, ss 50, 51; see also the reference below to the Statute Law Revision Teams and their Statute Law (Repeals) Bills.

17 The Deregulation and Contracting Out Act 1994, the Regulatory Reform Act 2001 and the Legislative and Regulatory Reform Act 2006.

the replacements or omissions, as well as with what can often be complex and enduring transitional and saving provisions.

## ACCESS TO LEGISLATION

It has always been, and remains, possible to purchase Queen's Printer's copies of Acts and statutory instruments from bookshops. In addition to that, it is now possible to obtain free electronic access to the text of all Acts, statutory instruments and devolved legislation from the Internet website of the Office of Public Sector Information ("OPSI"). Superficially, therefore, it could be said that the United Kingdom citizen has good access to all sources of legislation. In fact, however, for most practical purposes the access afforded by Queen's Printer's copies or the OPSI website is utterly useless. This is because of the fact that an enormous amount of new legislation, both primary and subordinate, operates by referential amendment of old legislation: the result is that the text of an Act as passed ten years ago is of no help at all in telling me the state of the law now. Indeed, recourse to the Queen's Printer's copy of an old Act in the hope that it will give the "general flavour" of the present law, despite not showing recent amendments, is a perilous exercise likely to mislead the reader very seriously.

It is open to debate whether the technique of referential legislation is on balance better or worse than the alternatives[18]. It is well known that the only reliable rule of legislative drafting is that there are no reliable rules of legislative drafting. Form and approach must be driven by what is simplest and clearest in each case, and not by academic dogma. That being so, there will be times when to replicate the entirety of a lengthy piece of legislation with a minor modification hidden somewhere in the middle would be immensely more confusing for all classes of reader than to have a short provision issuing an instruction to the mythical editor of the mythical statute book to make the required amendment. And there will be other times when the number and nature of the amendments proposed to a piece of old legislation makes a series of textual amendments confusing to read and difficult to apply, and the right approach is clearly to repeal and re-enact. Most cases fall between the two extremes and require a combination of techniques designed to assist the greatest number of readers as much as possible. But there will often be political or other constraints which prevent the adoption of whichever technique is likely to be optimal for some or all readers[19]; and the interests of different classes of reader will sometimes conflict[20].

Whether or not one approves of it in principle, however, the technique of referential legislation is clearly right for some purposes and is equally clearly here to stay at least for those purposes and probably for others as well. The result is that access to a database of laws passed along the lines of that made available by the Queen's Printer and OPSI is more or less useless to ordinary citizens for ordinary purposes. Every time I access an Act or instrument which amends an earlier one I am forced also to obtain the text of the earlier one[21] and to construct a revised version reflecting what will often turn out to be a

---

18  For a considered, although not necessarily complete, consideration of the issues see *The Preparation of Legislation* (the "Renton Report"), paras 11.27–11.31, ch XIII (Cmnd 6053).

19  Considerations of Parliamentary time, or the application of the procedural rules of scope (Commons) or relevance (Lords) may, for example, mitigate against adopting a wholesale re-enactment approach in favour of a set of minor amendments.

20  It may, for instance, be most helpful to legislators to have before them a complete re-enactment, so that they can consider the overall effect of what is proposed, while it may be most helpful for practitioners experienced in the field to see the legislation in the form of specific changes to provisions with which they are already familiar.

21  Noting that the OPSI site carries exhaustive electronic versions only for years 1988 onwards, and the paper version of some earlier Acts may be out of print.

complicated multilayered set of amendments. Difficult and time-consuming, but arguably not impossible: more problematically, however, I will have no practicable way of knowing that the Act or instrument I am reading has not itself now been amended by a later one.

What is needed is, of course, an up-to-date version of legislation, showing amendments and repeals and also containing information about the timing of commencement and the exercise of delegated legislative powers. One might think that the State would provide that, if it expected citizens to be willing and able to comply with the plethora of complicated laws enacted[22]. Until 1991 the Statutory Publications Office provided a looseleaf publication *Statutes in Force*[23] which fulfilled this function to some extent, but only for primary legislation; and it never managed to be sufficiently up-to-date for a citizen to be able to rely on it with a tolerable degree of certainty.

The official successor to that publication is the Statute Law Database, presently a project of the Statutory Publications Offices and the Ministry of Justice. Since the end of 2006 the database has been made available online without charge, which makes it a major advance towards the kind of accessibility that citizens are entitled to expect[24]. It does not, of course, help those without reliable access to the Internet, a class which could include some of the most vulnerable in society who might have a particular need to discover the law that affects them, whether to discover their rights or their obligations. Much more importantly, however, the database is not up-to-date[25], which greatly diminishes its usefulness for anyone who needs to be certain of the text of the law that applies today; there are, however, tables of legislative effects which would enable a citizen to construct a picture of later amendments, at least for primary legislation. It is hoped that the database will eventually be brought completely up to date and maintained in that state[26], at which point it will be a very significant resource for citizens, at least in relation to primary legislation.

Until that time, and beyond that time in relation to statutory instruments, which account for an increasingly important part of the practical legal burdens on the citizen, citizens of the United Kingdom must have recourse to commercial publications, electronic and paper, for an up-to-date text of legislation. Although there are a number of such publications, both in specialist fields and of a general nature, they are not authoritative and cannot safely be assumed always to be entirely accurate; nor are they free. So their effect stops short of providing the kind of access that is arguably essential.

---

22 Certainly the responsibility is accepted in principle. See, for example, "The Lord Chancellor recognises that he has a responsibility, on behalf of the Government, to ensure that satisfactory arrangements are made for the publication of the statute book, in order that the citizen may know by what laws he is bound." Hansard (HC Debates), 13 June 1991, WA 613–14.

23 Itself successor to the earlier project *The Statutes Revised*, which was produced with insufficient frequency to be sufficiently reliable for most purposes.

24 "The database ... contributes to our aims for improving access to justice" – Website of the Department for Constitutional Affairs, June 2007.

25 The database carries the following messages (as at July 2007): "What legislation is held on SLD? ... Most types of primary legislation are held in 'revised' form ... Most types of secondary legislation on SLD are not revised and are held only in the form in which they were originally made ... How up-to-date is the legislation on SLD? All legislation held on SLD in revised form has been updated at least to the end of 2001. Most of those items are also up-to-date to the present. For the remainder there are still effects outstanding for at least one of the years 2002 to the current year. Most of the effects of 2002 legislation have been completed. The effects of legislation enacted in the years 2003 to 2006 are now being applied."

26 "The primary legislation has been revised to 2002 and is expected to be completely up to date with revisions by the end of 2008" – Website of the Department for Constitutional Affairs, June 2007.

Reliable access is arguably all the more essential given the fact that the courts will uphold the effect of legislation even against the citizen who had no effective access to it[27]. Even the European Convention on Human Rights[28] does not include a right of access to knowledge of law as a precondition of being bound by it[29]. But the courts have continued to stress the importance of accessibility if the rule of law is to be fair, and successive governments have accepted this principle and bound themselves to apply it so far as reasonably practicable[30].

## PARLIAMENTARY SCRUTINY

In order to be satisfied with the fairness and propriety of the legislation binding them, citizens must not only be able to access accurate and authoritative texts of relevant laws: they must also be able to be satisfied that the process by which those laws are made has the authority and legitimacy of the democratic process. In particular, this requires being satisfied that effective arrangements are made within Parliament to ensure that legislation made by Parliament, or under powers conferred by Parliament, has been subjected to proper and thorough scrutiny in a form and at a level that is appropriate for its content and effect. The increasing volume of legislation obviously places strains on the mechanisms for Parliamentary scrutiny, which is an additional reason why the sheer pace and acceleration of the legislative machinery is a cause for concern. As a reaction to the increasing legislative burden, some significant developments have taken place in recent years in relation to the scrutiny of both primary and subordinate legislation.

The traditional rule for primary legislation was that most Bills received, in effect, a share of the limited amount of time on the floor of each House[31] and a few weeks in Standing Committee in the Commons.

The most significant change in respect of primary legislation has been the increasing use of different kinds of Parliamentary Committee. First, for pre-legislative scrutiny: once a rare exception, one of the first recommendations of the House of Commons Select Committee on Modernisation after its establishment in 1997 was that "Although it is unrealistic to expect all or most major bills to be published in draft, it can reasonably be hoped that such a practice will grow wherever appropriate. There is almost universal agreement that pre-

---

27 "It is beyond argument that an Act of Parliament takes legal effect on the giving of the Royal Assent, irrespective of publication." – *ZL v Secretary of State for the Home Dept and Lord Chancellor's Dept* [2003] EWCA Civ 25 at [17], [2003] 1 All ER 1062 at [17].

28 The Convention for the Protection of Human Rights and Fundamental Freedoms 1950, agreed by the Council of Europe at Rome on 4 November 1950.

29 Although publication and accessibility may sometimes be relevant to questions of due process under the Convention. "In cases where the justification for a prima facie invasion of a Convention right depends on the State's having acted "in accordance with a procedure prescribed by law" (art 5) or "in accordance with the law" (art 8) or "as … prescribed by law" (arts 9–11), [the European Court of Human Rights] declines to recognise national laws which are not adequately accessible: see *Sunday Times v UK* (1979) 2 EHRR 245 (para 49) – *ZL*'s case, above, also at [17].

30 See, for example, "My Lords, all Acts are published simultaneously on the Internet and in print as soon as possible after Royal Assent. It is important to ensure that an accurate approved text is published and that all users have access at the same time to the same text. To do otherwise might raise issues of fairness." – HL Deb 10 cols 464–66 (10 February 2003), Leader of the House of Lords, replying to oral Parliamentary Question about the case of *ZL* discussed above.

31 Typically, a day (which in practical terms generally amounts to about five hours of debate) in the House of Commons for Second Reading, and a day or half a day for Report and Third Reading together, plus a day in the House of Lords for Second Reading, anything from one to three days in Committee depending on the length of the Bill, a day for Report and a day for Third Reading.

legislative scrutiny is right in principle, subject to the circumstances and nature of the legislation."[32] Whether a Departmental Select Committee of the Commons is used, or an ad hoc Joint Committee of the two Houses, pre-legislative scrutiny is an important opportunity for front- and backbenchers to scrutinise the provisions of a Bill and to hear expert evidence about its likely effect, at a time when it can generally be expected that the government's plans will still be sufficiently flexible to enable ministers to be more receptive to comments and criticism than they may feel able to be, for practical and political reasons, during the passage of the Bill through Parliament after introduction. The government is committed to providing opportunities for pre-legislative scrutiny where practicable[33].

Perhaps the other most significant development for the scrutiny of primary legislation is the substitution for the old Standing Committees, which considered each Bill clause by clause in the House of Commons, of new Public Bill Committees[34]. These were introduced in 2007 again in response to a report of the Modernisation Committee[35] and the most significant differences from the old Committees are the powers to take oral evidence before commencing detailed consideration of the Bill and to receive written evidence[36].

The House of Lords has also increased its use of Committees taking place off the floor of the House for the detailed consideration of Bills. As well as relieving pressure on time in the Chamber, this enables a more thorough examination of the detail of Bills, sometimes including hearing oral expert evidence[37]. The Committee system in both Houses also ensures that those Members and peers with the greatest interest and expertise in a Bill are able to take a full part in its discussion.

Even before these changes primary legislation was always relatively well off, so to speak, in the matter of Parliamentary scrutiny. Each Bill has always received three or four separate stages of consideration in each House[38], and in both Houses the Committee stage can last for a sufficient length of time to give even a lengthy Bill a reasonably detailed level of scrutiny (although practical and political constraints often mean that, particularly in the case of a lengthy Bill, many provisions receive little or no scrutiny in Committee in either House).

---

32  *First Report of the Modernisation Committee* (1997–98) (23 July 1997) para 19.

33  See, for example, the undertaking "to proceed on the presumption that Bills will be published in draft for pre-legislative scrutiny unless there is good reason otherwise" – Hansard (HC Debates), 4 February 2003, WA col 134; for further information about the theory and use of pre-legislative scrutiny see House of Commons Library, Standard Note SN/PC/2822 *Pre-legislative scrutiny*, 8 February 2007.

34  Some might argue that the introduction of routine programming for all Bills, in place of the occasional guillotine motion for particularly controversial Bills, is an even more significant development: but it is a moot point (on which I express no opinion) whether the overall effect of programming has been to increase or decrease the effectiveness of Parliamentary scrutiny of primary legislation.

35  See Hansard (HC Debates (1 November 2006)) cols 304–411.

36  Although interested pressure groups always provided briefing for members of Standing Committees, and the briefing was sometimes referred to in debate, the system of having written evidence formally submitted and printed gives in practice additional weight to the views of different sections of the public, and significantly enhances informed expert briefing as a method of influencing the debate.

37  See *Companion to the Standing Orders and Guide to the Proceedings of the House of Lords*, The Stationery Office (2007) para 7.102.

38  Second Reading, which discusses the principle of the Bill, Committee, which examines it clause by clause and considers detailed amendments, Report, which is a further stage for amendments and is omitted in certain cases, and Third Reading, which returns to the principle of the Bill as amended.

Subordinate legislation was traditionally a very different story. The vast majority of instruments receive no formal Parliamentary scrutiny at all, either because no procedure is provided by the Act which confers the power or because the "negative procedure" is provided for and nobody chooses to table a motion to annul the relevant instrument. The various options for the scrutiny of statutory instruments, including the roles of the various Parliamentary Committees and the difficulties of their tackling effectively the volume of legislative material produced each year, are discussed by Lord Hope of Craighead in *R (on the application of Stellato) v Secretary of State for the Home Dept*[39].

Under the negative procedure, which is used for the vast majority of instruments that attract any specific procedure at all, an instrument becomes law without any action on the part of Parliament, but can be annulled if, within a specified period, either House of Parliament passes a motion to that effect. Apart from the obvious fact that there is little enough Parliamentary time for the consideration of primary legislation and even less for secondary legislation, there is also a traditional reluctance on the part of the two Houses, but particularly the Lords, to undo what the Executive has chosen to do in legitimate exercise of a power properly delegated to it by Parliament[40]. Only a small minority of powers are subject to the "affirmative procedure", under the most common form of which an instrument can be made only if a draft has been approved by resolution of each House[41].

So, despite the fact that one could argue that secondary legislation needs more careful scrutiny than primary legislation rather than less if the abuse by the Executive of the increasing number and range of powers delegated to it is to be avoided, under the traditional systems very little provision was made for the effective scrutiny of statutory instruments. But in recent years a number of developments have changed that, to a significant extent if not necessarily to a sufficient extent.

First, both Houses now make greater use of Committees, for which time is easier to find than time on the floor of the House[42].

Secondly, since its establishment in 1992 the House of Lords Select Committee now known as the Committee on Delegated Powers and Regulatory Reform has performed the task of considering all legislative powers conferred by Bills before the House with a view to

---

39  [2007] UKHL 5 at [7]–[12], [2007] 2 All ER 737 at [7]–[12].

40  Annulment does happen, however: see, for example, the rejection by the House of Lords on 22 February 2000 of the Greater London Authority Elections Rules 2000, SI 2000/208. Before that occasion, annulment might have been thought to be almost an obsolete procedure: according to an answer given in the course of a starred question in 1995 (Hansard (HL Debates), 28 June 1995, col 750) "since 1979 this House has rejected delegated legislation on only one occasion. In 1988 two special procedure orders relating to the harbour authorities of Harwich and Newport were annulled on motions moved by the Government and agreed to without Division, because they were found to be technically defective". On 20 October 1994, at the instigation of Lord Simon of Glaisdale, the House of Lords resolved "that this House affirms its unfettered freedom to vote on any subordinate legislation submitted for its consideration". That freedom relates both to motions to annul instruments already made and to motions to approve instruments laid in draft for approval by affirmative resolution: as to those, although again it is extremely rare for either House to deny the government its resolution it is possible to use various procedural devices to register opposition to particular aspects of the draft. The general attitude of the government to the House of Lords' reluctance to exercise the power to annul an instrument is encapsulated in the following observation of the Lord Privy Seal (Viscount Cranborne) – "Her Majesty's Government support the constructive way in which your Lordships have shown restraint in exercising the House's undoubted power to vote on subordinate legislation" – Hansard (HL Debates), 2 May 1995, WA 113–114; see also Hansard (HL Debates), 28 June 1995, cols 750–751.

41  There is also a variant form whereby an instrument comes into force without prior affirmation, but lapses unless approved within a certain period. And certain instruments concerning public finance are subject to procedure in the Commons only.

considering whether appropriate provision is made for the scrutiny of their exercise[43]. Although a report of the Committee has no formal effect, its reports are regularly referred to during debates on Bills, and the government corresponds with the Committee to explain provisions which confer legislative power, and frequently reacts to an adverse report by tabling amendments to alter the level of Parliamentary scrutiny provided for by a Bill.

Thirdly, although there had for many years been a Joint Committee to scrutinise certain technical matters relating to statutory instruments[44] in 2004 the House of Lords decided to establish a Select Committee whose terms of reference would involve inquiring into the substance of instruments with a view to considering the use made of powers conferred by Parliament, as part of the desire to improve the arrangements for scrutiny of legislation as a whole[45]. The present terms of reference allow the Committee to draw an instrument to the House's attention for a range of substantive reasons[46], and the Committee presently makes a number of reports each Session, which can found or influence debates on motions for annulment of negative instruments or for affirmation of affirmative instruments, or in other contexts.

All these changes, and others of a more minor nature, have been designed to enable Parliament to control and scrutinise more effectively legislation made by Parliament or under powers delegated by Parliament. But Parliamentarians are the first to recognise that there is room for further improvement. It is inevitable that with thousands of pages of legislation being passed or made every year not every page will receive the detailed consideration that it deserves, and problems will arise after enactment. There is therefore an increasing body of opinion that formal arrangements are also needed for post-legislative scrutiny, by which the operation of legislation after its enactment can be considered from time to time by Parliament, with a mechanism for drawing attention to specific difficulties. The Law Commission considered the issue of post-legislative scrutiny in a report in 2006[47]. They found a number of reasons for introducing more effective arrangements for post-legislative scrutiny, as well as a number of potential difficulties associated with it. They recommended the establishment of a Parliamentary Joint Committee on post-legislative scrutiny, as well as the use of informal departmental arrangements. They also found that

---

42 "In recent decades, the number of SIs considered in some form by the House of Commons has risen considerably. As a result the House has found it difficult to make enough time available for the debate of SIs. Debates, normally on Motions to approve or annul instruments, may take place on the floor of the House (usually late in the parliamentary day), or in Delegated Legislation Committees. These were first set up as Standing Committees on Statutory Instruments in the 1973–74 session in order to relieve pressure of time in the House itself. Their title was changed at the beginning of the 1995–96 session to Standing Committees on Delegated Legislation, and again in 2006–07 to Delegated Legislation Committees. Debates on the floor of the House on Statutory Instruments ... may generally be debated for an hour and a half." – House of Commons Information Office Factsheet L7 *Statutory Instruments* 2007 Revision p 6. For the Lords, statutory instruments are now frequently referred for consideration by a Grand Committee – see, for example, the referral of ten approval motions at Hansard (HL Debates), 27 April 2006.

43 The relevant part of the Committee's present terms of reference is "to report whether the provisions of any bill inappropriately delegate legislative power or whether they subject the exercise of legislative power to an inappropriate degree of parliamentary scrutiny".

44 The Joint Committee on Statutory Instruments, established by House of Commons Standing Order No 151 and House of Lords Standing Order No 74; the Committee considers *vires*, drafting and certain other technical matters, but does not as a rule become involved in questions of substance.

45 "The committee was an innovation set up by the House in April 2004, built out of the concern that the vast volume of secondary legislation that passed through Parliament often received scant attention in the Chamber itself because of the volume of legislation that was passed." – Hansard (HL Debates), 29 November 2006, col 805 (per Lord Filkin).

consideration should be given to applying new arrangements to subordinate legislation as well as to Acts. For the present no single formal system has been established; but the issue of post-legislative scrutiny has not gone away, and is regularly discussed inside and outside Parliament[48].

Whatever arrangements are provided for scrutiny, it is inevitable that subordinate legislation will receive less detailed consideration by Parliament than primary (it being one of the reasons for delegating certain legislation that Parliament wishes to preserve its time for consideration of the most important issues). That makes it essential to strike the right balance between primary and secondary legislation, a question on which much has been written and said over the years[49]. "In essence, the aim in striking a balance is to avoid leaving too much of significance to be determined by the executive or the courts while at the same time preventing the principal purpose of the primary legislation from being obscured by an excess of complicated detail. Like many balances between conflicting desiderata, this is both easy to state and impossible to achieve to everybody's satisfaction."[50]

COMMENCEMENT

Once legislation has been passed or made, and the citizen has obtained access to a text of it, he or she is confronted with the additional difficulty of knowing what the status of the text is at any particular moment, particularly as regards the question of commencement. Although the default position remains that Acts come into force on the day of Royal Assent[51], that simple rule is more often than not rebutted by a proposition conferring power on a Minister to appoint one or more days for the commencement of the Act.

The confusion and difficulty caused by the complexity of arrangements for commencement have frequently been the subject of public concern and discussion. One of the most important discussions, between the Law Society of England and Wales and the government, culminated in the issue of new guidance on commencement within government[52]. The most important points of that guidance are: a presumption, rebuttable in the case of particular need, that there will always be an interval of at least two months between Royal Assent and commencement to enable the world to discover and prepare for the new law; an undertaking to restrict the taking of commencement powers to cases where it is not reasonably practicable to specify a particular date in the Act itself; easy identification of commencement provisions in a separate place in each Act; and the issuing of notes on previous commencement when making an order under a commencement power.

---

46 "(3) The grounds on which an instrument, draft or proposal may be drawn to the special attention of the House are – (a) that it is politically or legally important or gives rise to issues of public policy likely to be of interest to the House; (b) that it may be inappropriate in view of changed circumstances since the enactment of the parent Act; (c) that it may inappropriately implement European Union legislation; and (d) that it may imperfectly achieve its policy objectives."

47 *Post-Legislative Scrutiny* (Law Com No 302) (October 2006) (Cm 6945).

48 See, for example, Hansard (HL Debates), 10 July 2007, cols 223–225 and Hansard (HL Debates), 11 July 2007, cols 1398–99.

49 A useful summary of the arguments will be found in *Making the Law*, the Report of the Hansard Society Commission on the Legislative Process, The Hansard Society for Parliamentary Government, (November 1992) paras 253–260 and the evidence referred to there.

50 Daniel Greenberg and Michael J Goodman *Craies on Legislation* (8th edn, 2004) para 1.2.3.

51 Interpretation Act 1978 s 4(b).

52 As described in a letter from the Lord Privy Seal to the Secretary to the Law Society on 16 June 1982.

Although these innovations, which have been implemented and sustained, have made it considerably easier for lawyers and other citizens to ascertain the state of the law at a particular time, the number of commencement powers continues to create difficulties and uncertainties. In particular, attention has been drawn from time to time to the amount of legislation which remains on the statute book although not having been brought into force and without there being any apparent plans to bring it into force, its continued presence acting therefore as a potential source of confusion for the unwary[53]. The government has also sometimes been challenged for appearing to use a power to commence at a convenient time and in an orderly manner as an excuse for failing altogether to implement Acts which are not, or are no longer, politically attractive to them[54].

Taking the difficulties posed by staggered and sometimes considerably delayed commencement, together with the difficulties of finding and deciphering what can be very complicated provisions for transitional provisions and savings when a new law is introduced, the question of commencement poses a significant additional burden for readers trying to ascertain the state of the law[55]. Once again, the citizen is in effect forced to rely on publications that will distil the effect of the technical provisions and present concise information on the status of the law and the periods or circumstances to which it applies. Until the government's Statute Law Database is able to fulfil that function, citizens will continue to rely heavily on such commercial publications as are available to them.

## PURPOSIVE DRAFTING AND CONSTRUCTION

It is sometimes suggested that the trend towards the proliferation and prolixity of legislation could be reversed if only drafters were to stop trying to foresee and provide for every conceivable eventuality and were to confine themselves to broad statements of principle and purpose, with the courts following suit by applying a purposive construction to the resulting legislation[56].

Although it is possible to adopt a dogmatic position either in favour of or in opposition to the use of purpose clauses or statements of principle, as in every other area of legislative drafting what matters is not the pursuit of theoretical dogma but the adoption of whatever techniques provide the greatest clarity and certainty in the context. Where the essential purpose of a law can be stated with sufficient clarity and precision to produce a justiciable proposition, the enactment of that proposition is preferable to the enactment of a

---

53 See, for example, the *Third Report from the Select Committee on Procedure of the House of Lords* (1995–96) (HL Paper 50), Hansard (HL Debates), 27 March 1996, cols 1705–1713 and the Cabinet Office Report *Bringing Acts of Parliament into Force* (Cm 3595) (March 1997). Note that the Law Commission of England and Wales has a Statute Law Revision Team whose continuing task it is to search for obsolete enactments with a view to their inclusion in periodic Statute Law (Repeals) Bills – but their function extends only to enactments whose obsolescence is obvious, not to those which have merely fallen into disuse whether by reason of not being commenced or otherwise.

54 See the decision of the House of Lords in *R v Secretary of State for the Home Dept, ex p Fire Brigades Union* [1995] 2 AC 513, [1995] 2 All ER 244.

55 A difficulty further compounded by the fact that there is often no easy or helpful answer to the question "What is the text" in relation to a particular law. Many laws are commenced not by reference to specific dates but by reference to particular circumstances – "persons born on or after X", "returns made for tax years on or after Y" – and so on. The result is that there will be parallel texts of a particular law for different purposes, particularly where an "old" provision is preserved by a saving provision in the commencement provisions for the "new" law, sometimes for the purposes of a transitional period which could last for many years. (The problem of parallel texts arises also occasionally in connection with devolution, where an Act which extends to more than one part of the United Kingdom is amended in its application to one part but not another.)

multiplicity of rules concerning individual cases and combining to achieve the overall purpose but without stating it simply. But where the statement of purpose will leave such doubt in the minds of readers about its precise application that nobody will know the law without applying to the courts to construe it, the essential purpose of legislation, the clear communication of the law, will have failed. Most cases will fall between these two extremes, and sometimes what is required is a combination of precise rules with a statement of an underlying purpose by reference to which they can be construed.

So each case must be judged on its own merits, and the government's policy remains one of constructive flexibility. As the then Leader of the House of Lords (Baroness Amos) replied in response to a Written Question on the subject of the use of purpose clauses –

> "Statements of principle have their uses and examples can be found in various Acts in recent years. Parliamentary draftsmen will continue to use this technique where it is helpful to do so. But where detailed provisions are required the addition of general statements can cause uncertainty and ambiguity. The Government agree with paragraph 11.5 of the 1975 report of the Committee on the Preparation of Legislation that draftsmen should not sacrifice legal certainty for simplicity of language."[57]

Taxation is an area of the law which is particularly troubled by complexity and where there are recurrent demands for simplification through the use of general principles drafting. In particular, it is often suggested that a general anti-avoidance rule, a relatively simple proposition prohibiting avoidance, could replace more efficiently and effectively a plethora of detailed rules each of which is designed to prevent or control a particular avoidance opportunity in a particular fiscal context[58]. There is certainly much to be said for legislating for general principles where they can be stated with justiciable certainty, in tax law as in every other area of law, and it is sometimes possible to provide anti-avoidance rules in relatively general terms but in specific contexts[59]. "But it is thought unlikely that a general anti-avoidance provision would be construed sufficiently tightly for the Government to feel able to rely on it and to resist making express provision where a particular avoidance opportunity could be identified. Apart from anything else, it is frequently very difficult to determine whether a particular commercial arrangement has been made for legitimate fiscal reasons, for evasive fiscal reasons, for accounting reasons, for commercial reasons or for a mixture of reasons. So although the courts have developed certain limited anti-avoidance doctrines themselves, and although there are specific anti-avoidance provisions of limited effect found in particular tax provisions, the hope that a single anti-avoidance provision of general application would significantly reduce the complexity of the tax code is unlikely ever to be realised."[60]

---

56 See, for example, Hansard (HL Debates), 12 November 2003, WA 202: "**Lord Renton** asked Her Majesty's Government: Whether they will ensure that in future legislation avoids enacting too much hypothetical detail but instead contains statements of principle, as recommended in the report of the Committee on the Preparation of Legislation." See also Hansard (HL Debates), 11 November 1997, cols 87–88; Hansard (HL Debates), 21 January 1998, cols 1583–1602; Renton Report (*Report on the Preparation of Legislation*) (Cmnd 6053) Recommendation 15; and *Making the Law*, the Report of the Hansard Society Commission on the Legislative Process, The Hansard Society for Parliamentary Government (November 1992) paras 223–252.

57 Hansard (HL Debates), 12 November 2003, WA 202.

58 The issues are discussed extensively in the 1998 Consultative Document issued by what was then the Inland Revenue, *A General Anti-avoidance Rule for Direct Taxes*.

59 See, for example, the Finance Act 2003 s 75A inserted by the Finance Act 2007 s 71 – "Stamp duty land tax: anti-avoidance".

So much for purposive drafting. As for purposive construction, the idea that a long-standing battle against the forces of darkness and literalism is gradually and painfully being won by the European inspired forces of light and teleology is simply a myth[61], albeit a popular one. But it is certainly true that in recent years the courts have begun to permit themselves greater freedom in the range of materials to which they will have regard in order to determine the background and context by reference to which legislation falls to be construed and applied.

In particular, in 1993 in the case of *Pepper v Hart*[62] the House of Lords famously abrogated a previous self-denying ordnance by virtue of which the courts refused to look at statements in *Hansard* for the purpose of illustrating the background to the Act (and therefore the mischief at which it was aimed), despite the fact that there had been a long tradition at looking at Law Commission reports and other travaux preparatoires for the same purpose. And the courts have also accepted that they can have regard to the Explanatory Notes to Bills and Acts, introduced in 1998, for the purpose of construing Acts[63].

These developments cut both ways for the citizen concerned about access to the law and how to obtain a clear understanding of it. On the positive side, the reader of an Act now has additional aids to understanding which can be relied on as having a degree of authority, at least in the sense that where they clearly help to illustrate the meaning of a piece of legislation the reader can rely on the courts to give effect to that meaning. And if the reader has happened to discover a document of whatever kind that sheds a light on the legislative intent where the text is itself unhelpful, he or she can have greater confidence than was once the case that the courts will be prepared to consider the document and give it whatever weight it deserves in the circumstances.

On the negative side, however, the greater use of explanatory material of all kinds means that the citizen who finally discovers an accurate text of legislation may still have to worry that unless all possible sources of elaboration are also considered a nuance of the legislation, to which the courts will have regard, may be overlooked. And discovering all possible elaboration could amount to a very considerable and costly research exercise involving examining all relevant debates in Parliament. It would be most undesirable for citizens trying to give effect to the meaning of legislation, according to their best efforts to construe it in its context, to be constantly vulnerable to being ambushed by a piece of explanatory material produced from some obscure source and advanced in support of a contrary construction. That would, in particular, tend to place the private citizen with limited resources at a disadvantage compared to many others. Indeed, in at least one case the courts have warned the government not to take unfair advantage of the greater research

---

60 Daniel Greenberg and Michael J Goodman *Craies on Legislation* (8th edn, 2004) para 1.10.7, footnote 45; note that this passage is cited by Sir Anthony Mason AC KBE, Distinguished Visiting Fellow, Faculty of Law, Australian National University in a paper delivered on Wednesday 23 August 2006 entitled "Income Tax Assessment Act 1936 – An Insoluble Problem", and the author concludes that as regards the prediction that a general rule would be unlikely significantly to reduce the complexity of the fiscal statute book in practice "The Australian experience with s 260 confirms the correctness of that opinion".

61 For further analysis see D Greenberg "All Trains Stop at Crewe: The Rise and Rise of Contextual Drafting" (2005) European Journal of Law Reform vol VII no 1 / 2 at pp 31–46.

62 [1993] AC 593, [1993] 1 All ER 42, HL.

63 "In so far as the Explanatory Notes case light on the objective setting or contextual scene of the statute, and the mischief at which it is aimed, such materials are therefore always admissible aids to construction. They may be admitted for what logical value they have." Lord Steyn in *R (Westminster City Council) v National Asylum Support Service* [2002] UKHL 38, [2002] 4 All ER 654, [2002] 1 WLR 2956.

resources available to it to adduce large quantities of supplementary material in an attempt to justify a gloss on the literal meaning of the legislation itself[64].

So although it is undoubtedly important that the courts are increasingly ready to look at any helpful material in construing legislation, one must remember that the whole notion of construction is not an ideal, but an inherently undesirable process to which citizens and courts are driven only by unclarity in the literal meaning of legislation as apparent from its immediate context. As Lord Carswell said in *Smith v Smith*[65] –

> "Statutory construction constitutes quite a sizeable proportion of the work of appellate judges. The instances and topics on which they have to engage in this exercise are multifarious, but its object is always the same, to ascertain the intention of Parliament as expressed in the instrument which has to be construed. In a judicial utopia every statute or statutory instrument would be expressed with such clarity and would cover every contingency so effectively that interpretation would be straightforward and the only task of the courts would be to apply their terms. Utopia has not yet arrived, however, and judges facing the interpretation of ambiguous or obscure provisions must use the well-worn tools of statutory construction to arrive at a result."

## CONCLUSION: HAPPY BIRTHDAY HALSBURY'S

The volume and complexity of legislation in the United Kingdom today presents a very serious challenge. At a number of points in his or her life every citizen is likely to need to discover with clarity and certainty just what the law is on a particular matter. Whether or not the citizen employs lawyers to assist in that discovery, more often than not it will be a difficult and confusing process. At the essence of the fairness of the rule of law is the attempt to meet, so far as is reasonably practicable, the challenge of making laws and their effect clearly and readily accessible to citizens and Parliamentarians alike. Commercial publications are and always have been an important partner with government in meeting this challenge, and their role looks set to continue. *Halsbury's Laws of England* is one of the most notable names in this context; it is a great pleasure to participate in this project marking the successful completion of its first century, and to offer good wishes for the future as it continues to play a central role in the vital enterprise of exposing and expounding laws to the citizens of this country.

---

64 *Lancashire CC v Taylor* [2005] EWCA Civ 284, [2005] 1 WLR 2668.
65 [2006] UKHL 35 at [79], [2006] 3 All ER 907 at [79].

# LAW REPORTING AND THE DOCTRINE OF PRECEDENT: THE PAST, THE PRESENT AND THE FUTURE

## LORD NEUBERGER OF ABBOTSBURY

### INTRODUCTORY

"The judicial decisions of the Superior Courts ... as reported in the volumes ... constitute ..., almost equally with the statute book, *the law of the land*", according to a Paper written in 1849. That is as true today as it was then. Law reporting plays a crucial role in the establishment and development of the law and in maintaining respect for the legal process. That is partly because it is closely linked to the doctrine of precedent. The two topics, law reporting and precedent, may strike many as being both rather dry and scarcely at the cutting edge. However, the two topics are not only important: they are interesting and influential. They are also significantly affected by technological and other developments. As in many other areas of life, if we do not control the effect of change, change will control us, and substantially alter things undesirably and irreparably.

### THE IMPORTANCE OF LAW REPORTING

There are three main reasons why the reporting of judges' decisions plays a crucial part in our legal system. First, it is a requirement of any modern democracy that the administration of justice is open and public. Secondly, reports of judicial decisions must be available for students of law. Thirdly, judicial decisions interpret and develop the law, above all in the common law system which prevails in England and Wales. An inevitable consequence of each of these factors is that complete and reliable reports of the decisions and reasoning of the judges must be freely (or at least cheaply), quickly and easily available to anyone who wants to understand use or analyse them.

As to the first factor, openness, or, to employ a popular, if rather over-used, word, transparency is of the essence of a genuinely free society. Nowhere is this more true than in the dispensing of law in the courts. Save where justified in an individual case by exceptional circumstances, secrecy in court processes, whether in connection with the hearing or the decision, is not merely wrong itself: the absence of public scrutiny almost inevitably leads to injustices.

The second factor justifying the need for reliable and full law reporting is to maintain "a record of what is decided to be the law [with] the object of having this record to facilitate the study of the law itself". This was the reason said to justify law reporting in a Paper written by Nathaniel Lindley QC in September 1863, (although he may have had wider notions of "study" than solely academic aspects). Without trustworthy law reports, there can be no reliable training for those seeking to practise, teach, or write about law. Without properly trained practising and academic lawyers, the legal system would quickly become unfit for the essential purpose that it serves.

As to the third factor, namely the role of judicial decisions in the law-making process, there are two sources of law in England and Wales. There is the legislature, which now effectively includes the European Parliament and the European Commission, and enacts Statutes and Statutory Instruments (as well as Directives and Regulations). And there is the court system, which now includes the Court of Justice of the European Communities ("the ECJ") and the European Court of Human Rights ("the ECtHR"). For present purposes, the courts have two functions. First, they have the task of interpreting much of this legislative documentation; this is increasingly important in the light of the enormous quantity of legislative documents and their varying drafting quality. Secondly, in the United Kingdom the domestic courts also pronounce and develop the common law, a feature of our legal system which is envied by many civil jurisdictions, and which it is so easy to take for granted.

## THE DOCTRINE OF PRECEDENT

The essential feature of common law is that it is judge made. The common law is established and developed through the medium of judicial decisions, which apply or adapt principles laid down in earlier cases to contemporary problems. Inherent in this is the doctrine of precedent or, to use the Latin, *stare decisis*, which is central to the common law. This is because, unless judicial decisions on issues of law are (at least in general) binding on inferior courts (and, to an extent, on courts of co-ordinate jurisdiction), the notion of a *corpus* of law, built up in a reasonably coherent and consistent way by the judiciary, becomes a dead letter.

Precedent involves rules or principles of law being made by decisions of the courts. In general, a court is bound by the essential legal reasoning, or *ratio decidendi*, of decisions made by courts superior to it, and it is either bound or normally will follow the *ratio* of decisions of courts of co-ordinate jurisdiction. This ensures a degree of predictability for those who give legal advice, as well as helping to enable orderly development and change in the law. It should; but it does not always do so. The arguments for and against a strong *stare decisis* rule reflect the familiar competing issues of certainty and fairness.

The precise extent of the role of precedent has always been a topic of debate. At one extreme, is the view of Lord Blackburn that it is "of more consequence that this point should be settled than how it is settled" – in *Tiverton & North Devon Railway Co v Loosemore*[1]. At the other, is Manisty J's view that "Common sense is a better guide ... than authority" – in *Henderson v Preston*[2]. As is so often the case, what appears to be a difference of principle is, to a substantial extent, an issue of degree. Nobody can seriously doubt the fundamental role of precedent in the common law, but, equally, nobody could disagree with the notion that it has its limits.

At any rate until recently, the law of precedent applied relatively strictly. Thus, the Law Lords, appropriately for the "voices of infallibility", were traditionally, indeed conventionally, bound by their own previous decisions and were also reluctant to interfere with principles long established by decisions in lower courts.

It has long been established that the civil division of the Court of Appeal is bound (not only by decisions of the House of Lords, but also) by its own earlier decisions – unlike the Criminal Division (see *R v Gould*[3]). However, this rule is subject to three exceptions, famously identified in *Young v Bristol Aeroplane Co Ltd*[4]. First, if the earlier decision was expressly or impliedly overruled by a subsequent decision of the House of Lords. (An earlier decision of the House will not do, in my view, unless it was overlooked in the Court of Appeal decision – in which case the third *Young* category would apply. By taking the House's decision into account, part of the *ratio* of the Court of Appeal's decision must be that the two decisions are consistent). Secondly, if the earlier decision was inconsistent with a yet earlier decision of the Court of Appeal. (Again, it seems to me that if the former decision was taken into account in the latter, this ground cannot be relied on, because part

1   (1884) 9 App Cas 480 at 499, HL.
2   (1888) 21 QBD 362 at 365, CA.
3   [1968] 2 QB 65, [1968] 1 All ER 849, CA.
4   [1944] KB 718, [1944] 2 All ER 293, CA (*affd* [1946] AC 163, [1946] 1 All ER 98, HL).

of the ratio of the latter decision must be that it is consistent with the former decision). Thirdly, if the earlier decision was reached *per incuriam* (ie without the court being referred to authority or statute requiring a different decision from that reached).

Consistently with the relatively strict approach to the doctrine of precedent, these exceptions were, at any rate until recently, rigorously applied. Thus, in *Duke v Reliance Systems Ltd*[5], the third exception was said only to apply where the Court "*must* have reached a contrary decision" if it had been referred to the overlooked material.

As for first instance judges, they should not depart from the reasoning of a superior court, unless perhaps fully satisfied that one of the criteria in *Young*'s case is satisfied. Even then, unless both satisfaction of the criterion and the consequence are absolutely clear, a more prudent course may be to follow the superior decision and enthusiastically give permission to appeal. A first instance judge should rarely refuse to follow a decision of a judge of co-ordinate jurisdiction (it has been said, somewhat charmingly, that this is on grounds of judicial comity). It has also been held that, if there are two inconsistent such decisions, a judge is free to follow either, unless the former was considered in the latter, in which case the latter should be followed, unless it was arrived at *per incuriam* – see *Colchester Estates (Cardiff) v Carlton Industries plc*[6].

This brief discussion of the doctrine of precedent should explain why it is so dependent on competent law reporting. If a court is bound by earlier decisions, it is very important that all such decisions are promptly and accurately reported. Such decisions represent the law, which will often provide the basis upon which legal advice is given and business decisions are made, as well as the basis upon which legal argument is advanced in court, and judges' later decisions are made. It is therefore not surprising that judges, as well as practising and academic lawyers, have always been keen to ensure that high standards are maintained in preparing, selecting and publishing reports of judicial decisions.

THE SKILL OF REPORTING

Law reporters are the unsung heroes and heroines of our legal system. In a speech given to a Conference on *Law Reporting, Legal Information and Electronic Media in the New Millennium*, in Cambridge in March 2000, Lord Bingham of Cornhill emphasised the importance of law reporting, and rightly said that the best British law reporting is "a work of scholarship". He also referred to "the amazingly high standards of accuracy" achieved by law reporters, which, as he pointed out, judges, practitioners and academics tend to take for granted. It would be unrealistic to expect the extraordinary quality of the most eminent (general and very long-standing) reports, namely the Law Reports, the Weekly Law Reports ("WLR") and the All England Law Reports ("All ER") to be equalled by all other reports (which are, in the main, more specialist and of more recent origin). Nonetheless, many of the specialist reports live up to that high quality, and all reports published by reputable legal publishers maintain a very good standard.

What are the skills required of a publisher of law reports in the modern age? First, there is the art of covering the many courts in and around the Royal Courts of Justice. This requires expert deployment of skilled staff. Secondly, there is the selection of cases to report. This is probably easier for the specialist reports, as, subject to length, almost any relevant case, which does not turn simply on fact, tends to find its way into such reports. Selection represents a very significant difficulty for the general reports: they can only report a limited number of cases. It is easy to say that they should limit themselves to (a) decisions which introduce a new principle, (b) decisions which modify an old principle, (c) decisions

5   [1988] QB 108 at 113, [1987] 2 All ER 858 at 860, CA.
6   [1986] Ch 80, [1984] 2 All ER 601.

which settle disputed or uncertain issues, and (d) decisions which are "peculiarly instructive". (These four categories, identified by Nathaniel Lindley in his 1863 Paper, are still applicable today – see Paul Magrath's Introduction to the Council's Special Issue of the Law Reports in September 2001.) It is often hard to determine whether a decision merits reporting on that basis, not least in the light of the competition.

Thirdly, there is the art of editing of the judgments: at least in my experience, however carefully one checks, a good law reporter will find mistakes, sometimes quite serious ones, in judgments as approved or handed down. Throughout my judicial career, I have had frequent cause to be grateful to a number of law reporters for saving my blushes in this connection.

Finally, there is the preparation of the other parts of the report. Depending on the report, these can include (a) identification of catchwords (for indexing), (b) writing the headnote, (c) identifying cases which are followed, applied, distinguished, disapproved, overruled or explained (d) listing cases referred to in argument and in the judgment, (e) explaining the procedural history including the essential features of court documents, and (f) a summary of the arguments. These all require skill and patience. The headnote is of particular importance as advocates' arguments on cases often go no further than the headnote. Even if they go further, the assessment of the judgment concerned is often coloured by the headnote, which tends to be fuller than 50 years ago. Headnotes now set out the facts (albeit in summary form) and often explain the *ratio* in some detail.

As I have mentioned, the quality of law reporting (which generally varies between good and Lord Bingham's "amazingly high") is taken for granted. But in our common law system, reliable reporting of judicial decisions is vital, and it is worth remembering that the law reporters have not always enjoyed such high repute. Indeed, judicial concerns about the quality and quantity of law reporting have been voiced continuously over the past four hundred years or more. Some of these concerns are of historical interest or amusement only; but others demonstrate that some things never change.

## LAW REPORTING UNTIL 1865

Decisions of the common law courts were initially recorded in the Record and were then published in the Year Books (which survive from the reign of Edward II). According to Blackstone[7], this practice ceased in the sixteenth century under Henry VIII, and, at the beginning of the next century, James I appointed two law reporters "with a handsome stipend". This in turn led to reports in all courts of record being prepared by individual barristers on an *ad hoc* basis (the "nominate reports", so-called because most, but not all, took their titles from the names of the reporters). According to Blackstone, these reporters "sometimes through haste and inaccuracy, sometimes through mistake and want of skill, have published very crude and imperfect (perhaps contradictory) accounts of one and the same determination".

As to quality, judgments from the seventeenth century onwards are replete with remarks, both unfavourable and (occasionally) favourable, about the multifarious nominate reports. For instance, Hyde CJ described the authority of Popham's reports as "none" in *R v Starling*, reported by Keble[8]. However, the biter was bit, as Keble was later described as a "bad reporter" by Lord Mansfield CJ in *Doe d Shore v Porter*[9], and Lord Kenyon CJ even reprimanded counsel for citing his reports, according to Park J in *Adams v Gibney*[10]. A very much fuller selection of judicial comments on the reliability of nominate

---

7   1 Bl Comm 71, 72.
8   (1664) 1 Keble 675 at 676.
9   (1789) 3 TR 13 at 17.
10  (1830) 6 Bing 656 at 664.

law reporters was collected by the indomitable Sir Robert Megarry in his *Miscellany-at-Law* at pp 293–294 (which includes Holt CJ's remark, in *Slater v May*[11], that "these scambling reports ... will make us appear to posterity for a parcel of blockheads") and in his *Second Miscellany-at-Law* at pp 117–133.

In addition to the concern about the quality of the nominate reports, there was also disquiet about the sheer quantity of law reports, including the duplicative nature of reporting. Thus, Sir James Wilde (President of the Court of Probate and Divorce, and later Lord Penzance) condemned the "vast agglomeration" of law reports, aggravated by "a competitive system of law reporting, and the record of useless decisions". Additionally, as a Paper in 1849 stated, because the reporters were self-appointed and unorganised, "we have chasms in our law reports", so that "the law expounded in Westminster Hall may ... remain for years concealed". Accordingly, there was unhappiness about the reporting of unimportant cases, as well as the failure to report important cases.

Concern about the unacceptable standards of law reporting came to a head during the nineteenth century. It was initially met by the publication in 1822 of the Law Journal Reports, followed by other commercial enterprises including the Law Times (1843) and the Weekly Reporter (1852) and the Solicitors' Journal (1856). Although these publications represented an improvement, the position was still not regarded as satisfactory. This was partly because these new publications increased the duplication of reports, but also because of their purely commercial nature. The concerns as to the state of law reporting was explained in two powerful Papers on law reporting published in 1849 and 1853 by the Society for Promoting the Amendment of the Law. The two Papers are reprinted, together with a number of other relevant documents, in William Daniel QC's "The History and Origin of the Law Reports".

The concerns highlighted in these Papers resulted in the founding of the Incorporated Council of Law Reporting which started reporting cases from 1 November 1865 (when, in those more relaxed times, the Michaelmas Law Term began). The Council was conceived as a result of the legal profession's rejection of the recommendation in the 1853 report that the government publish authorised law reports. The primary object of the Council was to prepare and publish "in a convenient form at a moderate price, and under gratuitous professional control reports of judicial decisions of the superior and appellate courts of England".

## LAW REPORTING FROM 1865 TO 1970

The Council, which has published The Law Reports (for nearly 150 years, often known as the Full Reports), and the WLR (for over 50 years), is a charity – see *Incorporated Council of Law Reporting for England and Wales v Attorney-General*[12]. It has always had heavy judicial and professional membership, but, very properly, its editors are given a free hand as to which cases to report. The Council's reports were characterised from the inception by clear headnotes, a summary of the facts (sometimes taken from the judgment) and the procedural history, and a verbatim report of the judgment. If the judgment was not reserved, the practice rapidly developed for a transcript of the *ex tempore* judgment to be sent to the judge, who could make such amendments as he or she saw fit. The WLR included all the cases which were to be in the Full Reports, and many more (perceived to be less important) cases as well. The principle differences between the two reports are that (a) cases in the WLR are published more quickly, (b) the WLR come out weekly, whereas the Full Reports come out about seven times a year, (c) the WLR contain more (now around

---

11 (1704) 1 Ld Raym 1071 at 1072.
12 [1972] Ch 73, [1971] 3 All ER 1029, CA.

300) cases of which about a third are in the Full Reports, and (d) the Full Reports include a summary of the advocates' arguments.

The competition to the Council has always come, at least in the main, from commercial bodies. In 1885, Nathaniel Lindley (by then Lindley LJ), in an article in the Law Quarterly Review, described it as "remarkable" that, although "the Government" published statutes, it "left entirely to private enterprise" the publication of judicial decisions. With our twenty-first century concern about the separation of powers, we should probably be relieved that the Executive has not seen fit to take on what Lindley LJ called the "authentic publication" of law reports (although, interestingly, the Reports of Tax Cases and the Reports of Patent Cases are published by the government).

By far the most prominent of the commercial competitors of the Council is and has been Butterworths (now LexisNexis and part of the Reed Elsevier International Group) who have published the All ER every week, for more than 70 years. Although there are significant cases only reported in one of the two famous weekly publications, these reports contain many of the cases which are in the WLR. The All ER have tended to be a little quicker in reporting cases than the WLR. Over the same period there have been the reports in the Solicitors' Journal and the Law Society's Gazette, as well as the abbreviated but speedy reports in The Times newspaper (published since 1785). As the twentieth century progressed, specialist reports started to emerge. The earlier ones included the Local Government Reports (started in 1910, as Knight's Local Government Reports) and Lloyd's Law Reports (1919). These reports adopted substantially the same format as that of the Council's reports.

Relatively little concern seems to have been expressed over the quality of the law reporting since the Council took on its responsibilities, although the reports in the Estates Gazette were viewed with suspicion until they were given over to a barrister in the 1970s (see *Birtwhistle v Tweedale*[13], where Denning LJ said that "there are quite enough cases that can be cited").

In terms of quantity, relatively limited disquiet was expressed until fairly recently, about whether too many cases were reported. There was some discussion about law reporters' influence over the development of the law by their ability to choose which decisions to report. This was one of the sources of anxiety expressed by Arthur Goodhart in his dissent in a Report commissioned in 1940 by the Lord Chancellor on law reporting, in which the majority expressed satisfaction with the then-current state of affairs. In 1975, during the course of the first High Court case in which I appeared (if only to take judgment), Templeman J referred with concern to "the remarkable power of the law reporters". There had been two contemporaneous and inconsistent first instance decisions on the same point. One of them had been reported and the other had not. As a result, the former had been followed and applied, unlike the latter (an earlier decision of Templeman J, which may partly have explained his concern). Despite my best endeavours, I can find no trace of either decision of Templeman J on any of the legal websites; that itself is a sign of how greatly things have changed in 30 years, a feature to which I now turn.

## LAW REPORTS SINCE 1970

Over the past few decades, it appears to me to be increasingly true that (a) many more cases are being decided, (b) a higher proportion of decided cases are being reported, and (c) a higher proportion of reported cases are being cited in subsequent cases. The combined effect of these changes is to effect a substantial alteration to legal advice, hearings and judgments.

---

13  [1953] 2 All ER 1598n, [1954] 1 WLR 190, CA.

In 1957, there were about 45 High Court Judges and ten (including the Lord Chief Justice) who sat regularly in the Court of Appeal. By 2007, the figures were about 108 High Court Judges and 40 in the Court of Appeal. The increase in judicial manpower is nearly three-fold; indeed, once one takes into account the substantial number of Circuit Judges and senior practitioners now sitting every day as Deputy High Court Judges, the number of sitting days in courts of record must have more than tripled since 1957.

It is true that hearings, especially at first instance, now last, at least on average, significantly longer than they used to last, partly because so many more cases are now cited. Even allowing for this, the substantial increase in judges sitting in courts of record must result in many more decisions. This is attributable to the fact that, while few, if any, areas of law have died off, many new areas have been appearing for the first time and many established areas have grown substantially. There has been a considerable increase in the volume of primary and secondary legislation, as examination of the bound annual volumes of statutes and of statutory instruments demonstrates. There has been an explosion in the quantity of regulation. Administrative law has grown out of all recognition in the past 50 years. EU law only came on the scene in the early 1970s, and has been on the march since then. Human rights came onto the domestic agenda less than ten years ago. The so-called culture of complaint, or blame culture, has had a marked and expanding influence on the law.

The increase in the number of reported cases is also plain to see. Over the past 35 years or so, Butterworths have vastly expanded their repertoire to include at least 12 sets of specialist law reports, starting with Industrial Relations Law Reports in 1972. It is interesting to note that of these twelve new sets of reports, eight began in or after 1995. The total number of cases these twelve new sets have reported to date exceeds 15,000; by comparison, since 1936, the All ER have published just under 25,000 decisions. Since 1970 or so, the vastly improved Estates Gazette Law Reports have published, on average, two full reports a week. Over that period, other companies also have started to publish specialist reports; examples notably include well-established legal publishers such as Thomson's Sweet & Maxwell (who publish, for instance, Common Market Law Reports and Housing Law Reports) and Jordans (whose publications include UK Human Rights Reports and Family Law Reports). Additionally, there has been the very significant development of the overnight reports (such as the Daily Law Notes, All ER (D) and Lawtel), consisting of electronically transmitted decisions (often of verbatim judgments) given the previous day.

Having said that, it is interesting to note that the number of cases reported in the leading established non-specialist law reports has actually fallen. The number of cases reported in [1937], [1957], [1987], [1997], and (up to 10 August) [2007] All ER were, respectively, 495, 382, 333, 227 and 163. As for the Council, the figures for [1907], [1977], [1997] and (up to 10 August) [2007] are 468 (the Full Reports, as that was all the Council published then), and 333, 281, and 190 (the WLR). I think that the fall in these numbers is attributable to three factors. First, more careful, even ruthless, editing; with the knowledge that most cases of any interest will be reported somewhere, the WLR and All ER reporters are trying, quite rightly, to ensure that they only report cases which really do fall into one or more of Lindley LJ's four categories. Secondly, judgments are increasingly long, as judges explain with greater particularity the reasons for their decisions, and have to deal with the increasing number of authorities raised in argument. Thirdly, there is the ever-growing number of specialist law reports, which make it easier for the general reports to eschew reporting cases, however important, if they are or may be largely of specialist interest.

There have also been two other very significant developments. First, there are non-commercial on-line publications of judgments (without any of the additional material found in law reports). Perhaps the two most notable are (a) the government sponsored House of Lords website, on which all decisions since 14 November 1996 of the Appellate Committee are published within two hours of delivery, and (b) the charitable BAILII website, which was incorporated here in December 2000, and publishes many Court of Appeal and High Court decisions promptly after they are delivered. Secondly, the commercial publishers of reports are also making available on-line judgments which they are not reporting. This started with LexisNexis, but now includes many other legal publishers, including Sweet & Maxwell.

The increase in reported cases (and the easy availability of many unreported cases) is, in my view, due to a number of factors. First, it reflects the wider information explosion. The relative ease of printing and distribution, and, even more, the advent of the Internet, has led to the expectation that any existing information should be made easily available to anyone who wants to see it (an expectation reinforced by the Freedom of Information Act 2000). While the Internet is by no means the sole cause, there can be no doubt but that it has directly enabled and indirectly inspired most of the revolutionary increase in the number of available judgments and reports and the speed with which they are provided. And the revolution is continuing. The official shorthand writers are currently intending to place all Court of Appeal decisions onto their website, and BAILII is starting to publish Tribunal decisions. There are, and no doubt will continue to be, many other proposals whose net effect is likely to be to increase (both the number and the degree of duplication) the stock of easily available judgments.

Secondly, the recent substantial increase in the number of specialist law reports is attributable to the increased specialisation within the legal profession. This has resulted in a significant number of separate new markets consisting of people who wish to know promptly of, and to study, every case decided in their particular field.

Thirdly, the increase in the number of law reports, and in the publication of unreported cases, is encouraged by the blame culture to which I have referred. While the actual claim figures may not bear this out, lawyers feel that they are much more at risk of being sued for alleged professional negligence than they were 30, or even 20, years ago. This inevitably means that the "no stone unturned" approach to legal research, whether for the purpose of advice or litigation, has become far more common. The climate is such that it is much easier to justify what turn out to be hours of expensive and useless research than it is to explain missing a relevant case as a result of deciding to limit one's research on reasonable cost-effective grounds.

Fourthly, the increasing internationalisation of legal services, especially with London being such a significant global commercial centre, has, I suspect, resulted in the approach to legal advice and litigation which has developed in the United States having a significant influence. That approach has been traditionally more exhaustive than the traditional English approach.

As to citation of cases, it is clear from even a cursory glance at the law reports that the number of cases relied on in argument, and the number of cases considered in judgments has increased enormously over the past century. Sasha Blackmore of Landmark Chambers (who has done much valuable research for this article) has compared the average number of cases cited in the argument and in the speeches in the cases heard in the House of Lords and reported in the Appeal Cases Reports for 1907, 1957, 1987 and 2007. In [1907] AC, the average number of cases cited in argument was five, and in [1957] and [1987] it was 23 and 20 respectively; by [2007] the average had increased to 41. Interestingly, these figures were roughly reflected in the average length of the Law Lords' speeches: six pages in [1907], 16 and 17 respectively in [1957] and [1987], increasing to 25 pages in [2007]. In each of those four years approximately half the number of cited cases found their way into the speeches.

The increase in the number of cited cases is, of course, in part due to the increase in the number of reported cases and the increase in the number of published unreported cases: the more decisions that are reported or otherwise available, the more potentially relevant reported decisions there are to be cited. Other reasons for the large increase in unreported cases are, I think, perhaps not surprisingly, the same as those which explain the increase in reported cases. I also suspect that the decision of the House of Lords in *Saif Ali v Sidney Mitchell and Co*[14] has had an effect. In that case, effectively taking advantage of the 1966 *Practice Statement*[15], the House departed from its previous view that an advocate could not be sued for negligence in relation to the conduct of a case in court. If my suspicion is right, this would be a case of a change in the common law having an effect on law reporting, rather than the converse.

## DIGESTING THE CHANGE

The large number of judicial decisions reported or otherwise available gives rise to significant challenges to the law reporters, legal advisers, advocates, judges, and academics, and thus to the common law itself. Before turning to those challenges, it should be said that the increased number of reported cases and published unreported cases does not only represent a problem: in principle, at least, the more decisions of courts of record that are available, the more informed legal advisers and judges will be, and the more informed they are, the less likely, at least in theory, it is that they will give the wrong advice or the wrong decision.

For the law reporters, the large number of judgments, particularly with many being given *ex tempore*, and therefore being unpredictable as to timing, renders covering the courts a difficult and expensive exercise. Although the rising proportion of reserved judgments mitigates the problem, it by no means neutralises the effect of the large increases in the number of judges and, hence, of judgments. As to the selection of the cases for reporting, the total number of cases reported in the All ER, the WLR and the Full Reports should not cause (and has not caused) the number of reported cases to increase. Accordingly, the growing tide of cases produces increasing challenges on selection.

The increase in the number of decisions, and, in particular, the introduction of overnight reporting, has resulted in editing of judgments being either more challenging or (in the case of many of the websites and the overnight verbatim reports) effectively abandoned. The contents of the report other than the judgment (for instance the headnote) represent a challenge which can only increase with the growth in both the number of decisions given, and the proportion getting reported.

For all those who wish to rely on case law, whether practising lawyers, academics, judges or students, there is a potential trade-off between speed and reliability. If a case is properly reported, it will be reliable, but, with the exception of House of Lords decisions (which are proof-read by reporters before they are given, and are reported normally within two weeks), there is a significant delay between the judgment and its reporting. Further, a substantial number of cases are never reported, and therefore never have the benefit of professional editing or a headnote. As pointed out by Diana Procter, one of the invaluable House of Lords law reporters (who has provided much in the way of information and thoughts for this article), because of the absence of editing or a headnote (or other information provided in a proper law report), an unreported judgment may well be less reliable and much more cumbersome to consider. Apart from giving a clear summary of

---

14 [1980] AC 198, [1978] 3 All ER 1033, HL.
15 *Practice Note (Judicial Precedent)* [1966] 3 All ER 77, sub nom *Practice Statement* [1966] 1 WLR 1234, HL.

the facts, issues and *ratio* of a case, a headnote enables one quickly to contextualise the judgment or judgments to which it relates. Particularly if there is more than one judgment, or there is a long judgment, the provision of a headnote acts like a road map, saving a lot of time and minimising the risk of misunderstanding. Overnight reports present an additional difficulty in the case of *ex tempore* decisions: in contrast to reported decisions, the judge is given no opportunity to approve (ie to edit and correct) what he is recorded as having said.

As to practising lawyers, the concern about being sued for professional negligence is reinforced and facilitated by an increase in the number of decisions which are reported, and also in the speed with which decisions are notified. Indeed, as mentioned, it encourages the proliferation of published decisions, reported and unreported. The inevitable consequence for clients is, of course, increased costs. The same point applies to argument in court: more reported cases and the possibility of a negligence suit result in fuller submissions and much more citation of authority, which produces longer and more expensive hearings. This in turn results in longer judgments, and has contributed to the increase in the proportion of reserved judgments. This produces an increased number of long judgments, which in turn feeds back into rendering legal advice and legal argument at hearings longer and more expensive.

Additionally, the welter of available case law leads to an increased risk of lawyers, whether advising or advocating, losing sight of the wood for the trees. With a morass of authorities, one risks becoming bogged down in other cases, when one should be concentrating on identifying the basic principles which apply to the case in hand.

The problems for the judiciary mirror those for the advocates. The increased citation of cases means more pre-reading, longer hearings, and longer judgments, and more reserved judgments, all of which mean more pressure and more work. There is also an increased risk of losing sight of the central issues.

One fairly obvious answer to the problems at each level is selectivity. Do not normally include (in your reports if you are reporter, in your advice if you are a legal adviser, in your argument if you are an advocate, or in your judgment if you are a judge) a case if it simply turns on existing principles, established by a reported case already referred to or cited, or merely illustrates application of those principles. This is easy to say, but often hard to do, and sometimes inappropriately strict, but it is a good general rule, advocated by Buxton LJ at the Cambridge conference in March 2000.

The judges have, quite rightly, been trying to stem the tide of over-citation of authorities, but there is a limited amount they can do. They have (a) admonished advocates who overload hearings of cases with unnecessary authorities, (b) occasionally made consequential adverse costs orders in such cases, and (c) issued the *Practice Direction (Citation of Authorities)*[16]. While these judicial attempts to hold back the flood should be welcomed, they are something of a mixed bag. To discourage the citing of more than one authority for a particular proposition seems sensible, but it cannot be an absolute rule. For instance, there can often be value in considering more than one judgment justifying a particular rule, or an advocate may reasonably want to rely on the sheer number of cases going the same way. Despite the welter of reports, there are, inevitably, unreported decisions of significance which remain unreported. It is not only for that reason that the proposition that an advocate cannot cite an unreported decision without permission appears questionable. In order to decide whether to give permission, a judge normally must look at the case to see what assistance it gives: once he has done that, quite apart from the paradox of refusing permission to cite a case which has been cited, it is hard to see what benefit would be gained by having to decide whether to permit the case to be cited.

---

16 [2001] 1 WLR 2001, sub nom *Practice Note* [2001] 2 All ER 510, CA.

It is often difficult for an advocate to know which authorities will be referred to at a hearing: much depends on the course taken by the evidence (at first instance) or the way the arguments develop. Particularly with the advent of skeleton arguments, it should be possible to have two bundles, one with cases that will be referred to, and the other with those that might be referred to. There is also much to be said for limiting the contents of bundles of authorities, at least in many instances, to the headnotes and those passages in a judgment which are to be relied on: indeed, that is provided for in para 32 of the current edition of the Chancery Guide.

Another suggestion, which is already taking root, for advocates and judges, is that greater use can be made of legal textbooks and articles. Particularly where the publication is well-established or by a well-known author, it may be possible and effective to cite a passage, which accurately encapsulates the law, rather than expending far greater time and effort in trawling through the primary material, namely the decisions themselves. Of course, if there is a challenge to what is said in the passage, one almost inevitably has to examine that material, but that is often not the issue. This suggestion fits in well with the marked and welcome increase in references to, and reliance on, legal textbooks and articles, in arguments and judgments.

I cannot speak with any authority about the problems, or indeed opportunities, faced by academics as a result of the increasing number of cases and reports, but one can easily imagine what they might be. What I can emphasise is the importance of fully educating law students how to find, understand and deploy the bewildering array of source materials (especially the raw materials of judgments, law reports, and, indeed, statutes), and to understand the common law including the doctrine of precedent. The use of cases and reports is an essential part of the technique of law, and the understanding of precedent is an essential part of the substance.

## EROSION OF THE DOCTRINE OF PRECEDENT?

While precedent is central to English law and should be fully taught to every law student, it is arguable that the tighter shackles of precedent have loosened over the currency of the past 40 years. The rule that the House of Lords is bound by its own decisions has changed following the *Practice Statement (Judicial Precedent)*[17], and the House can now overrule its previous decisions. The House may also be showing itself to be more ready than heretofore to overrule well established principles laid down by the Court of Appeal, as is evidenced by decisions such as *Hindcastle Ltd v Barbara Attenborough Associates Ltd*[18].

However, the need for certainty in the law is still very important, and the House's power to overrule its previous decisions should be used "sparingly" and, normally, only when "some broad issue is involved" and the answer appears tolerably clear – see *Jones v Secretary of State for Social Services*[19]. Accordingly, departures in the past 40 years have tended to be as much from previously established principle (as in *Pepper v Hart*[20]) as from specific previous decisions. However, the 1966 *Practice Statement* has been invoked on a number of occasions, a recent example being in *Horton v Sadler*[21]. Interestingly, although it states that there is an "especial need for certainty as to the criminal law", it is in that field

---

17 *Practice Note (Judicial Precedent)* [1966] 3 All ER 77, sub nom *Practice Statement* [1966]
     1 WLR 1234, HL.
18 [1997] AC 70, [1996] 1 All ER 737, HL
19 [1972] AC 944 at 966 and 1024–1025, [1972] 1 All ER 145 at 149 and 196–197, HL.
20 *Pepper (Inspector of Taxes) v Hart* [1993] AC 593, [1993] 1 All ER 42, HL.
21 [2006] UKHL 27, [2007] 1 AC 307, [2006] 3 All ER 1177.

that some of the best known cases invoking the *Practice Statement* have been decided, namely *R v Shivpuri*[22] and *R v Howe*[23].

As for the Court of Appeal, adherence to the strict principles established in *Young v Bristol Aeroplane* may be weakening. Over the past decade or so there have been at least three cases in which the Court of Appeal has refused to follow an earlier decision where none of the three categories in *Young* applies. They are *Esselte AB v Pearl Assurance plc*[24], *Wellcome Trust Ltd v Hamad*[25], and *Starmark Enterprises Ltd v CPL Distribution Ltd*[26] [2002] Ch 306. Although the Court of Appeal in *Desnousse v Newham LBC*[27] tried to squeeze these three decisions into the *Young* categories, they simply do not fit into any of them. In each decision, the Court of Appeal refused to follow its earlier decision on the simple ground that the reasoning in the earlier case was "fallacious" (the word used in *Wellcome*[28]). It is almost as if there is a fourth category, namely that the Court of Appeal is now no longer bound by earlier decisions if it thinks they are wrong. If that does transpire to be the rule, then, at least on the face of it, one should expect the Court of Appeal to be more reluctant than the House of Lords to refuse to follow its previous decisions, as it is not the final appeal court. Against that, however, the Court of Appeal deals with many more cases, and is under much more pressure, than the House of Lords, and in the overwhelming majority of cases it is the final arbiter.

Even in relation to the High Court, I have the fairly strong impression that first instance judges are rather less impressed than they used to be by the force of the rules of comity to which I have referred.

A recent significant change in a fundamental aspect of the law of precedent, which has been considered, but not decided, is whether the courts can limit the effect of a decision, which changes the common law, to the future. In other words, can a court say that, in relation to events or transactions after the date of its decision (or indeed from some other date), the law is changed, but, in relation to events or transactions before that date, the old law (now prospectively overruled) applies? Such a notion is inconsistent with the well-established fiction that the common law is and always was what the court declares it to be. That fiction was assumed to represent the law by the House of Lords in *Hindcastle*, and was reaffirmed less than two years later in *Kleinwort Benson Ltd v Lincoln City Council*[29]. However, although the point was left open, the House was much more receptive to the notion of prospective-only change in *National Westminster Bank plc v Spectrum Plus Ltd*[30]. If it had been thought to be appropriate in relation to the issue in that case, the impression one gleans from at least the speeches of Lord Nicholls of Birkenhead and Lord Hope of Craighead that they would have been prepared to give a prospective-only overruling.

## PRECEDENT AND THE EUROPEAN DIMENSION

There is more than one reason why the doctrine of precedent is being relaxed and at risk of being further relaxed. Some of those reasons reflect the challenges arising from the large increase in decided and reported cases, discussed above. There are other threats (if

22 [1987] AC 1, [1986] 2 All ER 334, HL.
23 [1987] AC 417, [1987] 1 All ER 771, HL.
24 [1997] 2 All ER 41, [1997] 1 WLR 891, CA.
25 [1998] QB 638, [1998] 1 All ER 657, CA.
26 [2001] EWCA Civ 1252, [2002] Ch 306, [2002] 4 All ER 264.
27 [2006] EWCA Civ 547, [2006] QB 831, [2007] 2 All ER 218.
28 [1998] QB 638 at 657, [1998] 1 All ER 657 at 671, CA.
29 [1999] 2 AC 349 at 379, [1998] 4 All ER 513 at 535–536, HL.
30 [2005] UKHL 41, [2005] 2 AC 680, [2005] 4 All ER 209.

that is not too strong a word) to the survival of the doctrine, at least in its present form, some of which come from the increasingly international nature of the world we inhabit. In terms of our legal system, this has manifested itself most markedly through the impact of our being parties to a European enterprise, and in particular the European Human Rights Convention and the European Union Treaties.

I believe that European law, and more specifically the jurisprudence of the ECtHR and the ECJ, may well have some effect on the doctrine of precedent. The doctrine has, of course, much less significance in a civil law system, such as prevails in the other signatories to the Convention or the Treaty of Rome (with the exception of the Republic of Ireland). It may therefore be that the duty of the courts of England and Wales to take into account the decisions of the ECtHR and to follow the decisions of the ECJ risks diluting the common law, not merely in content, but also in approach. Thus, the effect of the Human Rights Act 1998 is that, since 2000, common law has tended to develop so as to be compliant with the Convention, which almost inevitably includes compliance with decisions of the ECtHR. An example is to be found in *Venables v News Group Newspapers Ltd*[31], where the well-established rule that one could not have an injunction against a non-party (going back to *Iveson's Case*[32]) was held to be inconsistent with the Convention.

It is not merely that the decisions of the European courts have to be applied in our domestic courts. It is also that the more often domestic judges have to consider points on which ECtHR or ECJ decisions impinge, the more the approach of those courts enters the domestic judicial thinking and influences its approach.

It is interesting to note that in the *Spectrum Plus* case, the practice and approach of the European courts played a significant part in persuading the House that there was much to be said for the view that it was open to a court to change the common law on a "prospective-only" basis. Thus, the terms of the Convention, as interpreted by the ECtHR, were described as being "dynamic and evolutive", and the practice of the ECJ to "limit the temporal effect of some of its rulings" was also pointed out and relied on[33].

However, for those who regret this development, there is a mitigating factor. Even if we are being influenced by the civil law system as a result of the decisions of the ECtHR and the ECJ, close study of the judgments of the those courts (and perhaps even more of the opinions of the Advocates-General in the ECJ, above all Sir Francis Jacobs) suggests that the influence is a two-way process. It was not jingoism which prompted the remark earlier in this article that the common law system is envied by many people who practise in a civil law system. The cost and delay of taking cases to the ECtHR and the ECJ, coupled with the sheer volume of such cases, has, I think, served to impress the judges of those courts with the good sense and attraction of developing some sort of principle of precedent, by casting reasoning rather more widely than they may have done previously.

The development is perhaps more marked in the ECtHR, which has more ground to make up in this connection, I think, than the ECJ. Even now, one often sees stock quotations of principle being repeated in judgments from Strasbourg. Although this may be appropriate in some cases, it may sometimes conflict with a "living instrument" approach. On the other hand, in its judgments, the judges of the ECJ (and, even more, in their opinions, the Advocates-General) have for a long time apparently appreciated the desirability of giving general guidance, and I think one can detect in the ECJ judgments in recent times a greater awareness of the desirability of the court developing the law more generally.

---

31 [2001] Fam 430, [2001] 1 All ER 908.
32 *Iveson v Harris* (1802) 7 Ves 251.
33 The *National Westminster Bank* case [2005] 2 AC 680 at [23]–[25], [2005] 4 All ER 209 at [23]–[25].

A further mitigating point is that the burgeoning international dimension is not limited to Europe. There is an increasing tendency to refer to decisions of other common law jurisdictions, including the courts, particularly the High Court, of Australia, and also the courts of Canada and New Zealand, as well as the United States and South Africa.

The influence of the ECJ and the ECtHR has had a second, slightly more subtle, effect, which, at least at the moment, has been the subject of limited discussions. The European courts tend to give a single judgment. (It is true that there are occasionally concurring judgments, based on different reasoning. However, even dissenting judgments are normally short, and concurring judgments are not only relatively rare, but are always brief.) In this jurisdiction, single judgments in the House of Lords or Court of Appeal (ie a judgment of the court or a judgment from one member with which the other members agree) are quite common. However, it is equally, if not more common, particularly in cases of real significance, for there to be more than one judgment, even where the reasons are similar. In this connection, our domestic courts reflect the practice of other common law jurisdiction courts (eg Australia, New Zealand, and, rather less strongly, the United States), whereas the practice of the ECJ and ECtHR is the same as that of many of the domestic European courts.

This is not surprising. If the judicial function is simply to decide the case or to interpret the law, as in a civil law system, all that is ultimately needed from the court is a decision. On the other hand, if the function of the judges is to establish and to develop the law, then a wider or more detailed analysis is often appropriate. The common law rarely develops to a new stage, or even in a clear new direction, as a result of a single judgment in a particular case. It normally takes a series of judgments to achieve that end. The judges (with the benefit of the contents of earlier judgments, legal argument from practising lawyers, and academic articles and books) will test, change or extend the principles established or suggested in earlier judgments. This means that it is often very beneficial to have more than one judgment in a particular case, particularly where there is an issue of importance, or where some change in the law is being mooted.

It is undoubtedly true that there are disadvantages, as well as advantages, in having more than one judgment in a case. It requires more reading and analysis, and therefore leads to more cost and time. While more than one judicial contribution helps to ensures that the law developed and explained by the courts is less monolithic and more fully considered, it also means that the law may, for a time, be more uncertain. This is because different judgments in the same case almost inevitably give rise to arguments as to the precise *ratio* of the decision or about the *obiter dicta*. On the other hand, a single judgment will often involve a (sometimes substantial) degree of compromise between the judges as to what is included or omitted in the judgment, which often leads to lack of clarity or coherence. While each system has its advantages, the single judgment is the norm in a civil law system, whereas multiple judgments tend to result from a common law system.

There has been some discussion about whether appellate courts in England and Wales should be moving towards a single judgment of the court in each case. As already suggested, this may have been encouraged by the increasing awareness and influence of the ECJ and the ECtHR, as well as domestic European courts, whose decisions our courts look at rather more frequently than they did. The forthcoming creation of the United Kingdom's Supreme Court may prompt further interest in this issue. It was touched on in a judgment of the Court of Appeal given by Carnwath LJ (to which I was a party) in *Doherty v Birmingham City Council*[34]. If those discussions ever result in anything which even approaches a consensus, it could not occur before the establishment of the Supreme Court (currently projected for October 2009, but delay is not inconceivable).

---

34  [2006] EWCA Civ 1739 at [62]–[65], [2007] LGR 165 at [62]–[65].

On the single judgment/multiple judgments issue, it appears to me that, once again, the influence between Europe and the United Kingdom is not all one way. Indeed, so far, in terms of result, one could argue that the observable influence of the English and Welsh courts on the ECJ and the ECtHR in this connection is greater than the influence the other way. I do not detect an increase in the proportion of significant appellate decisions in this jurisdiction which have a single judgment. On the other hand, the number of ECJ and ECtHR decisions with concurring judgments appears to me to have increased, but this observation is based purely on the impression I have got from reading cases to which I have had cause to refer in my role as a judge. Even if there has been a change in the practice of the ECJ, it may well be attributable to causes other than the influence of the United Kingdom courts, such as the increase in the membership of the EU over the past two decades, and the concomitant increase in the number of ECJ judges.

## CONCLUSION

In his article in the Law Quarterly Review, Lindley LJ wrote that "a multiplicity of law reports is a great evil. The evil was once intolerable; it may become so again; whether it will or not depends on the profession and on the Council". By the time this was written, in 1885, the "evil" had abated. But, now in the twenty-first century, we again have a "multiplicity of law reports", which can result in needless complexity, pointless research and wasted time. However, the various reports fulfil different functions and serve diverse interests, and the publication of unreported decisions is unavoidable in the electronic age. It is also hard to deny that it is in the public interest that so many decisions of courts of record, which declare and fashion the common law, are published. The very large number of available judgments nonetheless presents a challenge, in terms of increased work, responsibility and powers of discrimination on the part of law reporters, practising lawyers, academics and students.

The sheer quantity of judicial decisions now available in the public domain represents a particular challenge to our common law system, with its doctrine of precedent. In the same way as the increasing influence of the international dimension, this challenge also represents an opportunity for the common law to show its well-established and enviable ability to evolve in an appropriate and principled manner. So far, at least, the doctrine of precedent has managed to develop and adapt to fast-moving change in a satisfactory manner without losing its essential character or the respect in which it is held. In the early years of the twenty-first century, the doctrine of precedent, like many other thriving organisms, is, I am glad to conclude, demonstrating, both by its activity and by its adaptability, that it is very much alive.

# IT LAW IN CONTEXT:
# A CRITICAL OVERVIEW

## STEVE SAXBY[1] AND CAROLINE WILSON[2]

## 1. INTRODUCTION

Commentators variously infer or describe the nexus of modern Information Technology law (hereafter, "IT law") as lying with computers[3], software[4] or the Internet[5]: what they have in common is that they identify this nexus as being technological, *not* legal. One can regard IT law, therefore, as sitting on the shifting sands of technology rather than on the traditional, firm regulatory bedrock, which, naturally, poses some difficulty when trying to define what constitutes IT law[6]. This mutability, in the view of the authors, means that the academic, the practitioner and the law maker should all be cautious about trying to define IT law by reference to *specific* technologies (eg personal computers, the Internet, etc). This, we would argue, is inflexible, technologically determinist and is reflective neither of the history of IT law nor its future development. Instead, the authors posit that two *general* technological developments (and the unfolding legal responses to how their application evolves), define the boundaries of modern IT law: *digitisation*[7] and *the networked computer*[8]. Indeed, it is the combination of digitisation with the mass communicative characteristic of the networked computer that, in our view, has both expanded and decentralised the capacity to reproduce, control, distribute and publish information and that gives rise to the fast moving nature and the regulatory challenges at the heart of modern IT law.

In this essay the authors offer a critical appraisal of modern IT law and its development, from a United Kingdom centric perspective. The legal and technological importance of other jurisdictions, principally the United States, is noted by way of overview only. Although a number of methodologies could be used in such a task, the authors wish to avoid mere

---

1   Professor of Information Technology Law and Public Policy, School of Law, University of Southampton. sjs@soton.ac.uk.
2   Lecturer in Intellectual Property Law, School of Law, University of Southampton. C.L.Wilson@soton.ac.uk.
3   Please note that throughout this essay the term "computer" is used to refer to *digital* computers; ie programmable electronic devices that process, store and retrieve digital data, comprising *hardware* (the tangible components) and *software* (the intangible instructions). Obvious modern examples of computers include personal computers ("PCs") but today computers are embedded in a wide range of products, ranging from cars and mobile phones to kitchen ovens.
4   As noted above, software is the intangible element of a computer (or, indeed, a computer network). Software is extremely pervasive today. For example, using the University of Southampton PC to draft this essay involved an operating system (Microsoft XP), an application (Microsoft Word) and online resources were accessed *via* a web browser (Microsoft Internet Explorer). The authors were able to "see" their work on a computer screen thanks to a GUI (a graphical user interface, one of the functions of Microsoft XP) and were able to exchange drafts using e-mail (Microsoft Office Outlook). As this basic (albeit Microsoft heavy) example illustrates, software can be multilayered. It is also important to realise that the technical standards (or protocols) that enable computers to connect and for data to be exchanged frequently take the form of software, eg TCP/IP (see note 34 below) or the MP3 format (MP3 being a standard for the compression of digital auditory content).
5   A definition of the term "Internet" is provided at note 42 below.
6   See section 2.1 below.
7   Digital content is functionally flexible (inasmuch as it can be easily manipulated and changed and can embrace multimedia communication: eg text, visual images, audio etc) and can be replicated without loss of quality. The legal challenges of digital content are explored in more detail in section 3 below.

description and to provide insight as well as overview; therefore both a strictly chronological approach[9] and a traditional intra disciplinary approach[10] have been eschewed. Instead, a more selective approach is taken; one that allows for critical reflection upon the symbiosis and conflict that exists between law and technology in the context of IT law.

There are three distinct parts to this essay, each necessarily brief: *context*, and an exploration of issues within Information Technology (IT) *infrastructure* and IT *content*. In section 2, the authors provide a critical overview of the academic, technological and legal context to IT law: thus the perennial academic question as to whether IT law is really law (section 2.1) is contemplated before a critical chronology of the technological historical context of IT law development (section 2.2) is undertaken. Then the boundaries (and sub-disciplines) of IT law (section 2.3), are considered and section 2 concludes with the authors proposing a United Kingdom model of regulation for modern IT law (section 2.4). Having thus provided this analytical context, the authors then critically reflect upon selected issues pertaining to modern IT infrastructure (section 3) and contemporary IT content (section 4). In section 5, the authors draw their conclusions and reflect on past, present and future challenges for United Kingdom IT law.

It is necessary, of course, in an essay of limited length for the authors to be highly selective. Thus a number of important topics are not discussed in detail. Comparative methodologies are not employed and neither is this intended to offer an exhaustive review of United Kingdom IT academic legal literature. Nevertheless, the authors believe that this essay contributes useful insights as to the development of IT law up to the present day. The modern story of the digital revolution may not span the full 100 years of *Halsbury's Laws* but it rightfully takes its place among the legal milestones of the latter half century of this important work.

## 2. CONTEXT

### 2.1. Is IT Law really Law?

The authors believe that the conceptual roots of both IT and IT law can be found in the English academic, Alan Turing's, theories of the Turing Machine and the Universal Machine[11]: thus, functionality became independent of the tangible. Accordingly, with the ever expanding sophistication and convergence of IT, we can identify the rationale of legal participation before us. The law must adapt and develop to meet the new challenges of products, activities and behaviours that information technology (IT) facilitates.

So, in answer to the question – is IT law really law? – the response must be very strongly that it is. Law must adapt to the new methodologies, norms and values of the present and

---

8   As Dewar (AJ Dewar *The Information Age and the Printing Press: Looking Backward to See Ahead*(1998) RAND paper P–8014 at p 4) argues, the networked computer is the foundation technology of modern IT law – being the first true mass market "many-to-many" technology assisted communications medium. In contrast, earlier key communications technologies can be characterised as being "few-to-many" (eg the printed book, radio, films and television). Some of the legal issues raised by networked computers are briefly considered in section 2 below.

9   To avoid a superficial and overtly technological treatment or a cursory law led treatment.

10  In the view of the authors, sole focus on key developments within the IT sub-disciplines – copyright law, data protection, etc – would be inappropriate in a work of this length, and would fail to provide an effective overview of IT law.

11  Details of both the Universal Machine and the Turing machine theory were first published as AM Turing *On Computable Numbers with an application to the Entscheidungsproblem, Proceedings of the London Mathematical Society* (1936–37) Series 2 vol 42 pp 230–265. Both "machines" are in fact abstract mathematical/philosophical constructs: for our purposes the import of the Turing Machine lies in its "programmable" features (ie it was the first conceptualisation of software): thus providing the model for the digital computer. The Universal Machine (simply a Turing Machine able to "read" and "interact" with any other Turing Machine) prefigures modern concepts of computer communication, networking and convergence.

within that process of adaptation can be found connections that bind legal development within fields of human endeavour. IT law emerged as a topic for academic study in the 1970s[12] and embedded itself within commercial legal practice and academia[13] in the 1980s. The 1990s saw convergence of technology, media, telecommunications and trade segments of activity within legal practice as well as within the manufacturing and service sectors supporting innovation and technological advance. These trends continue today as IT ever more deeply embeds itself into the fabric of daily life. The result, in legal terms, is of new legal rules and practices that have been specifically motivated and generated by the online world. Principles valid offline must now be adapted or redesigned for the digital environment. In this sense IT law has become pervasive of law itself.

On the other hand, just as is the case with other legal fields, a selective process can be undertaken to define those laws and legal issues that owe their rationale to IT and can therefore be grouped in various ways for the purposes of academic study and understanding (see section 2.3 below). That is the position today. Thirty years on from its beginnings, IT law is certainly advancing the case that it has a place among the established fields of academic legal study. Text books have been written in which the core principles that bind the field together have been exposed and discussed. Yet the significance of the question, as opposed to the conclusion, as to whether IT law is really law must be questioned. This debate, once popular amongst academics, is not one that the ordinary consumer or legal practitioner much cares about. While it may be fine for academics to assert the principles they say bind IT law into a coherent body of regulation worthy of academic study, the more important question relates to the adequacy and suitability of that regulation within the body of law as a whole. That remains a much harder question to answer tempered as it always must be with the ever present problem of the speed of the digital advance and the human ingenuity applied to its application.

In summary, the authors response to the question – is IT law really law? – is (to paraphrase Descartes[14]) to suggest that since IT law is both practised and taught, therefore it *is* a defined body of law.

## 2.2. *A Critical Technological Historical Chronology and Overview*

As noted at the beginning of this essay, the authors argue that it is within the confines of digital content and networks that modern IT law is placed. Within this paradigm, the authors posit that the development of modern IT – ie the innovations of the Information Age – can be characterised into five eras in the United Kingdom, each posing distinctive technological and legal challenges, as indicated in the sub sections below.

It should be noted that it is very easy to become fixated in the technicalities, and the acronyms, of modern IT; nevertheless, some grasp of the technical context of the key technologies (ie their inter-relationship and function) is necessary in order to comment critically upon their significance and legal regulation. In order to guide the reader and to avoid lengthy and turgid technical explanations, the authors have adopted the simplistic distinction between "pipes" (the conduits of information technology[15]) and "content"

---

12  Early United Kingdom pioneers in IT academia included Professor Harry Bloom's work at the University of Kent at Canterbury in the early 1970s.

13  For example, the first undergraduate course in United Kingdom IT law was established at the University of Southampton in 1981.

14  *"Je pense, donc je suis"* or "I think therefore I am". (See Descartes' seminal 1637 work, for example: R Descartes *"Discours De La Methode"*, Le Livre De Poche: Classiques (2000)).

15  Which we would define as not only including network *hardware* (eg the physical components of the modern telecommunications system and satellite technology) but also much *software*; from standards (eg the TCP/IP protocol), to search engines (eg Google).

(everything else[16]). The authors are aware that some practising IT lawyers use similar "pipes/content" analogies to *define* technologies, but we are not aware of any published work that utilises this distinction as a comprehensive tool of *legal analysis*.

Initially, the authors chose to use the "pipes/content" distinction in this essay for practicality[17] and for its' legal import[18]: reasons why one of the authors has previously used this distinction in her teaching activities. Latterly, the authors have come to the conclusion that the "pipes/content" distinction is even more fundamental than this. Much legal regulation and academic literature in IT to date is predicated on a "hardware/software" distinction[19], a distinction which is based on *form*, as opposed to the *functional* basis for the "pipes/content" distinction. The "hardware/software" distinction may have served IT law well in the past, but from a technological perspective form is no longer a good guide to function; moreover, hardware and software are (technically) more seamless than ever before, so it is submitted that little regulatory insight can be gained from the use of the "hardware/software" distinction any longer.

To clarify: hardware and software pervade both "pipes" and "content", but "pipes" (conduits for information) are *functionally* distinct from "content" (information conveyed in said conduits). The authors believe that the "pipes/content" distinction is now the centre of gravity for IT development but that academic legal analysis has not yet caught up with this transition.

### 2.2.1. The First Era: the Foundation of the Information Age[20] (1940–1968)

During the tail end of the Industrial Age[21], many of the foundation technologies for the Information Age were developed. Although a number of important analogue computing inventions predate what the authors have termed the foundation era, it is here – circa 1940 to 1968 – that the direct origins of the digital computer can be found. This era is characterised by the fruition and progression of earlier analogue computing developments: key technological milestones in this era include the development of the stored program computer. There was limited commercialisation of the early non-networked mainframe computers – such as the Ferranti Mark I computer[22] and LEO[23] –

---

16 For example, individual digital music files using the MP3 standard, conversations made *via* Internet telephony, word processing files etc.

17 Being (1) shorthand for technological context (it is a simple and useful way of describing the technical "place" of a technology) and (2) future proof (the semantics of the pipes/content distinction is relatively technology neutral).

18 See section 3.1 for the argument that proprietary rights have a different effect on each and that the appropriate regulatory models may differ.

19 Eg see section 3 below.

20 This essay is concerned with modern IT and modern IT law: this corresponds with the Information Age. Therefore, in this essay the authors do not discuss the information technologies of earlier Ages. Had this been necessary, the authors would have categorised time before the Information Age as follows: (1) the Hunter-Gatherer Age (circa 2.5m BC – 10 000 BC), which saw the development of human speech and art; (2) the Agricultural Age (circa 10 000 BC – 1700 AD) which saw the invention of writing and the first cultural depositories (prototype museums, libraries and archives), and; (3) the Industrial Age (circa 1700–1968) when printing, newspapers, photography, the typewriter, analogue computers, the postal system, the telephone, the phonograph, films, radio, television, the photocopier and other such information technologies were developed. See further: S Saxby, *The Age of Information* (1990) ch 2.

21 *Supra* note 20.

22 This was based on the Manchester Mark I computer and was the world's first commercially available general purpose computer.

23 It is a little known fact that LEO – The Lyons Electrical Office – was the world's first business computer, being in use within Lyons United Kingdom in February 1953.

but computer use largely took place within public bodies. It is noteworthy that, at the dawn of the Information Age, computer content was primarily numerical and many technological advances in this era had their genesis in the military sphere or academia.

A generic regulatory approach, ie one not distinguishing IT from other regulatory subject matter, is evident in this era. Specific, formal legal regulation of IT was absent and the field had not really caught the attention of United Kingdom legal academics, although there was a nascent United States literature. Overall, the challenges of the first era were largely technological with the focus on hardware development.

### 2.2.2. The Second Era: The Dawn of the Information Age (1969–1979)

This era saw a reduction in the size of computers, with the development of the microchip (also known as the semiconductor chip[24]), facilitating the subsequent introduction of personal computers and the development of further software applications[25] – marking the beginning of a move of IT usage beyond government and industry towards a mass market. However, computer use was still mainly institutional rather than personal[26]; residing in academia or industrial research, but also becoming well-established in businesses during this time. Although characterised by a rather narrow conception of IT, with particular emphasis on hardware (in the form of the computer), important software and network innovations took place during this period in the context of the development of the ARPANET[27].

The authors submit that there was a vital technological normative development during this era, namely the establishment of the principle of openness in modern IT engineering. This principle was not only a key technological feature of the ARPANET "pipes"[28]; it was (and still is) a defining characteristic of the process of network development – as evidenced by the RFC[29] (Requests for Comments) series[30].

Interestingly, although the authors would argue that IT was perceived as being *technologically* divergent from other technologies in this era, actual legal regulation in the United Kingdom at this time still tended not to draw a distinction between activities (or products) assisted by or involving IT, and those not. With a few exceptions, principally the discussion on the copyright protection of computer programs[31], there was little

---

24  See note 36 below.

25  From this point, enabled by software development, digital content began to expand beyond tabulating financial data, statistics, and other numerical information. For example, e-mail and word processing software were pioneered during this era.

26  Although at that time PCs tended to be developed and used by computer hobbyists; many such people becoming the workers and leaders of the then embryonic computer industry.

27  ARPANET, the network of the United States Advances Research Projects Agency (ARPA, now known as DARPA) went online in 1969. It is generally accepted that the ARPANET was the precursor of the modern Internet, but the authors would go further to state that the ARPANET was the foundation of the "pipes", both hardware and software, of modern networked computing.

28  Simply put, the "pipes" of the ARPANET were specifically designed to be used as a platform for other hardware and software (as is the case with the modern Internet and the World Wide Web), thus decentralising network innovation and enabling third party innovation "above" this platform.

29  RFCs are a collection of documents used by computer engineers to exchange IT ideas and theories. An RFC could variously constitute a work in progress, third party responses to the same or a draft proposal. The RFC series began in 1969 and quickly established a significant role in developing technical protocols or standards: a role that continues to this day.

30  RFCs were first circulated by "snail mail", then by e-mail. At the present time, there are a number of web sites that publish an index and repository of RFCs, one of the most comprehensive being found at http://www.ietf.org/rfc.html.

appetite for technology specific regulation. Technology specific academic writings, however, did take hold during this era.

### 2.2.3. The Third Era: Expansion (1980–1989)

Although computer hardware innovations continued apace, the growing importance of software is notable during the third era[32], which saw the rise of key multinational software companies (eg Microsoft) and networking (eg Cisco Systems). We can also see evidence of modern IT moving into the office and the home with the commercialisation of the first user friendly applications; for example, the launch of word processing programs[33]. Networks other than ARPANET began to proliferate – many of them rather small scale intranets, often based in academia. ARPANET itself underwent a transformation[34] to become part of a "network of networks" – the Internet.

In the context of this significant "pipes" innovation, it is only during the third era that we see the emergence of a technology specific regulatory model in the United Kingdom. This coincided with the establishment of the all party Parliamentary Information Technology Committee (PITCOM[35]) and the privatisation of United Kingdom telecoms *via* the Telecommunications Act 1984. Hereafter, we begin to see increasing evidence of a desire to change *existing* laws in the United Kingdom in order to meet the perceived needs of new IT industries and a willingness to *create* new laws to the same end[36]. It is notable, however, that some of the latter *sui generis* schemes have proved to be somewhat of a regulatory dead end[37].

Now, for the first time, a number of significant IT cases – mostly concerned with the application of intellectual property (IP) law to IT[38] – were litigated at the national level. It is unsurprising, therefore, that the third era also marked the development of IT law as a separate area of practice for legal practitioners and their clients[39] and of legal teaching[40] for the academic and student.

---

31 Both "pipes" and "content" software was affected by this, which is an example of existing law (copyright) being adapted in order to meet the perceived needs of the nascent software industry. Although it is documented that software *per se* was being treated as being literary works within United States law in 1964 (see the *Sixty-seventh Annual Report of the Register of Copyrights. For the Fiscal Year ending June 30 1964* (1965) Copyright Office, Library of Congress, Washington p 4) and international law accorded with this position in 1971 (ie the Berne Convention for the Protection of Literary and Artistic Works 1886, as amended in 1971), one can also see evidence of a national imperative to reform national copyright laws in the light of software developments in the United Kingdom Whitford Report (*Copyright and Designs Law: Report of the Committee to Consider the Law of Copyright and Designs*, HMSO 1976), and, in the United States, the CONTU Report (The National Commission on New Technological Uses of Copyright Works (CONTU) Report, July 31 1976 at pp 29–34), which resulted in, respectively, the Copyright, Designs and Patents Act 1988 ("CDPA 1988") in the United Kingdom and in the United States in the Copyright Act 1976 and later changes to section 117 of the same.

32 For example, the first IBM PC – IBM Acorn – went on sale in August 1981 complete with the MS-DOS 1.0 operating system. The Apple LISA computer (on sale in January 1983) was the first home computer with software that combined images, graphics and text (known as graphical user interface, or GUI) on a computer screen.

33 Such as MicroPro's WordStar – the first commercial word processing program.

34 Chief amongst these being the development of two key network protocols, the Transmission Control Protocol (TCP) and the Internet Protocol (IP). Together, TCP and IP created a flexible and enduring foundation "language" for the networked computer. The TCP/IP combination was officially adopted by ARPANET 1983 and this is generally accepted to mark the beginning of what we now know as the Internet.

Further legal developments enabled commercial entities to obtain proprietary interests in IT pipes and IT content: key exemplars here are *sui generis* database protection[41] and the patenting of software (see section 3 below).

In the third era, therefore, significant challenges were posed equally to technology, law and legal academe.

### 2.2.4. The Fourth Era: Transition (1990–2001)

This era is characterised by two technological leaps forward – first, the ARPANET technically ceded to the Internet[42] in 1990 and second the user friendly World Wide Web[43] was developed. The resultant increase in digital content, correspondingly significant growth in software applications developed by industry and a growing interest in establishing proprietary interests in IT content, all characterise this era.

Thus, technical innovations fuelled what can be regarded as a huge cultural shift from a quasi academic "science" based Internet culture to a commercialised Internet space. A wide variety of business models were explored during this era, fuelling the so-called dotcom boom. However, with the birth of e-commerce, attendant legal problems relating to jurisdiction[44], dispute resolution and intellectual property rights arose. Legal challenges posed by the Internet in this era were not confined to private law: privacy issues and "e-crime" concerns were also prevalent. Yet in both private and public law the legal response was frequently technology specific.

The fourth era, then, was one that posed great challenges and significant transition in a variety of contexts – technical, cultural, commercial and legal.

### 2.2.5. The Fifth Era: Social Diffusion (2002 onwards)

So far, the current era has witnessed further commercialisation and an exponential increase in the use of the Internet. It is during this time that we have seen the Web, in a meaningful sense, begin to realise some of its potential as a publishing medium. The most obvious

---

35  Which has proved influential in the United Kingdom (see R Sarson (ed) *PICTOM at 25*, available at http://www.pitcom.org.uk/pitcom25web.pdf). In more recent eras, other Associate Parliament Groups have been established, such as the All-Party Group on Telecommunications and the All-Party Internet Group (APIG).

36  There are examples here relating both to "pipes" and "content": (1) The development of data protection law, is probably the first example of *sui generis* content regulation – it is generally accepted that Sweden and Norway led the development of data protection in the second era – see, for example, J Bing *Data Protection in Norway* (1996) (http://www.jus.uio.no/iri/forskning/lib/papers/dp_norway/dp_norway.html), but it was only in the third era that the United Kingdom established by the Data Protection Act (DPA) 1984 (now the DPA 1998); and (2) the development of *sui generis* computer chip protection was probably the first such "pipes" regime. The protection of layout designs of integrated circuits as a specific subject matter was first mooted in the United States and resulted, in 1984, with the approval of the Semiconductor Chip Protection Act (the SCPA, which was codified at 17 USC sections 901–914 (1988)) and in the EU (EC Council Directive 87/54 of 16 December 1986 on the legal protection of topographies of semiconductor products). International negotiations led to the adoption, in 1989, of the Washington Treaty (the Washington Treaty on Intellectual Property in Respect of Integrated Circuits).

37  In the view of these authors, the Washington Treaty is now obsolete.

38  Eg *Merrill Lynch's Application* [1989] RPC 561 on patentability of software.

39  See section 2.1 above.

40  See note 13 above.

41  The introduction of a *sui generis* database right by the Copyright and Rights in Databases Regulations 1997, SI 1997/3032, following the EC Directive on the Legal Protection of Databases 96/9, to supplement copyright protection of databases as literary works (CDPA 1988 s 3A).

characteristic of this era is, again, a social *consequence* of technical developments to date – the rise of user generated online content, characterised today with the sobriquet "Web 2.0"[45]: thus the rise of applications as diverse as social networking[46], blogs[47], podcasts[48] and commercial Internet based virtual reality environments[49].

The rise of user generated content has meant that the English language, although still prevalent, is no longer dominant in Web content; however the globalisation of the Internet has thrown into sharp relief the digital divide[50], and we must question the effectiveness of the international response to this[51]. For those on the "right" side of the digital divide, the pervasiveness of technology in society is, today, extraordinary. However, meeting public expectations in areas such as enforcement and security (from national security to personal privacy) is a huge challenge. The public want a safe Internet environment in which to conduct their day-to-day activities and they also want the authorities to control illegal and harmful content that might threaten the individual and society, but they want this without the perception or reality of unwarranted intrusiveness by the state or commerce. Such concerns arise within the contexts of increased network capacity, the resultant increased content and technological sophistication of the general population (from tech savvy children to the over 55s – the "silver surfers").

One might characterise the fifth era as having a *community* rather than *individualistic* approach to IT usage. There is recognition of the need for public law to support, by regulatory means, a safer online community. Thus significant social change, supported by cheaper and ever more sophisticated and converging technology characterise the current era.

Where we are seeing true technical innovation today is in military[52] use of IT and in advances in surveillance techniques[53] that can monitor behaviour online and offline, for the benefit of government authorities, commercial enterprises or criminals. The resultant moral issues pose substantial regulatory challenges. Also, significant technical steps forward have been made in research and development on further reducing computer size, and the development of new networks for the future and software for said networks. Collective

---

42  Curiously, it was not until 1995 that a definition of the term "Internet" was agreed (see Federal Networking Council (FNC) Resolution, *Definition of "Internet"*, October 24 1995 (available at http://www.nitrd.gov/fnc/Internet_res.html). For our purposes, "Internet" can be defined as the global network of "pipes" that provides electronic connection between computers enabling them to communicate with each other.

43  The Web, as it is known, was a key "pipes" innovation developed by the United Kingdom academic Professor Tim Berners-Lee and first implemented in 1990. The Web is usually defined as the system of interlinked hypertext documents that can be accessed *via* the Internet. Simply put, the Web is a "place" on the Internet (websites such as www.soton.ac.uk) where one finds *interlinked* content that is based on an Internet standard – hypertext (http). So, when you use Google to find a website you are directly using the Web, but when you use a modern telephone system (mobile or landline) you are directly using the Internet.

44  See 2.4.1 below.

45  Despite confident media reference to "Web 2.0" there is no technical definition of this term. It is generally taken to refer to second generation web based communities and hosted services claiming to offer enhanced collaborative and information sharing applications to users.

46  Eg Facebook (http://www.facebook.com/).

47  Online diaries or "web logs".

48  User friendly digital audio software which can be used to record webcasts or to broadcast Internet based radio programmes.

49  Such as Second Life (http://secondlife.com/).

50  A euphemism commonly used to describe the "haves" and "have nots" of the Information Age.

51  The international response recently featured two conferences, known as the World Summit on the Information Society (WSIS). The WSIS process has, in the view of these authors, so far generated a wide range of documents, policy and targets, but with negligible results.

creativity is being facilitated by technology on a larger scale than ever before (for example, http://en.wikipedia.org/wiki/Main_Page): this, as well as the reduced cost of publishing content, is forcing established commercial content providers to reassess their traditional business models.

Lacking a historical perspective, it is difficult to discern at this stage the legal impact of the current era. At present there is some evidence to suggest a return to generic – rather than technology specific – regulation in the United Kingdom, and current and future technologies will certainly pose new challenges for United Kingdom law, but it is difficult to predict as yet what these will be and how the law will respond.

### 2.2.6. Summary

The authors believe that a number of technological and legal themes have evolved in the United Kingdom through the five eras. From a technological perspective, for example, we have seen hardware and software development that has evolved beyond rare, expensive, hard to use mainframe computers with numerical content to user friendly, digital multimedia content on decentralised but accessible networks, and cheap computers. Thus the evolution of the "pipes" (technologies which the Internet community is fighting to keep as "open" rather than becoming the property of one commercial entity) has driven the increasing availability and range of "content". Today, computers are pervasive and their increasing functionality and convergence can be expected to drive further increases in the quantity and forms of "content".

From a legal perspective we have seen a number of different formal legal responses, variously, generic and technology specific in their approach to technological development and commercial pressures; which is to say that the law appears to play a *reactive* regulatory role[54]. However, this may not be the whole picture and it will be argued below[55] that other models of regulation have an important part to play in the regulation of IT. Despite the technological value of openness (at least with regard to "pipes"), there is increasing pressure to establish proprietary rights in "pipes" and "content" (which contrasts with the technological value of openness and, in the fifth era, the increased community approach to IT usage); an issue which will be briefly revisited in sections 3 and 4 below.

### 2.3. What *is* IT Law?

Defining the boundaries of IT law was a difficult task in the early years. Indeed, early critics of the establishment of IT law as a separate discipline carped that IT law was merely a rag-bag of aspects of established legal disciplines such as contract law and intellectual property law. As noted above, IT law has since become established as a separate legal discipline; however, how should we define IT law? The problem here was identified at the beginning of this essay: the boundaries of IT law flex according to IT development. The authors assert that the boundaries of IT law were diffuse in the first era, but began hardening in the second and third eras[56]. However the authors suspect that, throughout the fourth and current eras, the boundaries have again become diffuse: indeed, the syllabi of academic United Kingdom IT law

---

52  For example, United States military forces currently use Artificial Intelligence assisted technology such as unmanned "drone" aircraft and are currently developing the first generation of "robot" soldiers.

53  Such as modern CCTV technology.

54  A number of questions flow from this that cannot be answered in this essay: does the (slower) pace of regulation act as a break on technological development? Can, and should, law lead technological development?

55  See section 2.4 below.

56  At which point IT law could be said to encompass – amongst others – telecommunications law, intellectual property law, the law of e-commerce and e-crime law.

courses has become highly diverse during this time and we see evidence that the more informal regulatory models are being used in practice (see section 2.4 below). Moreover, the formal regulatory impact of information technologies is increasingly found *within* more traditional legal disciplines[57]. Perhaps this is reflective of the ubiquity of IT and technology convergence? If these speculations are true – and further research is necessary here – then perhaps the question – is IT law really law? – has renewed practical, as well as academic, import.

### 2.4. *The Regulatory Context: a Critical Overview*

It was noted in section 2.2.6 above, that formal legal regulation provides only part of the regulatory framework for IT. In this section, these questions and the import of more informal regulation will be considered (in section 2.4.2) in proposing a theory of IT regulation. This theory, espoused in section 2.4.3, consists of five regulatory models; characterised as three standard regulatory models[58] and two alternative models[59]. It is these constructs that the authors argue can be discerned from the present study of IT law.

### 2.4.1. Jurisdiction: a Brief Note

Before these models are introduced, it should be noted that as modern IT facilitates communications and activities across national borders, an important aspect of its regulation must be enforcement: and that leads us to the topic of jurisdiction. As noted in the introduction to this essay, the authors have had to be selective in choosing the topics for critical discussion. Jurisdiction is one such omission, but it is relevant to note that the authors refute what has been termed "the cyberspace fallacy"[60], ie the view that the internet is a virtual space over which no jurisdiction has *de facto* or *de jure* control of activities. The authors, along with numerous commentators and most IT legal practitioners[61], accord with the view that the actors in internet activity are, in essence, human – using human designed software and physical equipment (hardware). Ultimately, both the human and hardware elements are based in legal jurisdictions and are, thus, within the reach of national laws and therefore subject to legal regulation.

### 2.4.2. The Role of Institutions in IT Regulation

In assessing what drives IT law development it is important to note the role of institutions working within their spheres to develop policy, standards and compliance processes. Both general and technological institutions have been very important in the genesis of both IT and IT law, with examples of the former including the United Nations ("UN") and the Organisation of Economic Co-operative Development ("OECD"). In this context much of what has been achieved thus far has largely been accomplished by "soft law" processes,

---

57  Eg the impact of the Electronic Commerce (EC Directive) Regulations 2002, SI 2002/2013, on United Kingdom contract law, and of the Sexual Offences Act 2003 on United Kingdom criminal law.

58  The *technological model* (regulating technology by technology), the *legal model* (regulating technology by law) and the *hybrid model* (regulating technology by a combination of law and technology).

59  These being *"soft" legal regulation* and the *trust based regulatory model*.

60  A term coined by Professor Chris Reed – see C Reed *Internet Law: Text and Materials* (2nd edn, 2004) p 1 – one of the many commentators who has written on the topic of jurisdiction in IT law.

61  A fair reflection of the average United Kingdom IT legal practitioner's perspective is that whilst it is not *legally* difficult to establish jurisdiction (the global nature of the Internet means that a single IT activity usually will fall within United Kingdom jurisdiction, and indeed, that of other countries: principally the United States), there may be *practical* barriers to achieving this and to then enforcing United Kingdom rights and laws; and the time and effort this can involve often meaning that the cost may preclude enforcement from being commercially feasible. In this area, as with so many other issues, the response of the practitioner is to reduce his client's risk *via* creative use of contract law.

ie not by the sledgehammer of legislation but by codes of practice, often negotiated voluntarily with regulatory authorities, designed to promote best practice and to minimise formal action. Technological measures taken as a result of industry collaboration and co-operation with public authorities may also provide a greater deterrent, for example to online criminal activity, than sterner criminal sanctions alone.

In some instances the issue has gone full circle with evidence, for example, that the police are increasingly calling on the banks to take necessary enforcement action to tackle credit card fraud rather than for the police themselves to investigate and prosecute such activity through the courts. Whilst the banking industry clearly has responsibilities to minimise fraud, there are dangers should this approach to policing extend to other less well supported crime victims where the individual may feel that he or she is on their own against the criminal.

The increasing complexity of the challenge is also encouraging the establishment of partnerships and national specialist agencies such as SOCA – the Serious Organised Crime Agency – which is an executive non-departmental public body sponsored by, but operationally independent from, the Home Office[62]. SOCA tackles a range of criminal activity and abuse involving the use of IT in perpetration. By contrast the Internet Watch Foundation[63] operates on a non-statutory basis, funded by the EU and the online industry, to minimise the availability of potentially illegal content online.

Internationally, the blend of "soft" and "hard" law activity continues through the auspices of technological organisations such as the International Telecommunication Union (the "ITU"). The ITU is a United Nations Agency within the information and communication technologies acting as a "global focal point for governments and the private sector" within the areas of radio communication, standardisation and development. Established by the first International Telegraph Convention in 1865, its 191 member states and 700 sector members and associates work together to establish global policies for the global telecommunication environment while developing standards for emerging new systems. At the apex the global summits and plenipotentiary conferences define the direction for exploitation and development of the global telecoms resource.

*Via* similar mechanisms of international treaties, working groups, meetings and assemblies, another international organisation – the World Intellectual Property Organisation (the "WIPO") – also works with more than 90 per cent of countries in the world, and a wide range of stakeholders and organisations, *inter alia*, "to promote the protection of intellectual property throughout the world through co-operation among states and, where appropriate, in collaboration with any other international organisation". Thus WIPO has been instrumental in developing international IP laws and standards consistent with the demands of the online world which have then been implemented within the domestic law of its member states.

So whilst there is little dispute that international collaboration is essential to enable the "pipes" to deliver what governments, business and consumers want, it is less clear what regulatory contributions are required when the technology and its applications filter though into everyday life. At that level, particularly in relation to "content", the priorities and politics of nation states kick in along with the everyday demands of business and the public, all of which will temper and influence the priorities and pressures for regulatory development. This means of course that regulatory differences may emerge between nations in the actions taken. This is particularly the case with regard to the sensitive issue of online content regulation which some governments see as vital to the maintenance of the regime in power.

---

62  See http://www.soca.gov.uk/aboutUs/index.html.
63  See http://www.iwf.org.uk/public/page.103.htm.

In assessing the contribution of public law towards information technology the approach in terms of legislation has always been to lay down parameters and to permit the law to evolve within the interpretation of the regulators, including the courts. This can be seen in the United Kingdom in the functioning of the Computer Misuse Act 1990 (as amended) and the Data Protection Acts 1984 and 1998. Public law has also been a facilitator of modernisation. For example, the Electronic Communications Act 2000 s 8 permits the appropriate minister to modify legislation so as to facilitate electronic communication or storage as an alternative to traditional hardcopy methods in a wide variety of formal contexts. This includes electronic alternatives to documentary evidence. Although used sparingly by government the measure does at least fulfil the modernising responsibilities that such provisions imply. The direct effect of such measures contrasts well against the achievements of international treaties. Despite their contribution to global or regional regulation, treaties can be slow in coming to fruition and inflexible when legally binding on signatory states.

If one can step outside public law for a moment and focus on public sector policy towards IT one can see governments striving to gain the financial efficiencies that IT can offer. In the United Kingdom, public sector policy towards e-government for example has grown from an aspiration to improve government services into a transformational government agenda designed to radically change the way government operates in the delivery of public services. However, despite much effort in this regard, reports of inadequacies and failings in the modernisation of public sector IT infrastructure and the evident needs of policymaking for a more sophisticated government information policy, demonstrate that there is still much to be done.

### 2.4.3. A Theory of IT Legal Regulation

The authors tentatively hypothesise that five distinct regulatory models can be discerned from the legal regulation of IT in the United Kingdom. It should be made clear from the outset that these regulatory models are not alternatives: they can be complementary to each other and can also be rather promiscuous (thus, combinations of the different models can evolve in practice). Below, each model is briefly described with their attendant advantages and disadvantages critically analysed in outline.

#### 2.4.3.1. The Standard IT Regulatory Models

It is difficult to think of examples of the technological regulatory model (technology regulating technology) outside computer engineering itself. The "architecture" of the "pipes" of the Internet is regulated by technology; what we might term *macro*-technological regulation, however it is difficult to see where else the technological model could be useful. A rare example might be so-called vigilante justice websites, such as http://hollabacknyc.blogspot.com/ (which "empowers" New Yorkers to "holla back" at street harassers). This rare (and antisocial) form of "content" could be characterised as a form of *micro*-technological regulation of social behaviour in public places. Overall the technological model does not appear to have great import outside computer engineering because, in practice, most regulatory use of technology takes place in concert with proprietary rights, contract or public law.

Yet, regulation of technology purely by law (the legal model) carries its own risks: principally that of legal obsolescence. As discussed earlier in this essay, two common forms of IT legal regulation are generic regulation and *sui generis* regulation: many of the examples discussed earlier have employed the legal regulatory model which appears to be the most common model employed in formal IT law. However, we are increasingly seeing new laws that would fall into the hybrid model, ie regulation that employs a combination of law and technology. The hybrid model would seem to be both more useful than the technological model and at less risk of legal obsolescence. A good example of this is digital rights management in the context of copyright law (see section 4.2 below).

### 2.4.3.2. The Alternative IT Regulatory Models

As pointed out above, the potential applications of the technological model are relatively narrow. Further, by their nature both the legal and hybrid models are dependent on legislative or common law developments (or at least on contractual relationships). However, these standard regulatory models do not appear to reflect the whole picture of legal regulatory practice within IT. Not only does IT provide a technical and fast moving environment for regulation, but we have to contend with the actions of important institutions (see section 2.4.2 above) as well as the ever evolving human activities that IT facilitates. Consequently, more flexible, policy based and "bottom-up" regulatory approaches are needed. It is therefore unsurprising that the academic legal literature suggests that other forms of regulation are evolving to fill this "regulatory gap". In generalist academic legal literature there is an acceptance that so-called soft law[64] has a regulatory role to play and in academic circles there is some discussion of trust based regulation. This accords with the authors' own experience as to how IT is regulated in practice: that there are alternative regulatory models, which we have characterised in this essay as the soft law model and the trust based model.

A "pipes" example of the soft law model would be IT protocols and standards (such as the TCP/IP protocol) and a content example would be the Internet Watch Foundation[65]. One can also see that soft law, combined with contract law, is increasingly used to deal with a range of private law issues over which there is relatively little formal legal regulation; this evolution of the soft law model might be characterised as a "hybrid-soft model" regulatory approach.

Trust based regulation is technically a feature of the decentralised infrastructure of the Web[66] and has traditionally been part of the "science" based ethos of IT. Although trust infuses the "pipes" of the web[67] it is difficult to see a trust ethos being widely used in a commercial environment, but there are some examples of this ranging from Google[68] to eBay[69].

### 2.4.4. Summary

As we have seen, there is a plethora of regulatory actors (law makers, judges, institutions, etc) in IT. It is our submission that there is also a wide choice of regulatory models that

---

64  For example, it has been used in EU law (eg L Senden *Soft Law in European Community Law* (2004)). Soft law can be defined as regulation by non-binding instruments: such instruments might include resolutions, codes of conduct, guidelines and recommendations.

65  The IWF plays an important, but informal, United Kingdom focused co-ordinating role in controlling Internet content that includes child sex abuse, obscene content and content that incites racial hatred. Individuals can notify the IWF of such content *via* the IWF hotline; the IWF subsequently alerts the relevant hosting service providers that criminal content is found on their servers (see http://www.iwf.org.uk/public/page.2.htm).

66  Professor Tim Berners-Lee refers to these as "social mechanisms" (eg see his testimony before the United States House of Representatives' Committee on Energy and Commerce Subcommittee on Telecommunications and the Internet Hearing on the "Digital Future of the United States: Part I – The Future of the World Wide Web". See http://dig.csail.mit.edu/2007/03/01-ushouse-future-of-the-web.html.

67  This is why the Web is, at a technical level, vulnerable to abuses of trust – spam (unsolicited e-mail) is the prime example of such an abuse.

68  Google has an informal corporate motto: "*Don't be evil*" (see http://investor.google.com/conduct.html).

69  Trust metrics are important to eBay users: see, for example, http://pages.ebay.co.uk/services/forum/feedback.html.

have been and are being used in the regulation of IT. The authors consider that this pluralism is a strength, rather than a weakness, of IT law, but concede that it may add credence to the argument that IT law is not law (see sections 2.1 and 2.3 above). Nevertheless, there is the regulatory flexibility to adopt different models for different contexts.

There are two additional factors that, in practice, can be expected to add complexity to this regulatory theory: (1) that the five regulatory models can variously be directed to the "pipes", "content", or a combination of both (to good or ill effect) and, (2) that the regulation of modern IT is a global task, while regulation is primarily at the national level, so this can lead to regulatory competition.

These regulatory insights, together with earlier elements from this essay, will now be brought to bear in a brief consideration of modern examples of "pipes" and "content" legal issues (respectively, sections 3 and 4, below).

## 3. IT INFRASTRUCTURE ("THE PIPES")

### 3.1. *An Exemplar: Software Patents*

As noted earlier in this essay, many key aspects of the "pipes" take the form of software. The purpose of this section is to briefly reflect on the issue of software patents.

First, a brief overview of United Kingdom patent law in this context is needed. Under the Patents Act 1977 ("PA 1977")[70] a patent, a property right, can be granted to inventions that are novel, capable of an inventive step and are industrially applicable. However, s 1(2)(c) provides that "a computer program ... is not an invention as such". United Kingdom patent law is heavily influenced by an EEA system – the European Patent Convention ("EPC") 1973, as interpreted by the European Patent Office[71] ("EPO")[72], and it was the influence of the latter that led United Kingdom courts over the years to make it clear that inventions incorporating software are not necessarily to be regarded as being "computer programs as such" (and thus, excluded from patentability): where a computer program has a *technical effect*, such inventions may be deemed to escape the restriction of s 1(2)(c).

There are a number of issues that arise here. Firstly, the PA 1977 can be categorised as an example of the legal regulatory model. Secondly, the wording of s 1(2)(c) is clearly influenced by the old "hardware/software" distinction: s 1(2)(c) providing that hardware is potentially patentable but software is not an invention "as such". However, latter interpretation of this section (which allows inventions incorporating software to be patentable where there is a technical effect) can be seen as an example of the adaptation of existing law to meet the perceived needs of the software industry[73]. An interesting development in this area is the presence of a collective and individual technological backlash – in the form of the Open Source and Free Software movements[74] – to the patenting of software applications. The result being that for basic personal and office use, there is a choice between patented proprietary software (eg Microsoft) or open source

---

70  Please note, further changes to the PA 1977 are expected: all references to this Act were correct at the time of writing.

71  See http://www.cpo.org/about-us/cpo.html.

72  Although United Kingdom patent jurisprudence has recently diverged from the EPC jurisprudence on computer programs (see the Court of Appeal's decision in *Aerotel Ltd v Telco Holdings Ltd* [2006] EWCA Civ 1371, [2007] 1 All ER 225).

73  Most commentators agree that the EPO's interpretation of the EPC 1973, and the subsequent United Kingdom, adaptation of the technical effect doctrine in relation to the PA 1977, were a result of regulatory competition with the United States (where software patents are more readily available).

74  These are examples of two of the social movements, with their origins in the technology community, which support and foster the development of non-proprietary software. For example, see the GNU Project at http://www.gnu.org/).

applications (eg Linux); thus, the IT community (*not* the legal system) has delivered consumer choice.

As implied above, software patents is an example of an area of law where the old "hardware/software" distinction was applied, but has subsequently broken down. It is interesting to speculate as to what might happen if United Kingdom patent law abandoned this old distinction entirely. Clearly this would necessitate the reference to software in s 1(2)(c) PA 1977 being removed[75] – while the "pipes/content" distinction in United Kingdom patent law might offer a useful alternative basis for lawmaking[76]. Opponents of software patents would clearly like to retain the "hardware/software" distinction, and strengthen the impact of s 1(2)(c), but the authors believe that this academic debate should be more realistic, and that adaptation of the "pipes/content" distinction could lead to better and more creative law making in patent law.

Further development of the "pipes/content" distinction might lead to a more nuanced approach to software patents. Given the existence (and growing success) of Open Source and Free Software, it is the authors' opinion that IT innovation and consumer choice does not appear to have unduly suffered from the patenting of software applications. What *is* of concern to the authors though is the growing trend of commercial entities trying (through patent law and other means) to establish proprietary rights in IT standards. Here, we would argue that the commercial monopolisation of IT standards can only have a detrimental effect on consumer choice and future innovation. Thus, we believe that establishing property rights in high level "pipes" such as IT standards is inappropriate, whereas establishing property rights in low level "pipes", such as software applications, may be less harmful in terms of innovation. Developing the "pipes/content" distinction along these lines[77] within patent law might address these concerns: distinguishing high level "pipes" (which would be excluded from patentability on policy grounds) from low level "pipes". This is an interesting suggestion which requires further research, but the key point here is that current patent law appears ill-equipped to deal with the monopolisation of IT standards, and, at present, it is left to competition law to attempt to regulate this issue.

## 4. IT CONTENT

### 4.1. *Content Generation*

There are a wide range of important legal issues relating to IT content. For example, how should the United Kingdom regulate children's access to dangerous Web content such as audio visual recordings of "tombstoning" stunts[78] and damaging "pro-ana" tips[79] on social networking sites such as *Bebo* and *Facebook*? If a person directs their avatar, their digital embodiment, to engage in undesirable behaviour in a virtual reality world such as *Second*

---

75 It should be noted that, as a signatory of the EPC 1973, the United Kingdom is not currently in a position to unilaterally make such important changes to the PA 1977.

76 It should be noted that United Kingdom patent law already contains restrictions on inventions to be used for certain functions (eg methods used in medical treatment, surgery and diagnosis in PA 1977 s 4) so there are prior examples, for policy reasons, of the use of functional distinctions in determining patentability.

77 The imprecise nature of this high level/low level "pipes" distinction is conceded, but a similarly imprecise distinction – that of macro-biological and micro-biological processes (PA 1977, Sch A2, s 3(f)) is already used in United Kingdom patent law. It should be noted that there may also be consumer and innovation benefits in distinguishing between "high level" and "low level" "content" in copyright law, but further discussion of this is beyond the scope of this essay.

78 Where untrained individuals jump off high vantage points (piers, harbour walls, cliffs etc) into the sea. The (consensual) recordings of such stunts usually include images of the serious injuries or deaths that result.

79 That is, pro-anorexia tips on dieting and the avoidance of medical intervention.

*Life* should this give rise to a criminal prosecution? Although, in these examples, contractual relationships would provide the basis for some content regulation; is it desirable for justice to be privatised in this way? Or, is contract law the best mechanism given the techno-legal obstacles to United Kingdom regulation of any website activity? As a *global* medium, with actors that are often geographically disparate and the servers for the relevant websites often being based outside the United Kingdom, there is only so much that can be achieved by the United Kingdom acting alone. Would Web content best be regulated technically (eg by making ISPs formally liable for Web content that they host)? Would legal regulation be helpful (some sort of international treaty on Web content)? Or some combination of the two? These are questions that require further research.

However, in the absence of international treaties, contract currently provides the most effective way of formally regulating general Internet content; but contract only provides an *indirect* form of content regulation. In section 4.2 below, the main example of *direct* formal regulation of original content, copyright law, is considered in more detail.

### 4.2. *An Exemplar: Copyright and P2P Music Networks*

A relatively recent issue within IT academe is the regulation of so-called peer-to-peer (P2P) computer networks[80] upon which MP3 music files are exchanged. As with any unauthorised use of copyright works, sharing an MP3 file, without the permission of the copyright proprietor(s) *via* an unauthorised peer-to-peer network, clearly constitutes copyright infringement. Although this fact causes some consternation amongst young United Kingdom music fans, this is both clear and appropriate in the eyes of the authors: what *is* of concern to the authors is the *extent* of copyright in this area.

First, a brief summary of the United Kingdom copyright regime is appropriate. Copyright is a property right, governed by the Copyright Designs and Patents Act 1988 ("CDPA 1988"), that subsists in certain categories of works, including: original literary works (most forms of written matter, including song lyrics); musical works (eg song melodies), and, sound recordings[81]. There is significant regional and international regulation of copyright, which has had great influence on the United Kingdom regime, with clear evidence that the international copyright regime has been adapted in the light of the challenges that digital content poses[82]. In the view of the authors, copyright is the *de facto* mechanism whereby the original content of the digital age is directly regulated.

However, academics such as Lessig[83] have pointed out that copyright is conceptually unsuited to regulate digital content. Copyright (*"copyright"*) developed around the concept of *copying* as the cornerstone to copyright infringement. But with digitised copyright material, mere *access* to a work[84] *technically* involves copying and thus, constitutes copyright infringement. It should be noted that the civil and criminal consequences of copyright infringement *per se* are both significant and broad[85]. At a fundamental level, therefore, copyright law is ill-adapted to the digital environment. There are additional complications relating to the regulatory "pipes" that many copyright works flow through. Permission to use copyright works is traditionally garnered from the network of national collecting societies[86] (to whom copyright proprietors traditionally cede the tasks of monitoring use of and collecting revenue from use of their copyright works). But with

---

80  A typical P2P computer network is based on an application which utilises the Internet to allow users to exchange content with each other, either directly or through a mediating server.

81  See CDPA 1988 ss 3, 5A.

82  For example, the WIPO Copyright Treaty (WCT) 1996.

83  First posited in L Lessig *Code and other Laws of Cyberspace* (1999).

84  Which, with non-digital works, typically does not constitute copyright infringement.

85  For example, see CDPA 1988 ss 96(2), 97, 107.

86  For example, the Performing Rights Society in the United Kingdom.

digital content it is technically possible to avoid or supplement this. Technologies for restricting and tracking usage (eg encryption and digital watermarking) and collecting revenue (eg iTunes) collectively are known as digital rights management (DRM). As in most other jurisdictions, controversially both common law[87] and statute[88] now afford direct protection to DRM. Thus, *via* copyright and *sui generis* DRM protection we have what the authors' term a *digital format dichotomy*, ie the same content is treated differently in law depending on whether it is in analogue or digital form.

Returning to our exemplar – let us illustrate the impact of this with two scenarios. Say person A buys a new analogue music record and listens to it both on his own record player and that of a friend (person B). A then lends, on a non-remunerative basis, the record to another friend (person C); none of these activities could constitute infringement under the CDPA 1988. However, undertaking *substantially the same* activities on an online, authorised MP3 music service would give rise to liability and penalties under the CDPA 1988: where A paid to access an MP3 file from such a service (company Z), both downloading and listening to the file is technically copyright infringement (although A's contract with Z would usually allow for this. However, A may only be able to access the music file for a certain period of time or a certain number of times[89]). It would almost certainly constitute copyright infringement[90] for A to listen to the MP3 file on a friend's computer and similarly for A to e-mail or otherwise distribute the MP3 file to C. To extend this scenario, if A became frustrated with the lack of functionality of the music supplied by company Z, "cracked" the DRM technologies applied and posted guidance on how to "crack" Z's DRM technologies on a website, this would give rise to criminal sanctions.

In summary, works in digital format are less functional and subject to more robust copyright regulation than those in analogue form. Whilst this may be justifiable in terms of the interests of the right holder (whose digital content can be more easily exploited without authorisation than equivalent analogue content), and may even have some benefits for the consumer (an authorised MP3 music file may well be cheaper than the equivalent offline version), the authors question whether copyright is an appropriate mechanism for regulating original digital content or whether *sui generis* regulation of original digital content might be the way forward. This is clearly an area that requires further research.

## 5. CONCLUSION

In this essay the authors have critically explored the relationship between technology and law in a way that, they hope, is of interest to the non-IT lawyer and specialist IT lawyer alike. By way of background, the authors have posited that the development of IT and United Kingdom IT law can be divided into five eras (section 2.2). More fundamentally, the necessity for a new paradigm for IT law has been discussed: the old hardware/software

---

87 See *Kabushi Kaisha Sony Computer Entertainment Inc v Edmunds (t/a Channel Technology)* [2002] All ER (D) 170 (Jan). Affording protection, thus, to DRM is a clear example of establishing proprietary rights in "pipes".

88 This *sui generis* protection has been achieved by the introduction in the CDPA 1988 of civil remedies against the act of circumvention as well as the making and dealing in circumvention devices and the provision of circumvention services (CDPA 1988 ss 296(2), 296ZA(3), 296ZD). Criminal sanctions (CDPA 1988 s 296ZB) are only available against the making and dealing in circumvention devices and the provision of circumvention services. This is controversial legally (because CDPA 1988 ss 296, 296ZA have had the effect of making DRM a form of quasi property when applied to copyright works) and in practice (because copy protected material often has reduced functionality, eg some forms of copy protection will prevent CDs from being played on a computer).

89 There are no such contractual restrictions in the analogue scenario, above.

90 Also, DRM would make this technically difficult. Further, circumventing any DRM would also give rise to a separate cause of action in copyright.

distinction is no longer useful from a technological perspective, so why should we expect it to be useful in academic analysis? Further research, including comparative research, will be required to explore how the best regulatory environment for "pipes" and "content" can be secured: as this is where the authors believe the future of IT law lies.

Other contributions of this essay are to be found in the consideration of the academic context of IT law (section 2.1, but also section 2.3). Here the authors suggest that IT law may have come full circle as a legal subject – from an ill-defined emergent topic to a separate legal subject, to now, where there is some evidence of IT issues "filtering back" to traditional legal subjects. The modern academic study of IT law arguably has parallels with that of jurisprudence: perhaps it is evolving into a "meta-subject", one that can provide insight as to how the law/technology relationship should be managed within the context of other traditional legal subjects.

Another contribution of this essay is to be found in the hypothesis that IT law can be characterised as utilising five different, sometimes complementary, regulatory models (section 2.4). Further insights into IT legal regulation are to be found in sections 3 and 4.

The authors believe that these insights may be fundamental in considering how IT law should evolve in the future.

# THE CRIMINAL LIABILITY OF ORGANISATIONS FOR MANSLAUGHTER AND OTHER SERIOUS OFFENCES

## JEREMY HORDER[1]

## 1. INTRODUCTION

The passing of the Corporate Manslaughter and Corporate Homicide Act 2007 in July 2007 ("2007 Act") makes this an appropriate time to reflect not only on the merits and demerits of the Act itself but, more broadly, on the approach that English criminal law should take towards the liability of organisations for serious offences. Does the 2007 Act provide a model that should be followed when making organisations liable for other serious crimes, or is the structure that the 2007 Act provides closely bound up with the special character of the crime in question; manslaughter by gross negligence[2]? I shall argue that there are unusual features of liability for corporate manslaughter that may make it the wrong model to employ in seeking to make organisations (and their officers) liable across a whole range of serious crimes. The offence of corporate manslaughter imposes liability on the organisation directly for the causing of the harm (death) as a principal offender, something made possible at least in part by the special nature of the fault element of manslaughter. With other serious crimes, it may be better in terms of appropriate labelling of an organisation as an offender to look to alternative forms of criminal liability. Two such forms are liability for permitting or tolerating the commission of the relevant offence by an employee, and liability for inadequate supervision or control of an offending employee.

My main concern, however, will be with an analysis of the 2007 Act. My thesis will be that, in the way that it has extended the Law Commission's recommendations for an offence of "corporate" manslaughter to public bodies, the government has given with one hand but then taken away with the other, by granting public bodies exemptions from liability that are unduly generous.

## 2. AN ANALYSIS OF THE NEW OFFENCE OF "CORPORATE" MANSLAUGHTER

### (i) *The residual importance of liability at common law*

The 2007 Act seeks to make a new start by abolishing the common law offence of manslaughter by gross negligence in so far as it applies to corporations and other bodies, such as public bodies, to which the 2007 Act applies (s 20), and by providing that individuals cannot be complicit in an offence of corporate manslaughter (s 18). Accordingly, in a manslaughter case where the prosecution wishes to proceed in essentially the same way against both the organisation itself and its directors individually, the latter will have to be charged separately with gross negligence manslaughter. To what extent will these changes produce a completely clean sheet on which prosecutors can write a new and in particular an *exclusive* story of corporate liability for manslaughter? The 2007 Act still leaves open two important possibilities at common law. First, there is the possibility that corporations (but not Crown bodies, to whom immunity would still apply) could incur

---

1 Law Commission for England and Wales. I am grateful to Ruth Pogonowski and Hafsah Masood for their research assistance in the writing of this essay.
2 The 2007 Act does not use the common law term, "gross negligence" manslaughter, but s 1(1)(b) instead speaks of a "gross breach of a relevant duty of care".

common law liability for "unlawful and dangerous act" manslaughter as principal offenders, or could be complicit in such liability when the principal offender is an employee[3]. Secondly, there is the possibility of individual liability (involving, for example, directors or company employees) for common law manslaughter arising on the same set of facts as corporate manslaughter.

This residual scope for the application of the common law may prove to be not without its significance. Speaking of unlawful and dangerous act manslaughter, Professor Celia Wells has argued plausibly that[4]:

> "Many workplace accidents could be considered as negligent killings in themselves, but there is no reason why they should not also be open to prosecution on the easier to prove unlawful act head."

Professor Wells maintains, in particular, that offences giving rise to danger on the roads ought to be regarded as a perfectly appropriate basis for unlawful act manslaughter when they lead to the causing of death, notwithstanding any views suggesting the contrary in the House of Lords decision in *Andrews v DPP*[5]. The special significance of this (as we will see below) is that the courts have shown themselves willing to hold companies liable as complicit parties in road traffic-related offences committed by their employees, on the basis of a culpable failure to take steps to prevent those offences being committed[6]. It is already the case that the courts have been willing to find a company complicit in an offence committed by an employee of causing death by dangerous driving, on the basis that the company counselled or procured the offence[7]. That offence (like other offences based on the causing of death on the roads[8]) is, of course, separate from – even though it may overlap with – gross negligence manslaughter, and is hence unaffected by the exclusion under the 2007 Act of companies from liability for gross negligence manslaughter. The inevitable implication is that such a basis for complicity may be relied on when an individual employee is charged with manslaughter by means of an unlawful and dangerous act, whether the unlawful and dangerous act takes place on the roads or in some other context.

That brings me directly to consideration of corporate complicity in individual instances of manslaughter by unlawful and dangerous act. Although the common law is not highly developed, as I have just indicated, liability – through the doctrine of complicity – can be imposed on a company if it fails to take steps to prevent offending by its employees. Such liability is based on the company's failure to exercise the entitlement that it has to control the actions of individual employees[9]. It seems that the courts may be willing to extend this application of the doctrine of complicity. A recent example concerns the failure of a manager to take steps to prevent one employee racially harassing another employee[10]. So it would, perhaps, not be such a large step to find a private company liable on this basis when,

---

3   There is a good discussion of the latter in James Gobert and Maurice Punch, *Rethinking Corporate Crime* (2003) pp 70–75.
4   Celia Wells, *Corporations and Criminal Responsibility* (2nd ed, 2001) p 120.
5   [1937] AC 576, [1937] 2 All ER 552.
6   *R v JF Alford Transport Ltd* [1999] RTR 51, [1997] 2 Cr App Rep 326. The offence in issue in this case was falsifying a tachograph record, and the question was whether the company could be complicit in the offence through a failure to take steps to prevent its employees committing it. For a list of ways in which a company might be found complicit in offending by another person, see Gobert and Punch, see note 3 above, p 72.
7   *R v Robert Millar (Contractors) Ltd; R v Millar* [1970] 2 QB 54, [1970] 1 All ER 577.
8   See the Road Safety Act 2006.
9   The well-known example is that of *R v JF Alford Transport Ltd*, see note 6 above, (although the conviction in this particular case was quashed because of a misdirection to the jury).
10  *R v Gaunt* [2003] EWCA Crim 3925, [2004] Cr App Rep (S) 37.

for example, it has failed to prevent the systematic physical mistreatment by employees of children, patients or prisoners in the company's care, and that mistreatment has caused death or led to the suicide of such an individual and hence to a conviction for manslaughter of the employee or employees responsible for the mistreatment[11]. It must be kept in mind, though, that the fault element for complicity in another's offence is not easy to satisfy. It would have to be shown that, at some time prior to the commission of the offence, a director knew or believed that the failure to control the actions of an employee or employees would (not merely might) assist or encourage the offending in question[12].

In these kinds of circumstances, could a company be found complicit in manslaughter by *gross negligence* committed by an individual employee? At first blush, this seems unlikely. Section 20 states:

> "The common law of manslaughter by gross negligence is abolished in its application to corporations, and in any application it has to other organisations to which section 1 applies."

Clearly, the intention is that an organisation's involvement in killing through carelessness should be dealt with through the new offence, and the language is unequivocal so far as liability for offending as a principal is concerned. However, s 20 does not explicitly rule out the possibility of an organisation's complicity in gross negligence manslaughter by an individual, even though the principles of complicity are explicitly addressed in a different context in the 2007 Act[13]. On balance, however, it seems probable that such liability is no longer a legal possibility.

The significance of this residual role for the common law may not be all that great, although the ability at common law – but not under the 2007 Act – to find individuals complicit in offences committed by corporations (and vice versa) may be important in some contexts. There may also turn out eventually to be significance in how Parliament develops the courts' general sentencing principles, principles that can be applied to corporations. Under the 2007 Act, a conviction for corporate manslaughter can be followed only by a fine (s 1(6)), although it will also be possible for the court to order that the organisation in question remedies the breach (s 9) – an order that that may include a ruling that the company make good deficiencies in provision for health and safety – and to order that the organisation publicise the fact that it has been convicted, with details of the offence and the punishment and remedial action imposed (s 10). By way of contrast, the punishment for manslaughter by unlawful and dangerous act remains entirely discretionary, although in practice the courts have confined themselves to fining corporate defendants. However, by way of contrast with the position under the 2007 Act, the courts have in theory a freedom to employ sanctions against those convicted of common law manslaughter as wide as is given to them by legislation affecting their general sentencing powers, and only limited either by law or by the nature of corporations as defendants (who cannot, obviously, go to prison)[14]. In so far, then, as Parliament sees fit to broaden the courts' general sentencing

---

11 On the possibility of conviction for manslaughter when mistreatment leads to suicide, see Jeremy Horder and Laura McGowan, "Manslaughter by Causing Another's Suicide" [2006] Crim LR 1035. The 2007 Act explicitly countenances the possibility of liability for corporate manslaughter respecting a victim who was in custody or care at the time of their death: see s 2. See the discussion in Pt 2(v) below.

12 *National Coal Board v Gamble* [1959] 1 QB 11, [1958] 3 All ER 203. The current archaic language of the Accessories and Abettors Act 1861 speaks of aiding, abetting, counselling or procuring, rather than of assisting and encouraging.

13 See 2007 Act s 18.

14 See M Jefferson, "Corporate Criminal Liability: The Problems of Sanctions" (2001) 65 J Crim L 235.

powers, their powers to deal with corporate defendants other than those convicted under the 2007 Act may well also be broadened.

### (ii) The fault element in the 2007 Act: wide or narrow?

Putting these issues on one side, what is the nature of the new scheme that will now govern the relevant corporate and public bodies? Under s 1, such a body will be liable for corporate manslaughter ("corporate homicide" in Scotland) if, "the way in which its activities are managed or organised":

> (a) causes a person's death, and
> (b) amounts to a gross breach of a relevant duty of care owed by the organisation to the deceased.

In that respect, the way in which an organisation's activities are managed or organised by its "senior management" must be a "substantial element" in the breach of the duty of care (s 1(3)), on which more will be said below[15]. "Senior management" is defined, in relation to an organisation, by s 1(4)(c) in terms of persons who play, "significant roles in – (i) the making of decisions about how the whole or a substantial part of its activities are to be managed or organised, or (ii) the actual managing or organising of the whole or a substantial part of those activities."

The 2007 Act thus takes a significant step beyond the limitations of corporate liability at common law. At common law, a company could only be found liable for an offence (such as manslaughter) with a fault element if that fault element was possessed by someone, such as a director or chief executive, who could be identified with the company itself (the "identification doctrine"). In *Lennard's Carrying Co Ltd v Asiatic Petroleum Co Ltd*[16], Lord Haldane said[17]:

> "Mr Lennard was the directing mind of the company ... his action was the action of the company itself ... [his] fault is not merely that of a servant or agent for whom the company is liable upon the footing *respondeat superior* but somebody for whom the company is liable because his action is the very action of the company itself."

In searching for criminal fault, the "simplistic"[18] identification doctrine treats companies as if they were individuals, confining liability to instances in which someone who can be said to be "the company itself" had the fault necessary for the commission of the offence[19]. That has always been a major limitation on liability, for the simple reason that it fails to take account of the degree to which in medium to large-sized companies crucial, strategic decisions are frequently delegated to lower levels of management than those granted plenary authority over the company's affairs in the company's articles of association[20]. It is true that the vast majority of British firms are very small, and are hence

---

15  This is perhaps unlikely to prove to be a very significant restriction on the scope of liability, as the courts do not interpret the term "substantial" to mean "main" or "major". They understand it to mean simply "not insignificant" or "not wholly trivial": see *R v Cato* [1976] 1 All ER 260 at 265–266. For the Law Commission recommendations on which this section is based, see Law Commission, *Legislating the Criminal Code: Involuntary Manslaughter* (Law Com no 237) (1996).

16  [1915] AC 705, [1914–1915] All ER Rep 280.

17  [1915] AC 705 at 713, [1914–1915] All ER Rep 280 at 283.

18  See A P Simester and G R Sullivan, *Criminal Law: Theory and Doctrine* (2nd ed, 2003), p 254.

19  See Wells, see note 4 above, p 85.

20  For explicit limitation of corporate liability in cases involving fault to this, highest level of management, see the speech of Lord Diplock in *Tesco Supermarkets Ltd v Nattrass* [1972] AC 153 at 199, [1971] 2 All ER 127 at 155.

unlikely to have many – if any – layers of management[21]. Nonetheless, it is unacceptable that a company should be able to escape liability for serious crime, even when the fault element for the crime was possessed by someone with authority to take strategic decisions, simply because that person was not a director or chief executive. As Simester and Sullivan rightly point out[22], the narrowness of this approach is illustrated by the case of *R v Redfern and Dunlop Ltd (Aircraft Tyres Divisions)*[23]. In this case, the knowledge of no less a person than the European sales manager was considered insufficient to fix a company with liability when charged with knowingly exporting combat equipment to Iran. Similarly, in *R v P&O Ferries (Dover) Ltd*[24], the company escaped liability for manslaughter following the Zeebrugge ferry disaster in which 192 people were drowned, in part because the ship's master was not someone who could be identified with "the company itself". In consequence, the only successful prosecutions for manslaughter against companies have involved very small companies where the directors are necessarily themselves involved in day-to-day management and decision making[25].

In some jurisdictions, the net of liability is also cast more widely by statute than by the common law but in a different way. For example, under s 12.3(1) of the Australian Model Criminal Code[26], the fault element of an offence can be attributed to a corporation if it expressly, tacitly or impliedly authorised or permitted the offence to take place. Section 12.3(2) sets out four means by which such authorisation or permission may be proved:

"(a) proving that the body corporate's board of directors intentionally, knowingly or recklessly carried out the relevant conduct, or expressly, tacitly or impliedly authorised or permitted the commission of the offence; or

(b) proving that a high managerial agent of the body corporate intentionally, knowingly or recklessly engaged in the relevant conduct, or expressly, tacitly or impliedly authorised or permitted the commission of the offence; or

(c) proving that a corporate culture existed within the body corporate that directed, encouraged, tolerated or led to non-compliance with the relevant provision; or

(d) proving that the body corporate failed to create and maintain a corporate culture that required compliance with the relevant provision."

The Tasmanian Law Reform Institute has recently recommended adoption of these provisions as a basis for corporate criminal liability in general, with the exception of (d) as a basis for liability. It regarded (d) as going too far in that, while undoubtedly a species of corporate fault, it is a negligence-based form of liability and hence an unsound basis on which to attribute to the company an offence involving intention, knowledge or recklessness[27]. Would provisions (a) to (c) have been a better model for corporate manslaughter and corporate liability in the United Kingdom more generally?

---

21 See Wells, see note 4 above, p 151.
22 Simester and Sullivan, see note 18 above, p 255.
23 (1992) 13 Cr App Rep (S) 709, [1993] Crim LR 43.
24 (1991) 93 Cr App Rep 72.
25 See eg *Kite and OLL Ltd* (1994) The Independent, 8 December.
26 Drafted by the Model Criminal Code Officers' Committee, *General Principles of Criminal Responsibility*, Report (1992) ch 2, p 109.
27 See E Colvin, "Corporate Responsibility and Criminal Liability" (1995) 6 Criminal Law Forum 1 at pp 2–3, 37, "[it is] questionable ... whether it is an appropriate ground on which to hold a corporation responsible for the intentional, knowing, or reckless commission of an offence".

It seems obvious that if fault can be attributed to a "senior manager" (2007 Act), or to a "high managerial agent" (Australian Model Criminal Code), then a case against a corporation involving proof of fault against a European sales manager[28], or the like, is likely to be soundly based under the reformed law even though it is not under current English law. Furthermore, in its concentration on "the way in which [the organisation's] activities are managed or organised", s 1 of the 2007 Act goes beyond simply fixing an organisation with liability by taking account of the individual culpability of a wider range of individuals within the organisation (under s 1(3), senior managers) than is possible at common law. As is the case with the "corporate culture" test under the Australian Model Criminal Code, the 2007 Act makes it possible to convict an organisation on the basis of, "aggregated or collective failings"[29], that (in the case of the 2007 Act) must include but are not restricted to failings on the part of senior managers. How much wider in this particular respect, if at all, is the "corporate culture" test of liability? A test case for any differences between the 2007 Act and the Model Criminal Code might be *R v P&O Ferries (Dover) Ltd*[30].

In this case, the company's ferry overturned having left Zeebrugge harbour with its bow doors open, leading to a large number of deaths. P&O and seven individuals (two of whom were sufficiently senior to be "identified" with the company itself) were prosecuted for manslaughter. As indicated above, the trial judge (Turner J) directed that the defendants be acquitted. Most pertinently, for present purposes, the judge was not prepared to aggregate the fault of the defendants collectively so that a "global" judgment that there had been a reckless disregard for safety could be found[31]. In the circumstances, that was fatal to the prosecution's case. Moreover, evidence that the assistant bosun responsible for shutting the bow doors had fallen asleep, that the chief officer whose responsibility it was to ensure that the bow doors were shut had failed to do so, and that there was no means by which the captain could confirm from the bridge that the bow doors were shut, did not assist the prosecution's case against the company. For, this evidence did not show that the company itself, as opposed to these individuals, had behaved with reckless disregard for safety.

Would that all still be true under the 2007 Act? Arguably not. At best, of course, the individuals just mentioned would be regarded as no more than junior – rather than senior – managers, since they do not really have, to use the words of the 2007 Act, "significant roles in – (i) the making of decisions about how the whole or a substantial part of [the company's] activities are to be managed or organised, or (ii) the actual managing or organising of the whole or a substantial part of those activities" (s 1(4)). However, it must be kept in mind that whilst any case of corporate manslaughter must rest, as a necessary condition of success, on proof of a gross breach of a duty of care on the part of senior managers, under s 1(3) the prosecution's case need only be that management failure was a "substantial" element in the breach[32]. The prosecution would also be able to rely on the conduct of others involved in management or organisation at lower levels (like the ship's chief officer and captain) to construct its case that the way in which the organisation was organised or managed as *a whole* caused death through a gross breach of a duty of care.

---

28  See *R v Redfern and Dunlop Ltd (Aircraft Tyres Divisions)*, see note 23 above.

29  Gobert and Punch, see note 3 above, p 105.

30  See note 24 above. An extensive discussion of the case can be found in Wells, see note 3 above, pp 107–111.

31  At that time, the fault element for manslaughter was considered to be recklessness; it is now gross negligence.

32  See note 15 above.

So, had P&O been prosecuted under the 2007 Act, it is likely that the case would have succeeded. The Sheen Enquiry into the Zeebrugge ferry disaster had concluded that, "from top to bottom the body corporate was infected with the disease of sloppiness"[33], and added that[34]:

> "a full investigation into the circumstances of the disaster leads inexorably to the conclusion that the underlying or cardinal faults lay higher up in the company. All concerned in management, from the members of the Board of Directors down to the junior superintendents, were guilty of fault in that all must be regarded as sharing responsibility for the failure of management."

That being so, it would have been easier to convict the company under the 2007 Act because, as I have already said, the Act permits evidence of fault to be aggregated to the extent that under s 1 the jury is entitled to consider in a holistic manner, "the way in which [the company's] activities are managed or organized", so long as in that regard the role of senior management was a substantial contributing factor to a gross breach of a duty of care.

The difference under the Australian Model Criminal Code would be the relevance of head (c) above[35], that has no precise equivalent under the 2007 Act; in other words, the possibility of proving guilt through a finding that, "a corporate culture existed within the body corporate that directed, encouraged, tolerated or led to non-compliance with the relevant provision". What, if anything, does this add? According to the Model Criminal Code Officers' Committee, one function of the "corporate culture" basis for attributing fault to a company is to catch the unwritten rules by which a company operates. It is meant to permit the prosecution[36]:

> "to lead evidence that the company's unwritten rules tacitly authorised non-compliance or failed to create a culture of compliance. It would catch situations where, despite formal documents appearing to require compliance, the reality was that non-compliance was expected. For example, employees who know that if they do not break the law to meet production schedules (eg by removing safety guards on equipment) they will be dismissed. The company would be guilty of intentionally breaching safety legislation."

So understood, the "corporate culture" basis for convicting organisations does not add significantly to the 2007 Act, because breaches of a duty of care by senior managers themselves – here, through the expectation that employees would ignore safety procedures – play a role in causing the offence to be committed. However, under s 12.3(6) the Model Criminal Code defines a corporate culture as, "an attitude, policy, rule, course of conduct or practice existing within the body corporate generally *or in the part of the body corporate in which the relevant activities take place*" (my emphasis). This seems to imply that the prosecution would have been able to rely on proof of a "culture of sloppiness" on the Herald of Free Enterprise *alone*, as a basis for their case against P&O, if the ship and its crew could be regarded as the "part of the body corporate in which the relevant activities [took] place". The prosecution would then have needed to look no further than evidence of the culture of neglect amongst those on board responsible for the ship's safety – such as

---

33  Sheen, *MV Herald of Free Enterprise Report of the Court No 8074*, Department of Transport (1987), para 14.1, cited by Wells, see note 4 above, p 109.

34  *Ibid.*

35  See text following note 26 above.

36  Model Criminal Code Officers' Committee, see note 26 above, pp 111–113; See also P Bucy, "Corporate Ethos: A Standard for Imposing Corporate Criminal Liability" (1991) 75 Minn Law Review 1095 at pp 1128–1146.

the bosun, the chief officer and the captain – whatever might have been going on in terms of (perhaps harder to prove) management practices higher up in the corporate chain of command[37].

Having said that, it is not necessarily a criticism of the 2007 Act that it failed to extend the bases for establishing corporate liability to include proof of a "corporate culture" of neglect or indifference, whether in the organisation as a whole or in some part of it. Although such a thing undoubtedly exists, there is an inherent vagueness in the notion of "corporate culture" – something that can apparently be found in any one or more of "an attitude, policy, rule, course of conduct or practice" – that makes it of doubtful value in the context of criminal liability. Further, in so far as "corporate culture" can be proved in law if it existed only in the part of the body corporate where the relevant activities took place, even if it was condemned by or completely unknown to the Board of Directors and senior managers, then (in the absence of a due diligence defence for the company) the doctrine in effect makes the company vicariously liable for the acts of those further down the chain of command who sustained the culture and hence committed the offence[38]. Whilst vicarious liability for fault-based offences is possible in some jurisdictions[39], and has gained a foothold in England and Wales[40], it is unlikely to be the approach taken across the board in the United Kingdom[41]. Having said that, we will see that the notion of "corporate culture" can play an important evidential role in supporting both the view that an organisation tolerated the commission of criminal offences by its employees, and the view that senior managers individually consented to or connived at such criminal activity. Moreover, in that regard, s 8(3) of the 2007 Act makes what looks very like "corporate culture" a factor that may be taken into account in deciding whether there was a "gross" breach of a duty of care. To that end, s 8 requires the jury to consider whether and to what extent the organisation failed to comply with health and safety legislation, and adds:

"The jury may also –

(a) consider the extent to which the evidence shows that there were attitudes, policies, systems or accepted practices within the organisation that were likely to have encouraged any such failure ... or to have produced tolerance of it ... "

The law thus makes proof of a corporate culture of neglect a possible building block in establishing a case that the required fault element has been made out, rather than turning proof of it into a necessary part of such a case, or even making proof of it *ipso facto* sufficient to establish such a case. With such an ambiguous notion as "corporate culture", that may be the best approach.

---

37  See further the Australian Model Criminal Code s 12.3(4).

38  Under s 12(4) of the Australian Model Criminal Code, if an employee reasonably believed that a high managerial agent would have authorised or permitted the commission of the offence, that is a factor relevant to whether there was a "corporate culture" in which the commission of such offences was tolerated; but this factor is not decisive.

39  See the discussion of United States law in Wells, see note 4 above, pp 132–136.

40  See the discussion in Simester and Sullivan, see note 18 above, p 256; Andrew Ashworth, *Principles of Criminal Law* (5th edn, 2006) p 116.

41  There is, of course, less of an objection to vicarious liability if senior managers of the organisations have a "due diligence" defence. For further reflections on this, and discussion of a more sophisticated version of the "corporate culture" theory, in terms of whether an organisation's, "system, its operating policies, displayed a reckless attitude to safety", see Wells, see note 4 above, p 158.

(iii) *The reach of the duty of care under the 2007 Act; public and private organisations*

The offence of "corporate" manslaughter applies not only to private companies – the traditional focus of scholars who have argued for the imposition of liability on organisations – but also to a large range of public bodies (including the police) for the most part set out in Sch 1 of the 2007 Act[42]. It is worth noting that under Sch 1 the new offence will apply to the Ministry of Defence, to the Department of Health and (eventually) to HM Prison Service[43]. The 2007 Act will hence in the end apply in some measure to all the public bodies the performance of whose functions are most likely to involve causing deaths, whether these occur (for example) in custody or in hospital. Having said that, as we will see, the 2007 Act (arguably, wrongly) restricts in important ways the range of activities engaged in by public bodies in respect of which a duty of care and hence liability can be imposed. The Act includes these exemptions for public bodies even though the government itself indicated that the Health and Safety Executive has censured a Crown Body only four times in the last six years in relation to the causing of a death[44].

The 2007 Act certainly spreads the liability "net" wider than some jurisdictions have thought appropriate. For example, in the Australian Capital Territory (ACT), the relatively new crime of "industrial manslaughter" can only be committed by an employer against a worker, in the course of their employment[45]. It would not apply to a case in which, for example, a member of the public was killed by a workplace explosion, or by a company's defective products or dangerous services[46]. By way of contrast, by virtue of s 2, the 2007 Act is of wider application. Section 2(1) sets out the scope of the duty of care not to cause deaths imposed on organisations to which the 2007 Act applies:

"(1) A 'relevant duty of care', in relation to an organisation, means ...

(a) a duty owed to its employees or to other persons working for the organisation ...

(b) a duty owed as occupier of premises;

(c) a duty owed in connection with –

(i) the supply by the organisation of goods or services (whether for consideration or not),

(ii) the carrying on by the organisation of any construction or maintenance operations,

(iii) the carrying on by the organisation of any other activity on a commercial basis, or

(iv) the use or keeping by the organisation of any plant, vehicle or other thing;

(d) a duty owed to a person who, by reason of being a person within subsection (2) [a detained person], is someone for whose safety the organisation is responsible."

---

42 The fact that the public bodies are set out in the schedule means that they may be added to or subtracted from relatively easily by the Secretary of State for Justice, who thus retains bureaucratic control over who can be an offender.

43 See the statement of the Secretary of State for Justice, at 463 HC Official Report (6th series) col 331.

44 Home Office, *Corporate Manslaughter and Corporate Homicide: A Regulatory Impact Assessment of the Government's Bill* (2006).

45 Crimes Act 1900 (ACT) s 49A, inserted by the Crimes (Industrial Manslaughter) Amendment Act 2003.

46 See the discussion in Tasmanian Law Reform Institute, *Criminal Liability of Organisations*, Final Report No 9 (2007) para 6.3.5.

It is clear from this wording that the scope of the duty is very considerably wider than that imposed under the legislation in the ACT, mentioned above. Third parties, such as those occupying neighbouring properties and consumers of public services, including health care services, may fall within the scope of the duty not to cause death (respectively, under s 2(1)(b) and under s 2(1)(c)(i)) just as easily as employees (under s 2(1)(a). In that regard, whether there was a duty on a particular organisation not to cause the death of a particular individual will be a question of law for the judge and not a jury question[47]. As well as making it possible to maintain consistency between the civil and the criminal law on this point, this precautionary measure will prevent a jury working backwards from the mere fact that death has been caused by the (in)action of an organisation to the conclusion that there must have been a duty not to cause it. By way of contrast, the question whether there was a "gross" breach is one for the jury. The jury must decide, "if the conduct alleged to amount to a breach of that duty falls far below what can reasonably be expected of the organisation in the circumstances" (s 2(4)(b)). In that respect, a good deal of scholarly attention has been focused on how extensive the notion of "in the circumstances" is meant to be. The Law Commission, in suggesting the phraseology, said that it would encompass[48]:

> "such matters as the likelihood and possible extent of the harm arising from the way in which the company conducted its operations [as compared with] the social utility of its activities and the cost and practicability of taking steps to eliminate or reduce the risk of death ..."

The courts have been resistant to the idea that unprofitability is a "cost" factor that can legitimately entitle a private company to cut corners on health and safety[49]. By way of contrast, government departments are likely to benefit (a) from the fact that what they can spend overall is ultimately determined centrally, and (b) from the fact that they will almost always be able to play the "social utility" card in a broader range of circumstances than private firms.

Nonetheless, the 2007 Act's starting point is that whether an organisation is providing a public service free or for a charge, or is a private company devoted to profit-maximisation, that organisation may find itself liable for homicide if it has caused death because it wrongly allowed its premises, plant, or vehicles (or the like), or the working conditions that it sustained, or the way that it provided its services, to become highly dangerous for employees or others who came into contact with, or used them[50]. Section 2(1) makes this the starting point in a way that has not been common in scholarly literature on the liability of organisations. Such literature has tended to focus almost exclusively on the way that the profit motive of private companies may lead to the maintenance of unsafe practices or premises. It is true, of course, that corporate law makes it possible for a company to sub-divide its operations in ways that make fault-based liability potentially harder to establish than would be the case with a public body (although the

---

47 2007 Act s 2(5). The offence of corporate manslaughter is triable on indictment only. Under s 2(5) the judge is also entitled to make any findings of fact necessary to come to a decision on the duty question.

48 Law Commission, see note 15 above, at para 8.6.

49 See *R v F Howe & Son (Engineers) Ltd* [1999] 2 All ER 249, and the good discussion of this issue in Gobert and Punch, see note 3 above, pp 105–107.

50 2007 Act s 2(6) specifically disapplies certain common law restrictions on liability: "For the purposes of this Act there is to be disregarded – (a) any rule of common law that has the effect of preventing a duty of care from being owed by one person to another by reason of the fact that they are jointly engaged in unlawful conduct; (b) any such rule that has the effect of preventing a duty of care from being owed to a person by reason of his acceptance of a risk of harm."

ability of a public body to contract out services narrows this difference)[51]. However, the dangerous perpetuation of negligence, idleness, indifference, inefficiency and unnecessary cost-cutting is not the preserve of private companies. It involves an all-too human set of institutional failings, a collective culture of neglect, that may well be found at work in government departments, hospitals, schools, and prisons not motivated by profit. As it was put in debate on the Bill in the House of Lords[52]:

> "[T]here is no reason why the death of an individual in one situation should be considered less of a death, or less deserving of justice, merely because that situation was presided over by government officials as opposed to privately employed foremen. Indeed, it is all the more of a tragedy and contravention of the natural principle of justice where the state itself acts with such gross negligence that the very lives of its own citizens are forfeit."

Having said that, as indicated earlier, there is an extensive set of circumstances in which public organisations, but not private ones, are exempted from a duty of care under the 2007 Act. Particularly common is an exemption bearing on any function public bodies have relating to the all-important s 2(1)(c) above, namely the supply of goods and services, construction and maintenance, commercial activities and the use or keeping of vehicles or plant etc. A cynic might say that the 2007 Act in fact does little more than the ACT legislation, mentioned above. It may be said that whilst the 2007 Act goes somewhat beyond the ACT's extension of liability to cover the deaths of employees (s 2(1)(a)), in that under the 2007 Act liability can also be extended to deaths arising from occupation of premises (s 2(1)(b)), the 2007 Act does not go much further so far as most of the public sector is concerned (and sometimes not even as far as that[53]). The government itself has said that it expects no more than a single prosecution against a public body annually[54]. The cynical view need only to some degree be tempered by the acknowledging that, at the House of Lords' insistence, there are now relatively extensive duties that will be owed to prisoners and detained patients under s 2(1)(d) and s 2(2), duties which cannot be reduced to duties owed by the relevant public organisation in its role as a simple occupier of premises where such people reside.

### (iv) *Are the exclusions under the 2007 Act too wide? Decisions based on "public policy"*

The cynic can point to the fact that although the extension of criminal liability to the public sector is the 2007 Act's starting-point, the exclusions of liability from which the public sector benefits are very broad. In that regard, it is appropriate to begin with an examination of s 3(1). This section excludes from the scope of the Act's duty of care not to cause death, "any duty of care owed by a public authority in respect of a decision as to matters of public policy (including in particular the allocation of public resources or the weighing of competing public interests)". The exclusion was justified by the government on the basis that decisions involving matters of public policy are subject to other kinds of accountability, such as public inquiries or reports. However, that argument was insufficient to persuade the House of Lords that an exemption should be held out to prison

---

51  See, for example, Wells, see note 4 above, at 125–126, "If there is one lesson from the P&O and other corporate killing sagas, it is that corporate defendants are highly motivated and well-placed to exploit the metaphysical gap between "the company' and its members". See also Gobert and Punch, see note 3 above, p 107.
52  688 HL Official Report (5th series) col GC189.
53  See s 3, which gives a blanket exemption in respect of deaths stemming from decisions by a public authority based on public policy considerations, and s 4 giving a blanket exemption for deaths arising from hazardous military activities of an operational or training nature.
54  Home Office, see note 44 above.

organisations respecting deaths in custody[55]. Moreover, the government itself has the power to resist calls for a public inquiry or a report, reducing the significance of that route as a means of ensuring that there are independent forms of accountability.

The exclusion brings into play the well-known distinction between "operational" and "public policy" matters, a distinction employed by the courts to assist in drawing the boundaries of the duty of care for the purposes of adjudicating civil claims against public authorities in the tort of negligence[56]. In *X v Bedfordshire CC*[57], Lord Browne-Wilkinson said that, "a common law duty of care in relation to the taking of decisions involving policy matters cannot exist"[58], and added[59]:

> "[the factors public authorities take into account when making decisions] will often include policy matters, for example social policy, the allocation of finite financial resources between the different calls made upon them or ... the balance between pursuing desirable social aims as against the risk to the public inherent in so doing. It is established that the courts cannot enter upon the assessment of such 'policy' matters."

In that regard, Lord Browne-Wilkinson drew a distinction between, on the one hand, (a) the manner in which a public authority exercises a statutory discretion and, on the other hand, (b) the way in which its duty has been implemented in practice. He thought that, for example, the exercise of a discretion to close a school would be an illustration of the former (policy factor), whereas the actual running of the school in accordance with statutory duty would be an illustration of the latter (operational factor). So, decisions taken falling within (b) would attract a duty of care at common law, whereas decisions taken falling within (a) would not[60].

What might be examples of how the distinction will work in the present context? Arguably, deaths attributable to a Health Trust's decision to economise by reducing certain kinds of expensive medical services could not lead to a prosecution for corporate manslaughter, no matter how poor the management thinking behind the decision. By way of contrast, a cross decision in furtherance of such a policy to change a series of individual patients' medication to something cheaper but entirely unsuitable, that then caused those patients' deaths, might fall outside the scope of the exemption in s 3(1). In like manner, a decision not to use limited resources to build more prison accommodation, with the result that prisoners must share cells because there is no other way of accommodating rising numbers, could not, in and of itself, give rise to liability for (say) a consequent suicide, even if that decision reflected glaring failures of strategic planning. On the other hand, management bungling that led to a decision to make two particular prisoners share a cell, with the entirely foreseeable result that one killed the other would – it is submitted – be a course of conduct falling outside the scope of the exemption in s 3(1) and would hence be covered by s 2(1)(d)[61].

It is, perhaps, ironic that the 2007 Act relies on the "public policy" nature of a decision as a basis for excluding the duty of care, because in recent years the courts have moved away from such a simplistic "all-or-nothing" test in determining whether a common law

---

55  See the discussion at the text to notes 61 and 77 below.
56  See *Anns v Merton LBC* [1978] AC 728, [1977] 2 All ER 492, HL.
57  [1995] 2 AC 633, [1995] 3 All ER 353, HL.
58  [1995] 2 AC 633 at 738, [1995] 3 All ER 353 at 356.
59  [1995] 2 AC 633 at 737, [1995] 3 All ER 353 at 370.
60  The 2007 Act specifically excludes from the scope of the duty of care the kind of decisions at issue in *Anns* (see note 55 above), namely inspections carried out as a matter of public duty: see s 3(3).
61  See, further, the discussion of the Zahid Mubarek case in the text preceding note 83 below.

duty of care exists for the purposes of the law of negligence[62]. For example, in *Barrett v Enfield LBC*[63], Lord Slynn of Hadley held that[64]:

> "Policy and operational acts are closely linked and the decision to do an operational act may easily involve and flow from a policy decision. Conversely, the policy is affected by the result of the operational act."

To similar effect, in *Phelps v Hillingdon LBC*[65], Lord Clyde held that[66]:

> "A distinction may be suggested between on the one hand matters of policy or discretion and on the other hand matters of an operational or administrative character. *But this kind of classification does not appear to provide any absolute test for determining whether the case is one which allows or excludes a duty of care.* The classification may provide some guide towards identifying some kinds of case where a duty of care may be thought to be inappropriate."

The key question may, then, turn out to be whether the courts will hold that s 3(1) excludes a duty of care, for the purposes of the 2007 Act, when there was *any* policy dimension to the decision(s) allegedly taken through – in effect – gross negligence and contravening s 1(1). For it may be open to the courts, as a matter of interpretation, to hold that s 3(1) only shields a public organisation from the scope of the duty of care under the 2007 Act if the decision was *predominantly* one based on public policy considerations. This would accord with Lord Wilberforce's view in *Anns v Merton LBC*[67] that, "the more 'operational' a power or duty may be, the easier it is to superimpose on it a common law duty of care"[68].

Should the courts take the wider or the narrower view of the scope of the exemption? An argument in favour of the wider view of its scope may come from paying closer attention to the "public" nature of the public policy basis for a decision that will take it outside the scope of the duty of care for the purposes of the 2007 Act. When the courts have described the distinction between policy and operational matters, it has sometimes been in terms of whether or not the authority had a "discretion" or choice between courses of action (policy) or was simply implementing a policy previously decided on (operational)[69]; but there is more than one way to understand "discretion", for the purposes of drawing the distinction. As Aronson and Whitmore put it, the notion of "discretion" in this context[70]:

> "may indicate that the official has a power to choose between two or more alternatives ... Alternatively, it may be used to indicate that an expert's or professional's sense of judgment is called for ... Or it may be used to indicate the power given to an official to formulate policy, to balance competing public interests by criteria which a court is not equipped to evaluate in terms of 'reasonableness.'"

---

62 There is a good discussion in Booth and Squires, *The Negligence Liability of Public Authorities* (2006) paras 2.29–2.54.
63 [2001] 2 AC 550, [1999] 3 All ER 193, HL.
64 [2001] 2 AC 550 at 557, [1999] 3 All ER 193 at 211.
65 [2001] 2 AC 619, [2000] 4 All ER 504, HL.
66 [2001] 2 AC 619 at 673, 674, [2000] 4 All ER 504 at 536 (my emphasis).
67 [1978] AC 728, [1977] 2 All ER 492, HL.
68 [1978] AC 728 at 754, [1977] 2 All ER 492 at 499.
69 See eg *X v Bedfordshire CC* [1995] 2 AC 633 at 735, [1995] 3 All ER 353 at 383–384 per Lord Browne-Wilkinson.
70 Aronson and Whitmore, *Public Torts and Contracts* (1982) p 69.

Aronson and Whitmore suggest that only the third kind of discretion is a kind that the courts should regard as outside the scope of any common law duty of care, and there is support for that interpretation in the case law[71]. On that view, perhaps, whenever a decision is based – even in part – on the exercise of discretion in this third sense, it is outside the scope of the duty of care for the purposes of the 2007 Act.

On the other hand, in favour of the narrower view of the scope of the exemption, it must be kept in mind that s 17 of the 2007 Act requires the consent of the Director of Public Prosecutions ("DPP") to any prosecution for corporate manslaughter, a means of "sifting" out and halting claims of liability that are not in the public interest, that has no equivalent in private law. As the Tasmanian Law Reform Institute[72] pointed out, the DPP may, for example, refuse consent to a prosecution if some other more satisfactory means (in the particular circumstances) of holding the public body to account is being pursued, such as a public inquiry. It goes almost without saying that the scope of a criminal statute should normally be construed more strictly than a rule or principle imposing mere civil liability. However, the courts should be vigilant to ensure that the advantages, in terms of protection from liability, given to public authorities are not construed so widely that in effect such authorities will only be held liable in circumstances where a private organisation would have been liable if it had agreed with the public authority to carry out at operational level what turned to be the death-dealing activity in question. Suppose, for example, that a death attributable to a gross breach of a duty of care can be put down to management failings in a joint venture between a public authority and a private organisation, and they are both prosecuted. In such a case, whilst s 3(1) may well apply to the public authority, the courts should not go out of their way to find that the exclusion shields the authority from liability simply because its part in the joint venture involved some policy-making element. To do that would effectively mean that only the private organisation was exposed to prosecution, something that may well leave not just the company itself, but also the victims' families and the general public with a well-founded sense that justice has not been done.

Section 3(2) sets out a more limited exclusion in respect of anything done, "in the exercise of an exclusively public function", meaning a function that falls with the ambit of the Crown prerogative, or is by its nature only exercisable with the authority conferred by the exercise of the prerogative or by or under a statutory provision[73]. This exclusion relates only to the public functions involved in s 2(1)(c), such as the supply of goods or services, construction work, or the use of vehicles and the like. It does not exempt the relevant organisation from liability arising from a breach of duty to an employee, or from a breach of a duty as an occupier of premises, or (perhaps most importantly) from a breach of duty owed to a detained person such as a prisoner or detained patient. The exemption was not supported by consultees in the government's consultation exercise[74], and it is worth noting that the Tasmanian Law Reform Institute has recently rejected this basis for exempting public authorities. The Institute said[75]:

---

71 See eg *Anns v Merton LBC* [1978] AC 728 at 754, [1977] 2 All ER 492 at 501 per Lord Wilberforce, "[P]ublic authorities have to strike a balance between the claims of efficiency and thrift ... whether they get the balance right can only be decided through the ballot box, not in the courts".

72 Tasmanian Law Reform Institute, see note 46 above, at para 5.1.11.

73 There is a further exclusion in s 3(3) respecting duties arising in respect of inspections carried out in the exercise of statutory functions, which disapplies the duty of care unless it falls within s 2(1)(a) or (b).

74 Home Office, *Summary of Responses to Corporate Manslaughter: The Government's Draft Bill for Reform*, March 2005, p 9.

75 Tasmanian Law Reform Institute, see note 46 above, at para 5.1.11.

"The Institute does not recommend a UK style exception for activities done in the exercise of a public function. Crown criminal liability is already possible in Tasmania in relation to some criminal offences ... While Crown prosecutions would no doubt be exceptional, as they are rarely in the public interest, a valuable message is sent by providing that all people, including the Crown and government bodies must obey criminal laws."

This is a point to which I will return in the next subsection. A similar exemption, limited to s 2(1)(c), is applied by s 5(3) to policing or law-enforcement activities other than operational or hazardous training activities (they have a broader exemption, examined below), and by s 7(1) to a variety of child-protection and probation functions[76]. So, the exemption from liability arising from activities covered by s 2(1)(c) is generous in terms of who it covers.

In fairness to the government, and in response to the cynic's view, it would be right to say that even this cursory look at exemptions for public organisations reveals that there has at least been no attempt, other than in very limited circumstances, to give a "blanket" exemption to public organisations simply because they are by nature involved in controversial, sensitive or dangerous work, such as managing prisoners, protecting children or detaining disordered patients. Nonetheless, the question is whether the exemptions granted to some of these public bodies do indeed go too far.

### (v) *Are the exclusions under the 2007 Act too wide? Prisons, the police and the military*

It will not be possible here to examine the proper scope of all the exemptions held out to public bodies, in particular the exemption applying to the provision of services under s 2(1)(c). However, a comparison can be made between the position in which prisons (and other custodial institutions) and secure hospitals find themselves, and the position in which police and armed forces organisations find themselves, so far as the scope of exemptions is concerned. It is arguable that the more generous exemption held out to army and police organisations is unwarranted. Not only does its wide scope effectively leave individual service personnel to "carry the can" when a death has been unlawfully caused because something went badly wrong, but it gives too little weight to the vital role of the Director of Prosecutions in preventing prosecutions under the 2007 Act when they are not in the public interest[77].

Section 2(2) specifically provides that someone for whose safety an organisation is responsible may be owed a duty when:

"(a) he is detained at a custodial institution or in a custody area at a court or police station ...

(c) he is being transported in a vehicle, or being held in any premises, in pursuance of prison escort arrangements ...

(d) he is living in secure accommodation in which he has been placed;

(e) he is a detained patient."

The inclusion of this subsection came at the insistence of the House of Lords, and was not in the original government Bill[78]. Given that there have been 1,000 suicides in custody within the last 13 years, it is hardly surprising that it gave rise to controversy. By way of contrast, deaths caused during active service, or during training in a hazardous military or police operational context, are expressly excluded from the scope of the duty of care under

---

76  In the civil law context, see by way of contrast, *Vicar of Writtle v Essex* CC (1979) 77 LGR 656.
77  Under s 17, the DPP's consent is required for all prosecutions under the 2007 Act.
78  See 694 HL Official Report (5th series) cols 135–138.

s 2[79]. Under s 6, similarly exempted are (with limited exceptions) the actions of the emergency services in responding to emergency circumstances[80]. No specific exemptions have been held out to prisons and secure hospitals.

The justification for this difference in treatment would seem to be this: it might be said that there is an overriding public interest in preventing what was described by the government as the growth of a "culture of defensiveness" in the conduct of military and police operations and training, because such a culture would be inimical to achieving the very aims of such activities[81]. So, if the introduction of an offence of corporate manslaughter in these contexts might encourage the growth of such a culture, then the offence should not be applied to them. By way of contrast, although the government sought to apply the same reasoning when arguing against the application of the offence to deaths in custody[82], the growth of a "culture of defensiveness" may ironically be precisely what is needed to promote good practice amongst staff and minimise the risk of deaths in custody or in hospital.

Here is a well-known illustrative example of this last point. In November 2000, Robert Stuart was convicted of the murder of Zahid Mubarek. Stuart was a prolific offender, disturbed, dangerous and a known racist with a history of disruptive and bizarre behaviour whilst in detention. On arrival at Feltham Young Offenders' Institution, Stuart was placed in a cell with Mubarek, and brutally killed him. An inquiry conducted by Mr Justice Keith came to this conclusion in 2006 about the way Stuart and Mubarek were dealt with[83]:

> "[B]ecause of a pernicious and dangerous cocktail of poor communications and shoddy work practices prison staff never got to grips with [Stuart] … [There was] a bewildering catalogue of shortcomings, both individual and systemic, at Feltham at the time … I name those members of staff who were in some way to blame for what happened to Zahid. But all this has to be seen in the context of the establishment as a whole. Feltham was identified in the mid-1990s as a prison which was failing on many fronts … [A]t present there is a disconnection between aspiration and reality, because insufficient attention is paid to 'outcomes rather than processes'."

The report added that the governor with line responsibility had very little operational experience, and did not get help from the manager of the department, "who had become complacent as his retirement beckoned"[84]. This was not an isolated instance of poor staff practice and inadequate leadership in custodial institutions. Speaking of Wormwood Scrubs, Lord Ramsbotham, a former Chief Inspector of Prisons, said in the debate on the Corporate Manslaughter Bill, "although there was no case of manslaughter, there was

---

79 See 2007 Act ss 4 and 5 respectively.

80 Other than a response that involves a medical treatment decision (excepting a decision concerning the order in which patients are treated): s 6(3) and (4). It is not made explicit that decisions taken by a prison governor during a prison riot would be covered by s 6, although it is almost certain that they are covered, because only duties at issue in s 2(1)(a) and s 2(1)(b) are "duties of care" for the purposes of s 6 of the 2007 Act even in an emergency. In other words, s 2(1)(d), concerned with prisoners and detained patients, is within the scope of the "emergencies" exception. On a generous reading, prison governors' decisions in emergencies would be covered by s 6(2)(d)(ii): "… any other organisation providing a service of responding to emergency circumstances … otherwise than on a commercial basis …" More probably, such a situation would be held to be covered by the "law enforcement" exemption in s 5, on which see below.

81 This argument is critically examined below.

82 See the response of Lord Bassam to the proposal to apply corporate manslaughter to the prison service, 688 HL Official Report (5th series) col GC198.

83 Cited by Lord Hunt, 688 HL Official Report (5th Series) col GC187–188.

84 Cited by Lord Ramsbotham, 688 HL Official Report (5th Series) col GC191.

extraordinarily bad behaviour by staff, brutality of prisoners and, over a number of years, management failure on a scale that I simply could not believe"[85]. Unsurprisingly, he concluded that[86]:

> "this [amended] Bill, which is based on the duty of care and which should be shown to everyone in charge of these authorities, is an appropriate weapon. I seriously believe that the Bill would energise the management system in a way that nothing else that I have come across in the past ten years seems to have been able to."

It is also highly arguable that the almost complete reliance that a detained prisoner or patient must place in the relevant organisation to ensure his or her health and safe-keeping during what may be a lengthy period of detention, overrides countervailing considerations and warrants placing the relevant organisation under an ongoing duty of care. As Lord Hunt said in arguing for the extension of liability to cover deaths in custody[87]:

> "The power lawfully to deprive an individual of his or her liberty must be one of the most serious responsibilities there can be. The duty of care owed to an individual in detention, where he cannot act freely in his own interests, is onerous and profound, yet the way in which the Bill is currently ordered suggests that that responsibility is not so regarded by the government."

This second argument in favour of the imposition of liability on prison organisations does not, of course, have the same application to police and army organisations, because their personnel have freely chosen their employment and are to a much greater extent responsible for their own welfare. However, that leaves the question whether the 2007 Act is right to leave police and army organisations immune from prosecution for corporate manslaughter, so far as deaths arising from hazardous training or operations are concerned, because of a supposedly overriding need to prevent a "culture of defensiveness" developing in training and operational contexts[88].

The exemption for policing and law enforcement (the military activity exemption in s 4 is in the relevant respects similar) in s 5 is as follows:

> "(1) Any duty of care owed by a public authority in respect of –
>
>   (a) operations within subsection (2),
>
>   (b) activities carried on in preparation for, or directly in support of, such operations, or
>
>   (c) training of a hazardous nature, or training carried out in a hazardous way, which it is considered needs to be carried out, or carried out in that way, in order to improve or maintain the effectiveness of officers or employees of the public authority with respect to such operations,
>
>   is not a relevant 'duty of care'.

---

85  688 HL Official Report (5th Series) col GC192.
86  688 HL Official Report (5th Series) col GC193.
87  688 HL Official Report (5th Series) col GC187.
88  I will in fact leave on one side here the s 6 exemption for organisations involved in the provision of emergency services in the course of which someone is unlawfully killed. The law is reluctant even to impose civil liability in such circumstances, let alone criminal liability: see *Capital and Counties plc v Hampshire CC; Digital Equipment Co Ltd v Hampshire CC; John Munroe (Acrylics) Ltd v London Fire and Civil Defence Authority; Church of Jesus Christ of Latter Day Saints (Great Britain) v West Yorkshire Fire and Civil Defence Authority* [1997] QB 104, [1997] 2 All ER 865, CA, approved on this point by Lord Hoffmann in *Gorringe v Calderdale MBC* [2004] UKHL 15 at [32], [2004] 2 All ER 326 at [32].

(2) Operations are within this subsection if –

(a) they are operations for dealing with terrorism, civil unrest or serious disorder,

(b) they involve the carrying on of policing or law-enforcement activities, and

(c) officers or employees of the public authority in question come under attack, or face the threat of attack or violent resistance, in the course of the operations."

The weakness of the argument for this immunity is that, first (and paradoxically), the existence of the exemption for police and army organisations may mean that *individual* police officers or army personnel are now more likely than individual prison officers or nurses to find themselves prosecuted when deaths have been caused through serious negligence. This will be for the simple reason that ss 4 and 5 prevent the relevant police or army organisation itself being prosecuted for corporate manslaughter, so recourse against individuals is more likely; whereas in a similar situation there is no such legal protection for the prison or hospital. As the European Court of Human Rights pointed out in the introduction to its judgment in *McCann v UK*[89]:

"The most important point which emerges from any study of the law on this subject is that the responsibility is an individual one. Any police officer who uses a firearm may be answerable to the courts or to a coroner's inquest and, if his actions were unlawful (or improper), then he as an individual may be charged with murder, manslaughter or unlawful wounding ... The fact that a police officer used his firearms under the orders of a superior does not, of itself, exempt him from criminal liability ..."[90]

Secondly, whilst it may seem right to prevent a "culture of defensiveness" developing in the way that individual police or army personnel carry out their duties in hazardous situations, it is questionable whether the same considerations apply with the same degree of force (in so far as a "culture of defensiveness" is just a negative term for the positive virtues of a "health and safety culture", or of a "human rights culture") to the organisations tasked with planning the context in which those duties will be carried out. I would not myself presume to pass judgment on the conduct of the authorities that led up to the killing of the IRA terrorists that was the subject of the litigation in *McCann*. However, the European Court was not persuaded that the killing of the three terrorists constituted a use of force which was no more than absolutely necessary in defence of persons from unlawful violence within the meaning of art 2(2)(a) of the Convention. A (bare) majority of the court found that[91]:

"there was a serious miscalculation by those responsible for controlling the operation. As a result the scene was set in which the fatal shooting ... was a foreseeable possibility if not a likelihood ... [There was] a lack of appropriate care in the control and organisation of the arrest operation."

The authorities had been planning the operation on Gibraltar for some months. In that regard, among the serious miscalculations and failures to which the court pointed were the decision by the authorities not to prevent the suspects from travelling into Gibraltar, and their failure to make sufficient allowances for the possibility that the intelligence assessments relied on might, in some key respects, have been erroneous. Crucially, the court cast doubt in that respect on whether the authorities adhered to their obligation to respect

---

89  Application 18984/91 *McCann v UK* (1996) 21 EHRR 97, [1995] ECHR 18984/91.
90  *McCann v UK* (1996) 21 EHRR 97 (para 137).
91  *McCann v UK* (paras 205, 212), see note 90 above.

the right to life of the suspects, in so far as the court doubted "whether they [the soldiers] had been trained or instructed to assess whether the use of firearms to wound their targets may have been warranted by the specific circumstances that confronted them at the moment of arrest"[92]. It is, of course, an open question whether the failures of the authorities to respect their obligations under art 2(2)(a), as found by the court, would necessarily amount to the kind of "gross" breach of duty of care due in part to management or organisational failings on the part of senior management (had there been no exemption in this respect) that is required for conviction under the 2007 Act. The latter does not necessarily follow from the former. The question is, should an exemption from liability be granted to the authorities in this kind of situation, even though it leaves as the only possible targets for prosecution individual soldiers who receive (*ex hypothesi*) erroneous advice that they will in all probability have to shoot to kill?

There is a case for saying that the exemption is undesirable and unnecessary. It means, for example, that military authorities will still be exempted from prosecution under the 2007 Act, even if they ignore or tolerate the development of a "shoot-to-kill culture" amongst soldiers called in to non-military operations, simply because such a development is seen as good for morale in that it is more "macho" than the culture developed by their counterparts training armed police officers[93]. It would have been better, in this context, to have taken the approach of the Tasmanian Law Reform Institute to the "exclusively public function" exemption, cited above[94]. In other words, it would have been better to have relied on the proper exercise of prosecutorial discretion and in particular on the judgment of the DPP (in deciding whether to give consent to a prosecution) as to whether the prosecution is in the public interest. As the Institute said, "The exercise of prosecutorial discretion should result in only appropriate cases being prosecuted. A factor relevant to this would no doubt be the extent to which the potential defendant had already been held accountable in another arena"[95]. It is unlikely to be easy to secure convictions or even to find adequate grounds to commence a prosecution, in these kinds of circumstances, and hence the police and military authorities would have scant grounds to fear that ill-founded prosecutions would ever be undertaken or succeed[96].

## 3. GROSS NEGLIGENCE MANSLAUGHTER AND OTHER SERIOUS CRIMES REQUIRING PROOF OF FAULT

### (i) *Committing gross negligence manslaughter as a principal offender*

The passing of the 2007 Act inevitably raises the question whether other serious offences should be reformed in such a way that organisations can be convicted of them more easily than at present, either through piecemeal reform of individual offences or through the introduction of a set of general principles of corporate liability for serious criminal wrongdoing. In that regard, Professor Wells has neatly encapsulated the key issue in the form of the question, "Should corporations be liable because of their own wrongdoing or

---

92  *McCann v UK* (para 212), see note 90 above.
93  On this point, see *McCann v UK* (para 211), see note 90 above.
94  See text at note 72 above.
95  Tasmanian Law Reform Institute, see note 46 above, at para 5.1.11.
96  A tragic case that might have led to prosecution is the De Menezes saga. Mr De Menezes was shot dead by armed police officers who, after administrative and intelligence errors arising from a surveillance operation, were led mistakenly to believe that he was a terrorist about to detonate a bomb on an underground train. The Independent Police Complaints Commission did not take proceedings against any of the individual officers involved, but the Metropolitan Police were charged under health and safety legislation with failing adequately to provide for Mr De Menezes" safety: see http://news.bbc.co.uk/1/hi/uk/6646537.stm.

because they are in a better position to control (or to be seen as responsible for) the wrongdoing of others?"[97]. The 2007 Act obviously takes the former approach, imposing direct liability on organisations as principals for causing death through glaring failings in whole or in part at senior management level. This approach makes sense, chiefly because the special nature of gross negligence manslaughter as a crime (corporate manslaughter being a species of it) makes it a peculiarly suitable vehicle for the imposition of liability on such a basis.

To begin with, there is no inconsistency in a finding that D1 committed the manslaughter of V by gross negligence as a principal offender, even when the immediate cause of V's death was the knowing and deliberate act of D2[98]. So, in the Mubarek case discussed above[99], it would be no bar to the prosecution of the prison authority for corporate manslaughter that the immediate cause of the victim's death was murder committed by another person in the victim's cell. Further, and most importantly, the fault element of "gross negligence" ("gross breach of a relevant duty of care", under the 2007 Act) need not necessarily be proven by reference only to a single act or omission, or a single course of conduct, such as falling asleep whilst on duty[100]. A judgment that negligence was "gross" can legitimately reflect the view that the whole is greater than the sum of the parts. So, proof of gross negligence can be founded on an analysis in terms of the aggregation of individual careless acts and omissions over a period of time in such a way that they can be regarded, cumulatively, as amounting to "gross" negligence[101]. A gross negligence fault element thus lends itself naturally to an approach to criminal liability that places emphasis on the context in which an unlawful act took place, and on systematic as well as individual failings, as the 2007 Act seeks to do through its focus in s 1 on, "the way in which [the organisation's] activities are managed or organised by its senior management". However, manslaughter has always been an unusual crime against the person at common law, in having a fault element that may be satisfied by gross negligence. Such a fault element is also rarely found in the definition of other serious crimes, especially those against the person, under statute in England and Wales[102]. It will be suggested here that a different approach (that could also have been taken to manslaughter) is generally to be preferred where serious crimes are in issue[103]. Such an alternative approach is also the only realistic course

---

97  Wells, see note 4 above, p 153.
98  For a discussion in the context of causing someone to commit suicide, see Jeremy Horder and Laura McGowan, note 11 above. See also *R v Kennedy (No 2)* [2005] EWCA Crim 685, [2005] 1 WLR 2159.
99  See the text at note 72 above.
100 See the text at note 29 above.
101 See Jeremy Horder and Laura McGowan, see note 11 above, pp 1044–1045. A difficult question for the courts in the early years of the 2007 Act's application will therefore be whether incidents and failures pre-dating the passing of the 2007 Act can be aggregated with those post-dating it, for the purpose of determining whether there was a "gross" breach of a duty of care. Bad practice *continuing* after the passing of the 2007 Act could perhaps have light shed on how bad or inexcusable it was by evidence of how long it had gone on before the passing of the 2007 Act.
102 Causing death by dangerous driving, contrary to the Road Traffic Act 1988, is perhaps the closest a statutory "result" crime with a high degree of seriousness comes to employing a gross negligence notion, but there are well-known differences between "gross negligence" and "dangerousness" that make this analogy far from exact. By way of contrast, under the Criminal Code (Tas), s 156, someone can be criminally responsible for wounding or causing grievous bodily harm brought about by an omission in breach of duty, if they were criminally negligent in breaching the duty.
103 However, I should not be taken to be suggesting that organisations cannot be found to have had the subjective fault elements, such as recklessness or intention, commonly required in more serious offences.

respecting crimes that – whether or not they have a (subjective) fault element – cannot be committed by organisations, such as rape or being "drunk and disorderly". This approach takes Professor Wells' second route of making an organisation responsible for a failure adequately to control and supervise the employees who committed the crime.

Lord Denman explained long ago what has often been taken to be the essential difficulty involved in holding organisations criminally responsible for serious crimes such as rape or murder[104]. Citing dicta from a range of older cases, he said[105]:

> "'A corporation cannot be guilty of treason or felony.' It might be added 'or perjury or offences against the person'. The court of Common Pleas lately held that a corporation might be sued in trespass; but nobody has sought to fix them with acts of immorality. These plainly derive their character from the corrupted mind of the person committing them, and are violations of the social duties that belong to men and subjects. A corporation which has no such duties, cannot be guilty in these cases: but they may be guilty as a body corporate of commanding acts to be done to the nuisance of the community at large."

I will not enter here into the longstanding debate over whether, and if so to what extent, there is a sense in which an organisation can indeed (*pace* Lord Denman) have a "corrupted mind" or "social duties", and can hence in theory commit almost any offence known to criminal law[106]. Instead, I shall work with the assumption that if and in so far as holding organisations directly responsible (as a principal offender) for the commission of some crimes – such as rape, sexual assault, or being drunk in a public place – seems impossible or at least counter-intuitive, and an equally effective and more intuitively plausible means of holding organisations responsible for the commission of such crimes exists, then the latter means of holding them responsible is to be preferred. This is not because intuitions are a reliable guide to sound moral insight; they are not. It is for the simple reason that the more intuitively plausible a basis for holding a person responsible for wrongdoing, the easier it will be not only to persuade prosecutors to seek to hold that person responsible on that basis, but also to persuade that person themselves to accept responsibility for the wrong done.

### (ii) *"Tolerating or permitting" the commission of an offence*

In terms of intuitive plausibility, as Lord Denman can be taken to be indicating at the end of the passage just cited, a better focus for corporate liability would be the attitude that the company (including, as under the 2007 Act, its senior managers) took towards offending by employees. The key issue should not be whether an organisation itself committed (or can commit) murder or rape, or could be drunk and disorderly, and so forth, but whether the organisation permitted or tolerated the commission of such offences by employees. For example, prisoners (or even members of staff) may brutalise other prisoners[107] by inflicting harm of a sexual nature on them up to and including rape. If the prison authorities could be shown to have turned a blind eye to such behaviour at senior management level, in the interests (say) of a quiet life, then in labeling terms it would be appropriate to convict the prison authorities not of rape itself, but of a new offence of high gravity: "permitting or tolerating" rape. I suggest that this way of describing the organisation's conduct is a more accurate label than that provided by the substantive offence for the wrong the

104  *R v Great North of England Railway Co* (1846) 9 QB 315.
105  *Ibid* at 326, cited by Wells, see note 4 above, p 89.
106  See further C M V Clarkson, "Corporate Liability" 2 Web JCLI (webjcli.ncl.ac.uk/1998/issue2/clarkson2.html); Wells, see note 4 above; Gobert and Punch, see note 3 above.
107  See the passage cited from Lord Ramsbotham's speech in the debate on the Corporate Manslaughter and Corporate Homicide Bill, in the text at note 85 above.

organisation has committed. If combined with a fault element such as a requirement that someone at senior management level "must have known" that the offending was being or might be being committed, it would be an offence of a gravity not far short of the completed offence itself[108]. Further, such an offence would sit neatly alongside the legislative practice of holding directors or company officers individually responsible for the commission of crimes by a company, if the commission of those crimes occurred with the "consent or connivance" of the directors or company officers (or, one might wish to add, the senior managers)[109]. Proof that the company must have known of the risk of – and tolerated or permitted – the commission of offences by employees would be compelling evidence that individual company officers or senior managers themselves consented to or connived at the commission of those offences. It would also be possible to buttress the serious offence (that has a subjective fault element of the kind just outlined) with a less serious offence of failing adequately to supervise employees with the result that an offence was committed by an employee, an offence that might come with a "due diligence" defence in relation to systems put in place to prevent offending of the relevant kind by employees.

There is more than one way of incorporating the notion of "permitting or tolerating" the commission of offences into a doctrinal scheme subjecting organisations to criminal liability. The route adopted under the Australian Model Criminal Code involves the imposition of direct liability on the organisation for the offence in question, where "permitting or tolerating" conduct (as I am calling it) can be proved. Section 12.3(1) provides:

> "If intention, knowledge or recklessness is a fault element in relation to a physical element of an offence, that fault element must be attributed to a body corporate that expressly, tacitly or impliedly authorised or permitted the commission of the offence."

As we have seen[110], the Australian Model Criminal Code has a very broad understanding of what is involved in "tacitly or impliedly" authorising the commission of an offence. It can be proved by showing that, "the body corporate failed to create and maintain a corporate culture that required compliance with the relevant provision"[111]; in other words, a species of simple negligence. This means that a company must be found guilty of an actual offence – such as murder – normally involving proof of intention or a high degree of recklessness, if the company is shown simply to have failed to maintain a corporate culture in which such an offence was regarded as impermissible. This may not be the right way to employ the "tolerating or permitting" notion. It risks distorting the offence label, by seeking to run together two rather separate concepts – the concept of committing an offence, and the concept of tolerating or permitting the commission of an offence – without maintaining parity of culpability and adequate linkage between the fault elements for them both. As Clough and Mulhern write, of s 12.3(1) of the Australian Model Criminal Code[112]:

---

108 The phrase, "must have known" is chosen deliberately, to make it clear that a jury would be entitled to infer from all the circumstances, and looking at management practices and culture generally, that this state of mind existed in one or more senior managers. The issue would be whether the company must have known that an offence, or one of a particular range of offences, might be being committed by employees. It should not be necessary to show that the company must have known that rape in particular, as opposed to (say) grievous bodily harm, was being committed, if it must have been known that one or other of these was being committed.

109 See eg the Health and Safety at Work Act 1974 s 37; and the Fraud Act 2006 s 12.

110 See text following note 26 above.

111 Australian Model Criminal Code s 12.3(2)(d).

112 J Clough and C Mulhern, *The Prosecution of Corporations* (2002) p 145.

"The fault element of the corporation is determined not by proving that the corporation exhibited that fault element or its equivalent, but by attributing the fault element to the corporation if it is proved that it authorised or permitted the commission of the offence. There is no link between proof of the authorisation or permission and the fault element that must be attributed to the company."

Of course, the "tolerating or permitting" offence that I support presupposes that the offence itself has in fact been committed by an employee, and is thus distinct from the inchoate approach to liability characteristic of the Health and Safety at Work Act 1974[113]. However, as the Tasmanian Law Reform Institute pointed out[114], this need not mean that an employee must be in law have been convicted of the offence before the organisation can be convicted of the "tolerating or permitting" offence, any more than the conviction of a secondary party to an offence depends upon the prior conviction of the principal.

In conclusion, it is worth pointing out that a focus on liability for something like an "inadequate supervision" offence has commended itself to European law reform bodies seeking to secure modernisation of the law of bribery. When it comes to bribery committed by companies, for example, art 18(2) of the Council of Europe's Criminal Law Convention on Corruption requires the parties to establish the liability of a legal person, "where the lack of supervision or control by a natural person ... has made possible the commission of the criminal offences mentioned in paragraph 1 [bribery offences] for the benefit of [a] legal person by a natural person under its authority"[115]. Similarly, art 5(2) of the European Council's framework decision 2003/568/JHA requires that:

"Each Member State shall take the necessary measures to ensure that legal persons can be held liable for [bribery] offences ... committed for their benefit by any person, acting either individually or as part of an organ of the legal person, who has a leading position within the legal person, based on...an authority to exercise control within the legal person ... each Member State shall take the necessary measures to ensure that a legal person can be held liable where the lack of supervision or control ... has made possible the commission of [a bribery offence] ... for the benefit of that legal person by a person under its authority."[116]

This approach may be a more appropriate way of dealing with the reality of modern corporate life. This can involve the quasi-autonomous operation of subsidiaries overseas, who may have powerful "local" reasons to commit offences, such as bribery, that do not apply to the parent company in its dealings within the jurisdiction in which it is incorporated[117]. In such circumstances, if the offence is committed by the subsidiary there may be an air of unreality about saying that the parent company also commits the offence as a principal (or even as a secondary party), although it may be possible to show that

---

113  For argument in favour of an "inchoate" approach to the criminal liability of corporations, one that does not depend on the commission of an offence by an employee, see Gobert and Punch, see note 3 above, ch 4.

114  Tasmanian Law Reform Institute, see note 46 above, at para 6.4.17.

115  It should be noted, however, that in typically exiguous fashion, art 18(2) says nothing about a fault element, and does not stipulate that "liability" must be criminal liability. This does not imply that a fault element is considered inappropriate, or that liability is meant to be civil rather than criminal.

116  See also art 3(2) of the Second Protocol of the Convention on the Protection of the European Community's Financial Interests.

117  See the discussion in Gobert and Punch, see note 3 above, ch 5.

individual company officers within the parent company consented to or connived at its commission. A morally and legally more powerful accusation may well be that the parent company either culpably failed to ensure that systems were in place to ensure that the offence was not committed by the subsidiary, or – given the local circumstances in which *ex hypothesi* they knew the subsidiary would be operating – must have at least turned a blind eye to (the risk of) its commission, or both. As indicated above, at least two kinds of offences could be created to accommodate this accusation against the parent company. First, a lesser offence of failing adequately to control or supervise employees with the result that the offence was committed, possibly subject to a due diligence defence. Secondly, a more serious offence of "tolerating or permitting bribery", committed in circumstances where the parent company must have known (of the risk) that offending was taking place. It is submitted that an approach that makes use of one or both of these offences is morally and legally preferable to an approach that seeks to make the parent company liable as a principal offender.

# THE REPRODUCTIVE TORTS

## JK MASON, MD, LLD[1]

### INTRODUCTION

The reader may wonder how it is a non-lawyer comes to be writing in what is one of the most prestigious publications in the field of English law. Here, I take refuge in the words of the author of a recently published monograph also devoted to pregnancy and the law: "To some degree", she wrote – "a legal education can rather blind us to what is going on in cases, given the tendency to see law through law, rather than to ask broader questions about whether the policy of the law is *fair* or sustainable outside the operation of legal rules"[2] – and nowhere can this be more appropriate than in the field that has become known as that of the reproductive torts. Widespread academic interest in these "harms" was stimulated by the now well-known case of *McFarlane v Tayside Health Board*[3] in which, as is now widely recognised, legal principle was overcome by a combination of legal legerdemain and policy driven emotion. Indeed, if, as the editors hope, this series of articles is to raise "interesting and topical – not to say controversial – issues", what better banner in the medico-legal field could there be than that raised by Mr and Mrs McFarlane in their quest for recompense for the birth by way of negligence of a healthy child?

*McFarlane* was a groundbreaking case at several levels. Firstly, it provided an unusual scenario in which a unanimous opinion reached in the Inner House of the Scottish Court of Session was overturned by an obversely unanimous finding in the House of Lords. Secondly, it reversed what had been taken, for at least fifteen years, to be the law regulating professional responsibility and liability for the birth as a result of negligence of an unwanted child. And, thirdly, in doing so, it introduced, on questionable grounds, a novel and significant exception to the currently recognised law of torts – we have Lord Hutton's appraisal in the later case of *Rees*[4]:

> "I think that the members of the House recognised that under the general principles applicable to the recovery of damages for negligent breach of duty the *McFarlane* parents would have been entitled to recover damages."

Thus, the case is fundamental to the understanding of the recent law in this area and it is essential to provide a précis within the introduction to the reproductive torts as a whole.

### *The McFarlane's case in outline*

The McFarlanes already had four children when Mr McFarlane underwent a vasectomy in 1989. Six months later, he was informed that his sperm count was negative and that he could safely resume sexual intercourse without contraceptive measures. Mrs McFarlane became pregnant 18 months later and was delivered of a healthy female child without further incident. It is significant from the point of view of later discussion that she did not seek a termination of pregnancy and that the child was accepted into the family with love

---

1  Professor (Emeritus) of Forensic Medicine and Honorary Fellow, Edinburgh School of Law.
2  N Priaulx "The Harm Paradox: Tort Law and the Unwanted Child in an Era of Choice" (2007), with reference to J Conaghan "Law, harm and redress: a feminist perspective" (2002) 22 Legal Studies 319–339.
3  Heard, ultimately, in the House of Lords 2000 SC (HL) 1, [2000] 2 AC 59, [1999] 4 All ER 961.
4  *Rees v Darlington Memorial Hospital NHS Trust* [2003] UKHL 52 at [98], [2004] AC 309 at [98], [2003] 4 All ER 987 at [98].

and affection. The case, however, proceeded on the assumption that the Health Board, through the obstetrician acting as its agent, had been negligent in advising Mr McFarlane that he could dispense with contraceptive methods during intercourse and failing to warn him of the possibility of a return of his fertility by way of natural recanalisation of his *vasa deferentia* – an example of information based negligence – actions for which are now commonplace in medical jurisprudence and which provide a major contribution to this article.

It is sometimes forgotten that the action followed two distinct lines. The first was brought by Mrs McFarlane for solatium in respect of undergoing the pregnancy and of the pain and suffering of giving birth. The second, brought by both parents, sought damages for £100,000 for the costs of rearing the child. The Lord Ordinary in the Outer House of the Court of Session dismissed both claims[5], a decision that was reversed unanimously in the Inner House[6]. The Health Board's appeal to the House of Lords[7] was dismissed as to the former – the "mother's" – claim but was unanimously allowed in respect of the latter – the "parents'" – claim. We will, of course, return to *McFarlane* later on. For the present, we need only note that, whereas the former decision was, virtually, uncontroversial, the latter, which dealt, in fact, with a very limited issue – namely, recompense for the upkeep of an uncovenanted[8] *healthy* child – raised a storm of academic protest and undoubtedly led to confusion within the whole field of the reproductive torts, much of which derived from misunderstanding of their nature and coherence.

*The reproductive torts*

The classification of the so-called reproductive torts has never been universally established and, even now, varies from one jurisdiction to another. What follows is, essentially, the present writer's personal assessment[9] although, as we will see, it is more than doubtful if a "classification" as such does much more than a disservice to the law.

Basically, there are three specifically recognised reproductive torts:

> *wrongful pregnancy* or *wrongful conception*[10] – generally taken as meaning an "uncovenanted" pregnancy[11]. Thus, it most commonly results from defective advice or surgical intervention which has led the parents to believe that further pregnancy is impossible;
>
> *wrongful birth* – which implies the birth of a disabled child as a result of inadequate antenatal management; and
>
> *wrongful life* – essentially, a claim *by the neonate* that he or she is suffering because his or her mother was wrongly advised as to continuation or termination of the pregnancy.

---

5  *McFarlane v Tayside Health Board* 1997 SLT 211.

6  *McFarlane v Tayside Health Board* 1998 SC 389, (1998) 44 BMLR 140.

7  Note 3 above.

8  This expression was first used in this context by Kennedy J in *Richardson v LRC Products Ltd* [2000] Lloyds Rep Med 280, (2000) 59 BMLR 185. It is used in Scots law to describe an event that was not so much unexpected as one which was not contemplated by the parties concerned.

9  Considerations of space dictate that this article is little more than an outline of the whole subject. For a far fuller exposition, see J K Mason *The Troubled Pregnancy: Legal Wrongs and Rights in Reproduction* (2007). It is to be noted that much of the recent literature on the subject comes from Australia – see, for example, D Stretton "The Birth Torts: Damages for Wrongful Birth and Wrongful Life" (2005) 10 Deakin Law Rev 310–364.

10  The phrases are often used as interchangeable. I prefer *wrongful pregnancy* as it is the pregnancy, not the conception, that causes any harm.

11  Note 8 above. The term should be perpetuated as it avoids applying the demeaning, and often inaccurate, adjective "unwanted" to a child.

The disadvantages of this and similar classifications are several. Firstly, it ignores the possibility of a wrongful pregnancy resulting in the birth of a disabled child. This lies at the heart of the problems thrown up by *McFarlane* which concerned only the birth of a healthy child; it is also essential to distinguish it from *wrongful birth* as defined above. For these reasons, I refer to this scenario in the text as *the McFarlane exception*. Secondly, and more importantly, the terms themselves are anomalous in that neither pregnancy, nor birth, nor life are, of themselves, wrongful and to describe them as such is falsely pejorative. To speak, particularly, of wrongful birth and wrongful life is to promote the concept that only healthy life is *rightful*. The terms themselves, thus, introduce major moral issues which, although of overwhelming importance in themselves, serve to obfuscate the *legal* issues which underpin the jurisprudence that has developed in respect of medical negligence. At the end of the day, however, it is well understood that moral and legal obligations cannot be separated – indeed, in the ageless wisdom of Lord Coleridge CJ, the latter are founded on the former[12]. The difficulty in sensitive areas such as human reproduction is to ensure that one does not dominate the other. In practice, the terms are deeply ingrained both in the academic literature and in legal understanding – on balance, they are probably better retained.

That having been said, it will be appreciated that the reproductive torts have it in common that they force a stark choice on the pregnant woman. Without prejudice to her subsequent right to sue the tortfeasor, the complainant can either accept the *status quo* or seek termination of the pregnancy[13]. It follows that the major moral issues of the sanctity of life and of abortion, as confined by the Abortion Act 1967, play a major role in the three major reproductive torts which we will now consider in more detail.

## ACTIONS FOR WRONGFUL PREGNANCY

As already stated, an action for wrongful pregnancy is most likely to arise following an unsuccessful sterilisation operation on either the male or female partner and, almost paradoxically, it will as often result from a failure to inform the parties adequately of the unavoidable vagaries of nature as it will to be due to technical inexpertise[14]. A number of cases, however, arise from undiagnosed pregnancies – generally those that have been missed in association with intended sterilisation – or from a mismanaged abortion where, again, the fault may lie in the realm of information disclosure or poor technique. *Scuriaga v Powell*[15], albeit very poorly reported, is the most significant of these on historical grounds and will be referred to later[16]. In any such event, the resulting child may be healthy or disabled, the incidence of the latter depending solely on natural chance which, as we will see, has major jurisprudential importance.

---

12 *R v Instan* [1893] 1 QB 450 at 453, [1891–94] All ER Rep 1213 at 1214.
13 I deliberately opt to resist confusing the issues of abortion and adoption – in so far as their outcomes are of totally different quality – the former results in fetal death while the latter leads to neonatal survival.
14 The "natural" long-term failure rate of competently performed vasectomy is about 1:2,000; that of tubal occlusion is in the region of 1:200. See E Jackson *Regulating Reproduction* (2001) pp 25–41.
15 (1979) 123 Sol Jo 406.
16 Other interesting and more recent examples include *Allen v Bloomsbury Health Authority* [1993] 1 All ER 651, [1992] PIQR Q50 (failure to ensure the patient was not already pregnant), *Crouchman v Burke* (1997) 40 BMLR 163 (failure of diagnostic curettage), *Chissel v Poole Hospital NHS Trust* [1998] Lloyds Rep Med 357 (unsuspected twin surviving an abortion). A surprising feature of such cases is the number of actions which are defeated on the grounds of "accepted medical practice", as established by *Bolam v Friern Hospital Management Committee* [1957] 2 All ER 118, [1957] 1 WLR 582.

Refusal of a claim for damages due to the burdens of pregnancy and childbirth resulting from a wrongful pregnancy – the "mother's" claim in *McFarlane* terms (see above) – is extremely rare. By contrast, controversy has always surrounded the question of reparation for the costs of upkeep of the resultant child and it is this issue alone that is addressed in the following commentary.

Recompense for the costs of an uncovenanted child has a chequered history in England and Wales. As mentioned above, possibly the first reference lies in *Scuriaga*, – albeit indirect – as there was, in fact, no such claim in that case. Nonetheless, Watkins J foreshadowed difficulties in stating:

> "Surely no one in these days would argue that [damages were irrecoverable] if the child was born defective or diseased. The fact that the child born is healthy cannot give rise to a different conclusion save as to a measure of damages" –

and he was supported in this in the Court of Appeal.

Whether the law of England recognised a principled difference between the negligent birth of a disabled and a healthy child was not, however, addressed directly until the case of *Udale v Bloomsbury Area Health Authority* – one concerning a failed sterilisation resulting in a fifth child – was heard[17]. Here, Jupp J was uncompromising:

> "It has been the assumption of our culture from time immemorial that a child coming into the world, even if, as some say, 'the world is a vale of tears', is a blessing and a reason for rejoicing."[18]

An award in respect of rearing the child was firmly rejected, this being on grounds which included the disadvantage to the child who later found that he had been rejected; the fact that to offset the joys of parenthood against the economic damage sustained would mean that virtue went unrewarded while "unnatural rejection of womanhood and motherhood would be generously compensated"; and that doctors would be under pressure to arrange abortions – these being views that had already been widely canvassed in trans-Atlantic jurisdictions[19].

The alternative view was expressed shortly afterwards in the information based case of *Thake v Maurice*[20] in which the economic nature of the damage done was recognised. Although the possibility that public policy considerations foreclosed the award of damages for the upkeep of a healthy child was not argued in *Thake*, that proposition was rejected in the intervening case of *Emeh v Kensington and Chelsea and Westminster Area Health Authority*[21]. Despite some very unsatisfactory aspects of the arguments deployed, *Emeh* thus established the principles of recompense without "strings" which were followed for some 15 years – including in Scotland[22].

A review of anglophone jurisdictions as a whole, however, reveals a picture as to the award of damages for the upkeep of a healthy child resulting from negligence which was still confused at the time of the *McFarlane* hearings[23]. The options which had been either accepted or rejected at various times were later summarised by Mr Justice Kirby in the

---

17 [1983] 2 ALL ER 522, [1983] 1 WLR 1098.
18 [1983] 2 All ER 522 at 531, [1983] 1 WLR 1098 at 1109.
19 In 1991, it was reported that all but nine of the United States insisted on "no recovery" for a healthy child: *Girdley v Coats* (1991) Mo App Lexis 1065.
20 [1986] QB 644, [1984] 2 All ER 513; on appeal at [1986] QB 644, [1986] 1 All ER 497, CA.
21 [1985] QB 1012, [1984] 3 All ER 1044, CA
22 *Allan v Greater Glasgow Health Board* (1993) 17 BMLR 135, 1998 SLT 580, CS (OH).
23 See, for example, O Radley-Gardner "Wrongful birth revisited" (2002) 118 LQR 11–15.

Australian case of *Cattanach v Melchior*[24]. It will be helpful to recapitulate these early in the discussion:

> Option 1 – the child is born healthy and no damages of any kind are awarded – which assumes that the child is in the nature of a "blessing".
>
> Option 2 – limiting compensation to the immediate damage resulting from pregnancy and childbirth – is what we have seen in outline to be the *McFarlane* solution.
>
> Option 3 – recovery is available for the extra costs of maintaining a disabled neonate – which we will see below constitutes the *Parkinson* solution[25] and is, now, the recognised United Kingdom policy within the appropriate scenario.
>
> Option 4 – offers the saving alternative of adhering to ordinary recovery principles but, at the same time, providing for the "offset" of the joys of parenthood. This has been extensively argued in the United States where the principle has been both accepted and rejected.
>
> Option 5 – compensation to include the foreseeable costs of child rearing, which could be described as the *Emeh* – or full recovery – option.

How, then, is it that these varied solutions, and their almost idiosyncratic acceptance or ejection, have survived? The answer lies in the resolution of, or a compromise between, the extremes of, on the one hand, a near spiritual attitude to maintaining human dignity in refusing the implication that the birth of a child can be a "harm" and, on the other, a determination to apply strict legal principle in decision making shorn of emotional overtones. And, judges being only human, there must be an element of subjectivity and, hence, variation in their opinions. All of which is well demonstrated in what might be termed the *McFarlane Saga*[26].

## THE *MCFARLANE SAGA*

The well-known history of the McFarlanes' claims has been outlined above. Lord Gill's rejection of both in the Outer House[27] was based on grounds similar to those of Jupp J – save that he, in addition, was unable to see a natural pregnancy as a compensable harm; Lord Gill, therefore, can be seen as standing at one extreme of the spectrum outlined above.

In direct contrast, the unanimous Inner House[28] represents the other – or "legal principle" – end. In effect, the Lord Justice Clerk applied the strict principles of delict. The court's task was made easier by the availability of the Scots legal concept of "*iniuria*". The concurrence of *iniuria* (the invasion of a legal right, in this case the provision of correct information) and *damnum* (prejudice to the McFarlanes' legitimate interests, that of not having any more children) derived from conception and pregnancy and provided grounds for an action for reparation – and the costs of rearing the child flowed directly from her conception. The incidental joys and benefits derived from the wrongdoing were "not of a kind that our law has ever recognised as being able to be set off against the calculable consequences of an injury"[29]. Thus, the Court of Session was able to circumvent the difficult concept of equating a natural process such as pregnancy with a "personal injury"

---

24  [2003] HCA 38, [2003] 5 LRC 1, (2003) 199 ALR 131, Aus HC.

25  *Parkinson v St James and Seacroft University Hospital NHS Trust* [2001] EWCA Civ 530, [2002] QB 266, [2001] 3 All ER 97.

26  I have expanded these thoughts in J K Mason "From Dundee to Darlington: An end to the *McFarlane* line?" (2004) Jur Rev 365–386.

27  Note 5 above.

28  Note 6 above.

29  See note 6 above – *McFarlane*'s case 1998 SC 389 at 403, (1998) 44 BMLR 140 at 152–153 as per Lord McCluskey.

and, at the same time, to dispose of the problem of balancing a financial loss against an emotional gain which has troubled, and continues to trouble, courts all over the world.

The difficulty is that there is no satisfactory English equivalent of the Scots concept of *damnum*. Thus, when the case came to the House of Lords, the panel had, effectively, to start from scratch in order to unify the law in both England and Scotland[30], each member following his own route to the terminus. In doing so, they reached the well-known conclusion that the "mother's" claim should stand while the Board's appeal against the "parents'" claim to the costs of upkeep of their uncovenanted child should

be allowed[31] – only Lord Millett commenting on the illogic of so doing[32] – and, as is equally well known, they reached the latter conclusion by diverse routes to justify their, effective, rejection of the normal rules of tort law[33].

Their reasons have been analysed by numerous academic authors and by the courts themselves[34]. It will be convenient to cite as an example Lord Hutton's summary in the important follow-up case of *Rees*[35]. Lord Hutton identified four main threads:

- It would not be fair, just or reasonable to impose on the Health Board a duty of care that gave rise to liability for the cost of bringing up the child[36] (Lord Slynn of Hadley and Lord Hope of Craighead);
- The principles of distributive justice would bar the claim (Lord Steyn – who famously called in aid the views of the commuter on the London Underground);
- Restitution of the costs would not take into account the benefits to the parents derived from a healthy child (Lord Clyde); and
- Society must regard the balance of advantage and disadvantage in having a normal, healthy baby as beneficial.

Most commentators believe that it is the first of these which carried the day – leaving one wondering why it is not equally unjust to deny compensation to those whose legitimate aspirations have been thwarted. Be that as it may, *McFarlane* has established that, negligence in its conception notwithstanding, the upkeep of a healthy child does not constitute a compensable harm in the United Kingdom. Yet, intuitively at least, one feels that there must be *some* harm in such a situation – why else should a partnership go to some lengths, and trust a third party in the process, to avoid what *they foresee* as a harm?

---

30 See note 3 above – *McFarlane's case* 2000 SC (HL) 1 at 4, [2000] 2 AC 59 at 68, [1999] 4 All ER 961 at 965 as per Lord Slynn.

31 What LCH Hoyano describes as a "slicing up of the professional relationship into several duties of care" in "Misconceptions about Wrongful Conceptions" (2002) 65 MLR 883–906 at p 886.

32 But the *logical* answer to *allow* both claims was barred on the grounds that "It is morally offensive to regard a normal, healthy baby as more trouble and expense than it is worth" (note 3 above – *McFarlane*'s case 2000 SC (HL) 1 at 44, [2000] 2 AC 59 at 114, [1999] 4 All ER 961 at 1005). Even so, he would have allowed the parents general damages by way of a conventional award of up to £5,000 "to reflect the true nature of the wrong done to them" by way of denial of "an important aspect of their personal autonomy" (note 3 above – *McFarlane*'s case 2000 SC (HL) 1 at 44, [2000] 2 AC 59 at 114, [1999] 4 All ER 961 at 1006).

33 "A majority of their Lordships in *McFarlane* clearly recognised that on normal principles the claim would be allowable": See note 25 above – *Parkinson* [2002] QB 266 at [76], [2001] 3 All ER 97 at [76] per Hale LJ.

34 See, especially, the judgments in *Rand*, *Hardman* and *Lee* to which we will return; see further note 75 below.

35 Note 4 above – *Rees* [2004] AC 309 at [83], [2003] 4 All ER 987 at [83].

36 Effectively applying *Caparo Industries plc v Dickman* [1990] 2 AC 605, [1990] 1 All ER 568. It is to be noted that the *Caparo* reasoning is not accepted in Australia. Hence, the divide between the leading cases of *McFarlane* and *Cattanach* (see below) may not be as wide as appears at first sight.

Interestingly, but, in the interests of space, only to be considered here as a diversion from the main theme, an almost identical case, *Cattanach v Melchior*[37], was threading its way to the High Court of Australia, which it reached shortly after *McFarlane* was decided in the House of Lords. The cause of the wrongful pregnancy here was a technically incompetent sterilisation of the woman; it also progressed differently in that the complainants won their case at every stage of the trial. The decision in the High Court was, however, reached by a 4:3 majority only; discussion was, therefore, rather more wide-ranging than in *McFarlane* and was certainly more impassioned.

*Cattanach* was, in essence, a victory for cold legal principle over communitarian sentiment in the guise of public policy. The majority opinion can be summarised in the words of Mr Justice Kirby who was deeply critical of the *McFarlane* decision. He had this to say as to generality (at [151]):

> "Neither the invocation of Scripture nor the invention of a fictitious oracle on the Underground ... authorises a court of law to depart from the ordinary principles governing the recovery of damages for the tort of negligence"

and, more particularly (at [149]):

> "To deny such recovery is to provide a zone of legal immunity to medical practitioners engaged in sterilisation procedures that is unprincipled and inconsistent with established legal doctrine."

I suggest that, while the minority views in *Cattanach* merit very considerable sympathy, the majority view is to be preferred – and, collaterally – *McFarlane* is to be disapproved. But this is *only* if it is appreciated that it is not the birth of an uncovenanted baby that constitutes the "harm" in wrongful pregnancy; rather, it lies in the moral and financial burdens that flow from that birth. Even so, it seems that the ordinary man, or the commuter on the Underground, who, acting through his elected representatives, will have the last word. The Parliaments of Queensland and New South Wales both reacted swiftly following *Cattenach* by passing legislation which ensures that the result cannot be replicated[38].

An alternative formula for the award of damages in such cases was floated in the Australian case of *CES v Superclinics (Australia) Pty Ltd*[39] – namely that expenses should be allowed until such time as the child could be offered for adoption. This concept was not carried through to a definitive decision and it is unlikely in the extreme that it would ever be revived in the United Kingdom[40]. Adoption and abortion however, occupy wholly different moral spheres and one wonders if the place of the former in the solution of the wrongful pregnancy dilemma may not, possibly, have been dismissed too lightly.

---

37  Note 24 above – [2003] HCA 38, [2003] 5 LRC 1, (2003) 199 ALR 131. For a comparison of *McFarlane* and *Cattanach* published in Australia, see S Todd "Wrongful Conception, Wrongful Birth and Wrongful Life" (2005) 27 Syd L Rev 525–542, where many other aspects of the reproductive torts are discussed.

38  Civil Liability Act 2002 s 71 (NSW); Civil Liability Act 2003 s 49A (Qd). Section 71(1) of the NSW 2002 Act now provides that, in any proceedings involving a claim for the birth of a child, the court cannot award damages for economic loss for: (a) the costs associated with rearing or maintaining the child. Section 71(2), however, modifies this so as not to preclude "the recovery of any additional costs associated with rearing or maintaining a child who suffers from a disability that arise by reason of that disability". The otherwise somewhat similar Queensland legislation does not include this last qualification.

39  (1995) 38 NSWLR 47.

40  See note 3 above – *McFarlane*'s case 2000 SC (HL) 1 at 15, [2000] 2 AC 59 at 81, [1999] 4 All ER 961 at 976 as per Lord Steyn.

*Causation and mitigation in wrongful pregnancy*

Although the doctrines of causation and mitigation apply to the tort of wrongful pregnancy in very similar fashion, the result in *McFarlane* separates the two in a practical sense. The common factor, however, lies in the question of whether a failure to terminate the pregnancy constitutes behaviour that is so unreasonable as to excuse the negligent professional of liability for his or her breach of duty, and/or to mitigate any damages awarded.

The latter problem is, in fact, self-answering given the decision in *McFarlane*. If no damages are awarded, there is nothing to mitigate and the question does not arise. It is, however, essential to remember that *McFarlane* is concerned *only* with the birth of a healthy child. Both Lord Steyn and Lord Clyde implied that the rule might change were the child to be disabled – and we discuss that possibility below.

The problem of causation is, however, of fundamental importance to the tort – does a failure to terminate break the causal chain between the negligence and the damage? This proposition was accepted at first instance in *Emeh* but that finding was very firmly reversed on appeal[41]:

> "Save in the most exceptional circumstances, I cannot think it right that the court should ever declare it unreasonable for a woman to decline to have an abortion in a case where there is no evidence that there were any medical or psychiatric grounds for terminating the particular pregnancy."

Considerable importance was placed on the fact that Mrs Emeh would have been subjected to a *late* termination and there was some doubt as to whether the same would apply to an early abortion. This was put to rest in *McFarlane* where *Emeh* was followed without qualification by the whole panel. The reverse question – whether the woman could *legally* opt *for* an abortion – was not directly considered but that uncertainty was raised in the very similar case of Mrs Greenfield – albeit arising from a "missed" pregnancy during contraceptive therapy – which resulted in the birth of a healthy girl[42]. Mrs Greenfield contended that she would have terminated the pregnancy had she been appraised of her condition early enough. Buxton LJ (at [4]) pointed out that:

> "[S]uch a course of action could not have been followed unless it would have been in the circumstances lawful to do so under the law ... [I]t is assumed for the purpose of this application that such a termination, if it had taken place, would have been lawful ... The matter, as I understand it, has not been decided, and is certainly not being decided by this court."

In my view, the general underlying assumption that a termination would be lawful in cases like these is correct. The Abortion Act 1967 s 1(1)(a) legalises a termination if:

> "the pregnancy has not exceeded its twenty-fourth week and that the continuance of the pregnancy would involve risk, greater than if the pregnancy were terminated, of injury to the physical or mental health of the pregnant woman."

This is a comparative test of *risk*. Put at its simplest, it is certainly arguable that the *risk* of injury to the mental health of a woman who has taken active steps to prevent a

---

41  Note 21 above – [1985] QB 1012 at 1024, [1984] 3 All ER 1044 at 10153 per Slade LJ.
42  *Greenfield v Irwin (a firm)* [2001] EWCA Civ 113, [2001] 1 WLR 1279, sub nom *Greenfield v Flather* (2001) 59 BMLR 43.

pregnancy will be greater if she is forced to continue an unwanted pregnancy than if she is relieved of her condition.

If that is so, it follows that the pregnant woman – and, certainly, the "wrongfully" pregnant woman – always has a choice, and this leads us into further legal and moral byways. In the first place it may be asked – has the negligent professional any right to assume that the wronged woman will take the "accepted" way out? The answer must, surely, be "no". Legally, the wrongdoer must accept his or her "victim" as she is, and this, in the present context, must include a woman's individual attitude to the unborn child; as it was said in *McFarlane* "the law does and must respect these decisions of parents which are so closely tied to their basic freedoms and rights of personal autonomy"[43].

Which leads, finally, to the ethical aspects. Much is spoken of "the autonomous right to govern one's bodily integrity" but, before taking this route, one must ask if it is properly called in aid in the reproductive field. The woman in Mrs McFarlane's position has determined to avoid a future pregnancy. The concept of "choice" should she *become* pregnant is, therefore, illusory[44]. Rather, it would seem that she is "accepting" a circumstance, and its consequent responsibilities, that have been forced upon her in defiance of her primary "choice". It is at this point that her autonomy has been breached and it is this which represents the ultimate "harm" in a wrongful pregnancy. I believe that the courts are coming round to this view and that this becomes apparent in the case of *Rees* which is addressed below.

## WRONGFUL PREGNANCY AND DISABILITY

*The McFarlane exception – the neonate with disability*

The question of what would happen to the *McFarlane* decision in the event that the child be found to have unsuspected disabilities was left open deliberately rather than by default[45]. Such situations must be very rare in modern obstetric conditions and it is fortuitous that a suitable test case – *Parkinson v St James and Seacroft University Hospital NHS Trust*[46] – arose within a year of the landmark decision[47].

Mrs Parkinson became pregnant ten months after an admittedly negligent sterilisation by way of tubal occlusion. It was not until some years later that the child was found to be autistic and we will see later that this confuses the jurisprudential issue (see the text at notes 49–51 below). Mrs Parkinson sued for her child's maintenance, the judge at first instance awarding damages for the costs of meeting the child's special needs but not for the basic costs of rearing a child. Both sides appealed.

The main interest in the Court of Appeal's various speeches lies not so much in their specifics as in their general, albeit – and of necessity – no more than underlying, dissatisfaction with the *McFarlane* decision and, for this, the case must be read in full. For the present, we will concentrate on the powerful opinion of Hale LJ who seized on the opportunity to be the first senior female English judge to address the topic of wrongful pregnancy. In essence, Hale LJ concentrated on the practical, rather than the purely

---

43  See note 3 above – 2000 SC (HL) 1 at 16, [2000] 2 AC 59 at 81, [1999] 4 All ER 961 at 976 per Lord Steyn.

44  The problem of choice is discussed in depth by N Priaulx; see note 2 above, Chs 5, 6.

45  See note 3 above – 2000 SC (HL) 1 at 18, 31, [2000] 2 AC 59 at 84, 99, [1999] 4 All ER 961 at 979, 992 per Lord Steyn and Lord Clyde.

46  Note 25 above – [2002] QB 266, [2001] 3 All ER 97.

47  In fact, a rather better case – *Taylor v Shropshire Health Authority* [2000] Lloyd's Rep Med 96 – was heard, and decided on *Emeh* principles, just before *McFarlane* went to the House of Lords. It is a pity that it was not appealed.

economic, aspects of unwanted maternity – the process of giving birth was, she considered "rightly termed 'labour'" and the hard work, accompanied by the curtailment of personal liberty, does not stop at pregnancy. All later consequences[48]:

> "flow inexorably from ... the invasion of bodily integrity and personal autonomy involved in every pregnancy [and the mother's financial claim] obviously represents the consequences of the fundamental invasion of her rights, which is the conception itself."

Hale LJ's approach leads to some interesting conclusions. First, it recalls Lord Millett's dissenting opinion as to the "mother's" award for pain and suffering in the face of a refusal to recompense the "costs" of child rearing – it is illogical to award one without the other, or, in Hale terms, it is illogical *not* to award one *with* the other. Secondly, it highlights the effects of an unwanted pregnancy in such a way that compensation can be readily justified on the grounds of distributive justice. Thirdly, it removes the label of "pure economic loss" from the wrongful pregnancy action and replaces it with that of economic loss consequent upon the invasion of a woman's bodily integrity. And, finally, everything that is said in this respect as to a child with disabilities is applicable to the birth of a healthy child. The analyst may well feel that *McFarlane* and *Parkinson* are incompatible – if one is right, the other is wrong. However, *Parkinson* has not been appealed and, so far as the neonate with disabilities is concerned, it remains good law.

In the event, the court considered that the disability in the resulting child was sufficient to distinguish the two cases and confirmed the trial judge's disposition. In short, the benefits and hardships of having a normal, albeit unsought, child were held, effectively, to balance one another but the additional costs attributable to a disability were compensable. While the logic of the ruling remains arguable – it is to be noted that it is an essential element of such cases that the health professionals had no reason to suppose that the child would be born with disabilities – it has the advantage of appearing to be a fair compromise. Perhaps the major remaining difficulty lies in the definition of the "cut-off" point at which the surgeon's liability in respect of the disability ends. Hale LJ indicated that this should be birth – in other words, the disability should, generally, have been present in the fetus[49].

This problem surfaced in the case of *Groom v Selby*[50], a case involving a missed pregnancy at the time of sterilisation. Here, the child developed salmonella meningitis at the age of three weeks having, it was presumed, contracted the organism from her mother's birth canal. Both the trial judge and the Court of Appeal considered this to be a foreseeable consequence of a negligent operation and applied the *Parkinson* formula in respect of damages. The logic of this depends on the rule that a child is not *born* until it is fully extruded from the mother – otherwise one might wonder why it is not equally foreseeable that a child will contract MRS infection in the maternity ward[51]. *Groom* is, in the writer's opinion, a complex case which defies classification in the reproductive torts[52]. It did, however, provide a further opportunity for Hale LJ to elaborate on her theme ascribing the

---

48  Note 25 above – *Parkinson* [2002] QB 266 at [73], [2001] 3 All ER 97 at [73].

49  Thus, *Parkinson*, itself, is a difficult case in so far as it assumes autism to be a congenital condition unaffected by infantile environment. Which leaves open the question of, say, late onset genetic disease.

50  [2001] EWCA Civ 1522, (2002) 64 BMLR 47, [2002] Lloyd's Rep Med 1.

51  A major difficulty in *Groom* was expressed by Brooke LJ: "The longer the period before the disability is triggered off, the more difficult it may be to establish a right to establish compensation" – *Groom* (2002) 64 BMLR 47 at [26], [2002] Lloyd's Rep Med 1 at [26].

52  See Brooke LJ's problems – (2002) 64 BMLR 47 at [18], [19], [2002] Lloyd's Rep Med 1 at [18], [19].

damage of a wrongful pregnancy to the uncovenanted invasion of and distortion of a woman's life for many years. This must be particularly relevant when an already disabled woman becomes pregnant and it is to this variation that we now turn.

### The disabled mother

In so far as *Parkinson* was dealing with the *exception* to *McFarlane*, the two cases were not in jurisprudential conflict despite the obvious disenchantment of the Court of Appeal with the decision in the latter. However, the baby born as a result of a negligent sterilisation in *Rees v Darlington Memorial Hospital NHS Trust*[53] was healthy. The cases differed in that Ms Rees was partially blind and had undergone sterilisation largely because she did not feel able to look after a child. Thus, while *Rees* provided a new ground for arbitration, it also offered the House of Lords – this time represented by a seven-man panel – the opportunity to review, and, possibly, to reverse *McFarlane*. This, they declined to do directly[54], although much of the case centred on modifying the *results* of *McFarlane*. It is these on which we will concentrate.

Meanwhile, Ms Rees, having lost her case for recompense for the upkeep of her child at first instance, went to the Court of Appeal where the outcome was predictable. Hale LJ, supported by Robert Walker LJ, maintained that, if the compensable harm in a wrongful pregnancy was related to the stresses of motherhood in the case of a child with disabilities, it was equally, or more so, related to the trials of a mother with disabilities. Accordingly, and despite a strong dissenting opinion from Waller LJ, damages were awarded so as to recompense Ms Rees for the extra costs in child rearing imposed by her blindness. This is, arguably, both a more logical and a more just decision in the case of a disabled mother than in that of a disabled neonate. Granted that a surgeon cannot be excused of negligence in *any* case, his lack of care is, nevertheless, more *reprehensible* when he is fully aware of a special need for his expertise.

It was inevitable that the subsequent proceedings in the House of Lords should be complex given the task as summarised by Lord Bingham[55]:

> "The appellant NHS Trust now challenges [the decision in the Court of Appeal] as inconsistent with *McFarlane*. The claimant seeks to uphold the decision but also claims the whole cost of bringing up the child, inviting the House to reconsider its decision in *McFarlane*."

We have, however, already seen that the House refused to do the latter, at least six of the panel confirming their agreement with an unmodified *McFarlane*. That part of the discussion relevant to this paper thus became a consideration of the interplay between *McFarlane* in the Lords and *Parkinson* and *Rees* in the Court of Appeal. Either the latter two are equally distinguishable from the former or *McFarlane* and *Rees* are united by virtue of the child being healthy in both – in which case *Rees* is not a legitimate extension of *Parkinson* but, rather, "an illegitimate gloss on *McFarlane*"[56]. The opinions given were, inevitably, varied and are quite beyond the compass of an article such as this[57]. Suffice it to say that the House allowed the appeal but only by the narrowest majority of 4:3. It is

---

53  [2002] EWCA Civ 88, [2003] QB 20, [2002] 2 All ER 177, (2002) 65 BMLR 117; rvsd [2003] UKHL 52, [2004] 1 AC 309, [2003] 4 All ER 987.

54  This was almost entirely on the procedural grounds that it was too early to do so.

55  Note 53 above – *Rees* [2004] 1 AC 309 at [1], [2003] 4 All ER 987 at [1].

56  *Ibid* [2004] 1 AC 309 at [113], [2003] 4 All ER 987 at [113] per Lord Millett.

57  My own analysis is to be found in Mason, note 25 above. For a feminist critique, see N Priaulx "That's One Heck of an 'Unruly Horse'! Riding Roughshod over Autonomy in Wrongful Conception" (2004) 12 Feminist Legal Studies 317–331.

probably fair to summarise the position as the presence of a normal infant being the ruling factor, this overriding the alternative view that the interpolation of disability of any sort provides an acceptable exception to the *McFarlane* rule. Nonetheless, it is impossible to avoid the impression that the majority of the House was anxious to mitigate the effects of *McFarlane* – particularly as to its admitted distortion of tort law – while, at the same time, retaining its basic authority.

*The conventional award*

This culminated in the introduction of the controversial conventional award[58], the origin of which lies in the intuitive belief that the parents of the uncovenanted child have sustained a legal wrong, albeit, at this point, of uncertain definition; as a consequence, Lord Bingham proposed that "in all cases such as these, there be a conventional award to mark the injury and loss" – and he set this at £15,000. The rationale for the award is, currently unclear. We have good evidence as to what it is *not*. Lord Bingham said it would be neither compensatory nor nominal[59]; Lord Hope, while expressing his own doubts, thought it was by no means punitive. It is to be paid in addition to the "mother's claim" and irrespective of the neonatal outcome – and, significantly it is to be paid to the mother rather than the parents. Since it is not "the product of calculation"[60], we must look for a common denominator in the form of wrong to be righted in all the variations on the tort of wrongful pregnancy – and this is to be found in the common affront to the mother's interest in controlling the size of her family and limiting the responsibilities that go with motherhood. In short, we are looking at an insult to one or both parents' personal autonomy – a wrong for which there is currently no appropriate form of reparation[61].

The main interest of *Rees*, on this analysis, is, then, to raise the question of whether the courts are engaged in defining a new tort – breach of personal autonomy. There is certainly other evidence of this[62] and to accept it would not be to undermine the moral foundation of the *McFarlane* decision – indeed, in coming very close to the Scottish concepts of *damnum* and *iniuria* (see above), it would serve to harmonise the apparently irreconcilable results in the Inner House of the Court of Session and the House of Lords in that pivotal case. And, if it be said that the law is now written in stone – well, *Parkinson* is still available as a portal for further review by the highest court.

THE ACTION FOR WRONGFUL BIRTH

A main feature of the action for wrongful pregnancy is that the woman or the couple concerned does not want *any* further children. A further factor is that the health of the child was immaterial to the original decision; the birth of a child with disability is no more than one element in the assessment of the extent of the wrong done to the parents.

By contrast, those bringing an action for wrongful birth have sought parenthood. They have, however, been concerned that their child should not be disabled and have taken medical advice to this end; the subsequent birth of a child who, in fact, has disabilities may

58  Only four members of the panel actually approved it. For discussion, see P Cane "Another Failed Sterilisation" (2004) 120 LQR 189–193.

59  He also said it would not be "derisory"; it certainly is not princely.

60  Note 54 above – *Rees* [2004] 1 AC 309 at [8], [2003] 4 All ER 987 at [8] per Lord Bingham.

61  A recent wide-ranging analysis in favour of the conventional award is to be found in V Chico "Wrongful conception: Policy, inconsistency and the conventional award" (2007) 8 Medical Law International 139–164

62  See, in particular, *Chester v Afshar* [2004] UKHL 41, [2005] 1 AC 134, [2004] 4 All ER 587 which was described as "a modest departure from traditional causation principles" per Lord Steyn at [24].

well be due to negligent, and actionable, antenatal care. However, while antenatal counsellors can assess the *risk* of disability occurring in a fetus, it is clear that, outside the sphere of assisted reproduction involving, say, in-vitro fertilisation and pre-implantation genetic diagnosis, they cannot control the *occurrence* of disability. The best they can do is to diagnose the condition and assist the parents in their choice of management of the remaining pregnancy – and, by and large, that choice rests between continuation and termination[63]. Thus, it follows that the wrongful birth action is intimately bound up with abortion – far from being a choice that is imposed upon a woman, it is the denial of that choice which forms the kernel of any subsequent action.

Although it is difficult to say precisely why, the action for wrongful birth has proved less controversial in the medico-*legal* field than has that for wrongful pregnancy. It is true that the latter raises major moral concerns as to "commodifying" the human fetus; an action for wrongful birth is, however, equally suspect as it inherently discriminates against the fetus with disabilities and, by extrapolation, against the child or adult who is consequently affected. Moreover, terminations on the grounds of fetal disability will almost always be relatively late in pregnancy and fetal maturity has a profound effect on women's attitudes to abortion, this being in addition to the increased physical dangers to the woman associated with termination as gestation advances. The difference in attitude may, in fact, be fostered by the isolation of fetal disability[64] as a legal justification for abortion in the Abortion Act 1967 s 1(1)(d) which legalises termination if:

"there is a substantial risk that if the child were born it would suffer from such physical or mental abnormalities as to be seriously handicapped."

Again, however, this is no place to delve into the intense moral arguments surrounding our attitudes to disability in general – the terms of the 1967 Act and the increasing acceptance of abortion as a part of contemporary life have virtually precluded critical judicial analysis of the wrongful birth action. The situation has been well summarised in an instructive Canadian case[65]:

"[T]he claim for wrongful birth slipped quietly into Canadian tort law as a type of medical malpractice case without any fundamental analysis or delineation of such a claim."

And the same is probably true of the United Kingdom jurisprudence[66].

The recognisable causes of congenital disabilities can, simplistically, be divided into: chromosomal disorders (Down's syndrome being the most significant); genetic disease (for example, cystic fibrosis and muscular dystrophy) which may be sex or, better, X-linked (haemophilia); environmentally induced – particularly by viral disease in or drugs taken by the mother; and those due to a combination of factors – for example, neural tube defects (especially spina bifida). The majority of these will be effective post-conception but a few – including haemolytic disease of the newborn – may be induced pre-conception.

---

63 Inevitably, disability must add a new dimension to the choice of adoption as an option. I am not considering here the further possibility of the child being taken into care – see *Re B (a minor) (wardship: medical treatment)* (1981) [1990] 3 All ER 927, [1981] 1 WLR 1421, CA.
64 It will have been noted already that this writer, at least, believes that, subject to the gestational limit, termination on the grounds of fetal disability could easily be justified under the 1967 Act s 1(1)(a).
65 *Mickle v Salvation Army Grace Hospital* (1998) 166 DLR (4th) 743 at 747 per Zuber J, Ont Ct.
66 The first properly reported case seems to have been *Salih v Enfield Health Authority* [1991] 3 All ER 400, (1991) 7 BMLR 1, CA, in which the cases referred to were essentially of wrongful pregnancy type.

Antenatal counselling consists of anticipation, demonstration, interpretation and advice. Thus, it will be seen, first, that many and varied health care professionals will be involved; they will be readily identified and their proximity to the complainant in terms of a duty of care is unlikely to be disputed. The nature of that duty will, however, differ. That of the technician is generally straightforward, as is the identification of his or her breach of that duty. There is little difficulty in attributing negligence to the laboratory technician who confuses two specimens of blood so long as it is appreciated that his or her failure lies in the faulty demonstration and interpretation of a significant *diagnostic* feature – there can be no suggestion that he or she *caused* the fetal disability. The duty of the counsellor, however, is quite different and is a matter of presenting the facts to the pregnant woman in such a way that she understands them and can, as a result, make an informed decision as to whether or not to continue with the pregnancy. Thus, a large proportion of wrongful birth actions will be based on information disclosure and whether or not that duty has been discharged will depend, even today, on *Bolam*, or accepted medical practice, principles[67]. The difficulty is, of course, that counsellors must have their own personal views and whether truly non-directional counselling is a practical reality is at least questionable. The case of Mrs Al Hamwi[68] illustrates many of these points.

Mrs Al Hamwi, who already had one healthy child, had a strong family history of chromosomal abnormality[69] but, at 11 weeks' pregnancy, she was informed by her primary carer that it was "too late to have genetic tests". It was not until she was 17 weeks' pregnant that she was offered amniocentesis which she, first, accepted but, after consultation, later refused. This was largely on the grounds that, whereas the hospital estimated the risk of miscarriage following amniocentesis was 1:100, she believed it to be 75 per cent. She also understood that the risk of her child having a chromosomal abnormality was 1:8396 – but the fact that the abnormality was of transmissible type does not seem to have been appreciated until after the event. Over and above this, we have a deeply religious Christian counselling an equally devout Muslim woman. The child born was severely affected by the familial condition. In dismissing Mrs Al Hamwi's action in negligence for being denied the opportunity to terminate her pregnancy, Simon J admitted that she might have been confused. But he went on to say[70]:

> "Clinicians should take reasonable and appropriate steps to satisfy themselves that the patient has understood the information which has been provided; but the obligation does not extend to ensuring that the patient has understood" –

which demonstrates vividly one of the major difficulties confronting the claimant in an action for wrongful birth.

The possibly greater obstacle to overcome, however, lies in the field of causation – in order to succeed, she must *convince* the court that, given the right advice, she would have terminated her pregnancy. And, as the pioneer case of Mrs Gregory[71] illustrates, this may be a hard task. Mrs Gregory was not informed that her amniocentesis test was

---

67  Note 16 above. The *Bolam* test would now be modified by *Pearce v United Bristol Healthcare NHS Trust* (1999) 48 BMLR 118, CA, where it was held that it is the responsibility of the doctor to inform the patient of significant risk if the risk was such as would affect the judgment of a reasonable patient (per Lord Woolf MR at 124).

68  *Al Hamwi v Johnston* [2005] EWHC 206 (QB), [2005] Lloyd's Rep Med 309.

69  It turned out to be of the rare trans-location type which is transmissible. The incidence of Down's syndrome as it commonly occurs depends almost entirely on the age of the mother.

70  Note 68 above – [2005] Lloyd's Rep Med 309 at [69].

71  *Gregory v Pembrokeshire Health Authority* [1989] 1 Med LR 81.

unsatisfactory until it was too late to undertake a termination[72]; the problem was whether or not she would have accepted a repeat test had she been offered one in time. Rougier J, at first instance, summed up the situation succinctly:

> "[W]e can only conjecture as to what would have been done had matters turned out differently, and that conjecture is bound to be influenced, subconsciously, by what has happened in the meantime. It is not integrity which is in question but objectivity ... This [evidence] provides an illustration of how the objectivity of an honest witness can fail in the circumstances of stress."[73]

And Mrs Gregory lost her case and her appeal.

### Recompense for wrongful birth

Once these hurdles have been surmounted, there seems to have been little difficulty in obtaining recompense for negligent antenatal care in the United Kingdom prior to 2000, although much of the evidence for this stems from two Scottish cases[74]. These, however, interwove with *McFarlane* as it passed through its various stages – and *McFarlane* had a profound effect on recompense for wrongful birth. Quite why this should be so is difficult to analyse. It is obvious from what has been said that wrongful pregnancy and wrongful birth are clearly distinguishable; there is no reason in principle why one should depend upon the other – and it is only fair to point out that the learned judges themselves fully appreciated the distinction. Nonetheless, the precedent has been firmly established in a trio of cases[75] each of which included an extensive analysis of *McFarlane* as part of the decision making process.

*Rand* resulted from the negligent failure of the ultrasonographist to diagnose Down's syndrome in the fetus. Here, Newman J avoided having to put a value on a child's life by concentrating on the costs associated with the degree of disability alone and, in so doing, set the pattern of awarding damages only for the *extra* costs involved in the upkeep of a disabled child. *Hardman* was an example of disability arising from viral disease in the mother. The court, here, noted the difficulty of awarding costs for the pain and discomfort of pregnancy and labour when these were freely accepted; instead, Henriques J assessed these so as to recompense the mother for having to undergo caesarean section and for the shock of having given birth to a child with disabilities[76]. The loss to the parents was considered to be purely economic but, given the different circumstances, it was "fair, just and reasonable", and morally inoffensive, to quantify, and recompense, the additional expenditure imposed by the child's disability. Interestingly, the two courts differed as to the assessment of quantum, Newman J believing that this was driven by the parents' means

---

72  Under the, then, terms of the Infant Life (Preservation) Act 1929 s 1(1).

73  Note 71 above – [1989] 1 Med LR 81 at 86. The problem of the objective (reasonable) and subjective woman is best discussed in the Canadian case of *Arndt v Smith* [1997] 3 LRC 198, [1997] 2 SCR 539, Can SC – a nine-judge decision of the Supreme Court.

74  See *Anderson v Forth Valley Health Board* (1997) 44 BMLR 108, 1998 SLT 588, OH; *McLelland v Greater Glasgow Health Board* 1999 SC 305, 1999 SLT 543, OH, 2001 SLT 446, IH.

75  *Rand v East Dorset Health Authority* (2000) 56 BMLR 39, [2000] Lloyd's Rep Med 181; *Hardman v Amin* (2000) 59 BMLR 58, [2000] Lloyd's Rep Med 498; *Lee v Taunton and Somerset NHS Trust* [2001] 1 FLR 419, [2001] Fam Law 103.

76  The parallel problem of dissociating the personal injury of pregnancy from the economic loss associated with child rearing was considered. For further discussion, see *Godfrey v Gloucestershire Royal Infirmary NHS Trust* [2003] EWHC 549 (QB), [2003] Lloyd's Rep Med 398.

while Henriques J considered the dominant factor to be the extent of the child's disability. The latter was, surely correctly, followed in *Lee*.

Mrs Lee's case involved the birth of a child with spina bifida and was concerned, in the main with the difficulty encountered in *McFarlane* of balancing the benefits of a healthy child against the burdens of bringing up a healthy child Toulson J, however, summed up what most critics of *McFarlane* will maintain[77]:

> "I do not believe it would be right for the law to deem the birth of a disabled child to be a blessing in all circumstances and regardless of the extent of the child's disabilities."

As a result, the law in cases of wrongful birth was unaffected by the decision in *McFarlane* – and *Lee* followed the pattern of recovery established in *Rand* and *Hardman*.

It is possible, in a way, to see this as a fair compromise. The health carers concerned have been explicitly involved in the avoidance of a child with disabilities; their proximity to the claimant is undisputed and they cannot find refuge in *Caparo*[78] in respect of the disability. On the other side, the women concerned have wanted children; what they have not wanted is children with disability. It is, therefore, logical that they should receive recompense such as is directly associated with that disability. What the compromise does not recognise is the emotional effect on the mother of having borne and having to care for a seriously ill child – but this, being a matter of personal injury, is, as noted in *Hardman*, a separate issue.

The more tangible dilemma, however, lies in the question of why all the harm should be seen as affecting the mother. Is there not a solid case for recompensing the neonate for his or her diminished quality of life? And this is the basis for the third form of reproductive tort – the action for wrongful life brought by the disabled child.

## THE ACTION FOR WRONGFUL LIFE

Actions for wrongful birth – brought by the mother – and actions for wrongful life – brought by the child – have a common aim, that is, restitution for the tortious birth of a child with disabilities. It follows that they have common features and they have usually been pursued together. Yet, while, as we have seen, the former is likely to succeed, the latter has, until very recently, been rejected in virtually every major jurisdiction[79] – to the extent that, in the remarkable Canadian case of *Cherry v Borsman*[80], a doctor, whose negligence had clearly caused a child to be born severely disabled, sought to have the case heard as one of "wrongful life" rather than of negligence *simpliciter*.

Certainly an action for wrongful life is, currently, very unlikely to succeed in England and Wales and this is for two main reasons – neither of which, in one view, is particularly compelling. Firstly, it is widely believed to be barred by way of the Congenital Disease (Civil Liability) Act 1976 s 1(2)(b)[81] and, secondly, the only precedent lies in the case of

---

77 Note 75 above – *Lee* [2001] 1 FLR 419 at 430.
78 Note 36 above.
79 None of the three well known successful American cases – *Turpin v Sortini* (1982) 31 Cal 3d 220, (1982) 643 P 2d 954, Cal SC; *Harbeson v Parke-Davies Inc* (1983) 656 P 2d 483, Wash; *Procanik v Cillo* (1984) 97 NJ 339, (1984) 478 A 2d 755, NJ SC – was a clear cut case but there is no space here for discussion.
80 (1992) 94 DLR (4th) 487, BC CA.
81 Which defines an antenatal occurrence for which a health care practitioner may be answerable to the resultant child as one which "affected the mother during her pregnancy ... so that the child is born with disabilities which would not otherwise have been present".

*McKay v Essex Area Health Authority*[82] which is an old case on which to depend. As to the first, the words of Ackner LJ in *McKay* are significant[83]:

> "Subsection (2)(b) is so worded as to import the assumption that, but for the occurrence giving rise to a disabled birth, the child would have been born normal and healthy – not that it would not have been born at all."

In other words, it is simply a matter of semantics – the problem disappears if one substitutes the term "diminished life", which the action is all about, for "wrongful life" which is a misnomer. Moreover, it is apparent that a similar action is now available, at least, within the provision of assisted reproduction services[84].

As to *McKay* itself, Mrs McKay's daughter was born severely disabled by way of the congenital rubella syndrome as a result of laboratory negligence. Mrs McKay's own action for wrongful birth was, so far as is known, not contested; her daughter's claim for "being burdened with highly debilitating injuries" was originally struck out but was reinstated at first instance. The Authority's appeal was upheld in the starkest terms by Stephenson LJ who gave the main opinion. His reasons had previously been widely rehearsed in the American courts and can be summarised, with comment:

- the only loss for which the health carers could be held responsible was represented by the difference between disability and non-existence and this was impossible to assess. But it becomes perfectly feasible if one speaks of diminished rather than wrongful life – there is nothing particularly difficult in comparing disability with normality;
- any right not to be born disabled implies a right to be "deprived of the opportunity to live" and to accept such a further inroad into the doctrine of the sanctity of life would be contrary to public policy – but, with lawful abortions now running at some 180,000 per annum in England, this now has something of a dated ring to it[85];
- the health carers certainly have a duty not to injure the fetus but, insofar as it was the rubella virus, and not the carers, that caused the child's injuries, there was no breach of duty on the part of the latter. Thus, the action for wrongful life fails simply on the grounds of *causation* and it is this which, in the author's view, constitutes the major barrier to a successful fetal action not only for wrongful life but also for diminished life.

Before continuing the discussion, however, it is worth diverting for a moment to consider two circumstances in which causation could be shown. The first is the pre-conception tort that has been mentioned already. Here, the damage to the fetus results from previous negligent treatment of the mother which rendered it foreseeable that children as yet unconceived would be disabled. The tortfeasor – and, hence, the cause – is readily identifiable; even so, there is some obvious difficulty as to how far into the future his or her liability persists – a matter of proximity and the consequent duty of care. Cases, therefore,

---

82  [1982] QB 1166, [1982] 2 All ER 771, CA.

83  [1982] QB 1166 at 1186, [1982] 2 All ER 771 at 786. For recent criticism of this interpretation of the Act, see A Morris and S Saintier "To be or not to be: Is that the question? Wrongful life and misconceptions" (2003) 11 Med Law Rev 167–193.

84  Congenital Disabilities (Civil Liability) Act 1976 s 1A inserted by Human Fertilisation and Embryology Act 1990 s 44.

85  The best modern judicial analysis of the wrongful life action is to be found in the Australian case of *Harriton v Stephens; Waller v James* [2004] NSWCA 93, (2004) 59 NSWLR 694, NSW CA, *Harriton v Stephens* [2006] HCA 15, (2006) 226 ALR 391, Aust HC. The minority opinion by Mason P in the Court of Appeal is particularly useful reading.

are fact sensitive and such actions may go either way[86]. The second exception lies in those instances of neonatal disability in which a drug that is known to be teratogenic has been administered to a pregnant woman. Here, the identity of the tortfeasor and causation appear well-established; again, however, the problem lies in the duty of care but, this time within the far more proximate relationship between the woman's physician and the woman's fetus – does it, in fact, give rise to a duty of care? This has, in the past, caused confusion[87]. In England and Wales, we can now take refuge in statute; the Congenital Disabilities (Civil Liability) Act 1976 was specifically enacted to ensure that the drug disabled neonate had a cause of action against the negligent prescribing agency.

Nonetheless, I suggest that, semantics apart – and to which I return in conclusion – it is the problem of causation that is at the heart of the paradox that, given the birth of a neonate with disabilities that results from negligent antenatal care, the mother will always receive recompense for the extra costs in rearing the child that are imposed by its handicap while the child's suffering as a result of the same negligence and the same handicap will go unrecognised. On the assumption that damages for the same tort should not be levied twice, many, the author included, would see the action for wrongful life as being more logical and more deserving of success than that for wrongful birth[88]. As has already been noted, it is, in the main, causation that stands in the way of that resolution of the problem and it is only comparatively recently that it has been revisited from this angle – but, this time, in the courts of the European Union.

### Wrongful life in Europe

The case of Mme Perruche[89] caused medico-legal uproar in France. The circumstances were precisely those of Mrs McKay. At first instance, the claims of both the mother and the child were upheld; the latter was dismissed by the court of appeal on grounds similar to those given in *McKay* and was dismissed again by way of causation. The case then went to the Assemblée Plénière which held that the hospital was negligent in preventing Mme Perruche from exercising her freedom to terminate her pregnancy, the harm resulting to the child from his handicap was caused by that negligence and he could, accordingly, claim compensation for it.

Which seems a reasonably logical solution of the causation problem and, when one adds the practical reasoning provided – that control of the damages should be in the hands of the person who is damaged rather than in those of his or her possibly fickle parents – it is clear that the *Perruche* judgment has much to commend it. Nevertheless, it took the French Parliament only a very short time to introduce a law making a repetition impossible – and, incidentally, at the same time, severely curtailing the scope of the parental wrongful birth action. The result is, therefore, extremely unlikely to affect the European jurisprudence and there is little point in discussing it further[90]. As for England and Wales, the solution of the wrongful life action remains governed by a combination of *McKay* and the Congenital Diseases (Civil Liability) Act 1976.

---

86 See the important article by A Whitfield "Common law duties to unborn children" (1993) 1 Med Law Rev 28–52.

87 Again, a most instructive case comes from the Commonwealth via Canada. In *Lacroix v Dominique* (2001) 202 DLR (4th) 121 it was held that no such duty arose.

88 Although it would seem right that the mother should, simultaneously, receive at least "conventional" damages for the mental trauma due to the unexpected birth of a child with disabilities.

89 *X v Mutuelle d'Assurance du Corps Sanitaire Français et al* (*Perruche*) (2000) JCP 2293.

90 For the same reason, I do not propose discussion of the somewhat convoluted reasoning of the Netherlands Court of Appeal which also allowed a wrongful life action shortly after *Perruche* was reported: *X v Y*, The Hague Court of Appeals, 26 March 2003.

## CONCLUSION

The majority of commentators would probably agree that the status of tort law in relation to reproduction is currently confused and, to some extent, unsatisfactory. There are a number of factors underlying this. First, the cornerstone of the law is provided by the *McFarlane* case which, as was admitted by its founders, introduced an exception to the law of tort as it is commonly applied. It is not easy to formulate principles on an exception and the greater part of the subsequent case law has been devoted to circumventing its rigid rule.

Secondly, much of the reasoning in the courts worldwide is still based on assumptions that have something of a dusty appearance. Attitudes to family planning, the increasing acceptance of voluntary termination of pregnancy as a normal part of life (or death) and, indeed, the emergence of an increasingly hedonistic society are all features of the twenty-first century that, rightly or wrongly, have received little attention in recent relevant judicial opinions.

Most importantly, the very terminology in use is self-defeating. It is neither the pregnancy, the birth nor the life that is wrongful. Rather it is wrongful negligence that is common to all. Looked at in this way, the emotive aspects of the reproductive tort – and, in particular, those concerned with what are predominantly philosophical problems – can be avoided and the standard rules of tort can be applied to what are, in essence, standard actions for negligence. There is nothing "wrong", and nothing denigrating to a child, in awarding compensation for the costs involved in undertaking a task which one has been at some pains to avoid. I cannot resist quoting, once again, the famous words of Peter Pain J[91]:

> "Every baby has a belly to be filled and a body to be clothed. The law relating to damages is concerned with reparation in money terms and this is what is needed for the maintenance of a baby."

---

91 *Thake v Maurice* [1986] QB 644 at 666, [1984] 2 All ER 513 at 526.

# THE FIELD OF PLAY

## MICHAEL J BELOFF QC[1] AND RUPERT BELOFF[2]

### (1) THE JUSTICIABILITY OF SPORTS DECISIONS

In *Czarnikow v Roth, Schmidt & Co*[3], Scrutton LJ memorably said "There must be no Alsatia in England where the King's writ does not run". We want to explore whether the sporting field, pitch, rink, pool or court constitutes another Alsatia where the official is himself absolute monarch and whence (furthermore) the civil and criminal law are excluded.

The rules of a game define how the game must be played, and who should adjudicate upon or enforce compliance with the rules themselves. In football, for example, such rules define how victory is achieved (by one team scoring more goals than the other), as well as how a goal is scored (kicking the ball across the goal line from an onside position) and who determines whether a goal has been scored (the referee, with the assistance of the linesmen).

The referee also has power to administer summary punishment for a breach of the rules which amounts to misconduct (such as deliberately fouling an opponent) by showing a red card, resulting in a player's dismissal from the field of play (and suspension for a number of matches thereafter).

The referee's *bona fide* exercise of judgment or discretion, nowadays aided in sports such as rugby, cricket and tennis by Hawkeye or equivalent technology, is beyond challenge[4] otherwise than in so far as the rules of the game themselves provide: for example, an appeal either during the currency of a competition[5] or (after the game) against a red card, which if successful, may lift the suspension, but has no retrospective effect on the match[6]. This is a fundamental element in sports law most fully elucidated in the jurisprudence of the Court of Arbitration for Sport ("CAS")[7], which has received the accolade of the Swiss Federal Tribunal as being the true world Court of Sport.

It is an apparent, but not an actual paradox, that one of the key objectives of sports law (or the *lex sportiva*) is indeed to immunise sport from the reach of the law, to create, in other words, a field of autonomy onto which even appellate sports tribunals should not trespass.

In *Yang v Hamm*[8], a CAS Panel (chaired by the first-named author) had to decide after the Athens Olympics whether to reallocate the medals in the Men's Gymnastics All Round

---

1 Michael Beloff QC practises from Blackstone Chambers, The Temple. He is Senior Ordinary Judge of the Court of Appeal of Jersey and Guernsey and Treasurer Elect of Grays Inn, a member of the Court of Arbitration for Sport and a former President of Trinity College Oxford.

2 Rupert Beloff, MA (Oxon), LLB, Pg Dip EC Law (Kings) practises from No 5 Chambers Birmingham.

3 [1922] 2 KB 478, [1922] All ER Rep 45, CA.

4 *Machin v FA* (unreported, 1993), CA.

5 In the recent World Track and Field Championships in Osaka (2007) in the Men's 1,500 metre semi-final, the French athlete Mehdi Baala knocked over two athletes in a sprint for the line. He was disqualified by a jury of appeal and the two victims generously instated into the final.

6 There is a difference between re-writing a result of a game on the basis of objective video-evidence, and maintaining a sanction against a player insofar as a result of what can be shown to have been an erroneous judgment (eg, as to whether a footballer "dived" or fell because fouled).

7 F Oschütz "The Arbitrability of Sports Disputes and the Rules of the Game" in *The Court of Arbitration for Sport 1984–2004* (2006) pp 200–209.

8 CAS 2004/A/704, p 37.

final when the bronze medallist had been a victim of erroneous marking by the judges as to the difficulty of his parallel bars exercise. The Panel summarised the state of the art in this way:

> "The extent to which, if at all, a Court including CAS can interfere with an official's decision is not wholly clear. An absolute refusal to recognise such a decision as justiciable and to designate the field of play as 'a domain into which the King's writ does not seek to run' in Lord Atkin's famous phrase[9] would have a defensible purpose and philosophy. It would recognise that there are areas of human activity which elude the grasp of the law, and where the solution to disputes is better found, if at all, by agreement. It would contribute to finality. It would uphold, critically, the authority of the umpire, judge or referee, whose power to control competition, already eroded by the growing use of technology such as video replays, would be fatally undermined if every decision taken could be judicially reviewed. And, to the extent that the matter is capable of analysis in conventional legal terms, it could rest on the premise that any contract that the player has made in entering into competition is that he or she should have the benefit of honest 'field of play' decisions, not necessarily correct ones."[10]

However, as the Panel went on to note "Sports law does not have a policy of complete abstention", and referred to earlier decisions of a Panel with a similar jurisdiction: *Segura v IAAF*[11], where the challenge was to a referee's decision that a walker had "lifted" contrary to the rules of walking; and *Korean Olympic Committee (KOC) v International Skating Union (ISU)*[12], where the challenge was to the disqualification of a Korean skater, Kim Dung-sung, in the final of the men's 1,500 metre short track skating event. The Panel there expressly characterised the approach as one of self-restraint, not absence of jurisdiction.

It is indeed pragmatisms rather than principle which draws the line between the justiciable or non-justiciable since, after all, "Such decisions may have direct or indirect financial consequences for the persons to whom such decisions are addressed"[13].

But such relative abstention can be justified for a variety of reasons: an arbitrator's lack of expertise in the technical side of sport; the inevitable element of subjectivity, resulting in part from different physical perspectives, in judging, for example, whether a tennis ball was in or out; the fear of constant interruption to the course of play; the opening of floodgates; the problems of rewriting a result after the event[14]; as well as the need to strengthen the match official's hand.

---

9  *Balfour v Balfour* [1919] 2 KB 571 at 919, [1918–19] All ER Rep 860 at 865.

10  Upon review I consider that it would be more logical [if *complete* abstention were the true position] to hold that the contract was that the player would accept (subject to internal appeal) the referees' decision, right or wrong, honest or dishonest.

11  CAS OG 00/013 Reeb 2 680. See too the decision in *Mendy v ABA* (1996) CAS-Digest p 409 (referee's decision as to whether a blow was below the belt was unjusticiable).

12  *KOC v ISU* OWG Salt Lake City 2002 007 Reeb 3 611.

13  Oschütz, *op cit*, p 208. An illustration was provided by one of the first matches of the 2007–2008 Premiership Football season where Chelsea were wrongly awarded a penalty (as the referee candidly admitted after the game). The points lost by Liverpool after Chelsea scored as a result a winning goal may yet be decisive in the championship with all the implications for TV monies, sponsorship etc: 'Styles rested after admitting Chelsea penalty was a mistake' (2007) The Times, 21 August. Oddly enough, a month later Chelsea were wrongly deprived of a valid goal on the basis admitted afterwards by the referee to have been wrongly ruled "offside": "Shevchenko's prognosis is poor as Mourinho's headache grows worse" (2007) The Guardian, 17 September.

"A video may show the objective fact but such fact must not be mingled with the limited information which was available to the referee in the situation at hand."[15]

And, as anyone who has watched endless replays from various angles of the pack of players converging over the try-line while resort is had to the umpire studying his own video to determine whether or not a try has been scored, the camera may not lie but it can be economical with the truth. As Mike Atherton, the former England cricket captain has written[16]:

"The desire to use more technology is based on two false premises: that the technology is completely accurate and that all decision-making can be reduced to an absolute truth."

The qualified immunity of field of play rule from quasi judicial review has accordingly been extrapolated to challenges to the efficacy of the accuracy of technical equipment. In the Sydney Olympics, the Bulgarian rower Nekyova finished second in the women's single sculls in the time of 7.28.783 behind Ekaterina Karsten, who finished in the time of 7.28.741, and requested the ad hoc Division to allocate gold medals to both athletes on the basis that the photo-finish was not accurate. Her reliance on a video of the race produced by a commercial television channel which appeared to contradict the assessment of the photo finish produced by the "officials" Swatch failed[17].

In *Hamm v Yang*, the immunity was extended even to the *admitted* judging error. The panel said[18]:

"An error identified with the benefit of hindsight, whether admitted or not, cannot be a ground for reversing a result of a competition. We can all recall occasions where a video replay of a football match, studied at leisure, can show that a goal was given, when it should have been disallowed (the Germans may still hold that view about England's critical third goal in the World Cup Final in 1966), or vice versa or where in a tennis match a critical line call was mistaken. However, quite apart from the consideration, that no one can be certain how the competition in question would have turned out had the official's decision been different, for a Court to change the result would on this basis still involve interfering with a field of play decision. Each sport may have within it a mechanism for utilising modern technology to ensure a correct decision is made in the first place (eg cricket with run-outs) or for immediately subjecting a controversial decision to a process of review (eg gymnastics) but the solution for error, either way, lies within the

---

14  In CAS 2004/A/704 in favour of Hamm, the Panel noted:
"The event was not a single apparatus event, but an all round one. After the parallel bars there as one more apparatus on which the competitors had to perform ie the high bar. We have no means of knowing how Yang would have reacted had he concluded the competition in this apparatus as the points leader rather than in third position. He might have risen to the occasion; he might have frozen; his marks on the high bar were in fact below expectation and speculation is inappropriate."

15  Oschütz, *op cit*, p 208.

16  Mike Atherton "Third Umpire referral rules are as confused as poor Mustard" (2007) Sunday Telegraph, 10 June.

17  CAS OG SYD 2000 Reeb 2.674.

18  The qualified immunity of the so-called *"game rule"* or *"field of play"* was reiterated in a number of cases at the Athens Olympics: the interim application in *CAS OG/005* at [2] and *OG/04/007* at [8.6] (rowing: trespass into another's lane).

framework of the sport's own rules; it does not licence judicial or arbitral interference thereafter. If this represents an extension of the field of play doctrine, we tolerate it with equanimity. Finality is in this area all important: rough justice may be all that sport can tolerate."

Sports Courts or Sports Tribunals may interfere only if an official's field of play decision is tainted by fraud or by arbitrariness or corruption. The panel noted in *KOC v ISU*[19]:

> "5.1 The jurisprudence of CAS in regard to the issue raised by this application is clear, although the language used to explain that jurisprudence is not always consistent and can be confusing. Thus, different phrases, such as 'arbitrary', 'bad faith', 'breach of duty', 'malicious intent', 'committed a wrong' and 'other actionable wrongs' are used, apparently interchangeably, to express the same test (*Mendy v/AIBA*, CAS OG 96/006)."

It could have added to the catalogue "contrary to general principles of law."[20]

It is not so much that there is a presumption of regularity as that there is a powerful bias in favour of a result already reached.

The rules of the game and rules of law are distinguishable. But game rules are not a species of sub- or non-law, or even what Michael Riesman has called micro-law[21]. They are justiciable: but sports bodies will exercise circumspection in their own adjudicative exercise.

> "'The Rules of the Game' (sometimes also called 'Technical Rules') are the rules which are intended to ensure the correct course of the game and competition respectively. The application of such rules cannot, save in very exceptional circumstances, lead to any 'judicial review'. The 'rules of law' are of a different nature. They are proper statutory sanctions that can affect the judicial interests of the person upon whom a sanction has been imposed other than in the course of the game or competition. For this reason they have to be subject to judicial review."[22]

Referees or umpires must, in particular, *apply* game rules[23] and not ignore them since "a deviation from a mandatory game rule undermines the utility of the rule, and, moreover, may affect the outcome of the game or tournament". In one case, having decided that, as a matter of construction of the IPC rules, the starter is the sole judge of whether a race shall be stopped when there has been a collision within 200 metres of the start, a CAS panel ruled that *whether* he stops a race in those circumstances is entirely a matter for him[24].

While game rules are generally beyond the reach of the general law, most sports provide for the ability to discipline participants who not only breach those rules but do so in such a way as to amount to misconduct[25].

In the controversial fourth match between England and Pakistan at the Oval in 2006, the umpire charged the Pakistan team for unfairly changing the conditions of the ball. In consequence, the Pakistan team initially refused to continue to play and forfeited the match. The Pakistan captain's disciplinary hearing took place before the ICC chief referee, Ranjan

---

19  *cit sup.*
20  *FIN v FINA* (1997) CAS Digest 351 96/157 and *Segura v IAAF* CAS OG 00/013.
21  Riesman *Law in Brief Encounters* (1999).
22  In *WCM-GP Ltd v FIM* CAS 2003/A/461 Reeb 3.43 at [29]–[30] and IHA, LHF and FIH CAS 2001/A/354 Reeb 3.489.
23  *IHF v LHF* CAS 2001/A/354 at [7]. CAS 2003/A/461 at [471]–[473].
24  *CPC v PC Reeb 2 567*, CAS 2000/A/305.
25  Lewis and Taylor *Sports Law and Practice* (2nd edn, 2002) para 3.11.

Madugalle, on 27 August 2006. In his decision, dismissing the charge of ball-tampering, the chief referee rejected the ICC's submission that he should overturn the ball-tampering decision of the umpires only if he was satisfied that it was perverse, in bad faith, or the result of a misinterpretation of the laws. The chief referee held (controversially) that his function was to reach his own view of whether there was ball-tampering. Given the physical state of the ball, allied to the fact that neither umpire had seen a fielder tampering with the ball, his conclusion was that there was no breach of the relevant rule.

It has been powerfully argued that[26]:

> "The chief referee's decision about his function in this case can only encourage more of the same, be it in the disciplinary forum or for broadcasting to the watching public. Regarding the former, there is now even more incentive for cricketers charged with disciplinary offences to wheel out former players and other experts as defence witnesses, and for their legal representatives to rely upon their evidence as the basis for cross-examination of the main in the middle. The same is likely to be true in other sports."

In this instance the internal appeal resulted in acquittal. Elsewhere, the decisions of internal disciplinary bodies have been challenged in the courts when the decision has been reached by an unfair procedure or is substantively irrational, disproportionate or in restraint of trade or breaches human rights[27].

## (2) THE CRIMINAL LAW APPLIED TO SPORT

The courts' procedures can directly be engaged when breaches of criminal or civil law are involved on the field of play, establishing that it is not the case that the sporting field is a closed shop, protected by its own special rules and procedures into which the law of the land cannot venture. In the case of *R v Barnes*[28], the Court of Appeal considered when it was appropriate for criminal proceedings to be instituted after an injury is caused by one player to another player during a sporting event.

The Court of Appeal drew a clear distinction between cases where no injury had been caused and those where it had. It was held that[29]:

> "When no bodily harm is caused, the consent of the victim to what happened is always a defence to a charge. Where at least bodily harm is caused, consent is generally irrelevant ..."

In the court's opinion:

> "[13] The general position as to contact sports was helpfully considered by the Law Commission in Consent and Offences Against the Person (1993) (Law Com No 134). The Commission indicated its approval of the approach adopted by the Criminal Injuries Compensation Board (1987) (Cm 265) which we would also approve. This is that (para 10.12) –
>
> > 'in a sport in which bodily contact is a commonplace part of the game, the players consent to such contact even if, through unfortunate accident, injury, perhaps of a serious nature, may result. However, such players do not consent to being deliberately punched or kicked and such actions constitute an assault for which the Board would award compensation.'

---

26  Griffiths and Whale "Not cricket" (2006) 156 NLJ 1897.
27  Lewis and Taylor, para 3.11.
28  [2004] EWCA Crim 3246, [2005] 2 All ER 113.
29  *Ibid* at [7].

[14] Subject to what we have to say hereafter we would in general accept the view of the Commission that (para 10.18) –

'the present broad rules for sports and games appear to be: (i) the intentional infliction of injury enjoys no immunity; (ii) a decision as to whether the reckless infliction of injury is criminal is likely to be strongly influenced by whether the injury occurs during actual play, or in a moment of temper or over-excitement when play has ceased, or "off the ball"; (iii) although there is little authority on the point, principle demands that even during play injury that results from risk-taking by a player that is unreasonable, in the light of the conduct necessary to play the game properly, should also be criminal.'

[15] On the other hand, the fact that the play is within the rules and practice of the game and does not go beyond them, will be a firm indication that what has happened is not criminal. In making a judgment as to whether conduct is criminal or not, it has to be borne in mind that, in highly competitive sports, conduct outside the rules can be expected to occur in the heat of the moment, and even if the conduct justifies not only being penalised but also a warning or even a sending off, it still may not reach the threshold level required for it to be criminal. That level is an objective one and does not depend upon the views of individual players. The type of the sport, the level at which it is played, the nature of the act, the degree of force used, the extent of the risk of injury, the state of mind of the defendant are all likely to be relevant in determining whether the defendant's actions go beyond the threshold."

And the court concluded:

"[28] We appreciate the difficulty that the judge had summing up this case because of the state of the authorities. The concept of 'legitimate sport' in itself is not unhelpful. However, it required an explanation of how the jury should identify what is and what is not 'legitimate' in the context of the relevant sport ... It should have been pointed out to the jury that even if the offending contact was a foul, it was still necessary for them to determine whether it could be anticipated in a normal game of football or was it something quite outside what could be expected to occur in the course of a football game. The summing-up should also have made it clear that even if a tackle results in a player being sent off, it may still not reach the necessary threshold to constitute criminal conduct.

[29] The jury were not given any examples of conduct which could be regarded as 'legitimate sport' and those which were not 'legitimate sport' for the purposes of determining whether they were criminal. The jury did not need copies of the rules, but they did need to be told why it was important to determine where the ball was at the time the tackle took place. They should have been told the importance of the distinction between the appellant going for the ball, albeit late, and his 'going for' the victim."

In R v Venna[30], reference was made to an earlier case, R v Bradshaw[31], "as supporting the view that unlawful physical force applied recklessly constitutes a criminal assault". This was not cited in Barnes, which must now be regarded as the locus classicus.

---

30  [1976] QB 421 at 429, [1975] 3 All ER 788 at 793.
31  (1878) 14 Cox CC 83.

One may differentiate those activities which constitute an excessive exercise of a game (connected action[32] – for example, an "over the top tackle"), from those which are entirely unconnected with the game, other than that they occur during it (such as a punch thrown in the course of play[33]). Therefore an act that does not breach the rules of the sport in question is unlikely to be criminal. Where an act does breach the rules of the sport, it may still not be criminal even though it may merit penalty under those rules.

Boxing, of course, creates its own insoluble problems. The House of Lords established in *R v Brown*[34] (a case about sado-masochism, not sport) that consent to actual bodily harm does not provide a defence to criminal prosecution. Lord Mustill considered the specific case of boxing. He determined that[35]:

> "For money, not recreation or personal improvement, each boxer tries to hurt the opponent more than he is hurt himself, and aims to end the contest prematurely by inflicting a brain injury serious enough to make the opponent unconscious, or temporarily by impairing his central nervous system through a blow to the midriff, or cutting his skin … The boxers display skill, strength and courage, but nobody pretends that they do good to themselves or others. The onlookers derive entertainment, but none of the physical and moral benefits which have been seen as the fruits of engagement in manly sports. I intend no disrespect to the valuable judgment of McInerney J. in Pallante v. Stadiums Pty. Ltd. (No. 1) [1976] V.R. 331 when I say that the heroic efforts of that learned judge to arrive at an intellectually satisfying account of the apparent immunity of professional boxing from criminal process have convinced me that the task is impossible. It is in my judgment best to regard this as another special situation which for the time being stands outside the ordinary law of violence because society chooses to tolerate it."

It is therefore only public policy that protects the boxer from prosecution for criminal activity.

## (3) THE CIVIL LAW APPLIED TO SPORT

### Negligence

As to civil law, the English law of tort (in its protection of the person) makes the standard of behaviour of the person who caused the injury determinative of whether liability arises. Assault and battery – respectively the threat of and the actual infliction of physical injury – require intent in the tortfeasor. Negligence requires the infliction of injury in circumstances where the tortfeasor had no intent, but his action or omission fell short of an appropriate objectively set standard.

The tort of negligence has three elements that the claimant must establish: (i) that the defendant owed him a common duty of care; (ii) that he breached that duty; and (iii) that damage resulted.

The primary aspect of the common law duty of care relevant to sport is the need to avoid foreseeable risk which results in foreseeable physical injury.

---

32 See E Grayson *Sport and the Law* (3rd edn, 1999) pp 260–264 for examples of criminal cases arising out of action on the foul play. As was noted in Barnes, criminal prosecutions arising out of actions on the field of play were very rare but in recent years there has been an increase.
33 For which 15 months' imprisonment was imposed at Gloucester Crown Court: (2006) Times, 6 January, p 6.
34 [1994] 1 AC 212, [1993] 2 All ER 75.
35 [1994] 1 AC 212 at 265, [1993] 2 All ER 75 at 107–108.

Three main issues arise: (1) whether there is a duty of care; (2) if so, what standard of care is required; and (3) whether, and to what extent such voluntary participation in or attendance at the sporting contest provides a defence to a claim.

As to the duty of care, it is elementary that[36]:

> "Firstly, a duty is owed to those who ought reasonably to be in contemplation as being affected by a particular act (the so-called 'neighbour' principle derived from the speech of Lord Atkin in *Donoghue v Stevenson*);
>
> Secondly, the duty itself is to take *reasonable* care to avoid injury to another person or property;
>
> Thirdly, since both the identification of the individuals to whom the duty is owed and the existence and extent of the duty *are* substantially determined by conceptions of reasonableness, the facts of and relating to any given case will determine whether or not a duty is established and, if so, whether or not breach of such duty can be shown."

In *Rootes v Shelton*[37] in the High Court of Australia (which arose out of a water skiing accident), Kitto J said:

> "I cannot think that there is anything new or mysterious about the application of the law of negligence to a sport or a game. Their kind is older by far than the common law itself. And though water skiing may be slightly faster than chariot-racing it is, like every other sport, simply an activity in which participants place themselves in a special relation or succession of relations to other participants so that adjudication under the common law upon a claim by one participant against another for damages for negligence in respect of injuries sustained in the course of the activity requires only that the tribunal of fact apply itself to the same kind of question of fact as arises in other cases of personal injury by negligence.
>
> ... the conclusion to be reached must necessarily depend, according to the concepts of the common law, upon the reasonableness, in relation to the special circumstances, of the conduct which caused the plaintiff's injury ... the tribunal of fact may think that in the situation to which the plaintiff's injury was caused, a participant might do what the defendant did and still not be acting unreasonably, even though he infringed the 'rules of the game'. Non-compliance with such rules, conventions or customs (where they exist) is necessarily one consideration to be attended to upon the question of unreasonableness; but it is only one, and it may be of much or little or even no weight in the circumstances.
>
> The question to be asked was 'was the defendants conduct which caused the injury to the plaintiff reasonable in all the circumstances, including as part of the circumstances the inferences fairly to be drawn by the defendant from the plaintiff's participation in what was going on at the time?'"

This antipodean approach was followed in the English Court of Appeal in *Condon v Basi*[38], where a foul tackle by the defendant, during a game of soccer, resulted in the plaintiff sustaining a fractured leg. The court, having noted:

---

36 "The issue of negligence cannot be resolved in a vacuum; it is fact specific." Judge J *Caldwell v Maguire* [2001] EWCA Civ 1054, [2002] PIQR P6, [2001] All ER (D) 363 (Jun).

37 [1968] ALR 33 at 37.

38 [1985] 2 All ER 453, [1985] 1 WLR 866.

"There is no authority as to what is the standard of care which governs the conduct of players in competitive sports generally and, above all, in a competitive sport whose rules and general background contemplate that there will be physical contact between the players" –

then concluded that the duty of care between players in competitive sports was a duty to take all reasonable care, taking into account the particular circumstances in which the completing players were placed. If one player injured another because either he had failed to exercise the degree of care, which was appropriate in all the circumstances, or because he had acted in a way to which the other could not have been expected to consent, he would be liable for damages in an action in negligence brought by the injured player.

This, with respect, confuses the existence of a cause of action with the existence of a defence.

The question posed by the first (and proper) test is, *what* are relevant circumstances? These may include:

- Is the sport a contact or non-contact sport? Different standards apply to boxing (where the object of the exercise is to engage in aggressive bodily contact) to rugby (where it is a necessary feature of the sport) and to lawn bowls (where such contact should not occur).
- Was the accident caused in the heat of the moment or in a quiet passage of play? It has been judicially noted that "The conduct of a player in the heat of a game is instinctive and not to be judged by standards suited to polite social intercourse"[39].
- Have the rules of the game been broken? The clear implication from *Condon v Basi* is that, in the case of contact sports, such as football or rugby, it will be almost impossible to establish liability unless the actions of the defendant are outside the rules of the game. Indeed the Court of Appeal appeared to be saying that a breach of the rules is virtually a *necessary*, albeit not necessarily a *sufficient*, requirement for liability to attach. Not every foul will constitute a tort, but something short of a foul will not do so.
- What is the cost and availability of precautions?
- What is the level of risk involved?

In *Caldwell v Maguire*[40], Tuckey LJ said that the scope of the duty is "to exercise in the course of the contest all care that is objectively reasonable in the prevailing circumstances for the avoidance of infliction of injury to such fellow contestants".

A controversial issue relates to whether different standards apply at different levels of the game for example, whether the game is at a professional or amateur level. In *Condon v Basi*[41] it was stated:

"The standard is objective but objective in a different set of circumstances. Thus there will of course be a higher degree of care required of a player in a First Division football match than of a player in a local league football match."

---

39 *Agar v Canning* (1965) 54 WWR 302 at 304. But where the sidecar passenger was injured during a motorcycle race because of the failure of the rear brakes detectable by the rider before the race began, his action for damages succeeded. It was held that the rider owed his passenger the normal standard of care and not the modified one, which usually applied to competitors in a sport, because the negligence had occurred in the relative calm of the workshop and not during the flurry and excitement of the race: *Harrison v Vincent* [1982] RTR 8.

40 [2001] EWCA Civ 1054 at [11], [2002] PIQR P6 at [11].

41 [1985] 2 All ER 453 at 454, [1985] 1 WLR 866 at 868 per Sir John Donaldson MR.

A contrary approach is, however, illustrated by *Elliott v Sanders and Liverpool FC*[42], where Drake J said:

> "The fact that the players are top professionals with very great skills, is no doubt one of the circumstances to be considered, but in my judgment the fact that the game is in the Premier League rather than at a lower level, does not necessarily mean that the standard of care is different."

It would be anomalous if, when a professional team plays an amateur team (as sometimes occurs for example in the early rounds of the English FA Cup), different standards of care applied to different teams, so that a striker in team A could injure a sweeper in team B with impunity when the same tackle by a striker in team B on a sweeper in team A could result in a bill for compensation of £100,000.

The resolution of the anomaly may be that the standard of care required in each case is the same, although the nature and level of the match in question (and, accordingly, the standards of skill to be expected from the players) would form part of the factual context within which such standard fell to be applied[43].

Mere errors of judgment do not amount to negligence: *Pitches v Huddersfield Town FC*[44]. And in golf, wayward shots must be tolerated as inherent in the game; likewise, loss of control in skiing[45].

In all these cases there are particular difficulties in the assessment of evidence in what is often an occurrence whose duration can be measured in seconds[46]. A charge or claim in law is one thing: proof in fact quite another. Judges are properly slow to rush in where regulators fear to tread.

In appropriate circumstances, those refereeing or otherwise controlling dangerous sports may themselves be liable for any failure to display reasonable competence resulting in injury to a player, including failure to implement relevant rules designed to protect against injury. This was established in *Smoldon v Whitworth*[47], where the referee of a game of rugby was held liable to a player who was injured when a scrum collapsed dangerously.

The level of care required of an official towards a player was again appropriate in all the circumstances, taking full account of the factual context in which he was exercising his functions as referee.

Lord Bingham of Cornhill CJ expressly, and negatively, declined to equate the duty owed by a referee to players with that owed by a participant to a spectator[48]:

> "In [the latter] cases it was recognised that a sporting competitor, properly intent on winning the contest, was (and was entitled to be) all but oblivious of spectators. It therefore followed that he would have to be shown to have very blatantly disregarded the safety of spectators before he could be held to have failed to exercise such care as was reasonable in all the circumstances.

---

42 (1994) 10 June, unreported. (Drake's Drumbeat for Sporting Injuries: E Grayson *Sport and the Law* (1991) All ER Rev pp 309–315.

43 Cases where damages have been recorded in association football include *McCord v Swansea FC* (Transcript, 19 Decemebr 1996), *Watson, Bradford City FC v Gray and Huddersfield Town FC* (1988) Times, 26 November, and in Rugby Union, *Ramsay Elshafay v Clay* CBD (Transcript, 6 April 2001).

44 QB Transcript: 17 July 2001.

45 Lewis and Taylor, *op cit*, E. 51–52.

46 See E Grayson *Sport and the Law* (3rd edn, 1999) pp 74–75; *Wooldridge v Sumner* (1963) 2 QB 43 at 52, 60, [1962] 2 All ER 978 at 980, 985, CA, per Sellers and Diplock LJJ.

47 [1997] PIQR P133, CA.

48 *Ibid* at 138–139

The position of a referee vis-à-vis the players is not the same as that of a participant in a contest vis-à-vis a spectator. One of his responsibilities is to safeguard the safety of the players. So, although the legal duty is the same in the two cases, the practical content of the duty differs according to the quite different circumstances."

He then expressly, and positively, set out the way in which the duty of care was to be applied in this particular context:

"The level of care required is that which is appropriate in all the circumstances, and the circumstances are of crucial importance. Full account must be taken of the factual context in which a referee exercises his functions and he could not be properly held liable for errors of judgment, oversights or lapses of which any referee might be guilty in the context of a fast moving and vigorous contest. The threshold of liability is a high one. It will not easily be crossed ... [the learned trial judge] did not intend to open the door to a plethora of claims by players against referees, and it would be deplorable if that were the result. In our view that result should not follow provided all concerned appreciate how difficult it is for any plaintiff to establish that a referee failed to exercise such care and skill as was reasonably to be expected in the circumstances of a hotly contested game of rugby football ..."

So while the players' duty to other players and to spectators is now on the same level, a referee's duty to players is on a higher one.

## Contributor's negligence

There may well be occasions where the player, as an ordinary prudent participant in the game and calling upon his experience in the sport generally, will foresee dangers and will anticipate the likelihood of negligence of his fellow players. In such circumstances, the player may have his damages reduced on account of his contributory negligence. Just as in rescue cases, a court ought to make all proper allowances where the speed of the activity on the playing field has reduced the time available to the plaintiff to take stock of his situation and, hence, his opportunity to take evasive action either to avoid the accident or to reduce the degree of damage suffered.

In *Feeney v Lyall*[49], during a round of golf, the pursuer had hooked his drive from the ninth tee on to the adjacent sixth fairway. In order to play his second shot he crossed over to the sixth fairway, where he was struck and seriously injured by a golf ball driven off the sixth tee by another golfer, who could not see the presence of the pursuer on that fairway. Liability in negligence was not established but, if it had been, the opinion was expressed that the pursuer would have been held 25 per cent contributorily negligent.

## Volenti

The maxim *volenti non fit injuria* describes a defence to a claim in circumstances where it is shown that the plaintiff had consented to the breach of the duty of care which is alleged and had agreed to waive his right of action in respect of it. It can be seen, therefore, that the defence is founded upon the concept of consent. Furthermore, while such consent may be express, it is usually to be implied from particular circumstances.

Unlike contributory negligence it offers a complete not merely partial defence.

---

49  1991 SLT 156.

In *Rootes v Shelton*[50], the water skier brought an action against the driver of the towing speedboat, where he, one of a group of skiers which included the driver, was performing a complicated manoeuvre and was injured by a collision with a stationary obstruction of which the *driver* had given him no warning. It was held that the onus was on the driver to establish voluntary acceptance of a risk not inherent in the pastime.

By way of distinction, the doctrine of *volenti* was held inapplicable in *Smoldon*[51], as there was no consent to a breach of duty by the referee:

> "... this argument is unsustainable. The plaintiff had of course consented to the ordinary incidents of a game of rugby football of the kind in which he was taking part. Given, however, that the rules were framed for the protection of him and other players in the same position, he cannot possibly be said to have consented to a breach of duty on the part of the official whose duty it was to apply the rules and ensure so far as possible that they were observed."

## (4) CONCLUSION

From this brief survey we may conclude that judicial interference on the field of play is a step taken reluctantly. Whether in considering the reach of the criminal or civil law onto the sports field, or the even more delicate business of the law becoming embroiled in the rule of the game, the circumstances in which courts are prepared to act have so far been narrowly construed. So while the field of play is not a wholly delegalised zone – not another Alsatia, in other words – it can fairly be said that although the King's writ does run, it is perhaps more likely to proceed with caution.

---

50  [1968] ALR 33.
51  [1997] PIQR P133 at 147.

# JURY ISSUES

## MICHAEL ZANDER QC, FBA[1]

The jury system has existed in this country for hundreds of years. The jury stands high in public esteem. Yet there is rarely a time when the topic is not actively under discussion. The issues that have arisen lately which are dealt with here are: the rules of allocation of cases between Crown Court and the magistrates' court; removal of the right of trial jury for long and complex fraud cases; eligibility for jury service; who actually serves on juries; research in the jury room; what to do about impropriety in jury decision making; race and jury decisions; juries and the effect of pre-trial publicity; abolition of the double jeopardy rule; and a prosecution right of appeal against perverse jury acquittals.

## ALLOCATION OF CASES AS BETWEEN CROWN COURT AND MAGISTRATES' COURTS

The cost of Crown Court cases is much greater than the cost of cases in the magistrates' courts. Unsurprisingly, governments seeking for economies have been keen to find acceptable ways of increasing the number of cases dealt with by magistrates. One way is to reclassify "either way" cases as "summary only". This occurred in 1977 in relation to drink driving and other motoring offences, in the teeth of opposition from the motorists' lobby. In a foretaste of battles to come, however, the same approach to cases involving thefts of, or to the value, of under £100 ran into massive opposition and was dropped by the government. The other way was to change the allocation process. The Runciman Royal Commission on Criminal Justice (1993) unanimously proposed that the allocation decision should be made by the magistrates after hearing representations by both sides, thus taking away the defendant's absolute right to have trial by jury in any either way case. The Royal Commission put its proposal as a matter of principle rather than to save resources. The allocation decision should be made by the system not by the defendant. In so far as the defendant opted for jury trial in the hope that it gave him a better chance of an acquittal, he should no more be permitted to choose the trial court than the trial judge. In reality he often opted for jury trial principally as a delaying tactic. Moreover, the great majority of defendants charged with either way offences who claimed the right to trial by jury ended by pleading guilty, often at the door of the court.

The Royal Commission's report made 352 recommendations. This was the one that attracted the most criticism, led by the Lord Chief Justice, Lord Taylor of Gosforth, who thought it would lead to two-tier justice.

The government attempted to implement the proposal in the Mode of Trial Bill 1999 but it was defeated in the House of Lords and was withdrawn. A revised Mode of Trial (No 2) Bill was introduced in the following year but it was again defeated in the Lords and it too was withdrawn. In its White Paper *Justice for All* the government announced that it had decided to abandon the whole idea of removing the defendant's right to elect for jury trial.

I was a member of the Royal Commission and have never been shaken in my belief that the Commission was right to propose that the allocation decision should be made by the system through the court rather than by the defendant. But I believe that the matter is now dead. I do not think that any government will feel able to implement the proposal.

---

1   Emeritus Professor, London School of Economics and Political Science.

## THE ABOLITION OF JURY TRIAL FOR LONG, COMPLEX FRAUD CASES

The argument over jury trial for long and complex fraud cases has been going on for decades. In the 1960s Lord Chief Justice Parker urged that such cases should be tried by some form of specialist tribunal. In 1983 the idea was supported by the chairman of the Law Commission, by the then Lord Chief Justice, Lord Lane and by Lord Hailsham, the Lord Chancellor.

In 1986 the report of the Roskill Committee concluded that long fraud cases were so complex that it was not reasonable to expect jurors to be able to cope. The evidence often ran into hundreds or even thousands of documents. ("The background against which frauds are alleged to have been committed – the sophisticated world of high finance and international trading – is probably a mystery to most or all of the jurors, its customs and practices a closed book" (para 8.27).)

There was one dissentient, Mr Walter Merricks, today the Financial Services Ombudsman. Mr Merricks pointed out that the evidence given to the Committee had been overwhelmingly in favour of retaining the jury. It had become a convention of the unwritten constitution that citizens should not be subjected to more than a short period of imprisonment otherwise than on a jury's verdict. Parliament should not be asked to abrogate this constitutional right unless there was clear evidence that jury trial had broken down in serious fraud cases. The issue in most fraud trials came down usually to one of dishonesty. The legal standard of dishonesty was the standard of the ordinary man.

His powerful dissent carried the day. The Committee's recommendation was not implemented.

In 1998, a year into the life of the Blair government, the topic was re-opened by a Home Office consultation paper, *Juries in Serious Fraud Trials*. The consultation paper canvassed a number of possible options: special juries, a judge sitting on his own, a special tribunal and a judge sitting with a jury.

Auld LJ, in his report on criminal courts in 2001 recommended that in serious and complex fraud cases the trial judge should have the power to order trial by himself sitting with lay members selected from an official list, or, if the defendant agreed, by himself alone. The two arguments that weighed most heavily with him were "the burdensome length and increasing speciality and complexity of these cases" and the length of these cases. The average length of cases brought by the Serious Fraud Office was six months. ("The fact is that many fraud and other cases ... now demand much more of the traditional English jury than it is equipped to provide."[2])

The government's White Paper *Justice for All* (2001) agreed that a small number (15–20 per year) of serious and complex fraud trials placed unreasonable burdens on jurors' personal and working lives. As a result it was not always possible to find a representative panel of jurors. It rejected Auld LJ's suggestion of trial by judge with selected lay members and proposed that such cases should be tried by judge alone.

In 2002, the Criminal Justice Bill provided for trial by judge alone on grounds of the length or complexity of the case if two conditions were satisfied. One was an excessive burden for the jurors. The second related to the kind of evidence the case involved. The clause was rejected by the House of Lords. The government reintroduced it in the Commons but in order to get the Lords to agree, the Home Secretary, Mr David Blunkett, gave an undertaking that it would not be implemented before there had been further consultation.

---

2  *Review of the Criminal Courts System* (2001) p 204 (para 183).
   See www.criminal-courts-review. org.uk.

Consultation consisting of a half-day conference, chaired by Lord Goldsmith, the Attorney General and attended by all relevant interest groups, duly took place. In June 2005, Lord Goldsmith announced that the government would be pressing ahead with implementation of the provision. In the event, however, this did not happen and in March 2006 Lord Goldsmith announced that it would not be implemented but that, when parliamentary time allowed, a fresh bill would be brought forward to deal with the matter. The pundits, including the writer, predicted that this signified that the topic had been kicked into the long grass. Confounding that expectation, in November 2006 the Blair government introduced the Fraud (Trials Without a Jury) Bill to activate the Criminal Justice Act 2003 s 43. Again, however, the House of Lords intervened. On 20 March 2007 it voted by 216 to 143 to delay the Bill to the next session of Parliament. At the time of writing, it is not known whether the Brown government will pursue the matter.

I firmly believe that serious criminal cases should generally be tried by juries, but I accept that there are some circumstances where jury trial is not appropriate. The situation in Northern Ireland in the time of "the Troubles" was such a circumstance. Research in the first six months of 1973 in Belfast showed an acquittal rate of 16 per cent for Protestant defendants as against 6 per cent for Catholics. That led to an inquiry headed by Lord Diplock. The Committee identified intimidation of witnesses by terrorists and the danger of perverse acquittal of Loyalist terrorists by predominantly Protestant juries. Its recommendation of the suspension of jury trial for "scheduled offences" was implemented in 1973.

Trial by judge alone in "Diplock courts" was subject to a requirement of a reasoned judgment in cases ending with conviction. A major study published in 1995 stated that well over 10,000 defendants had passed through Diplock courts. Although the acquittal rate ran somewhat below that in ordinary trials, in seven years it was over 40 per cent and in three years it was over 50 per cent[3]. I believe that the record of the Diplock courts is impressive.

The 2003 Act s 44 provided for trial by judge alone where the prosecution satisfies the judge that there is evidence of a real and present danger that jury tampering would take place and that the danger is such as to make it necessary in the interests of justice for the trial to be conducted without a jury. This provision was uncontroversial.

Auld LJ in his report on the criminal courts recommended that a defendant in any case tried on indictment should be permitted to ask for trial by judge alone. The judge would decide after hearing representations from both sides. Such "jury waiver" was widely used in the United States, and to some extent in Canada, New Zealand and Australia. The government accepted the recommendation and included it in the Criminal Justice Bill in 2002 but it was rejected by the House of Lords and was not re-introduced. I personally would support such a provision. If the defendant is content to be tried by judge alone, I see some advantage in permitting it – not least in the fact that a conviction would be based on a reasoned judgment.

Trial by judge alone in a small number of long and complex fraud cases raises difficult issues. I do not share the view of those who regard this as the thin edge of the wedge leading to abolition of trial by jury. I believe that ministers are genuine in asserting a determination to preserve trial by jury for serious criminal cases. I see force in the argument that such long trials are incredibly disruptive in the lives of ordinary citizens. On the other hand, I am not persuaded that jurors cannot master the evidence in such cases. Obviously, at the outset the jurors are likely to be completely at sea. But as the case grinds on week after week, month after month, it seems possible that gradually they will learn the jargon and come to

---

3   J Jackson and S Doran *Judge without Jury: Diplock Courts in the Adversary System* (1995).

understand the issues. Persuasive evidence that this can happen now exists in the report into the collapse of the *Jubilee Line Case*. The jury was discharged and the case abandoned on 22 March 2005 almost two years after it began on the ground that no jury could be expected to remember and assess evidence that had been given a year or eighteen months earlier.

The Attorney General asked the Chief Inspector of the Crown Prosecution Service to inquire into the reasons for this costly fiasco involving the waste of some £25m of taxpayers' money. The Chief Inspector's report totally exonerated the jury from any blame. ("No responsibility for the inconclusive outcome of the case can properly be attributed to the capabilities or conduct of the jury.") Eleven of the twelve members of the jury had been interviewed by the review team. They had been furious when they discovered from the newspapers that the case had been terminated because of their assumed inability to remember the evidence. They claimed that when the case collapsed they had a clear understanding of the evidence. That this was actually so emerged from a group interview conducted by the review team:

> "During a group interview in early August 2005 they showed quite impressive familiarity with the charges, issues and evidence, despite the length of time that had elapsed and the fact that they did not have their notes or access to documents nor an opportunity to think back and refresh their memories. They recalled particular parts of the evidence, particular witnesses and the substance of their evidence. They recalled different counts ... Occasionally there were individual failures of recollection, but one advantage of the jury system is that not all jurors are likely to have forgotten the same piece of evidence, if it is of any importance."

This does not prove that all juries in such long cases can cope. But it does dispose of the argument that no jury can be expected to cope.

An indication that the Jubilee Line jury may not have been untypical came in a survey of English judges who had handled fraud trials. The survey was conducted by Justice Julian of the Supreme Court of New York, who obtained permission to interview all the judges who had conducted such trials in a recent randomly selected year (not identified to preserve their anonymity)[4].

Nine judges were interviewed. Justice Julian summarised his findings:

> "Permeating every interview was the strong belief expressed by each of the judges that trial by jury was entirely appropriate in serious fraud cases and that trial by judge should not replace trial by jury. The judges unanimously voiced their faith in, and commitment to the jury system. The common rationale of the judges interviewed was that juries were usually able to understand a complex fraud case upon the completion of the trial, explaining that usually the complexity of a serious fraud case gradually evaporates as the trial progresses when the proof is competently and carefully presented."

On balance, I would favour keeping the jury even for these long, complex cases – but I believe that the arguments are finely balanced and, whilst not especially welcoming, reintroduction of the Fraud (Trials Without a Jury) Bill I would not strenuously oppose it.

---

4   Robert F Julian "Judicial Perspectives on the Conduct of Serious Fraud Trials" [2007] Crim LR 751.

Again, on balance I think that trial by judge alone is the least bad of the various alternatives to trial by jury.

## WHO IS REQUIRED TO SERVE ON A JURY?

For hundreds of years eligibility to serve on a jury was dependent on owning property. This excluded most adults. Especially it excluded most women. When the Morris Committee reported on jury service in 1965 it found that only 22.5 per cent of those on the electoral register were eligible for jury service. The Committee's recommendation that the property qualification be removed and that the electoral register be made the basic criterion of eligibility was adopted in the Juries Act 1974. Under the 1974 Act a person on the electoral register is eligible for jury service if he is between the ages of 18 and 70 and has been resident in this country for at least five years since the age of thirteen.

Certain persons, however, were "ineligible", "disqualified" or "excused". Those ineligible were persons who it was thought might exercise undue influence in the jury room by reason of their occupation – judges, lawyers, court staff, police officers, prison officers, probation officers and, in a different category of influence, clergymen of any denomination. Auld LJ in his report on the criminal courts in 2001 recommended that this category of exemption should be abolished, as it had been in several American states. The recommendation was implemented in the 2003 Act. There is now no category of exemption based on occupation. But the court has the duty to ensure a fair trial. In October 2007 the House of Lords by 3-2 allowed appeals from two defendants because the jury had included in the one case, a police officer and in the other, a Crown Prosecution lawyer. In a third case, where the jury had included a police officer the Law Lords unanimously upheld the conviction. There was no conflict in that case between police and defence witnesses[5].

Persons are disqualified under the 1974 Act by reason of their criminal convictions. The 1974 Act as amended by the 2003 Act spells out the details. Previously checks of disqualifying convictions were somewhat haphazard. However, jury summoning is now done for the whole country by the Central Summoning Board. The handling of the checks for disqualifying criminal convictions is now an automatic electronic process through a link to the criminal records system.

Persons were excused as of right because it was considered that they had more important business elsewhere – members of either House of Parliament, full-time members of the armed forces, persons in the medical profession and the like. Auld LJ recommended that excusal as of right should be abolished and this too was implemented in the 2003 Act. The new principle is that no one is excused from jury service unless they can show good reason – in which case jury service should normally be deferred to another date.

The Solicitor-General told the House of Commons that removing the categories of "ineligible" and "excused as of right" would add an estimated four million names to the pool from which jurors are drawn.

It has always been possible to ask to be excused on an individual *ad hoc* basis and this is in fact very common. A Home Office study in 1999 based on a sample of 50,000 people summoned for jury service, found that 38 per cent were excused. The reasons were various: medical (40 per cent); care of children or the elderly (20 per cent); the juror being an essential worker or financial reasons (20 per cent); not being a resident (9 per cent); being a student (6 per cent); transport problems (overall only 1 per cent but in some areas, as much as 30 per cent).

---

5   *R v Abdroikof; R v Green; R v Williamson* [2007] UKHL 34, [2007] All ER (D) 226 (Oct).

The Home Office study also found that as many as half of those who were eligible had had their jury service deferred to a later date, sometimes more than once. The reasons were similar to those for being excused except for the addition of prior holiday arrangements which accounted for one third of deferrals.

Applications for excusal or deferment which previously went to the summoning officer of the court in question now have to be made to the Central Summoning Bureau, but there is a right of appeal to a judge. The *Practice Direction* on excusal after the elimination of the "ineligible" and "excusal as of right" categories recognised that there would be an increase "in the number of jurors with professional and public service commitments". Applications for excusal, it said, should be considered "with common sense and according to the interests of justice".

A study conducted by Dr Cheryl Thomas[6], published by the Ministry of Justice in June 2007 was based on all those summoned for jury service for all the 94 Crown Courts in England and Wales in one week in 2003, 8,599 jurors, and in one week in 2005, 7,055 jurors[7]. The study showed that the proportion who served for the date summoned in 2005 was 47 per cent (up from 36 per cent in 2003); that the proportion who served at a later date was unchanged (18 per cent in 2005, 17 per cent in 2003); and that the proportion who did not serve because they were excused was 28 per cent (down from 35 per cent in 2003). The tightening up in the new rules therefore had had an effect.

## IS THE JURY REPRESENTATIVE OF THE LOCAL POPULATION?

The main thrust of Dr Thomas' study was concern about the under-representation of ethnic minorities on juries. Her study included an examination of the summoning of jurors with special reference to the question whether black and minority ethnic ("BME") persons are under-represented at that stage of the process. The study examined this question court by court comparing the profile of those summoned in 2005 with that of the local population based on the most recent census data. The ethnic minority information was based on a questionnaire sent to prospective jurors together with the jury summons. There were only two Crown Courts in which the differences between BME jurors summoned and the BME population in the court catchment area were statistically significant. In one, Grimsby, the proportion of BME jurors summoned was significantly *higher*; in Manchester it was significantly *lower*. The conclusion was that the computerised random selection of jurors based on local electoral lists reaches a representative selection of the local population.

The study showed that only 20 of the 94 Crown Courts have a local BME population in excess of 10 per cent. Of these, 12 are in London – unsurprising considering that almost half (45 per cent) of the country's non-white population live in the London region. Where BME groups comprise under 10 per cent of the local population there is statistically little likelihood of BME representation on juries.

## THE SOCIAL CLASS COMPOSITION OF JURIES

There is a widespread belief that juries are mostly composed of the unemployed and the retired, or those not important or clever enough to get out of jury duty.

The *Crown Court Study* (1993) which I conducted for the Runciman Royal Commission on Criminal Justice (1993) was based on every case decided during two weeks in every Crown Court in the country, save three courts used in the pre-pilot. At the end of

---

6   Director of the Jury Diversity Project at the University of Birmingham and Honorary Professor in the Faculty of Laws at University College, London.

7   *Diversity and Fairness in the Jury System* Ministry of Justice Research Series 2/07 June 2007.

the case, all the participants – judge, lawyers, police, defendant and jurors – received questionnaires. The jury questionnaire included questions about socio-economic factors. The social class measures were somewhat crude but it appeared that 19 per cent were skilled manual, compared with 21 per cent in the general population, seven per cent were unskilled manual, the same as in the general population, and 29 per cent were professional or managerial, compared with 31 per cent in the general population. Over four-fifths were working either full time (69 per cent) or part-time (13 per cent). Seven per cent were unemployed; six per cent were retired.

Dr Thomas' study examined whether socio-economic factors affected whether a person summoned actually served. The factors considered were gender, employment status, religion, ethnicity, income, prior jury service, and whether English was the juror's first language. Income, employment status, ethnicity and first language were found to be predictive. Thus for instance among those whose first language was English, 62 per cent of black jurors summoned did jury service, compared to 78 per cent of asian and 72 per cent of white jurors summoned. Of those whose first language was not English, only 51 per cent served.

But income and employment status were much more significant than either ethnicity or language in determining whether a summoned juror served or did not serve. Those with the lowest household income were by far the least likely income group to serve. Under half in this group (46 per cent) served compared with four-fifths (79 per cent) of the highest income group. Employment status was equally significant. Four-fifths (80 per cent) of those who were economically active, whether employed or self-employed, did jury service, compared with half (49 per cent) of those who were economically inactive. Contrary to received wisdom, the economically active are over, not under, represented on juries.

When the reasons for not doing jury service were examined, there was no difference in the proportion excused who were white or BME (28 per cent for both groups). Taking all those who were excused, the largest proportion did not serve because of medical reasons (34 per cent), child care (15 per cent), work related reasons (12 per cent) and age (11 per cent). But among BME persons the reasons for the largest proportions not serving were residence for an insufficient period (24 per cent) and language reasons (21 per cent). A significantly higher proportion of BME jurors summoned were disqualified (15 per cent as against 5 per cent for white jurors).

Doing jury duty does not mean actually sitting on a jury, which requires that one's name be drawn by the court clerk in the final stage of selection (empanelling). This is the only stage of the whole process that is not now done by electronically random methods. The computer generates cards with the names. The cards are supposed to be shuffled by the court clerk and the first 12 names are then read out in open court. Each juror enters the jury box and when 12 names have been read without challenges or excusals the jury is sworn.

Unlike the American system, where the challenging of jurors is an important part of the process, in England challenges are rare. The right to challenge without reasons, peremptory challenge, was abolished in 1988. There is a right to challenge for cause but, *Catch 22*, one cannot normally ask questions to establish whether there is cause. In the United States of America the process of questioning jurors can takes hours, days or even weeks. In England it virtually never takes place at all. The English jury is therefore a more genuinely random selection of the local population.

Dr Thomas looked at jury pools, jury panels and actual juries in three courts to see whether there was any evidence of distortion or bias. She found some evidence that BME jurors on jury panels appeared to be selected to serve on juries less often than white jurors on jury panels. She suggested a possible reason might be clerks avoiding reading out juror names that are difficult to pronounce!

## SHOULD RESEARCH BE PERMITTED IN THE JURY ROOM?

In 2005, the Department for Constitutional Affairs issued a consultation paper ("CP") inviting views as to whether the Contempt of Court Act 1981 s 8 should be amended to permit research on the jury process to extend into the jury room[8]. In the result nothing came of this exercise. I was one of those who responded to the CP. As a member of the Runciman Royal Commission I had subscribed to its unanimous recommendation that such research be permitted. In my response to the CP I explained why I had changed my mind. There were two reasons. One was doubt whether such research would produce anything of much value that could not be obtained from other kinds of jury research. The second, more important, reason was concern that the results of such research might *wrongly* destabilise a functioning institution that had worked to general satisfaction for hundreds of years. It was not that I thought the jury system was working badly. On the contrary:

> "My view, based both on impression and on what is known from existing research, including my own, is that the system works remarkably well and fully justifies public confidence. I believe it would confirm what seems to be a broad agreement among both regular participants such as judges and lawyers and among members of the general public that generally the jury either 'gets it right' or at least reaches an understandable verdict. My concern is that because the research would show that jurors are ordinary human beings who display the failings of ordinary human beings, some might mistakenly conclude from the research that the system was working badly by confusing the possibly messy process with the generally accepted results of cases ...
>
> The result would be rational in terms of the weight of the evidence, the details of the case and all relevant factors, but the process might not show this to be so. Such a finding would not necessarily be a commentary on the IQ of the jurors. The intelligent and the educated are as capable of meandering or illogical argument as anyone. Discussing issues in a sometimes vague or emotional or unfocused way is what human beings do. My fear is that the discovery that the jury is composed of ordinary human beings could for some create a sense of unease about jury decision-making. It might, for instance, lead some to argue that jury decision-making should be structured by a series of questions posed by the judge. This view was put by Lord Justice Auld in his report, but, rightly in my view, was rejected by the government. It might lead some to argue that the jury should be required to give written reasons – a task which they would be unable to perform. That could fuel the argument that, if the jury cannot give reasons, it should be scrapped ...
>
> I believe that anyone who supports the jury system has to be prepared to accept that such shortcomings, if that is what they are, exist. My fear is that

---

8  *Jury Research and Impropriety* DCA CP 04/05 March 2005.
   The Contempt of Court Act 1981 s 8 provides that:
   "(1) Subject to subsection (2) below, it is a contempt of court to obtain, disclose or solicit any particulars of statements made, opinions expressed, arguments advanced or votes cast by members of a jury in the course of their deliberations in any legal proceedings.
   (2) This section does not apply to any disclosure of any particulars
   (a) in the proceedings in question for the purpose of enabling the jury to arrive at their verdict, or in connection with the delivery of that verdict, or
   (b) in evidence in any subsequent proceedings for an offence alleged to have been committed in relation to the jury in the first mentioned proceedings,
   or to the publication of any particulars so disclosed."

many of those who place their confidence in the system have not given thought to the fact that such shortcomings are inevitable and would be upset if they came to realise it through research. My concern therefore is that some of the public's confidence in the jury system as the best available system would be shaken if such 'shortcomings' were exposed to view – because of unrealistically high expectations as to how it does work and should work. I do not believe that that would serve the public interest."

That remains my view.

In fact many forms of jury research not involving "bugging" the jury room can be conducted without breaching the terms of the 1981 Act – as was shown by the Crown Court Study conducted for the Runciman Royal Commission[9], in which we asked jurors a slew of questions about the case.

## WHAT TO DO ABOUT JURY IMPROPRIETY?

The 2005 Consultation Paper also invited views as to whether anything further should be done about impropriety in jury decision making. Again I quote from my own response to the CP:

"I favour the approach to the problem of jury impropriety put forward in the CP para 5.8.1 as the government's present view: basically, leave the matter to be handled by the courts through the developing common law.

My main concerns are, first, that frank discussion in the jury room should not be impeded and second, that the finality of verdicts should not be disturbed by encouraging disgruntled jurors, or a convicted defendant, to raise issues after the case is over.

My approach is similar to that expressed by Lord Hope in his speech in *R v Mirza*: 'Full and frank discussion, in the course of which prejudices may indeed be aired but then rejected when it comes to the moment of decision-taking, would be inhibited if everything that might give rise to allegations of prejudice after the verdict is delivered were to be opened up to scrutiny.'[10]

Jurors' disagreements as they work to arrive at their verdict may generate powerful emotions even involving angry exchanges. That is not to be discouraged either directly or indirectly. The system must provide the necessary protection to enable them to hammer out their differences in private without fear that sharp disagreements will lead to judicial scrutiny of the jury's deliberations. The system must be robust enough to allow for struggle in the jury room.

On balance, I prefer the traditional common law approach that the 1981 Act s 8 applies to the courts – as opposed to the approach of the Law Lords in *R v Mirza* holding that the courts are exempt from the 1981 Act. I believe that the decision in *R v Mirza* opens the door to undesirable inquiries as to what occurred in the jury room. But I do not feel strongly enough on this issue to urge that legislation be introduced to change the law back to what it was before the decision.

---

9  The authors of the CP seemed to be unaware of the existence of the Crown Court Study – a surprising example of governmental incompetence.
10  *R v Mirza; R v Connor* [2004] UKHL 2 at [116], [2004] 1 AC 118 at [116], [2004] 1 All ER 925 at [116].

I would, however, be against any move to further widen the scope of inquiry into what happens in the jury room. Legislative clarification of the limits of inquiries into jury impropriety, though theoretically desirable, is in practice very difficult. As the CP says (para 5.7.1), it bears the risk of being either too broad and fundamentally undermining the principle of confidentiality within the jury room or too narrow and excluding a form of impropriety that had not previously been thought of. Wisest would be to leave it to the courts to develop the concept on a case by case basis, supervised, as it will be, by the European Court of Human Rights.

I would warn against giving either the trial court or the Court of Appeal the specific power to investigate allegations of discrimination on any of the long list of grounds suggested by the CP: sex, race, colour, language, religion, sexual orientation, political or other opinion, national or social origin, association with a national minority, property, birth or other status. I believe this would open a Pandora's box of endless footling or misconceived allegations which would then need to be investigated."

In November 2005 the government stated that its decision was to allow the common law to develop on a case by case basis and that there would not be any legislation on the subject.

RACE AND JURY DECISIONS

The question whether the ethnic make-up of juries affects their decisions and, if so, what should be done about it, has been an issue for many years. In the 1980s there were conflicting judicial decisions as to whether the trial judge had the power to interfere with the jury selection process in order to secure a racial mix. In 1989 the Court of Appeal settled the matter when it held that the judge had no such power[11]. Fairness required random selection.

The Runciman Royal Commission on Criminal Justice was persuaded by the Commission for Racial Equality to recommend that this rule be changed. In a racially sensitive case the judge should be able to allow names to be drawn from the jury panel until three ethnic minority jurors had been empanelled. Auld LJ made the same recommendation in his report. The government rejected the recommendation. In the White Paper *Justice for All* (2001) it said that implementing the proposal would:

- undermine the fundamental principle of random selection;
- assume bias on the part of the excluded jurors;
- place the ethnic minority jurors in a difficult position – as if they were supposed to represent the defendant;
- generate tensions and divisions in the jury room;
- create new burdens for the courts in having to decide which cases merited this exceptional procedure and, in addition, provide a ground for unmeritorious appeals.

I joined with my fellow Commissioners in Runciman's unanimous recommendation but I now accept that we were wrong and that the government's reasons for rejecting the idea of special selection methods for juries in racially sensitive cases are convincing.

The first evidence in this country as to decision making by racially mixed juries emerged in Dr Cheryl Thomas' study (2007). As part of her project on *Diversity and Fairness in the Jury System*, Dr Thomas conducted a special inquiry into how the racial composition of a jury affects the deliberations and the final verdict. The method used was to make a one and

11  *R v Ford* [1989] QB 868, [1989] 3 All ER 445.

a half hour edited film from the transcript of a real trial and play it to 27 mock juries consisting of persons who had just completed their jury duty. The trial was filmed in Blackfriars Crown Court with real judge, barristers, court clerk and witnesses. The study varied the race of the defendant – white, asian, black. The three different defendants were of much the same appearance and age and were dressed identically.

All but one of the 27 juries in the study were racially mixed. Each jury was shown a randomly selected version of the case. At the end of the film, jurors were given a brief questionnaire asking how they would vote, guilty or not guilty, and how confident they felt about their vote at that stage. They were then given 20 minutes to deliberate and to try to reach a verdict. They were then given the same questionnaire to record their final vote and a further more detailed questionnaire about the evidence and the witnesses.

The case was a difficult one to decide. The real jury in the actual trial on which the film was based was itself unable to reach a verdict. Whether for this reason or because of the short time allowed for deliberation, there was a very high proportion of hung juries – 16 out of 27. In the 11 cases ending with a verdict, the ethnicity of the defendant made no difference to the result. The defendant was found guilty in only one case (white defendant, majority verdict). In all the other cases the defendant was found not guilty.

Altogether 319 jurors took part in this part of the study. Pooling the results showed that when juror ethnicity and defendant ethnicity were examined together some significant differences did emerge. BME defendants were less likely to be found guilty than white defendants, while the white defendant was much more likely to be found guilty by BME jurors than by white jurors. However, jury verdicts are the product of a group decision-making process and these differences in jurors' individual votes did not produce any significant differences in the verdicts of the jury as a whole.

The evidence from Dr Thomas' study of the effect of race on decision making by racially mixed juries is encouraging. She is now conducting a further study to apply the same test to all-white juries.

## JURIES AND THE EFFECT OF PRE-TRIAL PUBLICITY

The law of contempt of court is designed to minimise risks to the possibility of a fair trial. In recent years it has seemed that successive Attorneys General have been regrettably lax in enforcing this law. Certainly the press are bolder than in former times in publishing material that arguably could prejudice a fair trial. As a result, the courts have increasingly had to deal with defence applications that a case be stayed or that a conviction be quashed on account of prejudicial pre-trial publicity. Generally, such applications have been resisted. In 1996 the Court of Appeal upheld the conviction of Rosemary West[12], who with her husband Fred West had been accused of multiple horrendous murders. After his suicide she was convicted of ten murders. There had been massive pre-trial publicity. The question, the Court of Appeal said, was whether it was possible to have a fair trial after such intensive, unfavourable publicity. Lord Chief Justice Lord Taylor said: "To hold otherwise would mean that if allegations are sufficiently horrendous so as inevitably to shock the nation, the accused cannot be tried. That would be absurd." Provided that the jury had been adequately directed to act only on the evidence given in court, a fair trial was possible.

Recent research conducted for the New Zealand Law Commission suggests that the impact of prejudicial pre-trial publicity even in high profile cases is in fact not great[13]. As Lawton J had said in the trial of the notorious gangster Reginald Kray: "The drama ... of

---

12  *R v West* [1996] 2 Cr App Rep 374, CA.
13  W Young, N Cameron and Y Tinsley *Juries in Criminal Trials Part Two* ch 9 para 87 (New Zealand Law Commission preliminary paper no 37 November 1999) – www.lawcom.gov.nz.

a trial most always has the effect of excluding from recollection that which went before." But obviously one cannot be sure that that will be so.

The issue came up again in an appeal by Abu Hamza, the Imam of the Finsbury Park Mosque, who in February 2006 had been sentenced to seven years' imprisonment after conviction at the Old Bailey of, six counts of soliciting murder, three counts of stirring up racial hatred and of possessing an item likely to be useful to someone preparing an act of terrorism. In support of his argument that a fair trial was impossible, counsel for Abu Hamza produced 600 pages of newspaper reports, articles and comments as samples of a sustained campaign against the defendant, almost entirely hostile to him, some of it couched in particularly crude terms. The Court of Appeal said that some of it treated Abu Hamza as an ogre.

In the first of three rulings on this issue at different stages of the case, the trial judge said he had no doubt that the publicity created a risk that the fairness of the trial might be affected. As a result he postponed the trial so that it took place more than a year after the most intense publicity. He accepted that it was likely that jurors might even then remain generally aware that this was a defendant who was the object of intense publicity and of a campaign against him. That meant that the jury would have to be warned in much more than formulaic terms to put out of their minds what they had read in the papers. He was confident that with such a direction the jury would be able to decide the case fairly.

The Court of Appeal accepted that the trial judge had been right to conclude that the pre-trial publicity here had created a risk to the fairness of the trial. The question was whether he had done enough to neutralise this danger. His task had been an exacting one. The court said it had read the judge's direction to the jury with admiration. It noted that as well as convicting the defendant on some counts, the jury had acquitted him of others, showing that it had differentiated between stronger and weaker counts. The judge had been right to allow the trial to proceed. There was no basis for quashing the conviction[14].

## RE-OPENING JURY ACQUITTALS

It has for centuries been a generally accepted principle that a person should not be put in peril of conviction twice for the same offence – expressed in the ancient common law doctrine of *autrefois acquit*, better known as the rule against double jeopardy.

Recently however this principle was overturned in the English system. In 1999 the Macpherson Report into the murder of Stephen Lawrence recommended that the Court of Appeal should be given the power to authorise a prosecution appeal against an acquittal where "fresh and viable" evidence had come to light. The recommendation was supported by the House of Commons Home Affairs Committee, by the Law Commission and by Auld LJ in his report. The government accepted the recommendation in its White Paper *Justice for All* and implemented it in the 2003 Act ss 75–97.

The provisions affect a person who has been acquitted anywhere, except Scotland, of a qualifying offence as defined in a schedule which lists 29 offences all carrying a maximum sentence of life imprisonment. The provisions are retrospective and apply therefore to acquittals that occurred prior to the 2003 Act. An application must be made to the Court of Appeal with the personal written consent of the Director of Public Prosecutions. Only one such application can be made. The Director of Public Prosecutions and the Court of Appeal must both be satisfied that there is "new and compelling evidence" against the acquitted person in relation to a qualifying offence which is highly probative against him, and that a second trial is in the public interest. When deciding whether to allow a second trial to take place, the factors the Court of Appeal must take into account include whether

14  *R v Hamza* [2006] EWCA Crim 2918 at [91], [2007] QB 659 at [91], [2007] 3 All ER 451 at [91].

the trial could be fair, the length of time since the offence was committed and whether an officer or prosecutor failed to act with due diligence or with due expedition.

So far the new provisions have been used only once, in the case of Billy Dunlop. Dunlop had been tried twice for the murder of Julie Higgs. In both trials the jury failed to reach a verdict and in 1991 he was formally acquitted. Later, while in prison for assaulting a girlfriend, he confessed that he had killed Julie Higgs. He was tried for perjury and was given a six-year sentence. Julie Higgs' mother was active in the campaign to get the double jeopardy rule changed. When her campaign succeeded, Cleveland police reopened the case. On 11 September 2006, Dunlop pleaded guilty to the murder and was sentenced to life imprisonment.

## THE JURY'S INALIENABLE RIGHT TO REACH A PERVERSE VERDICT

Auld LJ, in perhaps the most controversial recommendation in his report on the criminal courts, urged "that the law should be declared, by statute if need be, that juries have no right to acquit defendants in defiance of the law or in disregard of the evidence". The jury's role was "to find the facts and, applying the law to those facts, to determine guilt or no". They were not there "to substitute their view of the propriety of the law for that of Parliament or its enforcement for that of the appointed Executive, still less on what may be irrational, secret and unchallengeable grounds".

I regard this proposal as wholly unacceptable. The right to return a perverse verdict in defiance of the law or the evidence is an important safeguard against unjust laws, oppressive prosecutions or harsh sentences. In former centuries juries notoriously defied the law to save defendants from the gallows. In modern times the power is used, sometimes to general acclaim, sometimes to general annoyance, usually one imagines to some of each.

Happily, the government rejected Auld LJ's suggested approach. ("Nor do we intend to legislate to prevent juries from returning verdicts regarded as perverse where the verdict flies in the face of the evidence, as has happened very occasionally."[15])

Auld LJ quoted EP Thompson's eloquent passage in describing the function of the jury[16]:

> "The English common law rests upon a bargain between the Law and the People. The jury box is where people come into the court; the judge watches them and the jury watches back. A jury is the place where the bargain is struck. The jury attends in judgment, not only upon the accused, but also upon the justice and humanity of the law."

This exactly captures the position, which one could say is part of the unwritten constitution of this country. Auld LJ said that he regarded the ability of juries to acquit and to convict in defiance of the law and in disregard of their oaths, as a "blatant affront to the legal process and the main purpose of the criminal justice system – the control of crime – of which they are so important a part". This reflects deep distrust of the jury. It is based on an attitude that disregards history and reveals a misjudged sense of the proper balance of the criminal justice system.

---

15  White Paper *Justice for All* (2001) para 4.50.
16  E P Thompson *Writing by Candlelight* (1980).

# THE CONFLICT OF LAWS – THE LAST HUNDRED YEARS

## SIR PETER NORTH[1]

## I. PREFACE

The first challenge in surveying the development of this subject over the past hundred years is to decide how to describe it – itself a matter of change over the century. *Halsbury's Laws of England* has always described this area of the law as "the conflict of laws", whilst acknowledging from the outset that there is an alternative title – "private international law". However, the first edition of *Halsbury's Laws*[2] chose the former name, relying on the judgment of Holland who is quoted as regarding the former as the best title and "private international law" as "indubitably the worst"[3]. Over the intervening hundred years there is no doubt that "private international law" has become much more widely used, indeed predominantly used, not least because of the influence of civil law jurisdictions particularly through the European Union. Nevertheless, out of consistency and piety, this essay will retain *Halsbury's Laws'* original, and still current, description of the subject.

## II. BACKGROUND

Although there is no doubt that 1907 was a landmark year for *Halsbury's Laws*[4], for the conflict of laws it was a pretty ordinary year. It could boast obscure decisions on the recognition in England of the status of the curator of a French lunatic[5] and on the discretion to refuse service of a writ out of the jurisdiction[6], as well as decisions on the staying of an English action on the basis that it was oppressive[7] and on illegality in contract[8]. Only one of them merited an appearance in *Halsbury's Laws* in 1909[9]. 1909 itself does not figure much more prominently with just five reported decisions and none of them significantly influenced the development of the subject; and nor did the legislature do so in any way in the first decade of the century. Developing from this low base, the story of the last hundred years is one of the subject's growing importance and significance. A crude, but interesting, basis for assessing the development of the conflict of laws is to compare the first and current editions of the treatment of the subject in *Halsbury's Laws*. The conflict of laws occupied some 130 pages of the original vol 6, whilst it now occupies a whole volume (vol 8(3)), some 450 pages long, in the latest edition, published in 2003.

Like most areas of law do, or should, the state of the conflict of laws provides a reflection of its age. The reflection is usually a distorted one as the law is always playing

---

1 This essay draws very substantially from my chapter "Private International Law in Twentieth-century England" in *Jurists Uprooted* (2004) pp 483–515; and on my 24th FA Mann Lecture "Private International Law: Change or Decay?" (2001) 50 ICLQ 477.
2 *Halsbury's Laws of England* (1st edn, 1909) vol 6 para 180.
3 *Jurisprudence* (10th edn, 1906) p 405 et seq.
4 It should be pointed out that vol 6 which contains the discussion of the conflict of laws was not published until 1909.
5 *Re De Larragoiti* [1907] 2 Ch 14.
6 *Watson v Daily Record (Glasgow) Ltd* [1907] 1 KB 857.
7 *Egbert v Short* [1907] 2 Ch 205.
8 *Moulis v Owen* [1907] 1 KB 746.
9 *Egbert v Short*, above.

"catch-up" in that new problems or legal devices invented by clever lawyers take time to attract the attention of the legislature or, via the vagaries of litigation, to become the subject of legal decisions. In this context, the conflict of laws has some unusual characteristics. By definition, it is fundamentally concerned with a trio of cross-border issues: Do the English courts have jurisdiction to hear a case? What law is the court to apply? And will the judgments of the courts of any other country be recognised in England? This means that the development of the subject has been fundamentally and distinctively dependent on the development of international travel and communication opportunities, so far as both companies and individuals are concerned. At a time when those opportunities were less extensive than today, the role of the legal author was unusually important in speculating on the problems that might arise and in offering possible solutions to practitioners in the course of providing advice to clients or to the courts in the event of litigation. It is not by chance that the conflict of laws provided one of the earliest instances of the courts having recourse to and, indeed, at times of being heavily dependent upon academic opinion.

The cross-border nature of this area of the law engenders another characteristic. It is self-evident to state that it has a major international dimension. That is not, however, a uniform characteristic of all cases, in that there can be disputes whose elements do no more than cross the legal borders within the United Kingdom; and in the USA most conflict of laws issues arise in an inter-state rather than an international context – a factor which has had a strong influence on the way that rules there have developed differently from those in, for example, England where most cross-border disputes are, in fact, truly international. The characteristic that flows from this international dimension is that the last century has seen, in this field, a quest for international agreement, whether in terms of uniform laws – thus eradicating the need for a structure of conflict of laws rules – or of uniform conflicts rules, thus contributing to a greater uniformity of approach to cross-border issues amongst legally like-minded states. One of the interesting themes of the twentieth century development of the subject in England is to see the extent to which this characteristic has developed and with what consequences.

## III. DAWN OF THE TWENTIETH CENTURY

### 1. *Jurisdiction of the courts*

Let us start by looking at the state of the law a hundred years ago, although space constraints mean that this can be no more than a sampling exercise. Taking the first issue that arises in a cross-border dispute (and leaving family law proceedings to one side for the moment) – does the English court have jurisdiction to entertain the proceedings? – the answers to be given depended on the nature of the proceedings, but those answers were very domestic in nature. In an action *in personam*, jurisdiction depended on satisfaction of the procedural requirements of the Rules of the Supreme Court on service of a writ[10]. So if, for example, the defendant was in England when the writ was served on him, then the English court could take jurisdiction, irrespective of the country in which the cause of action arose. If the defendant was not in England, then there were various exceptional grounds of jurisdiction – as when the subject matter of the claim was English land[11], the defendant was domiciled or ordinarily resident in England[12] or the claim was founded on the breach in England of a contract (wherever made) which was to be performed in England[13]. A similarly insular and procedurally based approach can be seen in relation to the exercise of

---

10  RSC Ord 11 (now CPR, Pt 50, Sch 1).
11  RSC Ord 11, r 1(a).
12  RSC Ord 11, r 1(c).
13  RSC Ord 11, r 1(e).

admiralty jurisdiction *in rem*. Jurisdiction entirely depended on the ship in question being in harbour in England or within three miles of the English coast[14].

## 2. *Recognition of foreign judgments*

The other side of the coin from establishing rules for the assumption of jurisdiction is the issue of the recognition of the judgments of foreign courts; and the rules here had become quite fully developed at common law by the beginning of the twentieth century. English courts would recognise foreign judgments in actions *in personam* based on the defendant's presence in the foreign jurisdiction at the time of the action, or his voluntary submission to the jurisdiction of the foreign court[15]. The latter had been held to include an agreement to submit – whether express or implied[16]. There was also support for the view that a foreign judgment would be recognised if the defendant was a national of the foreign state[17]. An important negative rule which was finally established in 1908[18] was that, for recognition purposes, the jurisdiction of the foreign court could not be founded on the fact that the defendant possessed movable property in the foreign jurisdiction – a rule in sharp contrast to that already long established in Scotland that jurisdiction could be based on arrestment of movables[19]. It is also the case that the courts had, by the beginning of the twentieth century, developed criteria for determining the characteristics of foreign judgments that could be recognised, in that the judgment had to be final and conclusive, notwithstanding that an appeal might be pending, and be for a fixed sum[20]. It had been settled that the foreign judgment could not be impeached on the merits, even to the extent that claims would not be entertained that the foreign court was mistaken as to the facts, its own law or English law[21]. However, a foreign judgment could be impeached on the basis of fraud[22] and on the basis that its recognition would be contrary to public policy[23]. Furthermore, the courts were moving towards the establishment of a rule that recognition would be denied if the foreign judgment contravened rules of natural justice[24].

## 3. *Range of cross-border issues*

It is, perhaps, worth reflecting on the background to the foreign judgments cases at the end of the nineteenth and the beginning of the twentieth century because they give a flavour of the geographical and commercial range of the cross-border issues being addressed at that time. The cases range from a claim for damages by the Rajah of a protected Indian state which was considered to be a foreign country[25]; to disputes between two Englishmen in Sweden over an agency agreement to be undertaken there by the defendant[26]; a dispute in France between Danes, the defendants living in London, over a shipment of oats from Sweden to France[27]; between former partners over the working of a goldmine in Western Australia[28]; a claim in Russia against an English company for the return of goods to the

---

14  Dicey, *Conflict of Laws* (2nd edn, 1908) pp 251–253; *The Clara Killam* (1870) LR 3 A&E 161.
15  *Carrick v Hancock* (1895) 12 TLR 59.
16  *Copin v Adamson* (1875) 1 Ex D 17.
17  *Rousillon v Rousillon* (1880) 14 Ch D 351 at 371.
18  *Emanuel v Symon* [1908] 1 KB 302.
19  *Young v Arnold* (1683) Mor 4833.
20  *Sadler v Robins* (1808) 1 Camp 253; *Nouvion v Freeman* (1889) 15 App Cas 1.
21  *Henderson v Henderson* (1844) 6 QB 288; *Godard v Gray* (1870) LR 6 QB 139.
22  *Duchess of Kingston's Case* (1776) 2 SLC 644; *Ochsenbein v Papelier* (1873) LR 8 Ch App 695.
23  *Rousillon v Rousillon* (1880) 14 Ch D 351; *Huntington v Attrill* [1893] AC 150.
24  Eg *Rudd v Rudd* [1894] P 72.
25  *Sirdar Gurdyal Singh v The Rajah of Faridkote* [1894] AC 670.
26  *Carrick v Hancock* (1895) 12 TLR 59.
27  *Schibsby v Westenholz* (1870) LR 6 QB 155.
28  *Emanuel v Symon* [1908] 1 KB 302.

Russian plaintiff[29]; an action in Sicily by an Italian broker against an English businessman for money due on bills of exchange[30]; a dispute in South Africa over a loan between an Englishman and a South African[31]; between French brothers who were champagne merchants and the Swiss nephew of one of them over restraint of trade laws[32]; a dispute in Spain over the purchase of mines there, the defendants being the estate of an Englishman, the buyer of the mines[33]; a dispute between French and English seed merchants over the quality of trefoil seed[34]; and, finally, a claim in France by a French army officer against an American woman for damages for injuries caused by a riding accident in the Bois de Boulogne[35]. Whilst this is a fairly random selection of significant cases of the day concerned with the recognition of foreign judgments, the cases do reveal some interesting facets. Almost all of the parties were either private individuals or small partnerships. Many of the disputes involved relatively minor commercial issues or more directly personal matters. The countries in which the disputes were first litigated were either part of the British Empire or geographically quite close to England – with the possible exception of Russia. None of that may be surprising, but it does illustrate the relatively limited reach of the conflict of laws a century ago as compared with today.

### 4. Choice of law

Turning to other fields, it has tended to be assumed in recent years that much of the development of the conflict of laws in the first two-thirds of the twentieth century came in the areas of choice of law and the rather particular rules relating to family law matters. In asking how true that assumption is, it is significant to consider the position at the start of the century. Let us take first choice of law in contract and tort. There was no doubt that a contract formally valid by the law of the place of contracting would be regarded as valid in England[36]. More contentious was the negative proposition that no other law could confer formal validity on a contract. For example, Dicey in his second edition in 1908[37] upholds the force of the negative rule, while Cheshire nearly three decades later in his first edition[38] forcefully advances the view that compliance with the formal requirements of the "proper law of the contract" would also suffice. Turning to capacity to contract, there was no certainty here either, with writers providing support for the applicable law being the law of the domicile, the law of the place of contracting or the proper law of the contract, and with no clear judicial authority for any of these[39]. As for essential validity more generally, it had become clearly settled that the parties could choose the law to govern their contract[40]. What remained unsettled was whether there were limits to that choice and, if so, what. It was, however, clear that in the absence of choice the contract was governed by the proper law of the contract and that presumptions could aid the determination of the proper law, though with no resolution of the issue as to whether that determination was to be based on the

---

29  *Abouloff v Oppenheimer & Co* (1882) 10 QBD 295.
30  *Vadala v Lawes* (1890) 25 QBD 310.
31  *Taylor v Hollard* [1902] 1 KB 676.
32  *Rousillon v Rousillon* (1880) 14 Ch D 351.
33  *Nouvion v Freeman* (1889) 15 App Cas 1.
34  *Ochsenbein v Papelier* (1873) LR 8 Ch App 695.
35  *Raulin v Fischer* [1911] 2 KB 93.
36  *Compton v Bearcroft* (1769) 2 Hagg Con 430.
37  *Conflict of Laws* (2nd edn, 1908) pp 541–542; and see *Halsbury's Laws of England* (1st edn, 1909) vol 6 paras 236–237.
38  *Private International Law* (1935) pp 176–180.
39  *Ibid* pp 150–152.
40  *Gienar v Meyer* (1796) 2 Bl 603; *Lloyd v Guibert* (1865) LR 1 QB 115 at 120; *Jacobs v Credit Lyonnais* (1884) 12 QBD 589.

presumed intention of the parties or upon an objective assessment of all the connecting factors in order to determine with what country or its law the contract was most closely connected. Again, this was a fruitful ground for academic debate[41]. It appeared settled that the validity of a contract would not be upheld if it was illegal by English law or by its proper law[42]. While there seemed little doubt that illegality under the law of the place of performance would vitiate a contract, uncertainty and debate surrounded the issue of whether illegality by the place of contracting would affect the validity of the contract in England. In the case of tort claims, the pattern of the common law rules had become settled by the turn of the century. The wrong had to be actionable in England as a tort and not justifiable under the law of the country where it occurred[43].

Moving on to the law of property, it had been made clear by the end of the nineteenth century that the English courts had no jurisdiction to adjudicate over claims to title to, or rights of possession in, foreign land. The decision to this effect in *British South Africa Co v Companhia de Mocambique*[44] again bears one of the hallmarks of the conflict of laws cases of the period, the foreign jurisdiction, South Africa, being part of the British Empire. As for the law to govern the validity, both formal and essential, of the transfer of immovables, much of the authority that was to govern this area throughout the twentieth century dates from around the turn of the century[45], making clear that the law of the country of the situs of the land is to be applied. In the case of the transfer of tangible movables, Cheshire in his first edition[46] takes issue with the view expressed in Dicey[47] as to the governing law, favouring the proper law of the transfer, rather than Dicey's main propositions in favour of the law of the place of the goods or the place where the transfer was made. Three comments might be made on this. First, Cheshire writing in 1935 examines[48] what he regards as the seven leading cases[49], all but two of which are nineteenth century cases. Secondly, those decisions remain today as the major corpus of authority on this issue; and, thirdly, the difference between the approaches of the two major text books has not been finally resolved, either by the legislature or by the judiciary.

These choice of law examples drawn from the fields of obligations and property all indicate that by about the start of the twentieth century the fundamental rules to guide the courts throughout much of the century to follow had been substantially settled – or remained unsettled for much of the period.

## 5. Family law matters

A rather different picture presents itself in the field of family law. Let us look briefly at the four areas of marriage, matrimonial proceedings, children and family money. In all

41 Contrast Dicey, *Conflict of Laws* (5th edn, 1932) p 628 et seq, with Cheshire, *Private International Law* (1935) p 181 et seq.
42 *P&O Steam Navigation co v Shand* (1865) 3 Moo PC (NS) 589.
43 *The Halley* (1868) LR 2 PC 193; *Phillips v Eyre* (1870) 6 QB 1; *Machado v Fontes* [1897] 2 QB 231.
44 [1893] AC 632.
45 *Nelson v Bridport* (1846) Beav 547; *Adams v Clutterbuck* (1883) 10 QBD 403; *Duncan v Lawson* (1889) 41 Ch D 394; *Re Piercy* [1895] 1 Ch 83; *Bank of Africa v Cohen* [1909] 2 Ch 129.
46 *Private International Law* (1935) p 323 et seq.
47 *Conflict of Laws* (5th edn, 1932) p 608 et seq.
48 At pp 332–338.
49 *Cammell v Sewell* (1858) 3 H & N 617; (1860) 5 H & N 728; *Inglis v Usherwood* (1801) 1 East 515; *Freeman v East India Co* (1822) 5 B & Ald 617; *Liverpool Marine Co v Hunter* (1868) LR 3 Ch 479; *Re Korvine's Trusts* [1921] 1 Ch 343; *Alcock v Smith* [1892] 1 Ch 238; *Embericos v Anglo-Austrian Bank* [1905] 1 KB 677.

marriage cases and other matrimonial proceedings, the English courts would not take jurisdiction to entertain the case if the marriage in question was polygamous in fact or form – a proposition clearly laid down in *Hyde v Hyde*[50], a case concerning a Mormon marriage in Utah. As for choice of law in marriage, it was clearly settled that formal validity was to be governed by the law of the place of celebration of the marriage[51], even if the choice of the place of celebration was made in order to avoid a limitation imposed by the law of the country of the domicile[52]. Whilst, as will be seen, the absolute nature of this rule came to be somewhat eroded during the course of the twentieth century, influenced as with other aspects of the family law rules by the incidence of war and patterns of migration, there is also here an early example of intervention by the legislature in the choice of law field, in that the Foreign Marriage Act 1892[53] made provision for the formal validity in England of marriages abroad by British subjects which were solemnised by British diplomatic or consular officers, and of British forces serving abroad whose marriages were solemnised by forces' chaplains.

In the case of capacity to marry, it was clearly and crisply stated by Dicey in 1896[54] that the capacity of a person to marry is governed by the law of his or her domicile. Although this proposition lacked crystal clear judicial authority at the time, it remained unchallenged until Cheshire, after very careful analysis of the inconclusive authorities, propounded the view in his first edition in 1935 that capacity to marry is governed by the law of the intended matrimonial home[55]. What is interesting is that this debate continued through successive editions and editors of the two books throughout the rest of the twentieth century, without ever having been clearly and categorically determined by judicial decision. Furthermore, despite the uncertainty, the Law Commission, towards the end of the century[56], concluded that final clarification of the law should be left to judicial decisions, rather than be determined by legislative intervention. It must be said, however, that the greater weight of authority now supports the dual domicile approach[57], although even now that authority tends to be constituted by dicta in cases where the choice between the two approaches was not a real issue or decisions where the facts pointed to the adoption of the dual domicile approach but the court did not discuss the issue[58].

Turning to matrimonial causes, a hundred years ago the jurisdictional rules were simple. The English court would only take jurisdiction in the case of proceedings for divorce if the husband was domiciled in England at the time of the proceedings[59] and, as a matter of law, a married woman had the same domicile as her husband[60]. In the case of proceedings for judicial separation, jurisdiction could also be assumed on the basis of residence in England[61]. The harshness of the main divorce rule can be well illustrated by the case of an English wife who was deserted by her foreign domiciled husband and returned to England to live permanently. She could not acquire an English domicile of her own and

---

50  (1866) LR 1 P&D 130.
51  *Scrimshire v Scrimshire* (1752) 2 Hagg Con 395.
52  *Simonin v Mallac* (1860) 2 Sw & Tr 67.
53  Now amended by the Foreign Marriage Act 1947 and the Foreign Marriage (Amendment) Act 1988.
54  *Conflict of Laws* (2nd edn, 1896) p 613.
55  *Private International Law* (1935) p 152 et seq.
56  Law Com no 165 (1987) paras 2.13–2.14.
57  See *Padolecchia v Padolecchia* [1968] P 314.
58  Eg *Brook v Brook* (1861) 9 HL Cas 193; *Mette v Mette* (1859) 1 Sw & Tr 416; *Radwan v Radwan (No 2)* [1973] Fam 35; *Pugh v Pugh* [1951] P 482.
59  *Le Mesurier v Le Mesurier* [1895] AC 817.
60  *Warrender v Warrender* (1835) 2 Cl & F 488.
61  *Armytage v Armytage* [1898] P 178.

thus could not take divorce proceedings before an English court. Although, as will be seen, much has changed over the century in relation to the jurisdictional rules, the choice of law rules relating to divorce and judicial, now legal, separation still remain the same: the court always applies English law in English proceedings.

In the case of nullity decrees, English courts had jurisdiction if the marriage had been celebrated in England[62], and, possibly, if the respondent was resident in England[63], but not on the basis of domicile[64]. As for choice of law issues, those relating to the formal or essential validity of the marriage were governed by the relevant choice of law rules, mentioned above.

The rules for the recognition of foreign matrimonial decrees were relatively undeveloped. It was, however, clear that a foreign divorce decree obtained in the courts of the spouses' domicile would be recognised[65], as would a divorce obtained in a third country but which was recognised in the country of the domicile[66]. Dicey suggested[67], though in the absence of any clear authority, that a nullity decree obtained in the courts of the country where the marriage was celebrated would also be recognised – a view later confirmed in 1923[68].

At the beginning of the last century, some, but not all, conflict of laws rules relating to children (or infants as they were then known) were undeveloped. It was established that whether a child was legitimate depended on the child's domicile at birth[69]; though confusion had been sown by the decision of the House of Lords in *Shaw v Gould*[70] raising the question of the effect of the non-recognition of a foreign divorce in England on the legitimacy of a child domiciled at birth in the country where the divorce had been obtained – an issue which was to continue to exercise commentators for most of the twentieth century. Legitimation, especially by subsequent marriage, reveals a very non-insular approach by the English courts. Although legitimation was not introduced into English law until 1926[71], English courts had for forty years or more been prepared to recognise a foreign legitimation by subsequent marriage if the father was domiciled in the country of the legitimation both at the time of the child's birth and of the later marriage[72].

Other aspects of the law relating to children were very undeveloped, or non-existent. Adoption was not permitted in England until 1926[73] and there was no inclination to recognise foreign adoptions before that date[74]. As for orders regulating the custody or care of children, the only international development by the end of the Victorian era concerned guardianship. It had been made clear that an English court would exercise jurisdiction to appoint a guardian if the child was either in England[75] or, though abroad, was a British subject[76]. A foreign guardian had, as such, no rights over a child in England; such rights were regarded as wholly territorial in effect. Nevertheless, an English court might itself

---

62  *Simonin v Mallac* (1860) 1 Sw & Tr 67.
63  *Roberts v Brennan* [1902] P 143.
64  *Niboyet v Niboyet* (1878) 4 PD 1, 9.
65  *Harvey v Farnie* (1880) 5 PD 153; *Le Mesurier v Le Mesurier* [1895] AC 817.
66  *Armitage v A-G* [1906] P 135.
67  *Conflict of Laws* (2nd edn, 1896) pp 387–389.
68  *Mitford v Mitford* [1923] P 130.
69  *Birtwhistle v Vardill* (1835) 2 Cl & Fin 571; (1839) 7 Cl & Fin 895.
70  (1868) LR 3 HL 55.
71  Legitimacy Act 1926.
72  *Re Goodman's Trusts* (1881) 17 Ch D 266; *Re Grove* (1888) 40 Ch D 216.
73  Adoption of Children Act 1926.
74  Dicey, *Conflict of Laws* (2nd edn, 1908) pp 459–460.
75  *Johnstone v Beattie* (1843) 10 Cl & Fin 42.
76  *Re Willoughby* (1885) LR 30 Ch 324.

appoint a foreign appointed guardian as the guardian of the child, or agree not to interfere with a foreign guardian's exercise of his discretion over children in England[77]. As for financial orders, such as maintenance orders whether for a spouse or a child, it was not until well into the twentieth century that the cross-border implications of such orders came to the attention of the English courts – and then it was to deny the enforcement of foreign alimony orders on the basis that the foreign judgment[78] was not final or conclusive. If it was, as in the case of a judgment for arrears already due, then it became established that it could be enforced[79]. Although the first significant legislation in this field was passed at about the same time as these decisions, – the Maintenance Orders (Facilities for Enforcement) Act 1920, providing a scheme for the reciprocal enforcement of maintenance orders between the United Kingdom and Commonwealth countries – the limited significance of this area of the law can be illustrated by the fact that by 1932 it merited no more than an obscure footnote in Dicey[80] and failed to be discussed at all by Cheshire until 1952[81].

## IV. DEVELOPMENTS OVER THE LAST CENTURY

So much for a selective snapshot of some aspects of the conflict of laws as they stood early in the twentieth century. In looking at how the subject has changed over the past century, it is proposed to consider some of the main drivers of change, the impact that they had and the forms that change took.

### 1. A smaller world: the human impact

The conflict of laws develops and changes as the incidence of cross-border activity grows. One manifestation is a growth in trade and commerce stimulated by improved forms of communication and travel, and this has an obvious impact on the development of those aspects of the conflict of laws concerned with commercial activity, of which more later. The growth of cross-border trade also has a more human aspect. With increased cross-border commercial activities comes an increase in personal travel, with more people working in countries which are not their original "home". The pace of such developments has increased hugely with the greater ease and lower cost of air travel. There have, however, been other major causes of substantial migration. Economic migration has been encouraged, though subject to controls, in for example the USA, Canada and Australia, and now within the EU. Not long after the end of the Second World War, such migration to England from the West Indies was warmly encouraged. Similar patterns, coinciding with decolonisation, are identifiable in migration from the Indian sub-continent and West Africa. For the last half century or more, war, oppression and famine have led to migration to the United Kingdom. We have in recent decades seen, for example, migration to this country from Nazi persecution in Europe, from racial oppression in East Africa, from tribal and religious conflict in Afghanistan and from civil war in former Yugoslavia. Indeed, early in the twenty-first century, we are all too familiar with problems relating to refugees, asylum seekers, or economic migrants, however one describes those wishing to move to a country with greener, or any, grass compared with home.

---

77  Eg *Nugent v Vetzera* (1866) LR 2 Eq 704; cf *Re Willoughby*, above.

78  Eg *Re Macartney* [1921] 1 Ch 522 – Maltese maintenance order for a child; *Harrop v Harrop* [1920] 3 KB 386 – order of a court in Perak for maintenance of a wife and child.

79  *Beatty v Beatty* [1924] 1 KB 807.

80  *Conflict of Laws* (5th edn, 1932) p 476; and the same is true of *Halsbury's Laws of England* (2nd edn, 1932) vol 6 para 307.

81  *Private International Law* (4th edn, 1952) p 617, n 1.

All of these movements of people, for whatever reason, have had a very real impact in the last fifty or sixty years on the conflict of laws rules relating to family law issues. The influx into England of people from states where polygamy is accepted, mainly but not exclusively Muslim states, or the movement to such states of English companies and their employees, has required new thought to be given to old rules, such as that which denied the jurisdiction of the English courts to any dispute relating to an actual or potentially polygamous marriage[82]. Many people have become domiciled in England whose marriages fell outside the ambit of English family law simply because the marriage, entered into abroad, had been in the form appropriate to a potentially polygamous marriage. The Victorian abhorrence of such marriages became tempered gradually over the second half of the twentieth century, with the eventual outcome that now all marriages which are effectively monogamous will be so regarded[83] and some, but not full, recognition is also afforded to actually polygamous marriages which have been validly entered into abroad[84].

The more people travel the more they are likely to marry and divorce abroad. From this developed a clearly perceived need to address issues of divorce jurisdiction (and jurisdiction over other less practically significant matrimonial proceedings) and the recognition of foreign divorces in terms of both domestically initiated changes and those which have come from wider international initiatives. The expansion of the grounds of divorce jurisdiction was achieved, first, by a series of statutory provisions addressing piecemeal problems which had arisen from, for example, the predicament of a deserted wife whose English domiciled husband had gone abroad or a wife who had been resident in England for three years but whose husband remained a foreign domiciliary[85]. More sweeping change came in 1973 whereby jurisdiction was based on the domicile or one year's habitual residence in England of either spouse at the time of the proceedings[86]. Recently this broad approach has substantially been confirmed in the implementation of EU legislation[87]. So, world traveller though you may be, you only have to live in England on a settled basis to be able to gain access to English divorce law.

Liberalisation similar to that in relation to divorce jurisdiction can be seen in the field of the recognition of foreign divorces. The start of the second half of the twentieth century saw the judiciary taking the first steps to broaden the bases of recognition from that of divorces obtained or recognised in the country of the domicile to any foreign divorce obtained in circumstances where, *mutatis mutandis*, an English court would have had jurisdiction[88]. So expansion of the domestic rules expanded the recognition rules. In 1969, the House of Lords took the broader step of declaring that English courts would recognise a foreign divorce obtained in a country whenever there was a real and substantial connection between the petitioner (or perhaps also the respondent) and that country[89]. While all agreed that the bases of recognition had been broadened, few were sure as to how

82  *Hyde v Hyde* (1866) LR 1 PD 130, above.
83  Eg Private International Law (Miscellaneous Provisions) Act 1995, Part II.
84  See Cheshire and North, *Private International Law* (13th edn, 1999) pp 755–760.
85  Matrimonial Causes Act 1937 s 13; Law Reform (Miscellaneous Provisions) Act 1949 s 1. In fact, many of these problems disappeared with the change in the law (Domicile and Matrimonial Proceedings Act 1973 s 1) which allowed a wife to acquire a domicile separate from that of her husband; thereby getting rid of what has been described as "the last barbarous relic of a wife's servitude": *Gray v Formosa* [1963] P 259 at 267.
86  Domicile and Matrimonial Proceedings Act 1973, Part II.
87  Council Regulation (EC) 1347/2000, on jurisdiction and the recognition and enforcement of judgments in matrimonial matters and in matters of parental responsibility for children of both spouses; OJ 2000 L160 p 19.
88  *Travers v Holley* [1953] P 246.
89  *Indyka v Indyka* [1969] 1 AC 33.

far. Two years later Parliament, on advice from the Law Commission[90] and consistently with a convention concluded by the Hague Conference on Private International Law[91], placed the recognition rules on a statutory basis[92], though under a rather complex scheme with the common law continuing to apply to divorces obtained before 1972; essentially the scheme provided for automatic recognition of divorces obtained elsewhere in the British Isles, and rather different rules for divorces obtained outside the British Isles depending on whether they were obtained through judicial proceedings or extra-judicially. Despite this complexity, essentially confirmed in later legislation[93] (again on advice from the Law Commission)[94], there is no doubt that first the judges and then Parliament carried through a liberalising process of granting considerably greater recognition than had been the case to divorces obtained outside England. The latest developments continue this process by, in essence, extending the regime for the automatic recognition in England of divorces obtained elsewhere in the British Isles to divorces (and other matrimonial orders) obtained throughout the EU[95].

In the light of this marked willingness to entertain a broader range of divorce proceedings with cross-border connections and to grant recognition to foreign divorces obtained in a much wider range of jurisdictional circumstances, it is almost paradoxical that there has been relatively little activity on the part of judges, law reform agencies or the legislature to reformulate the choice of law rules governing the validity of marriages. The fundamental rules on the choice of law to govern form and capacity (whatever those rules may be, as considered earlier) remain essentially unchanged from the beginning of the twentieth century. The one significant area of development in the context of formal validity has been the extent to which the application of the law of the place of celebration can be displaced on the grounds of its inappropriateness in favour of English common law rules, as exemplified by marriages entered into by those affected by the tides of war – for example when no register offices were open in Germany in 1945[96], or as the German army advanced across the Ukraine in 1942[97], in Ho Chi Minh City in 1978[98], in a displaced persons' camp in Germany in 1945[99] or between occupying forces in Italy in 1946[100].

In the field of essential validity of marriage, there are two aspects where some change and development can, however, be identified. First, in relation to capacity to enter a polygamous marriage, after a series of judicial[101] and legislative[102] developments, Parliament made clear that persons domiciled in England have capacity to enter a foreign marriage which is polygamous in form, provided it is not actually polygamous[103]. It remains the case, however, that a valid polygamous marriage cannot be entered into in this country; though it is clear from recent newspaper reports that people do go through religious ceremonies in this country in polygamous form despite such ceremonies' lack of legal effectiveness. Secondly, the extension of the circumstances in which recognition will

---

90  Law Com no 34 (1970).
91  Convention on the Recognition of Divorces and Legal Separations (1970).
92  Recognition of Divorces and Legal Separations Act 1971.
93  Family Law Act 1986, Part II.
94  Law Com no 137 (1984).
95  Council Regulation (EC) 1347/2000; and see Council Regulation (EC) 2201/2003.
96  *Savenis v Savenis* [1950] SASR 309.
97  *Kuklycz v Kuklycz* [1972] VR 50.
98  *Re X's Marriage* (1983) 65 FLR 132.
99  *Kochanski v Kochanska* [1958] P 147.
100  *Taczanowska v Taczanowski* [1957] P 301; *Merker v Merker* [1963] P 283.
101  *Radwan v Radwan (No 2)* [1973] Fam 35; *Hussain v Hussain* [1983] Fam 26.
102  Matrimonial Causes Act 1973 s 11.
103  Private International Law (Miscellaneous Provisions) Act 1995 s 5(1).

be granted to a foreign divorce or, indeed, annulment led to confusion as to the extent to which such recognition in England affected a person's capacity to remarry in England or elsewhere if the foreign decree was not recognised by, for example, the law of that person's domicile[104]. The conflict was resolved by Parliament in favour of there being capacity to marry by reason of the recognition of the divorce or annulment in England, rather than lack of capacity because of its non-recognition under the foreign law[105].

It seems clear that, over the last two or three decades, there has been a declining interest in the conflict of laws rules relating to marriage. Indeed, as mentioned earlier, the Law Commission in 1987 having examined the rules in some depth saw no case for recommending significant legislative intervention[106]. It is probably not going too far to say that this is accounted for, in part at least, by the liberalisation of divorce laws across many countries in the world, coupled with a rise in the number of couples in stable, indeed lifelong, relationships who choose not to marry.

When one turns to money and children, the picture is very different. Change over the century has been dramatic. The growth in opportunities for travel, whether for business reasons, study or pleasure has resulted in a marked increase in financial or custody disputes between spouses with links to more than one jurisdiction, whether they are an English married couple who had lived together abroad and one had returned to England on the breakdown of the marriage, or where the spouses were originally from different countries with differing social and legal cultures. In the case of disputes over financial relief, problems and development have centred around the impact and effect of foreign orders in England, and most of the developments have been statutory. Starting in 1920, provision was made by statute[107] for the reciprocal enforcement of maintenance orders between England and those Commonwealth countries to which the legislation had been extended by Order in Council. Similar reciprocal machinery was extended in 1972[108] to any reciprocating foreign country, and then in 1982 and 1991 to the recognition and enforcement of maintenance orders made elsewhere in the EU[109] or in the EFTA states[110]. What is important to note is that the recognition and enforcement of foreign orders is essentially founded on international agreement between states – whether in terms of a series of standard form bilateral agreements or of uniform recognition and enforcement rules negotiated within the context of a broad political relationship, as with the EU. One particular difficulty in relation to financial relief arose from the increase in the circumstances in which foreign divorces would be recognised in England in that a spouse in England could not seek financial relief from an English court if her marriage was recognised as having already been dissolved by a foreign court[111]. While there were some judicial attempts to ameliorate the full impact of this legally impeccable analysis[112], it was Parliament which, in 1984[113], on the recommendation of the Law Commission[114], eventually conferred powers on an English

---

104 *Perrini v Perrini* [1979] Fam 84; *Lawrence v Lawrence* [1985] Fam 106.
105 Family Law Act 1986 s 50.
106 Law Com no 165 (1987) paras 2.11–2.15.
107 Maintenance Orders (Facilities for Enforcement) Act 1920.
108 Maintenance Orders (Reciprocal Enforcement) Act 1972.
109 Civil Jurisdiction and Judgments Act 1982, implementing the Brussels Convention on the recognition and enforcement of judgments in civil and commercial matters. See now Council Regulation (EC) 44/2001; OJ 2001 L12 p 1.
110 Civil Jurisdiction and Judgments Act 1991, implementing the Lugano Convention on Jurisdiction and the Enforcement of Judgments in Civil and Commercial Matters.
111 Eg *Turczak v Turczak* [1970] P 198.
112 Eg *Torok v Torok* [1973] 1 WLR 1066; *P (LE) v P (JM)* [1971] P 318.
113 Matrimonial and Family Proceedings Act 1984, Part III.
114 Law Com no 117 (1982).

court to grant financial relief after the marriage had been dissolved by a foreign divorce which was recognised in England.

A not dissimilar general pattern is seen in the development of the rules relating to children, ie a real human problem only ameliorated by legislation created as the result of international agreement. For much of the century, as has been seen, an English court in the case of a custody dispute, being charged with making an order which is in the best interests of the child, would not, as such, recognise a foreign custody order[115]; though it might, but did not have to, make its own order to similar effect. Not only were new jurisdictional rules introduced by statute in 1986[116] to determine when English courts might make custody orders (again on the recommendations of the Law Commission)[117], but also three separate initiatives have transformed the rules relating to recognition of foreign orders – all established by legislation stemming from different forms of cross-border agreement, ie intra-United Kingdom recognition rules[118] resulting from joint work by the English and Scottish Law Commissions[119], a worldwide regime of recognition created by the Hague Conference on Private International Law[120] and an overlapping and similar scheme established by the Council of Europe[121]. The development over the last twenty years of international regimes for tackling the problems of child abduction and other forms of international custody disputes provides a striking example of the way in which cross-border problems created by the ease of international travel have had to be addressed not by the development of separate sets of rules, state by state, but by international agreement. What is also striking is that, while the new rules are intended to minimise the number of custody disputes where court orders are defied or children are unlawfully removed, the paradox is that there is a very large number of litigated cases not only in this country but throughout the jurisdictions which are a party to the relevant conventions, thus revealing just how large a human problem this still is and how important international legal co-operation has become[122].

## 2. A smaller world: commercial activities

The impact over the century of improved communications – from the telephone to telex, to fax, to email and electronic money transfer – and improved transportation – from sail to steam, to diesel shipping, tankers, container ships and cargo aircraft – on the development of conflict of laws rules in the field of obligations, especially relating to commercial issues, can be exemplified in a variety of ways. Many more commercial disputes arise and are contested. This can be simply illustrated in two ways. There has been an increase in the number of reported decisions directly involving contract choice of law issues. Taking a crude sampling over the century[123], there are two such cases identified in the decade 1901–1910, three in the two decades 1931–1950, eight from 1961–1970, twenty one in the last

---

115  *McKee v McKee* [1951] AC 352.
116  Family Law Act 1986, Part I.
117  Law Com no 138 (1985).
118  Family Law Act 1986, Part I.
119  Law Com no 138 (1985).
120  Convention on the Civil Aspects of Child Abduction (1980), implemented by the Child Abduction and Custody Act 1985, Part I.
121  Convention on Recognition and Enforcement of Decisions concerning Custody of Children and on the Restoration of Custody of Children (1980), implemented by the Child Abduction and Custody Act 1985, Part II.
122  For recent EU development, see Council Regulation (EC) 1347/2000; OJ 2000 L160p 19; and see the Hague Convention on Jurisdiction, Applicable Law, Recognition, Enforcement and Co-operation in Respect of Parental Responsibility and Measures for the Protection of Children (1996).

decade of the twentieth century and twelve so far this century. While there are other decisions which might be classed as significant in the contract choice of law context, there is undoubtedly a pattern revealed of increased litigation over conflict of laws contract issues over the last hundred years. Furthermore, as compared with the beginning of the twentieth century, there has been a change in the character of the litigants from individuals and small businesses to much larger enterprises; and the claims are relatively much larger as well. The substantial nature of the parties can be illustrated by recent cases involving claims, for example, by or against banks, insurance companies, major shipping companies, state enterprises and global corporations.

A second way of evidencing the increased significance of commercial disputes is by looking at the field of arbitration. This is, of course, just one aspect of the development of the means of dispute resolution, but one which is of particular significance in the field of cross-border disputes, and also a method of dispute resolution which is most generally used in the current context for the resolution of commercial disputes. These developments can be illustrated in two ways. First, there has been a steady development of the common law principles for determining when a foreign arbitral award will be recognised and enforced in England[124]. More significantly, however, this has been an area where change has come through international agreement, such as the 1927 Geneva Convention[125], the New York Convention of 1958[126] and other more limited agreements[127]. The second context is that of the effect of an arbitration agreement on the question of recognition of a judgment from a foreign court. The significance of arbitration is emphasised by reason of the fact that an English court may, by statute[128], deny recognition to a foreign judgment if the court proceedings in the foreign country were brought in breach of an agreement to take any disputes to arbitration[129].

The last hundred years have also seen an increased focus on the development of particular sets of rules, whether jurisdictional rules or choice of law rules, to be applied to specific commercial areas or circumstances. For example, the rise in consumerism and the perceived need to protect consumers from the inequality of their bargaining position in relation to the commercial organisations with whom they contract is seen in the context of the conflict of laws, as it is in domestic law[130]. So, legislation[131] has led to the introduction of special jurisdictional rules in consumer contract areas which are of undoubted benefit to consumer claimants, enabling a consumer to sue in the country of his or her domicile, rather than having to go to the courts of the defendant supplier's domicile[132]. Similarly, special jurisdictional provision is made in the case of employment contracts[133], again carrying protective rules through into the conflict of laws sphere. The same approach is to

123 Using the Law Reports Digest and the Law Reports Index, and relying, albeit flexibly, on the classifications in those indices.
124 *Norske Atlas Insurance Co Ltd v London General Insurance Co Ltd* (1927) 43 TLR 541; *James Miller & Partners Ltd v Whitworth Street Estates (Manchester) Ltd* [1970] AC 583; *Cie d'Armement Maritime SA v Cie Tunisienne de Navigation SA* [1971] AC 572.
125 Implemented by the Arbitration Act 1950.
126 Implemented by the Arbitration Act 1975; see now the Arbitration Act 1995, Part III.
127 Eg the Arbitration (Investment Disputes) Act 1966.
128 Civil Jurisdiction and Judgments Act 1982 s 32.
129 *Tracomin SA v Sudan Oil Seeds Co Ltd (No 1)* [1983] 1 WLR 1026.
130 See Harris and McClean, "The Conflict of Laws", in Hayton *Law's Futures* (2000) pp 173–174, 182.
131 The Civil Jurisdiction and Judgments Act 1982 and now Council Regulation (EC) 44/2001; OJ 2001 L12 p 1.
132 Council Regulation (EC) 44/2001 arts 15–17; OJ 2001 L12 p 6–7.
133 *Ibid* arts 18–21; OJ 2001 L12 p 7.

be found in the choice of law field, with the relevant legislation[134] also laying down special choice of law rules for consumers[135] and for individual employment contracts[136]. Again, the purpose has been to provide added protection for the individual involved in, for them, the most common types of cross-border contracts.

The development of particular rules in the sphere of cross-border contracts and commercial disputes has not been restricted to consumer and employee protection. Indeed, Dicey, at the end of the nineteenth century, thought it helpful not only to provide an account of the general choice of law rules applicable to contracts[137], but also to examine "Particular Contracts" separately[138], an approach which has consistently been carried through successive editions[139]. It has been accepted that the increased complexity of commercial life is such that a "one rule fits all circumstances" approach is no longer tenable. So we have seen, for example, the development, again primarily by legislation, of specialised choice of law rules for carriage of goods[140] and of jurisdictional rules for insurance contracts[141]. Furthermore, there is a large body of international conventions which govern carriage of both goods and passengers, by air, road, rail and sea, concluded during the course of the twentieth century, starting with the 1924 Hague Rules on carriage of goods by sea and the Warsaw Convention of 1929 on the carriage of passengers and goods by air[142].

The increasing economic importance of world trade coupled with the importance of the development of legal rules which can accommodate the complexities of such commercial activity has led over the last half century to new approaches to the subject. An important interface in the commercial field which has been developed is that between conflict of laws rules and the detailed, often internationally agreed, rules relating to international trade law. This has led, for example, to an examination of the role to be played by the *lex mercatoria* in, on the one hand, the context of classical contract choice of law rules[143] and, on the other, in the resolution of disputes through arbitration[144]. Similarly, the recent enthusiasms for the development of uniform rules, laws or a complete code in the commercial law field[145] have raised important issues as to the interrelation of such new uniform laws with the freedom to choose the applicable law to govern an international contract[146].

## 3. *Extra-judicial development*

The conflict of laws rules established at the beginning of the twentieth century were, almost without exception, rules established by the judiciary. This had many merits – not least the

---

134 Contracts (Applicable Law) Act 1990, giving effect to the Rome Convention on the Law Applicable to Contractual Obligations (1980).
135 Rome Convention art 5.
136 *Ibid* art 6.
137 *Conflict of Laws* (2nd edn, 1896) Chapter XXV.
138 *Ibid* Chapter XXVI.
139 See Dicey, Morris and Collins, *Conflict of Laws* (14th edn, 2006) Chs 32, 33.
140 Contracts (Applicable Law) Act 1990, implementing the Rome Convention art 4(4).
141 See Council Regulation (EC) 44/2001 arts 8–14; OJ 2001 L12/5-6.
142 See Dicey, Morris and Collins pp 1762–1785.
143 See Nygh, *Autonomy in International Contracts* (1999) pp 177–198.
144 Carbonneau (ed) *Lex Mercatoria and Arbitration* (revised edn, 1998).
145 See Goode, "Insularity or Leadership? The Role of the United Kingdom in the Harmonisation of Commercial Law" (2001) 50 ICLQ 751; Berger, "Harmonisation of European Contract Law: The Influence of Comparative Law" (2001) 50 ICLQ 877.
146 See Honnold, *Uniform Law for International Sales* (3rd edn, 1999) sections 96–98. For a broader discussion of problems to which uniform laws may give rise, see Mann, *Further Studies in International Law* (1990) Ch 10.

ability to respond rapidly to new circumstances and problems as they were thrown up by the developments of trade and travel which was the legacy of the Victorian age. Being judge-made rules, and as long as they were not the outcome of decisions of the House of Lords[147], they also had the advantage that they could be developed to meet changing commercial and other circumstances – whether by refinement, the development of exceptions and variations for particular issues or, occasionally, replacement. Nevertheless, this approach had its disadvantages. Many judges in the first half of the twentieth century were inclined to resolve no more than the particular issue before them rather than to examine the concerns raised more broadly. Furthermore, the development of new rules depended on the accident of litigation, and it is very striking just how few reported decisions there were in the whole conflict of laws field during the first half of the twentieth century. For example, the Law Reports Digest from 1901 to 1950 contains reference to fewer than two cases a year, averaged over the period, which are classed as falling within this general area. What judicial development could rarely do in this field of law, as in so many others, was to provide new sets of rules for a whole range of issues arising within the particular field. Indeed, the formulation of such new rules might be thought to require wider advice, including commercial and political advice, than would necessarily be available to an appellate court[148]. Furthermore, and this is a particular characteristic of the subject under review, decisions of the judges of national courts could rarely create rules which would serve as the basis for international agreement on how to tackle cross-border issues. One reason for that was that judges, certainly English judges, in the first half of the twentieth century rarely looked beyond other legal decisions within their own jurisdiction in reaching their conclusions.

Herein lies another paradox. Judicial willingness to look beyond the confines of the writings of other English judges has changed markedly, in this field as in many others, over the last half century; but, at the same time, new drivers of change have appeared on the domestic and the international scene, and the medium for implementing their ideas and approaches has been legislation. Here we have almost the mirror image of the judicial approach. Legislation can tackle a whole range of issues at once; it does not need to wait for a litigant bold or wealthy enough to raise the issue before a court (though it does need to wait for legislative time), and it can embody the concluded agreement of a range of states, as well as the fruits of broad national consultation. However, legislation is much harder to change or develop if the legislature gets it wrong, the world has changed, or if states agree that change is needed but cannot agree on what.

Nevertheless, the last half century has seen the conflict of laws affected very widely by a whole range of new law reform approaches[149]. At home, the Private International Law Committee, and then the Law Commission, between them have produced a substantial number of recommendations for change, while the United Kingdom's membership of the European Union has led to the transformation of our rules on jurisdiction and the recognition of foreign judgments[150], on choice of law in contract[151] and to the introduction

---

147 It was not until 1966 that the House of Lords had power to overrule its own decisions: *Practice Statement (Judicial Precedent)* [1966] 1 WLR 1234. One of the most significant examples of the exercise of this power in the conflict of laws field was in *Miliangos v George Frank (Textiles) Ltd*; but even then Lord Simon of Glaisdale took the view that it was for Parliament and not the courts to change the law on the giving of judgments in foreign currency: [1976] AC 443 at 490–491, [1975] 3 All ER 801 at 832.

148 See [1976] AC 443 at 490, [1975] 3 All ER 801 at 832.

149 See North, "Private International Law: Change or Decay?" (the 24th FA Mann Lecture) (2001) 50 ICLQ 477 at pp 478–496.

150 See Council Regulation (EC) 44/2001; OJ 2001 L12 p 1.

151 See Contracts (Applicable Law) Act 1992.

of a new regime on jurisdiction and recognition in the area of matrimonial proceedings[152], with more change to come[153]. United Kingdom membership of the Hague Conference on Private International Law since 1955 has led to some seven areas of legislative reform[154], again with possibly more to come[155]. Amongst other international bodies whose work has led to legislative change in this field one can include UNIDROIT, UNCITRAL and the Council of Europe[156]. There is then an enormous range of bilateral conventions which the United Kingdom has entered into under the umbrella of various pieces of facilitating legislation, to say nothing of the range of conventions, especially in the field of transportation, whose purpose has been to establish uniform laws, thus eradicating the need for choice of law or recognition rules. A quick survey of the statute book reveals fifty statutes in the last fifty years which have had a direct impact in this field – some very substantial, such as the Civil Jurisdiction and Judgments Act 1982, others less so. Nevertheless, a statute a year marks a huge change in the nature and form of development of this area of the law.

It is worth pausing for a moment to consider the impact of the work of these varied agencies and of the legislation flowing from that work on different aspects of the conflict of laws and on the role of the judicial lawmaker. In the area of family law, as we have seen, there has been little legislative intervention in the central field of marriage, and the Law Commission felt it right that there should not be any more. Elsewhere, however, almost all of the family law rules are based on statutory provisions. The recognition of foreign divorces was, for the last third of the twentieth century, governed by a statutory regime[157] founded on activity stemming from the Hague Conference on Private International Law[158] and the Law Commission[159]. That is now supplemented by legislation from the EU[160], which has also replaced the statutory bases[161] for jurisdiction over matrimonial proceedings which again stemmed from the work of the Law Commission[162]. We have seen already that cross-border issues relating to family money and custody disputes were placed on an internationally negotiated statutory basis, through bilateral and multilateral conventions developed by the Hague Conference, the Council of Europe and the EU.

As a result, landmark judicial developments in, for example, divorce recognition have been swept aside and judicial decisions are now left simply to exemplify or occasionally explain the meaning or effect of legislative provisions, but even then reference is often made back to the report of the advisory body whose work lies behind the legislation. Furthermore, the explosion of reported decisions (enhanced by the arrival of new series of reports and electronic access to unreported cases) in the field of cross-border child custody disputes really amounts to a large number of factually illustrative decisions, coupled with just a few which explain the workings of the relevant legislation.

---

152 See Council Regulation (EC) 1347/2000; Council Regulation (EC) 2201/2003.
153 See below.
154 Wills Act 1963; Adoption Act 1968; Recognition of Divorces and Legal Separations Act 1971; Evidence (Proceedings in Other Jurisdictions) Act 1975; Child Abduction and Custody Act 1985, Part I; Recognition of Trusts Act 1987; and by Order in Council under the Maintenance Orders (Reciprocal Enforcement) Act 1972.
155 Eg a Convention on Choice of Court Agreements was concluded in 2005.
156 See North (2001) 50 ICLQ 477 at pp 493–495.
157 Recognition of Divorces and Legal Separations Act 1971.
158 Convention on the Recognition of Divorces and Legal Separations (1970).
159 Law Com no 34 (1970).
160 Council Regulation (EC) 1347/2000; OJ 2000 L160 p 19.
161 Domicile and Matrimonial Proceedings Act 1973, Part II.
162 Law Com no 48 (1972).

Turning to obligations much the same can be said of choice of law in contract since the coming into force of the Contracts (Applicable Law) Act 1990, implementing the Rome Convention (1980) concluded within the EEC. The role of the courts has become that of explaining the meaning of the statutory provisions in a very limited number of cases. The earlier common law decisions on how to determine the applicable law are now only of significance in terms of use as analogies for explaining the meaning of statutory provisions to similar effect. One of the novelties of the Rome Convention was the introduction of the presumption of "characteristic performance" to determine the applicable law in the absence of choice by the parties[163]; but here again the courts have had to do little more than provide guidance on how to determine the characteristic performance of different types of contract[164] and, even then, often with reference back to the report which accompanied the original convention[165].

The story is very similar in relation to torts. A range of leading cases has been stood on one side[166], having been replaced in 1995 by a statutory regime[167] based on proposals from the Law Commission[168]. Again, the role of the courts will be to determine the limits and effects of the legislation. One difference from the position in relation to contract is that the latter stems from EEC activities which means that there are likely to be decisions of the courts of other member states which may be of interest and assistance in interpreting the contract convention, whereas in the case of tort, for the moment, the legislative rules apply only in the United Kingdom; though the 1995 Act is itself due to be replaced in the near future by EU legislation in this field[169].

An area of international law-making activity of great practical importance is that relating to the jurisdiction of the courts and the recognition of foreign judgments in civil and commercial matters. For most of the last hundred years, the basic jurisdictional rules were, as has been seen, a mixture of common law rules, essentially providing for jurisdiction to be assumed on the basis of the procedural service of the proceedings on the defendant within the jurisdiction or on the defendant's submission to the jurisdiction of the English court, coupled with subsidiary statutory provisions under which the Rules of the Supreme Court determined the circumstances when proceedings could be served on a defendant abroad. As a result of European law-making activity, first embodied[170] in the Civil Jurisdiction and Judgments Act 1982 and the Civil Jurisdiction and Judgments Act 1991, a further layer of jurisdictional rules has been created which applies to cases which have statutorily defined links with the EU or EFTA states. In the context of the recognition of foreign judgments, there is, as we have seen, a similar mixture of common law rules, statutory rules giving effect to a wide range of multilateral conventions, and then separate rules, again originally created by international convention, to give effect in England to judgments from other EU or EFTA member states. So, again, the story of the last century here has been one of a movement from common law to statute, from national rules to internationally agreed ones, the movements being driven by a combination of bilateral and multilateral international negotiations.

---

163 Article 4(2).
164 Eg *Credit Lyonnais v New Hampshire Insurance Co* [1997] 2 Lloyd's Rep 1 at 6; *Sierra Leone Telecommunications Co Ltd v Barclays Bank plc* [1998] 2 All ER 821.
165 Giuliano and Lagarde Report, OJ 1980 C282 p 1.
166 *Phillips v Eyre* (1870) LR 6 QB 1; *Machado v Fontes* [1897] 2 QB 231; *Boys v Chaplin* [1971] AC 356; *Red Sea Insurance Co Ltd v Bouygues SA* [1995] 1 AC 190.
167 Private International Law (Miscellaneous Provisions) Act 1995, Part III.
168 Law Com no 193 (1990).
169 Proposal for a Regulation on the law applicable to non-contractual obligations (known as Rome II) (C6-0142/2007).
170 See now Council Regulation (EC) 44/2001; OJ 2001 L12 p 1.

A striking feature of the first few years of the twenty-first century has been the speed with which the EU has come forward with new proposals for the reform and harmonisation of the conflict of laws rules within the Community. This activity includes a new regulation on the recognition and enforcement of judgments in matrimonial matters and matters of parental responsibility[171], proposals for regulations on choice of law relating to non-contractual obligations[172] and to contractual obligations[173], on choice of law in matrimonial causes[174] and on jurisdiction, applicable law and recognition in relation to maintenance[175]. In addition, there are Green Papers under discussion on the conflict of laws relating to matrimonial property regimes[176] and on succession and wills[177], as well as the start of the process to review the major regulation on jurisdiction and recognition of judgments in civil and commercial matters[178]. What is fascinating is that the range and content of new proposed activity has not been considered wholly acceptable within the United Kingdom, with the result that the Government has decided not to opt into the discussions on choice of law in contract, choice of law in matrimonial causes and the proposals relating to maintenance. It is also possible that a similar view will be taken of the matrimonial property proposal.

There are two characteristics of internationally negotiated rules which should be mentioned in the present context. The first is that rules which emanate from such negotiations do not necessarily fit clearly into the pattern of rules drawn from one state or, for example, from the common law system rather than the civil law system, or *vice versa*. A simple illustration is provided by the use of domicile as a major connecting factor in the jurisdictional rules established by the Brussels and Lugano Conventions. Essentially, it is a common law term, but one which did not form a main basis of the common law jurisdiction rules, but which was then, by statute[179], given an English meaning more akin to the civil law understanding of the concept. Another example, drawn from the contract choice of law rules agreed within the EEC, and mentioned earlier, is the use of the place of "characteristic performance" of a contract as a connecting factor for determining the law applicable to that contract. In this instance, a concept has been adopted[180] which was substantially unknown in both the civil law and common law systems within the EEC, its origin apparently to be found in Swiss law[181].

The second characteristic is one which is currently most clearly illustrated by the provisions on jurisdiction and recognition created within the EEC. That legislation, first in convention form and now a regulation, is subject to the jurisdiction of the European Court

---

171 Council Regulation (EC) 2201/2003.

172 Proposal for a Regulation on the law applicable to non-contractual obligations (known as Rome II) (C6 – 0142/2007).

173 Proposal for a Regulation on the law applicable to contractual obligations (COM 2005/650 final).

174 Proposal to amend Brussels II Regulation (2201/2003) as regards jurisdiction and introducing rules concerning applicable law in matrimonial causes (COM (2006) 399 final).

175 Proposed Council Regulation on jurisdiction, applicable law, recognition and enforcement of decisions and co-operation in matters relating to maintenance obligations (COM (2005) 649 final).

176 Green Paper on Conflict of Laws in Matters Concerning Matrimonial Property Regimes, Including the Question of Jurisdiction and Mutual Recognition (COM (2006)400 final).

177 Green Paper on Succession and Wills (COM (2005) 0065 final).

178 Council Regulation (EC) 44/2001.

179 Civil Jurisdiction and Judgments Act 1982 ss 41–46.

180 Contracts (Applicable Law) Act 1990, giving effect to the Rome Convention on the Law Applicable to Contractual Obligations art 4(2).

181 Lipstein (1981) 3 Northwestern J Int L & Bus 402.

of Justice. This has two significant effects. The first is that this area of private law is subject to binding interpretation and application by a "hybrid" court, founded neither in civil nor common law. The outcome is that the rules are interpreted on a "European" basis, with rarely a reference to national law approaches. Secondly, as the rules are uniform throughout the member states, and the judgments of the European Court of Justice are binding on all, litigation in individual member states which raises issues in this field is increasingly likely to lead to decisions from the courts of other member states being considered and, indeed, applied. As EU legislation moves into other fields of the conflict of laws, as has recently occurred in the case of matrimonial proceedings, and is soon to occur with choice of law for non-contractual obligations, this trend is likely to continue.

There is one major area where the voice of the advocate for change, whether in national law reform bodies or in international organisations, has been muted, and consequently the intrusion of statutory provisions into the common law rules has been limited, and that is the whole field of property law – relating to both immovables and movables, whether tangible or intangible, and including succession. The voice has not, however, been completely silent as may be seen, first, from the fact that the statutory regime[182] for determining the law applicable to trusts, and the rules for recognising foreign trusts, stems from a Hague Convention on the topic[183]. Secondly, the Rome Convention on the Law Applicable to Contractual Obligations applies to govern the voluntary assignment of rights[184]; and, thirdly, as mentioned earlier, the statutory provisions governing the formal validity of wills find their origin in a 1961 Hague Convention. It must be said, however, that the limited degree of statutory development of this area of the conflict of laws has been well matched by the limited nature of judicial development over the past century. Little of fundamental significance has changed over a hundred years. There have been a few areas of judicial activity, such as addressing problems concerned with derivative claims and retention of title clauses[185], but unresolved fundamental issues from earlier times such as "what law governs the transfer of movables or of a negotiable instrument?" still remain unresolved. Authors continue to provide their varied solutions[186] but there has been remarkably little opportunity for the courts to address some of these basic questions. All this may be set to change for two reasons. First, there is, some evidence of courts having to address the complex cross-border issues thrown up by the world of electronic financial transfers[187]. Secondly, as we have seen, there is a developing interest within the European Union for the harmonisation of conflict of laws rules in the areas of matrimonial property and of wills and succession.

## 4. The role of the jurist

Something of a caricature of judicial attitudes towards academic writing during the first half of the twentieth century was that academics were rarely to be cited to or by the courts, and certainly not if they were still alive or were not members of the Bar[188]. This attitude was perhaps less true of the conflict of laws than of almost any other area of the law.

---

182 Recognition of Trusts Act 1987.
183 Convention on the Law Applicable to Trusts and on their Recognition (1986).
184 Article 12.
185 Cheshire and North, *Private International Law* (13th edn, 1999) pp 945–948.
186 *Ibid* pp 936–953, 965–969; Dicey, Morris and Collins, *Conflict of Laws* (14th edn, 2006) Ch 24; *Halsbury's Laws of England* (4th edn, 2003 Reissue) vol 8(3) para 307.
187 Eg *Macmillan Inc v Bishopsgate Investment Trust plc (No 3)* [1996] 1 WLR 387; Potok, *Cross-Border Collateral: Legal Risk and the Conflict of Laws* (2002); Dicey, Morris and Collins, *ibid*, pp 1189–194. For other issues arising from an electronic age, see North (2001) 50 ICLQ 477at pp 501–504.
188 Duxbury, *Jurists and Judges* (2001) pp 62–77.

Various reasons can be given for this. The cross-border nature of the subject meant that it was perceived to be more complex than most – "like playing three-dimensional chess", as it has been described – which may have prompted a reliance on academic writing, although at times, this complexity seems to have led judges to prefer to ignore the cross-border aspects of a case altogether and to treat it as though all the facts thereof were solely connected with England[189].

Whatever the reasons may have been for this atypical reference to academic opinion, there was a period when the relatively few decisions in the field seemed to have been dominated by "the battle of the books". Was the court to prefer the views expressed in *Dicey*, especially once John Morris had taken over the General Editorship in 1949[190], or those expressed by Cheshire? One example of where the courts have weighed these views without ever reaching a clear conclusion, as we have seen, is as to the law to govern capacity to marry; but as striking an example as any is provided by the decision in *Re Egerton's Will Trusts*[191], on the related issue of what law should govern a widow's rights of succession to matrimonial property. The only authorities cited by Roxburgh J were the writings of Cheshire[192] and Morris[193], on an issue "which might almost be said to set the professors by the ears"[194] – and Morris was declared the winner.

What also became evident in the latter part of the twentieth century was that a far broader range of conflict of laws scholarship, whether treatises, monographs or law review articles, came to be written and then to be cited and to be relied on by the courts. One facet of the change throughout the century, and one of particular importance in the commercial context, might be described as "the rise of the monograph". Before the Second World War, it would be hard to identify many non text books in the English conflict of laws field. However, the last thirty years have seen a great deal of scholarly endeavour devoted to the conflict of laws with the publication in the United Kingdom of well over fifty new works on the subject, many of them specialised monographs. It is clear that the most recent decades have seen the development of a greater scholarly and practical interest in the conflict of laws than probably ever before.

## 5. A broader approach

The second half of the twentieth century saw the adoption of a less insular approach in England to conflict of laws issues in that minds became opened to civil law, and indeed to other common law, influences, at a particularly significant time. The move towards a greater internationalisation of approaches to conflict of laws issues, whether through the regional approach of the EU, or the wider scope of The Hague Conference on Private International Law, required all involved in this field of law, judges, practitioners, academics and students, to become more familiar and more at ease with different ways of examining familiar issues. Perhaps this was to be seen at its sharpest in the context of the EEC dimension, first added to English private international law in the 1970s. Those who negotiated United Kingdom accession to the Brussels Convention on Jurisdiction and the

---

189  Eg *Schneider v Eisovitch* [1960] 2 QB 430, [1960] 1 All ER 169 – a tort claim stemming from a traffic accident in France, where no reference is made to French law or to any rules of private international law.

190  (6th edn, 1949).

191  [1956] Ch 593.

192  *Private International Law* (4th edn, 1952) pp 491–493.

193  Dicey, *Conflict of Laws* (6th edn, 1949) pp 541–542, 795.

194  [1956] Ch 593 at 600, [1956] 2 All ER 817 at 820. For a further example of a "battle of the books", see *The Hollandia* [1982] QB 872, [1982] 1 All ER 1076, affd [1983] 1 AC 565, [1982] 3 All ER 1141, where the contestants were Morris and Mann, with the former declared the winner.

Enforcement of Judgments in Civil and Commercial Matters or the creation of the Rome Convention on the Law Applicable to Contractual Obligations had to be fully aware of the implications of proposal and counter-proposal not only for the law within the United Kingdom but also within the then member states of the EEC. The greater awareness of a comparative approach to the issues under review was invaluable.

This need has not stopped. The fact that an increasing range of conflict of laws rules are now uniform throughout the EU, and subject to the jurisdiction of the European Court of Justice, has meant that, increasingly, decisions not only of the European Court of Justice but also of national courts in the member states are relied on both in academic writings and in judicial decisions[195]. To a degree, the same is happening in relation to those Conventions of The Hague Conference on Private International Law which have achieved widespread international acceptance, the most striking being the Convention on Civil Aspects of International Child Abduction (1980)[196], where a wide range of decisions from both common law and civil law jurisdictions has been relied on in England.

These developments have provided a further dimension to the role of the jurist in the conflict of laws field. The growing desire in the last half century to address the need for change through agencies other than the courts has meant that a much wider range of (usually) lawyers became involved in the process, and this has been particularly true of the conflict of laws. So, judges, academics and scholar practitioners have served on the Private International Law Committee, the Law Commission and its varied working parties addressing conflict of laws matters, as United Kingdom representatives in negotiations within the EEC on a very wide range of conventions, directives and regulations, as members of United Kingdom teams at the Hague Conference on Private International Law or on behalf of other bodies there, at UNIDROIT and UNCITRAL, at the Council of Europe and, perhaps less visibly, as members of advisory committees providing advice to government on how those varied negotiations might best be conducted from a United Kingdom standpoint. More recently, this broad input into the development of the subject has been recognised by the formal establishment, now within the Ministry of Justice, of the Standing Advisory Committee on Private International Law.

For much of the twentieth century, the conflict of laws was developed by judicial decision and academic debate. In the twenty-first century, judges and academics are joined with practitioners and public servants in the subject's further development, often on the international stage, and primarily through the medium of legislation.

---

195 See Hartley "The European Union and the Systematic Dismantling of the Common Law of Conflict of Laws" (2005) 54 ICLQ 813.
196 See Child Abduction and Custody Act 1985, Part I.

# THE LAWS OF ENGLAND AND WALES

## TIMOTHY H JONES[1]

It is well understood that England and Wales is one of three jurisdictions within the United Kingdom, alongside Northern Ireland and Scotland[2]. This jurisdictional division provides the three legislative areas to which Acts of Parliament can extend, either expressly or by implication. Parliament may legislate either for the United Kingdom as a whole or for its constituent parts[3]. Thus it can legislate for England and Wales, or for England or Wales alone, although in either of the latter instances the statute would be said to extend to England and Wales.

The purpose of this paper is to discuss the impact upon these basic understandings of the devolution of legislative powers to the National Assembly for Wales (the Assembly or NAW), under the Government of Wales Act 2006 (GOWA or 2006 Act). This is a development that has been accommodated so far within "what remains the formal jurisdictional umbrella of 'England and Wales'"[4]. The establishment of the NAW in 1999, first under the Government of Wales Act 1998 and now under the 2006 Act, has led to a growth in separate law applicable in Wales, distinct from that in England. In parallel to this growing body of Welsh legislation, there has been an increase in the amount of England-only primary legislation[5]. The Marine Bill proposed by the United Kingdom government provides a clear example. It has been made clear the legislation is within a devolved field and that the proposed draft legislation will only apply to England[6]:

> "We will work closely with the National Assembly for Wales, the Scottish Executive, and the Northern Ireland Executive to consider what approaches may be suitable in each of their countries. Where they have responsibility for the management of their territorial waters it will be for the devolved administrations to determine the need to bring forward any new legislation."

## THE LEGISLATION OF WALES

It has been suggested on a previous occasion that the traditional focus upon the all-encompassing legal system of England and Wales has led many to miss how different Wales has always been[7]. It is not just a result of devolution. Wales is a territory legally separate from England. At one time a reference to England in any Act of Parliament included a

---

1 Professor of Public Law, Swansea University
2 To the extent that there remain elements of the civil law in Scotland, the United Kingdom might also be said to possess a bijural legal system. See, generally, A Breton and M Trebilcock, *Bijuralism: An Economic Approach* (2006).
3 See R Hazell, "Westminster as a 'Three-In-One' Legislature" in R Hazell and R Rawlings (eds) *Devolution, Law Making and the Constitution* (2005) pp 226–251.
4 CMG Himsworth, "Devolution and its Jurisdictional Asymmetries" (2007) 70 Mod LR 31 at p 35.
5 See, for example, the Regional Assemblies Act 2003 (although this Act avoids any explicit recognition of its England only status).
6 http://www.defra.gov.uk/environment/water/marine/uk/policy/marine-bill/key.htm.
7 TH Jones and JM Williams, "Wales as a Jurisdiction" [2004] PL 78. R Rawlings, "Hastening Slowly: The Next Phase of Welsh Devolution" [2005] PL 824 at p 825, refers aptly to "the overarching unity" of the legal system of England and Wales as "a uniquely powerful geo-political concept".

reference to Wales[8], but this rather demeaning provision was removed by the Welsh Language Act 1967[9], which established (in its preamble) the legislative principle "that Wales should be distinguished from England in the interpretation of statutes". Wales was not, of course, invisible to the observer of the legal landscape prior to 1967. Parliament continued on occasion to pass legislation taking effect only in Wales, although most Westminster legislation was intended to have effect in both England and Wales. As a consequence, most of the legislation in effect in Wales is the same as that in England. (And the common law is that of England and Wales.) The origins of this assimilation are in Henry VIII's Laws in Wales Act of 1536, which provided that England and Wales were united and that Englishmen and Welshmen were to be subject to the same laws. The proclaimed intention of Henry VIII's "Act for Laws and Justice to be administered in Wales in like form as it is in this realm" was to incorporate Wales into England. Justice was to be administered according to the law of England and the Welsh language was abolished in all courts[10]. Despite this legislative fiat, Wales retained a distinct identity. There remained significant cultural, linguistic and religious differences between Wales and England. There continued to be Acts of Parliament taking effect in Wales, but not in England.

The legislative history of Wales has three main periods. The first is from 1536 until 1868. During this phase there was a large amount of legislation taking effect only in Wales. Most is concerned with the better securing of the hold of English law upon Wales[11]. There is also occasional legislation intended to make allowance for the different conditions prevailing in Wales, including the historically significant Welsh Bible and Prayer Book Act of 1563, which required their translation into Welsh.

The second period runs from 1868 (the year of the first general election after the Reform Act 1867) to 1998. The Reform Act extended the franchise and gave to Wales greater representation in the Westminster Parliament. This heralded the modern era, with a growing recognition of Wales as a "nation". There were increasing demands that Welsh needs and interests should be recognised in legislative policy. Of particular note is the Sunday Closing (Wales) Act 1881, which provided for a different policy for the closing of public houses. Unlike most of the earlier legislation only taking effect in Wales, it was not a measure of assimilation. The preamble to this Act proclaims the people of Wales to be desirous of its provisions. More constitutionally significant is the Welsh Church Act 1914, which provided for disestablishment of the Anglican Church in Wales. Following the establishment of the Office of Secretary of State for Wales in 1964, more "all Wales" legislation began to emerge. This includes the Welsh Language Acts of 1967 and 1993. The significance of this intermittent, separate legislation for Wales is that despite its incorporation within the jurisdiction of England and Wales, Wales has continued to have a distinct national persona. This was recognised in Westminster. The devolutionary idea of a separate public and legislative policy for Wales is something that has long been accommodated within the legal system of England and Wales.

The passage of the Government of Wales Act 1998 (now replaced by the 2006 Act) marks the beginning of the third period of Welsh legislative history. Devolution has led to a growing legislative divergence between Wales and England. It is true that the National Assembly does not yet possess primary legislative powers, but much of that which can be achieved by primary legislation can also be done by other legislative techniques. It is a question of the breadth of the powers conferred upon the Assembly. Like the Scottish

---

8   This legislative policy was not introduced until 1746, by the Wales and Berwick-on-Tweed Act 1746; see now Interpretation Act 1978 Sch 2 para 5(a).
9   Welsh Language Act 1967 s 4 (see now Interpretation Act 1978 and Welsh Language Act 1993).
10  This latter restriction was removed by the Welsh Courts Act 1942.
11  See I Bowen, ed, *The Statutes of Wales* (1908).

Parliament, the NAW is a devolved legislature[12]. It is empowered to make law applicable within Wales. What is significant for the legal system of England and Wales is the existence of a body of identifiably Welsh law. Devolution has created an opportunity for policies developed within Wales to be given legislative effect. This can either be by means of legislative activity on the part of the Assembly itself, or primary legislation passed by Parliament at the behest of the Assembly. An integral part of this policy process has been the creation of law that has application only within the territory of Wales. The quantity of such separate law has increased exponentially as a result of devolution. It will continue to do so, as the Assembly further develops its own distinctive approach to a range of issues of public policy.

## THE WHITE PAPER, GOVERNMENT OF WALES ACT 2006 AND BEYOND

The Government of Wales Act 2006 (which came into full effect following the Assembly election in May 2007) furthers the devolution of government in Wales, in particular by separating the executive (Welsh Assembly government) and legislative (NAW) arms of government and by conferring greater legislative power. There is no doubt that Welsh devolution is legislatively complex, as a consequence of the mode of devolution adopted. The Act purports to specify in some detail the powers to be transferred to the NAW. This means that there is a significant difference in the way that the Assembly's competence is delineated compared to the arrangements for the Scottish Parliament. In the Scotland Act 1998 the principal legislative powers of the Scottish Parliament are not listed. There is instead a list of subjects on which the Parliament cannot make law ("reserved matters"). The reverse applies in the 2006 Act, which lists 20 fields in which the NAW will be able to legislate (once all its provisions come into effect), although it does also specify some retained powers.

The Secretary of State for Wales gave two practical reasons for taking a different approach to that found in the Scotland Act 1998: (1) that the list of reserved matters in respect of Wales would be very long; and (2) that a list of devolved fields is easier to create with accuracy since it derives from the existing executive functions carried out in Wales. However, it appears that the overriding reason was a constitutional one: "If the Assembly had the same general power to legislate as the Scottish Parliament then the consequences for the unity of the England and Wales legal jurisdiction would be considerable."[13]

The White Paper that preceded the Act, *Better Governance for Wales*[14], included proposals for new legislation to: (1) effect a formal separation between the executive and the legislative branches of the Assembly; and (2) enhance the legislative powers of the Assembly. In particular, the White Paper proposed increasing the Assembly's legislative powers in three stages[15].

*(1) Stage one: framework powers*

The first stage is that of conferring wider powers on the Assembly to make subordinate legislation. The White Paper confirmed the government's intention immediately in drafting primary legislation relating to Wales "to delegate to the Assembly maximum discretion in making its own provisions using secondary legislative powers"[16]. The White Paper noted that this proposal would not require legislative amendment. The first examples of

---

12  R Brazier, "The Constitution of the United Kingdom" (1999) 58 CLJ 96 at p 111.
13  House of Commons Welsh Affairs Committee, *Government White Paper: Better Governance for Wales*, First Report of Session 2005–06, HC 551, EV 62.
14  Cm 6582 (for academic discussion, see Rawlings, note 3, above).
15  White paper, notes 13 above, paras 1.19 to 1.26 and 3.9 to 3.29.
16  *Ibid* para 1.24.

"framework" provisions of this kind were legislated in the NHS Redress Act 2006 and the Education and Inspections Act 2006. These two Acts confer wide legislative discretion in the form of framework powers. The NHS Redress Act 2006 provides for the establishment of a scheme to provide for the out-of-court settlement of claims in tort arising out of services provided as part of the health service in Wales. Section 17 of the Act gives a regulation-making power to the NAW. This broad framework power enables the Assembly, through regulations, to make any provision that could be made by an Act of Parliament (subject to certain limitations). The Education and Inspections Act 2006 has a rather complicated territorial application. Because of the use of framework powers for Wales, there are a significant number of England-only provisions, as well as provisions applying to Wales only and to England and Wales. Part 10 of the Act contains a framework power which enables the NAW to make by regulations any provision that could be made by an Act of Parliament about any of the matters set out in s 178 of the Act (subject to certain limitations set out in s 179). Section 178 permits the NAW to make regulations for a wide range of matters which are relevant to education and training in Wales. The scope of the powers is broad enough to allow the Assembly to determine arrangements that are most relevant to its policies and plans for education and training in Wales[17].

Although presented in the White Paper as the first stage of a process, it remains possible for Parliament to confer further framework powers on the NAW, and indeed it seems likely that further such powers will be granted. The First Minister has made clear that a pragmatic approach will be taken to the enhancement of the Assembly's legislative powers[18]:

> "Moreover, and most importantly, the Assembly will continue to be the beneficiary of further framework powers, in future Westminster legislation. ... I know that, in some circles, framework clauses were regarded as a temporary step, to be used only until the 2007 Assembly comes into being. That is not my view – or, I know, that of the Secretary of State. We will continue to explore all the possibilities which arise from Westminster Bills to enhance the Assembly's legislative clout."

*(2) Stage two: enhanced legislative competence and Assembly Measures*

The second stage is the establishment of an Order in Council mechanism through which Parliament can confer enhanced legislative powers on the Assembly in relation to specified subject matter within devolved fields (which are listed in Sch 5 to the 2006 Act)[19]. This mechanism enables the Assembly to pass its own legislation within the scope of the powers delegated by Parliament (as defined by the Order in Council). The main function of these Orders in Council (known as Legislative Competence Orders or LCOs) is to provide a means by which "matters" may be added to Sch 5. Where the Assembly wishes to legislate

---

17  By means of an Order in Council under s 162 of and para 31(2) and (4) of Sch 11 to GOWA 2006, the framework powers granted by s 17 of the NHS Redress Act 2006 and s 178 and 179 of the Education and Inspection Act 2006 have been converted into legislative powers of the Assembly (see the National Assembly for Wales (Legislative Competence) (Conversion of Framework Powers) Order 2007, SI 2007/910). These framework powers have become new "matters" listed in Sch 5 to GOWA 2006. If this step had not been taken, the powers would automatically have become executive powers of the Welsh Ministers under Sch 11 of GOWA 2006, rather than law making powers of the Assembly itself.

18  Rt Hon Rhodri Morgan, AM, *New powers, New Purposes: Policies and Priorities for the Assembly's Third Term*, National Centre for Public Policy's Annual Public Lecture at Swansea University, Monday 19 March 2007.

19  See GOWA, Pt 3 (ss 93–102).

in respect of a matter contained in Sch 5, the instruments by which it may do so are a new category of subordinate instrument known as Assembly Measures. The Assembly will no longer exercise functions of making the traditional forms of subordinate legislation (orders, regulations and rules). The power to do so will transfer to the Welsh Ministers and their delegates. The extension of the Assembly's legislative competence over time, by amending Sch 5 by Order in Council so as to add new "matters", is the mechanism for conferring enhanced legislative competence on the Assembly which was identified in the White Paper[20]. It will enable the legislative competence of the Assembly to be enhanced incrementally. The first draft LCOs were introduced to the NAW in June 2007. One relates to Education and Training (Additional Learning Needs). It inserts one new matter in the education field of Sch 5. The second concerns environmental protection and waste management, and inserts two new matters in the environment field of Sch 5.

One way in which the power to make Measures may come to be used is to consolidate Welsh legislation. A potential model has been provided by Westminster in the form of the National Health Service (Wales) Act 2006[21]. This is an illustration of the kind of consolidation that could be effected by a Measure made by the Assembly under an enabling Order in Council. Areas of public law in Wales could be consolidated. The First Minister has stated[22]:

> "There are parts of the Welsh statute book which are crying out for consolidation and codification. The law in relation to education and social services, for example, has grown up, piece-meal over more than 50 years of the welfare state. One Act follows another, amending, repealing, augmenting the law which has gone before. It is a brave head teacher or health visitor or social worker who, faced with the real-life complexities of individual lives, has to make immediate decisions which have to be rooted in legal powers and authority. I think we can do better than this in Wales. We can put our new abilities to work in drawing up a statute book which is more comprehensible to workers and users and which, as a result leads to better decision-making and more effective use of services in the future."

In this way, the statute law in important areas of government activity in Wales and England could come to look quite different in the near future. This is the more true when one considers that the Welsh consolidating measure will be bilingual in form. (It is worth noting that the National Health Service (Wales) Act 2006 was the result of initial work by the Law Commission, which raises the issue of whether an equivalent to the Law Commission might not be needed in Wales, to work on consolidation proposals.)

It should not be thought, however, that LCOs provide the only means by which legislative competence may be granted by Parliament. The option remains open of doing this by an Act of Parliament. For example, the Further Education and Training Bill 2006–2007, cl 27, gives to the Assembly a power to make Measures under new matters in a Field listed in Sch 5 to the 2006 Act. As noted in respect of stage one ("framework powers"), the various methods of granting Measure-making powers are complimentary rather than exclusive. There are two main sources of powers to make Measures: powers in Acts and powers in Orders in Council. It remains to be seen which of the two methods will be used more than the other. The choice of method is a political and practical matter. One important difference is that while the NAW as a legislature has a major role to play in

---

20  White Paper, note 13 above, para 3.16.
21  Equivalent provision for England is contained in the NHS Redress Act 2006. Both Acts extend to England and Wales.
22  Morgan, note 18, above.

LCOs, this is diminished in respect of Westminster legislation. In respect of the latter, it is the Welsh Assembly government that must negotiate with the United Kingdom government.

### (3) Assembly Acts

The third stage is that, following a referendum, the Assembly will be authorised to make law on all the matters within its devolved fields of competence without further recourse to Parliament. A referendum can only be triggered with the approval of both Houses of Parliament and of two-thirds of all Assembly members. Part 4 and Schs 6 and 7 of the 2006 Act make provision for the Assembly to acquire "primary" legislative competence, and specify the subjects on which the Assembly will be able to legislate. Provision is also made for these subjects to be adjusted and updated. Part 4 confers on the NAW the power to make "Acts" which can do anything (with a few narrow exceptions[23]) within devolved fields that an Act of the United Kingdom Parliament can do. If its provisions do come into force, they will not, however, override the continuing rights of Parliament to make legislation for Wales[24]. As a result, something would be needed akin to the "Sewel Convention," under which Parliament does not normally legislate for Scotland in devolved matters without the consent of the Scottish Parliament[25].

### CONCLUSION

This paper has explained how the law in Wales is diverging from that of England. The jurisdictional framework of England and Wales contains three types of statutory provision: those common to both England and Wales; those exclusive in effect to England; and those exclusive in effect to Wales. All must be accommodated within the common legal system of England and Wales, since all three kinds of provision are said to extend to England and Wales. The obvious question is for how long the current jurisdictional structure will be sustainable, as the depth of legislative divergence increases. At the very least, some adaptation may be necessary to the legal system of England and Wales to deal with the fact that Welsh public bodies are increasingly going to be operating under (bilingual) legislation that is quite distinct to that governing their English equivalents. Among the possibilities could be: (1) judges authorised to hear Welsh cases; (2) a separate division of the High Court; or (3) separation of Welsh judicial process from English at levels below the House of Lords/Supreme Court[26].

One source of tension within the current arrangements is that the boundaries of the jurisdiction (England and Wales) are not aligned to the boundaries of (devolved) government in Wales[27]. It has been seen that this shared jurisdiction has impacted definitively upon the way in which legislative powers are devolved under the 2006 Act. The particular problem raised by Welsh devolution, of course, is that the Act confers legislative powers in respect of one half of the jurisdiction of England and Wales. Those powers are limited to the territory of Wales, but at the same time are subject to the authority of the courts of England and Wales. One solution might have been to realign the jurisdictional

---

23  These relate to matters such as the functions of ministers of the Crown, modification of certain legislation (including the European Communities Act 1972, the Human Rights Act 1998, the Data Protection Act 1998, and the 2006 Act itself); see Sch 7.

24  See *ibid* s 107(5).

25  See B Winetrobe, "A Partnership of Parliaments? Scottish Law Making under the Sewel Convention at Westminster and Holyrood", in Hazell and Rawlings, note 3, above.

26  Lord Justice Thomas, *Legal Wales. Some Reflections on our Future Tasks*, speech at The St David's Hotel, Cardiff Bay, 19 January 2007.

27  Himsworth, note 4 above, p 33.

boundary to match the governmental boundaries and to reconstitute England and Wales as two separate jurisdictions. That policy has not been adopted and the 2006 Act does not overtly disrupt the unity of the legal system. It is often said not to be possible, in terms of territorial extent, to distinguish between England and Wales, since they both form part of a single jurisdiction. The Assembly's legislation therefore extends to England and Wales and the courts of that jurisdiction have the authority to enforce the legislation of the NAW. Professor Himsworth observes[28]:

> "This may appear to involve a small element of sleight of hand. There is no general power to legislate beyond Wales. But there is a power to engage the courts of a jurisdiction which does extend beyond Wales for the purposes of enforcement and this may indeed square the jurisdictional circle."

Courts in Wales do not have the exclusive jurisdiction over legislation that extends to Wales only. If an issue arose in a court in England where it was established that the matter was covered by legislation of the NAW, it would apply the statute without the need to go through the proofing process that usually follows when the law of another jurisdiction (as in the case of Scotland) comes into the matter. This approach is premised on the conventional understanding that the effect and extent of a legislative provision are distinguishable. Some have argued the improbability of the assertion that a statutory provision having effect only in Wales should extend beyond Wales[29]. The House of Lords Select Committee on the Constitution is correct in its assessment[30]:

> "Westminster is able to legislate exclusively for Wales; but whenever it does so, it is at least laying the partial foundations for Welsh law to become a distinct jurisdiction. To the extent that this is in process of occurring, common sense suggests that Westminster must be able to distinguish between legislating for England and for Wales."

---

28 *Ibid* p 43.
29 TH Jones, JH Turnbull and JM Williams, "The Law of Wales or the Law of England and Wales?" (2005) 26 Stat LR 135 at p 138.
30 House of Lords Select Committee on the Constitution, 15 Report of Session 2003–04, *Devolution: Its Effect on the Practice of Legislation at Westminster*, para 17 (citation omitted).

# THE *STAIR MEMORIAL ENCYCLOPAEDIA* AND THE INSTITUTIONAL TRADITION

## NIALL R WHITTY[1]

### 1. INTRODUCTION

In this centenary year of *Halsbury's Laws of England*, the main theme of this paper is to give an account, in its historical, comparative and contemporary context, of the foundation and development of a Scottish sibling of *Halsbury's Laws of England* whose first volume was published 20 years ago, namely *The Laws of Scotland, Stair Memorial Encyclopaedia*.

The year 2007 also happens to mark the tercentenary of the Union of the Parliaments of England and Wales and of Scotland and of the creation of the United Kingdom of Great Britain, which, whatever the future holds, should be regarded as one of the most successful constitutional settlements in world history. In the Acts of Union, art 18 preserved the identity and autonomy of Scots private law which thereby became a minority legal system with an absentee legislature within a unitary state. This state of affairs subsisted until the establishment by the Scotland Act 1998 of the Scottish Parliament in 1999 sitting in Edinburgh and exercising functions devolved from the United Kingdom Parliament.

It has to be borne in mind that Scots law is the only "mixed legal system" in Europe, using "mixed" in the technical sense of comparative law. Of course all the main Western legal systems are "mixed" to some extent, growing from a variety of different historical sources and subject to many different influences. Even English law, the greatest *original* legal system since Roman law, has been much influenced by the European civil law tradition over time[2] and especially in the nineteenth and twentieth centuries when English lawyers replaced the system of forms of action (eg assumpsit, trespass, case, and money had and received) with a system based on juridical headings such as contract, tort and unjust(ified) enrichment (or restitution) largely borrowed from the continental civilian tradition[3]. So common law and civil law systems are emanations of a single Western legal tradition. Nevertheless they have their own distinctive features and are correctly regarded as two distinct "families" of legal systems. The term "mixed legal system" is usually reserved for a third "family" of legal systems (such as those of Scotland and South Africa) which have been influenced strongly by both the civil law and the common law traditions, generally in that order.

In these mixed systems, "civilian jurisprudence has, to a larger or lesser extent, survived within a common law environment"[4] and Scots law was for long an isolated minority mixed system in a sea of common law systems within the British Empire or

1 Visiting Professor at the Law School in The University of Edinburgh; General Editor of *The Laws of Scotland, Stair Memorial Encyclopaedia* Reissue. The author wishes especially to thank Ms Eve Moran, Managing and Text Editor of the *Encyclopaedia*, for her guidance and help in preparing this paper; to acknowledge the vital contribution of herself and Ms Rosie Finlayson, text editor, to the Reissue; and to thank and to pay tribute to all his colleagues in Lexis NexisUK/Butterworths past and present, and particularly Ms Joan Lyle, former Managing and Text Editor.
2 Eg R H Helmholz "Continental law and Common law: Historical Strangers or Companions?" 1990 Duke LJ 1207; J Gordley "The Common Law in the Twentieth Century: Some Unfinished Business" (2000) 88 California L Rev 1815.
3 J Gordley *Foundations of Private Law, Property, Tort, Contract, Unjust Enrichment* (4th edn, 2006).

Commonwealth. With the move towards European integration or harmonisation of laws, the roles are reversed. Now English law and Irish law are isolated minority systems within a sea of civil law systems and sometimes have to adapt to conform to continental European standards.

This paper has three aims. First, as above mentioned, it seeks to give a factual description of the foundation, aims and development of the *Stair Memorial Enyclopaedia*. Second, it describes the Institutional and alphabetical traditions of arranging legal literature in Scotland, acknowledging the value of the Institutional tradition and arguing that (despite the claims of critics) the Institutional tradition need not be prejudiced, and can even be strengthened, by an alphabetically arranged legal encyclopaedia. Third, the paper shows how the *Stair Memorial Encyclopaedia* strengthens writing on Scots law, a small system in a globalised world whose literature struggles to cover the whole field. By its mission to be comprehensive (which no other Scottish legal publication has) together with the great goodwill of the Scottish legal profession, the *Stair Memorial Encyclopaedia* mobilises untapped writing talent as well as experienced authors in the service of Scots law and thereby fills many gaps and black holes in legal literature which would otherwise remain unfilled.

For reasons of space, the paper concentrates on private law though the *Stair Memorial Encyclopaedia* includes some very distinguished writing in the titles on criminal law[5] and public law[6] as well as private law.

## 2. THE HISTORICAL BACKGROUND PRIOR TO THE 1980s

### 2.1. *The strength of the Institutional tradition in Scotland*

#### 2.1.1. Preliminary

Although the role of the civilian tradition in Scots law can be more or less controversial depending on the context, very few Scots lawyers seem to question the value and importance of the civilian Institutional tradition. At least in civil law and mixed legal systems, it seems to be generally agreed that "the Roman institutional system covering persons, property, obligations, succession and actions, provides a useful working model of a private law system"[7]. In those systems, the subjects contained within the institutional sytem of private law, and within its modern manifestation the codes of civil law, are regarded as forming "a related body of law that constitutes the fundamental content of the legal sytem"[8]. "It is studied first, and subsequent study builds on it. It forms the matrix of thought of the lawyer in the civil law tradition". In England the system has a different role. Writing as a teacher in Cambridge University, Professor Peter Stein added[9]:

> "Apart from its intrinsic interest as the model for modern civil law codes, it serves to counteract the fragmentary character of the English common law. Our habit of presenting contracts, torts, land law, family law, and so on, in discrete boxes means that only rarely do our students catch any glimpse of the way those boxes fit together into a coherent system."

---

4   R Zimmermann "Roman law in a mixed legal system – The South African experience" in R Evans-Jones (ed) *The Civil Law Tradition in Scotland* (1995) p 41 at p 43.

5   See eg Reissue titles on Criminal Law and Criminal Procedure.

6   See eg Reissue titles on Administrative Law, Constitutional Law and Local Government.

7   P G Stein "Fundamental legal institutions" (1982) 2 Legal Studies 1 at p 3.

8   J H Merryman *The Civil Law Tradition* (1st edn) p 7 quoted in A Watson *Legal Transplants* (1974) Ch 6 on "Roman Systematics in Scotland".

9   P G Stein "Fundamental legal institutions" (1982) 2 Legal Studies 1.

This theme was taken up later by Peter Birks in an assault on *Encyclopaedias* to which I revert below.

### 2.1.2. The Romanist watershed: from forms of action to abstract headings of substantive law

The story must begin with Roman law. In the period of the praetorian formulary system, Roman substantive law developed around different individual forms of action[10]. The formulary system consisted of "an enumerative list of actions matched to the particular substantive right asserted"[11]. Although the systematic Institutional template was devised by Gaius in the second century AD (whom Birks called the Darwin of the law) and copied with modifications in Justinian's *Institutes* in AD 533, the Romans did not reorganise their law under juridical headings of substantive law. The role of Justinian's *Institutes* was merely to give students a coherent overview of the whole law which otherwise was set out haphazardly and unscientifically in the other parts of Justinian's *Corpus Iuris Civilis*, namely the *Digest*, the *Codex* and the *Novels*. So for example the 432 titles subsumed within the 50 books of Justinian's *Digest* (the most important source) were arranged unsystematically broadly on the pattern of the praetor's Perpetual Edict (which contained an authoritative list of the actions which the praetor would allow). The process of reorganising the Roman law texts under substantive law headings only began in the Middle Ages and took many centuries[12]. It followed that in the European *ius commune*, the law of actions and procedure had to be separated from the substantive law, a process begun by Huguenot humanist jurists in the sixteenth century such as Hugues Doneau (Donellus) and François Douaren (Duarenus)[13] and continued by the northern natural lawyers such as Hugo Grotius[14]. The last two jurists were expressly commended by James Dalrymple, Viscount Stair, a natural lawyer and the father of Scots law, in dealing with the classification and arrangement of private law in his great *Institutions of the Law of Scotland*[15]. Duarenus "argued that law should be expounded in the same way as other sciences, by proceeding from what is universal and familiar to what is particular. To this end he commended the briefer and more systematic approach of the *Institutes* as "superior to any other"[16]. Peter Stein highlighted the key role of Donellus (1527–1591) in developing the modern European institutional systems of private law[17]. It was Donellus who for the first time made a clear distinction between substantive law, which deals with our rights, and

---

10 As Stair *Institutions*, 4,3, 43, pointed out, "even after the taking away of the strict terms of the *formulae*, all their actions had known names": eg *actio venditi et empti; condictio indebiti; actio de in rem verso; rei vindicatio; hereditatis petitio*.

11 A Blomeyer "Types of relief available (judicial remedies)", in XVI *International Encyclopaedia of Comparative Law* (1982) Chs 4, 14.

12 G Dolezalek "The moral theologians' doctrine of restitution and its juridification in the sixteenth and seventeenth centuries" 1992 *Acta Juridica* 104 at p 106.

13 F Duarenus *Epistula de ratione docendi discendique iuris conscripta* (Venetiis, 1564).

14 H Grotius *De Iure Belli ac Pacis* (1625) Prolegomena.

15 Stair *Institutions*, 1.1.17.

16 P Stein *Roman Law in European History* (1999) p 80.

17 See eg P Stein "Roman Law, Common Law and Civil Law" (1992) 66 Tulane L Rev 1591; P Stein "Donellus and the origins of the modern Civil Law", in J A Ankum et al (eds), *Mélanges Felix Wubbe* (1993) p 442; P Stein "The quest for a systematic Civil Law" (1995) vol 90 *Proceedings of the British Academy* 147 at pp 156, 157; P Stein *Roman Law in European History* (1999) pp 80–82. Stein's view is accepted by R Feenstra "The development of European private law: a Romanist watershed?", in Carey Miller and Zimmermann *The Civilian Tradition and Scots Law* (1997) p 103 at p 113.

civil procedure which deals with the enforcement of our rights. At the same time in his *Commentaries* Donellus produced a wholesale rearrangement of the civil law in 28 books[18].

In the domain of civil procedure, since the praetorian forms of action were obsolete even in Justinian's time, they were not resurrected after the European reception of Roman law and their place was taken by a general and unitary form of action developed within romano-canonical procedure from the general *cognitio extraordinaria* of later Roman law. In Scottish secular civil procedure this development occurred when the mediaeval, Scoto-Norman, formulary system of brieves ceased to grow after an Act of 1491[19] and was largely superseded by the widespread use from the sixteenth century till the present day of the unitary and general signeted summons which was readily adaptable to an infinite variety of different claims. The originating writs in petition and summary application processes were also general and adaptable. So in the early nineteenth century, modern Scots law emerged from the Institutional period as a typical civil law system on the European pattern at least in this respect, that (unlike both Roman law and, until the abolition of the forms of action in 1854, English law) it made a sharp distinction between substantive law and procedure.

### 2.1.3. The Institutional scheme enters Scots private law

In the domain of substantive private law, Scotland was one of several civil law European legal systems which developed a new taxonomic structure in the seventeenth and eighteenth centuries through works organised under headings of substantive law, based with modifications on the classic pattern of Justinian's *Institutes*, and now known to legal historians as the institutes of national law[20]. The five major Scottish institutional works on private law from the first edition of Stair's *Institutions* in 1681[21] through Bankton[22], Erskine[23] and Hume[24] to the fourth and last personal edition of Bell's *Principles* in 1839[25] belong in this European tradition[26].

### 2.1.4. The Institutional scheme enters Scottish constitutional law (1998)

In establishing a separate Scottish Parliament with devolved functions, the Scotland Act 1998 s 126(4) provides:

---

18 *Commentariorum de jure civili libri viginti octo* (Frankfurt 1596) (16 books on substantive law and 12 books on civil procedure).

19 APS 1491 II, 224 (c 5); H McKechnie *Judicial Process Upon Brieves 1219–1532* (1956) p 28; J W Cairns "Historical Introduction", in Reid and Zimmermann *A History of Private Law in Scotland* (2000) vol 1, pp 61–62.

20 K Luig "The Institutes of National Law in the Seventeenth and Eighteenth Centuries" (1972) Juridical Review 193. See also eg P Stein "The Quest for a Systematic Civil Law" (1995) vol 90 *Proceedings of the British Academy* 147; P Stein *Roman Law in European History* (1999) Ch 4.

21 Viscount Stair *Institutions of the Law of Scotland Deduced from its Originals and Collated with the Civil, Canon, and Feudal Laws and with the Customs of Neighbouring Nations* (1st edn, 1681); (2nd and last personal edn 1693); (6th edn, 1981).

22 Lord Bankton *An Institute of the Law of Scotland in Civil Rights: with Observations upon the Agreement or Diversity between them and the Laws of England* (three volumes; 1751–1753) reprinted by the Stair Society vols 41–43 (1993–1995). For some reason W Forbes *Institutes of the Law of Scotland* (two volumes; 1722–1730) was not influential.

23 J Erskine *Institute of the Law of Scotland* (1st edn, 1773); (8th edn, 1871).

24 G Campbell, H Paton (ed) *Baron David Hume's Lectures 1786–1822* (Stair Society, vols 5, 13, 15, 17, 18, 19).

25 G J Bell *Principles of the Law of Scotland* (4th edn, 1839); (10th edn, 1899).

26 In English law for much of this period a system of forms of action matched to substantive rights was the cement of the English common law (but not equity) till the fusion of law and equity in 1873 when that system was discarded in England (as it had been slightly earlier in the United States) and replaced by a unitary, general form of originating writ.

"References in this Act to Scots private law are to the following areas of the civil law of Scotland –

(a) the general principles of private law (including private international law),

(b) the law of persons (including natural persons, legal persons and unincorporated bodies),

(c) the law of obligations (including obligations arising from contract, unilateral promise, delict, unjustified enrichment and negotiorum gestio)[27],

(d) the law of property (including heritable and moveable property, trusts and succession), and

(e) the law of actions (including jurisdiction, remedies, evidence, procedure, diligence, recognition and enforcement of court orders, limitation of actions and arbitration)

and include references to judicial review of administrative action."

The influence of the Institutional template is plain.

### 2.1.5. The survival of the short systematic overview of Scots private law

One reason for the survival of the Institutional template is the fact that, as Alan Watson observed, "The concept of a single comprehensive book on the whole law, fundamental for students and practitioners alike, still flourishes in Scotland in the 20th century"[28]. Since the late seventeenth century, Scottish students of law have been able to rely on relatively short (single- or double-volume) systematic overviews of Scots private law beginning with Mackenzie's *Institutions*[29] through Erskine's *Principles*[30], and Bell's *Principles* to the pre-eminent modern text of *Gloag and Henderson*[31] which has outlived its two main competitors[32]. It was even taken as a model in England for the new two-volume systematic, Institutional-style overview of English private law[33]. Criminal law was excised from *Gloag and Henderson* in the the tenth edition of 1995.

As mentioned above, Scots private law is a "mixed" legal system, that is one mixing civilian and English common law elements. In this mixture, civilian systematics are seen to

---

27  The original precursor of para (c) carried an impure classification, viz "voluntary and conventional obligations, obligations of restitution, and obligations of reparation". See Scotland Bill, cl 111(3)(b) (HC, Bill 104; print of 17 December 1997).

28  A Watson "The Rise of Modern Scots Law" in (1977) 3 *Formazione storica del diritto moderno in Europa* 1167 at p 1171.

29  Sir George Mackenzie *Institutions of the Laws of Scotland* (1st edn, 1684); (9th edn, 1758); see also A Bayne *Notes for the use of students of Municipal Law in the University of Edinburgh, being a supplement to Mackenzie's Institutions* (1731; 1749).

30  J Erskine *Principles of the Law of Scotland* (1st edn, 1754) (4th and last personal edn, 1769); (21st and last edn by Professor Sir John Rankine, 1911).

31  W M Gloag and R C Henderson *Introduction to the Law of Scotland* (1st edn, 1927); renamed *Gloag and Henderson, The Law of Scotland* (10th edn, 1995); (11th edn, 2001). It is understood that the 12th edition due to be published soon will have 51 chapters grouped in Institutional style under the following five headings namely (1) Legal System; (2) Obligations (contract; unjustified enrichment and negotiorum gestio; delict); (3) Property (including succession and trusts); (4) Persons (capacity; family law; partnerships; companies; associations); and (5) Debt Enforcement and Insolvency (diligence and bankruptcy).

32  T B Smith *A Short Commentary on the Law of Scotland* (1962); D M Walker's *Principles of the Law of Scotland* (4th edn, 1988) (three volumes): vol I (Introductory, International Private Law, Persons); vol II (Obligations); vol III (Property).

33  P Birks (ed) *English Private Law* (1st edn, 2000) (two volumes); A Burrows (ed) *English Private Law* (2nd edn, 2007) (two volumes).

be of paramount importance[34]. Indeed Dr Eric Clive, the foremost law reformer of his generation, has advocated the introduction of a code of Scots private law[35] which would enshrine the systematic Institutional template in statute, but at present his is as yet a rather lonely voice in Scotland.

On the other hand, Lord Rodger has recently emphasised the value of combining civilian systematics with the English case law methodology observing[36]:

> "For me one of the chief advantages of having a mixed system of law is that it has been expounded and analysed in the past by reference to some version of the template to be found in Roman law: persons, property, obligations, succession, actions, etc. It is true, of course, that the Institutional writers adopted various different models, not all of them particularly helpful. But, at least, we have these systematic expositions of the law and we had them long before there was anything similar in English law. We have the advantages of the case law approach of English law coupled with a degree of civilian rigour. That is a benefit of our civilian background that I, for one, would very much wish to foster. Certain aspects of the template can and should be improved ... But, if the system is refined in the light of modern thinking, it offers significant advantages.
>
> Unfortunately, often too little is done by teachers of the law to explain to students how the various parts of the law relate to one another: how contract and delict interconnect, how unjust enrichment should not be allowed to trump contract, how property and succession go hand in hand. The result is that practitioners and judges often overlook these connections and relationships too."

Later he continued[37]:

> "So the more systematic mode of expounding the law is an advantage which mixed systems derive from the civil law and which we certainly should not throw away. Rather we should cherish it, not as dreary introductory matter to be fed to bored students but as having a real practical role in deciding cases. Happily, there are signs that in English law the advantages of that kind of systematic approach are more and more appreciated by text-book writers. [Citing Peter Birks, Preface to *English Private Law* vol 1 at xxix–xxx.]"

## 2.2. The alphabetical tradition of the digest, dictionary and encyclopaedia in Scotland

The dominance and justified prestige of the Institutional tradition in Scots law, however, should not blind us to the practical utility of legal dictionaries and other works arranged alphabetically. The second last title of Justinian's Digest – D.50,16 *De verborum significatione* ("about the meaning of words") was, as its name and context suggest, a general legal dictionary. The title attracted commentaries in the European *ius commune*[38] especially by humanist jurists, including Donellus[39] and Cuiacius (Jacques Cujas)[40] as well as lesser

---

34  See eg Watson *Legal Transplants* (1974) Ch 6 on "Roman Systematics in Scotland".

35  See E M Clive "A Scottish Civil Code" in H L MacQueen (ed) *Scots Law into the 21st Century, Essays in Honour of W A Wilson* (1996) 82; E Clive "Current Codification Projects in Scotland" (2000) 4 Edin LR 341; E Clive "The Scottish civil code project" in H L MacQueen, A Vaquer and S E Espiau (eds) *Regional Private Laws & Codification in Europe* (2003) Ch 3.

36  Lord Rodger of Earlsferry "'Say Naught the Struggle Not Availeth': The Costs and Benefits of Mixed Legal Systems" (2003) 78 Tulane L Rev 419 at p 425.

37  *Ibid*, at p 426.

figures[41]. In 1597 the Scottish humanist lawyer Sir John Skene published a legal dictionary of Scots law terms arranged alphabetically also entitled *De verborum significatione*[42] which went through several editions[43].

Since then while legal dictionaries, style books[44] and case-digests for lawyers[45] and compendia of Scots law written for non-lawyers[46] have been arranged alphabetically, few other works on substantive law written for lawyers have been so arranged[47] and none of the latter have enjoyed a particularly high reputation at least until the coming of the *Encyclopaedias*. Between 1808 and 1826, as if to show the continuity of the dictionary tradition, Skene's *De Verborum Significatione* was appended to three editions of a new work by a Writer to the Signet, Robert Bell's *Dictionary of the Law of Scotland*[48]. This work was replaced in 1838 by another dictionary, written by an advocate William Bell. Though this was claimed by its author to be an entirely new work, it is usually seen as a fourth edition of Robert Bell's *Dictionary*. So regarded, the seventh and last edition was published in 1890 jointly by the publishing firms of Bell and Bradfute in Edinburgh and Butterworths in London[49]. This very useful work was not mere a dictionary but also a digest of branches of Scots law and half-way to being an encyclopaedia.

This was then replaced in 1896 by a much larger work in 14 volumes, *Green's Encyclopaedia of the Laws of Scotland*[50] two editions of which (and not merely one edition as commonly supposed) were published before the First World War[51]. The pattern was set by the first volume. The arrangement was alphabetical. Besides references there were over 250 articles written by 61 contributors[52]. The majority were advocates. The Encyclopaedia was the brainchild of the dynamic publisher Charles Edward Green of W Green & Son described by T B Smith as a "perfervid encyclopaedist ... [who] also published encyclopaedias in accounting, medicine and agriculture, as well as an encyclopaedia of English law and the English Law Reports"[53]. It is interesting to note that the first volume of Charles Green's Scottish *Encyclopaedia* in 1896, which is said to have been the

---

38  Often combined with a commentary on the last title D.50,17 (*De diversis regulis iuris antiqui*) a source of many maxims; see A A Roberts *A South African Legal Biography* (1942) p 256 sv "*Regulis juris, De* and *De verborum significatione*". The title *De Verborum Significatione* is also found in the *Corpus Iuris Canonici*.

39  *Commentarii ad tit De Verborum obligationibus* (Frankfurt, 1577).

40  *De verborum significatione* (Frankfurt, 1595).

41  Eg Barnabé Brisson *De verborum quae ad jus civilem pertinent significatione* (1st edn, 1587); (2nd edn by J G Heineccius, 1743). Brisson was President of the Parlement of Paris.

42  *De verborum significatione, The exposition of the Termes and Difficill Wordes, conteined in the Foure Buikes of Regiam Majestatem, and uthers, in the Actes of Parliament, Infeftments, and used in Practique of this Realme, with Diverse rules, and commoun places, or principalles of the Lawes: Collected and expound by M John Skene, Clerke of our Souveraine Lordis Register, Councell and Rolles* (1597). It consists of 146 pages in the 1846 reprint.

43  Editions or reprints in 1597, 1599, 1641 (two editions), 1644, 1681 (two editions), often bound together with Skene's editions of *The Lawes and Actes of Parliament*; reprinted as an appendix to Robert Bell's *Dictionary* (see note 48 below) and in 2007 by the Law Book Exchange Ltd. On Skene's legal-humanist background, see J W Cairns, T D Fergus and H L MacQueen "Legal Humanism in Renaissance Scotland" (1990) 11 Jo of Legal History 40 especially at pp 44–48.

44  Eg *The Scots Style Book* (eight volumes) (1902–1911); *Encyclopaedia of Scottish Legal Styles* (ten volumes) (1935–1940).

45  Eg W M Morison, *Decisions of the Court of Session* [1540–1808] *in the form of a Dictionary* 21 volumes (1801–1805) ("Morison's Dictionary"); *Scots Digest of Appeals in the House of Lords from 1707, and of Cases in the Supreme Courts of Sotland* (1800–1944; in several series) ("the Scots Digest"); Faculty of Advocates, *Digest of all reported Decisions in the Court of Session* (1868–1970; in several series) ("the Faculty Digest"); *Sheriff Court Digest* (1885–1944; five volumes).

prototype for his jointly ventured English Encyclopaedia in 1897[54], anticipated by a decade the commencement of publication of Halsbury's *Encyclopaedia* in 1907. Then between 1926 and 1935 the *Encyclopaedia of the Laws of Scotland* (commonly known as "the Dunedin Encyclopaedia")[55] was published by W Green & Son in 16 large volumes arranged alphabetically followed later by a two-volume Supplement in 1949 and 1951. At times the alphabet was used not only to order the material but also to order the authors. As T B Smith recalled, "the sole reason why the present Sheriff J Aikman Smith may become an authority on 'Emergency Powers' and the present writer on 'Fire Services' and 'Forestry' is because the appropriate sections in the Supplement to the Encyclopaedia were allocated in alphabetical order – and J A S took precedence over T B S"[56].

In 1926 in the Preface to vol 1, Lord Dunedin observed:

> "there has been since the date of last edition a very important fact, the appearance of *Halsbury's Laws of England*. It is explained in the preface to that book [sic] that its object is to provide by unofficial and unauthoritative work arranged in a series of treatises what might be done by codification. Being unofficial, it may be added, it escapes the congenital curse of codification, perpetual argument on what is the exact meaning of the words that now become binding in law. The book itself was so efficiently written that it might occur to some to question whether the field was any longer open. The answer is the simple one that the present work is intended to be the presentment of Scottish law as such; and that though in many branches they overlap, yet the English and Scottish systems are not identical."

Nowadays it seems remarkable that Lord Dunedin should have felt the need to explain why *Halsbury* did not render a separate Scottish *Encyclopaedia* otiose. Lord Dunedin went

---

46  Eg H Barclay, *Digest of the Law of Scotland for Justices of the Peace* (five editions between 1852 and 1894); R A McCreadie and I D Willock (eds), *Reader's Digest: You and Your Rights; an A to Z of the Law in Scotland* (1984).

47  For an exception, see Lord Dirleton *Doubts and Questions in the Law* (1698) arranged by topic alphabetically.

48  R Bell *Dictionary of the Law of Scotland* (1st edn, 1807–1808, two volumes); (2nd edn, 1815); (3d edn, 1826).

49  W Bell *Bell's Dictionary and Digest of the Laws of Scotland, with short explanations of the most ordinary English Law Terms* by William Bell, Advocate, (4th edn, 1838); (5th edn, 1861); by George Watson, Advocate (6th edn, 1882); (7th edn, 1890).

50  See Book Notice of vol 1 in 1896 SLT (News) 277: *Green's Encyclopaedia of the Laws of Scotland* edited by John Chisholm, MA LLB, Advocate, and of the Middle Temple, barrister-at-Law; vol 1 "Abandoning" to "Banker's Lien"; Royal 8vo; Wm Green & Sons; 15s net.

51  *Green's Encyclopaedia of the Laws of Scotland* (1st edn: 14 volumes 1896–1904); (2nd edn: 12 volumes 1909–1914).

52  Drawn from the Court of Session and shrieval bench, the Universities of Edinburgh and Glasgow, St Mungo's College Glasgow, the Faculty of Advocates, two solicitors, and court and other public officials including the Auditor of the Court of Session, the Accountant of Court, the Clerk of Justiciary, the Clerk of Teinds, the Solicitor of Inland Revenue, and the procurator fiscal of Elgin.

53  T B Smith "Viridis; One Hundred Years of Law Publishing" 1975 SLT (News) 1 at p 1. Charles Green took over the business from his father in 1885 aged 20 and died in 1920 aged 54.

54  *Encyclopaedia of the Laws of England* vol 1 with a General Introduction by Sir F Pollock Bart, "Abandonment" to "Bankruptcy" edited by A Wood-Renton, Barrister-at-Law, London. See book notice (1897) 4 SLT 220.

55  Lord Dunedin was the consultative editor. A Court of Session judge Lord Wark was the general editor.

56  T B Smith "Viridis; One Hundred Years of Law Publishing" 1975 SLT (News) 1 at p 1.

on to remark that though the 1926 *Encyclopaedia* "admittedly only seeks to set forth the law of Scotland, that law will be illustrated by copious citation of English authority". Whether he thought this was a good or bad thing is not clear. It is interesting that the founders of the *Stair Memorial Encyclopaedia* viewed the influx of English cases with a degree of disfavour.

One important trend is that in successive encyclopaedias culminating in the *Stair Memorial Encyclopaedia*, the articles on private law subjects have become fewer but longer and more thorough, sometimes resembling monographs of several hundred pages.

### 2.3. *A comparison with English law*

English law and its literature developed in a quite different way. First, the mediaeval English forms of action provided the cement of the substantive law till their abolition in 1854. Until the nineteenth century the main form of legal literature was the Abridgments of cases[57] which were normally arranged by topic alphabetically. Apart from *Blackstone's Commentaries*[58] there was nothing comparable to the Scottish Institutional writings. The dominance of the forms of action in English law meant that monograph literature on substantive law also developed late. In England, a substantial treatise on contract did not appear till 1794[59], on tort till 1860[60], and on unjust(ified) enrichment (or restitution) till as late as 1966[61]. Monograph literature has flowered in modern times and is now very strong indeed but there was and is no strong tradition of a relatively short overview-book to counterbalance the fragmentary organisation of the categories of English law. It was in a self-conscious attempt to remedy that perceived deficiency that the two-volume *English Private Law*, edited and inspired by the late Peter Birks, was published in 2000[62]. In summary, compared with Scots law, in England the systematic Institutional tradition is relatively weak (at least until recently) and the tradition of alphabetically arranged practitioners' books for working lawyers is relatively strong.

In English law opposition to the "top-down" imposition of the Institutional system on private law is much stronger than in Scotland. So for instance Stephen Waddams remarks[63]:

> "Since the nineteenth century it has been common to make distinctions in respect of Anglo-American law between public and private law, and within private law between property and obligations , and within obligations among contracts, torts and unjust enrichment. Legal issues and rules have been supposed to belong to one of these subcategories, and the rules applied to determine the result in particular cases. But this scheme has failed to account for many actual judicial decisions , a failure that led, in the twentieth century, to scepticism of formal explanations of law, to alternative explanations, and in turn to counter-reaction."

---

57  Eg C Viner *General Abridgment of Law and Equity* (1741–1758).

58  W Blackstone *Commentaries on the Law of England* (four volumes) (1st edn, 1765–1769). A Watson "The Impact of Justinian's Institutes on Academic Treatises: Blackstone's *Commentaries*" in *Roman Law and Comparative Law* (1991) Ch 17 traces the significant influence on *Blackstone's* structure of Justinian's *Institutes* and contemporary European studies thereon as well as his English forerunners especially Hale's *The Analysis of the Law* (1713).

59  J J Powell *Essay on the Law of Contracts and Agreements* (1794). See A W B Simpson "Innovation in Nineteenth Century Contract Law" (1975) 91 LQR 247.

60  C Addison *The Law of Wrongs and their Remedies* (1st edn, 1860).

61  R Goff and G Jones *The Law of Restitution* (1st edn, 1966).

62  See note 33 above.

63  Cf S Waddams *Dimensions of Private Law, Categories and Concepts in Anglo-American Legal Reasoning* (2003) Preface p vi.

Proceeding from the particular to the general, Waddams argues that many important legal issues have not been resolved by their allocation to a particular sub-category but by simultaneous application of several or all of the concepts mentioned in the quoted passage. Not all of his arguments apply in Scotland where for example, there is no distinction between Law and Equity and where by virtue of the Institutional *mentalité*, the distinction between property (real rights) and obligations (personal rights) is much sharper and clearer than in English law[64].

The history of English law, though once reputed to be entirely judge-made, is in fact symbiotically entwined with the development of English legal literature, the one influencing the other in many ways. This relationship has been well described by Tony Weir who pointed out that[65]:

> "the categories and compartments thought of and used by English lawyers tend to be of a much lower level of abstraction than those used as divisions of the system by civilian lawyers; furthermore, English lawyers indiscriminately use compartments of varying levels of abstraction. Thus most English legal categories are not provinces but departments, but one sometimes finds provinces listed among the departments."

This mixing up of taxonomic tiers is emblematic of the types of defect in legal taxonomy against which the late Professor Peter Birks ceaselessly campaigned. Though the life of the great *Halsbury* encyclopaedia is short relative to the long history of English law, yet in its life-time *Halsbury's Laws* is taken to have become (in Weir's phrase) "the basic source book of current English law as a whole". *Halsbury* must therefore bear its share of the blame for the defects of English law as well as claiming credit for the maintenance of its manifold strengths. Tony Weir found evidence of the mixing-up of taxonomic tiers in *Halsbury*:

> "A glance at *Halsbury's Encyclopedia of the Laws of England*, the basic source-book of current English law as a whole, demonstrates this[66]. For the editor and users of this indispensable work, the law of England falls into no fewer than 175 parts. Juxtaposed to such high abstract categories as Constitutional Law and Tort one here finds not only inferior and subsumable abstract categories such as Parliament and Crown Proceedings, Trespass and Nuisance, but also concrete categories like Explosives and Ferries. Electricity comes before Equity. As an intellectual disposition of the law it is quite deplorable. Yet almost identical headings are used by the two other major sourcebooks of English law, namely *Halsbury's Statutes*[67] and the *English and Empire Digest*[68]."

---

64  See eg K G C Reid "Unjustified Enrichment and Property Law" 1994 JR 167; K G C Reid "Obligations and property: exploring the border" 1997 *Acta Juridica* 225; G L Gretton "Constructive Trusts" (1997) 1 Edin LR 281 (Pt I); 408 (Pt II); G L Gretton "Scotland" in W Swadling (ed) *The Quistclose Trust; Critical Essays* (2004) p 169.

65  T Weir, Section III, "The Common Law System" in R David et al *Structure and the Divisions of the Law* (no date) at pp 78, 79 in R David (ed), Ch 2 of *International Encyclopedia of Comparative Law* vol 2 (*The Legal Systems of the World, Their Comparison and Unification*).

66  (43 volumes) (3rd edn by *Viscount Simonds*, London 1952–1962).

67  (26 volumes) with annual continuations (2nd edn London 1948–1951). A third edition is appearing.

68  (54 volumes) continually replaced. (See note 65 above. NB footnote numbering of T Weir's original changed).

It has to be conceded that the *Stair Memorial Encyclopaedia* with its 137 titles in 25 volumes[69] has not been able to avoid some of these defects. "General Legal Concepts" is squeezed between "Game" and "Guardianship"; the inferior and apparently subsumable categories of "Crown" and "Nuisance" are separate from higher-tier categories such as "Constitutional Law" and "Obligations" respectively. And so forth.

## 3. THE FIRST ISSUE OF THE *STAIR MEMORIAL ENCYCLOPAEDIA* 1987 TO 1996

### 3.1. *Origins*

#### 3.1.1. The crisis in Scottish legal literature in the mid-twentieth century

It is generally thought that before the First World War Scottish legal literature was at least adequate to the needs of the legal profession and that it declined thereafter till by the late 1950s it reached its nadir[70]. The Dunedin *Encyclopaedia* was beginning to age and in any event, with some honourable exceptions, had not been notable for fundamental research. In 1954 a committee was set up under the chairmanship of Lord Guthrie (a Court of Session judge) to consider the feasibility of a new edition of the Dunedin *Encyclopaedia* but nothing came of it[71]. Although the Stair Society, founded in 1934, kept up a steady flow of annual publications on the history of Scots law (including the publication of Baron Hume's Lectures which were to be of fundamental importance, for example in the renaissance of property law), very few books on the modern law of Scotland were being written; very few cases were being reported or even decided; there were only 3,000 practising lawyers (about one-third of the present number); and a tiny market for buying books. So practitioners turned increasingly to English law and English cases to fill the gap, augmenting a long established trend. Legal literature was universally acknowledged to be grossly inadequate and the viability of the system itself was under threat. The Carnegie Trust for the Universities of Scotland, in a report submitted on 27 February 1961, observed[72]:

> "The Law of Scotland has been said to be the country's most distinctive national heritage, containing elements which, when clearly discerned, are the admiration of other systems; yet by the end of this century this legal system will have decayed beyond hope of revival unless strenuous and far-reaching measures are taken now to restate Scots Law, by applying and adapting traditional principles to the needs of the twentieth century."

The threat of swamping by English law books and cases was keenly felt by those who cared about the survival of Scots law *as a system*. Roman law and comparative law studies might have provided a counterweight and were supported not merely by neo-civilian academics like T B Smith but also by some of the most senior and highly respected judges such as Lord Normand and Lord Cooper. In a famous passage Lord Normand wrote[73]:

> "We have in the tradition of Roman law a vast and unexhausted treasure house of principle, highly rationalized and deeply humanistic which we must not neglect if we are to maintain the identity of Scots Law in the necessary changes and modifications of the future. For unless our law continues to grow

---

69  See Annexe 1 below.
70  See eg D M Walker "Legal Scholarship in Scotland" 1960 SLT (News) 10.
71  T B Smith "Planning an Encyclopaedia of the Laws of Scotland" (1982) 27 JLSS 285 at p 286.
72  Quoted in T B Smith "The Scottish Universities Law Institute, The First Year" 1961 SLT (News) 97 at p 97.
73  The Rt Hon Lord Normand of Aberdour, Lord of Appeal, Foreword to J S Muirhead *An Outline of Roman Law* (2nd edn, 1947).

in accordance with that tradition it will run a grave risk of becoming a debased imitation of the Law of England, stumbling and halting before every new problem where we have no English precedent to guide us. From that fate our law students and future practitioners can save us by a right appreciation of the Roman tradition in the Law of Scotland and by accepting it as an active principle of natural growth and development."

This passage reflects a neo-civilian legal nationalism sometimes called the Cooper-Smith ideology[74]. In a series of learned articles too numerous to cite in full, Lord Rodger of Earlsferry, a Scottish Lord of Appeal and renowned academic Roman lawyer, has trenchantly criticised this ideology, at least as expressed in the writings of Lord Cooper and T B Smith, as unrealistic, undesirable and even corrosive[75]. In fact the ideology has met with a variety of complex responses, positive as well as negative, the merits of which continue to be debated to this day[76].

### 3.1.2. Back from the brink: a turning point

It was only in 1960 that a turning point was reached though it was not apparent at the time. In that year full-time study for the LLB degree was introduced and the Scottish Universities Law Institute (SULI for short)[77] was established with Professor T B Smith as its first Director. SULI began commisioning and publishing a series of monographs on Scots law. In 1965 the Scottish Law Commission was founded whose main function was legislative law reform but which incidentally conducted fundamental research into Scots law supplementing the work of legal scholars. Thus began a renaissance of Scottish legal literature. In describing the progess up to 1995 Kenneth Reid[78], doubting his own tongue-in-cheek claim that we live in "a golden age" of legal literature, remarked "perhaps this is only a silver age, and one with occasional lapses towards bronze. But at least it is not the stone age"[79]. The founding of the *Stair Memorial Encyclopaedia* in the 1980s can be seen as an important stage in this renaissance.

---

74  I D Willock "The Scottish legal heritage revisited" in J P Grant (ed), *Independence and Devolution* (1976) 1; H L MacQueen "Two Toms and an Ideology for Scots Law: T B Smith and Lord Cooper of Culross" in E Reid and D L Carey Miller (eds) *A Mixed Legal System in Transition, T B Smith and the Progress of Scots Law* (2005) p 44.

75  See eg A Rodger "Roman law comes to Partick" in R Evans-Jones (ed) *The Civil Law Tradition in Scotland* (1995) 198; A Rodger "Thinking about Scots Law" (1996) 1 Edin LR 1; A Rodger "The Use of Civil Law in Scottish Courts" in D L Carey Miller and R Zimmermann (eds) *The Civilian Tradition and Scots Law, Aberdeen Quincentenary Essays* (1997) p 225; Lord Rodger of Earlsferry "'Say Naught the Struggle Not Availeth': The Costs and Benefits of Mixed Legal Systems" (2003) 78 Tulane L Rev 419.

76  Among the burgeoning literature see eg the contributions in R Evans-Jones (ed) *The Civil Law Tradition in Scotland* (1995); D L Carey Miller and R Zimmermann (eds) *The Civilian Tradition and Scots Law, Aberdeen Quincentenary Essays* (1997); articles by K G C Reid, J du Plessis, G L Gretton, H L MacQueen and Lord Rodger of Earlsferry in (2003–2004) 78 Tulane L Rev; and E Reid and D L Carey Miller (eds) *A Mixed Legal System in Transition, T B Smith and the Progress of Scots Law* (2005).

77  See T B Smith "The Scottish Universities Law Institute, The First Year" 1961 SLT (News) 97.

78  K G C Reid "The Third Branch of the Profession; The Rise of the Academic Lawyer in Scotland" in H L MacQueen (ed) *Scots Law into the 21st Century; Essays in Honour of W A Wilson* (1996) p 39 especially at pp 43–46 entitled "Growth of a Legal Literature".

79  K G C Reid "The Third Branch of the Profession; The Rise of the Academic Lawyer in Scotland" in H L MacQueen (ed) *Scots Law into the 21st Century; Essays in Honour of W A Wilson* (1996) p 39 at pp 39, 40.

## 3.2. The establishment of the Stair Memorial Encyclopaedia

In 1980 the vice-president of the Scottish Law Agents Society suggested to the Law Society of Scotland (the Society) at its Annual General Meeting that the Society should accept responsibility for the publication of a new encyclopaedia of Scots law. In 1981 the tercentenary of the publication of the first edition of Stair's *Institutions* – the first of the series of Scottish Institutional writings – was celebrated[80]. In the same year the Society resolved to sponsor a new legal encyclopaedia in Stair's memory. A financial commitment was agreed to by the profession at the Society's AGM in 1982 and a capitation levy of £5 per annum was raised on members of the Society to meet the running costs of the General Editors. The Society authorised the General Editors to select authors each of whom entered into a contract with the Society which owns the copyright of the whole Encyclopaedia. The Society established a small Publications Committee to oversee publication with Professor Ross Harper as Convener who held the post from 1983 till the last of the 25 volumes (no 15) was published in 1996. T B Smith was the first General Editor and three senior academic lawyers acted as deputy general editors[81]. Smith's role was crucial. As Lord Hope observed "The *Stair Memorial Encyclopaedia* could not have been achieved without him"[82]. On Smith's death in 1988, he was succeeded as general editor by one of the deputy general editors, Professor Robert Black.

## 3.3. A description of the Stair Memorial Encyclopaedia

### 3.3.1. The basic policies: and comparison with Halsbury's Laws of England

The primary object of the *Stair Memorial Encyclopaedia* is to provide a complete record of Scots law[83] and thereby "to meet the needs of the profession and of scholars"[84]. The notional user referred to by the *Encyclopaedia* committee in the 1980s was the solicitor in general practice in Wick who did not have easy access to a law library. The Internet has improved accessibility of sources to an extent previously unimaginable but the aim remains the same with the difference that the *Encyclopaedia* in updated form is now accessible online.

It has been pointed out that "[t]he resources at the command of *Halsbury's Laws of England* enable it literally to comprehend all the laws applicable at given dates in England. But it is surely not being faint-hearted but only realistic to say that a work of that size and comprehensiveness must be far beyond the finance and manpower available in Scotland. Moreover it would be wasteful to duplicate the many works of diverse sizes which are already available from English sources on these topics"[85]. Against that background there was no choice but to make a virtue out of necessity by planning a different type of *Encyclopaedia*. Well before the first volume was published, T B Smith declared that the "*The Laws of Scotland*, as planned from the outset, firmly rejects the concept of appearing as a Scottish edition of *Halsbury*. The conceptual organisation and basic policies regarding comment and analysis differ substantially from those adopted by Messrs Butterworths in publishing *Halsbury's Laws of England*"[86]. The latter for example has traditionally had no

80  See eg D M Walker (ed) *Stair Tercentenary Studies* (1981) (Stair Society vol 33).
81  Professor Robert Black and Mr Hamish McN Henderson, both University of Edinburgh, and Professor Joseph M Thomson, University of Strathclyde.
82  Lord Hope in Preface to D L Carey Miller and D W Meyers (eds) *Comparative and Historical Essays in Scots Law* (1992) p xiii.
83  Professor Robert Black, second general editor, writing in The Herald, 10.1.97.
84  T B Smith "Indexing an Encyclopaedia" 1985 SLT (News) 193 at p 194.
85  [1981] SCOLAG 358 (Editorial comment).
86  T B Smith "The Name of the Encyclopaedia" 1985 SLT (News) 197.

separate autonomous title for "public law", "private law", "property", "obligations", "quasi-contract" or "unjust(ified) enrichment"[87]. Smith determined that in the *Stair Memorial Encyclopaedia* there should indeed be broad separate titles on "property" and "obligations" (the latter subsuming an extended treatment of obligations to redress unjustified enrichment) though not for "public law" or "private law".

The editorial policies vary depending on the topic. These policies include comprehensive systematic treatment of the core subjects of Scots law (eg child and family law; property law, succession and trusts; the core principles of the law of obligations namely unilateral promise; contract; unjustified enrichment; *negotiorum gestio*; and delict) supplemented by separate titles on specific topics (eg the specific contracts) arranged alphabetically[88]. For titles on large cross-border statutory regimes (eg pensions and social security) the aim would be to direct the reader's attention at least generally to all relevant legislation and at the same time to identify any Scottish specialities. The style would be more discursive and less uniform and impersonal than in the *Halsbury* house-style. An attempt would be made not to select the authors of existing standard works because second opinions on doubtful issues are valuable checks on possible unconscious bias or error. Where the law is doubtful the author is entitled to state his own personal opinion on the issues but would be expected to give a fair wind to conflicting opinions. A remarkable example of a "highly personal" approach[89] was T B Smith's contribution to the original title on Constitutional Law, especially his robustly polemical treatment of two of his favourite hobby-horses, namely "Fundamental Law"[90] and "Pretensions of English Law as 'Imperial Law'"[91]. The result could be a variety of different approaches even within the same title if multi-authored. So for instance one reviewer of "Constitutional Law" said that some sections of the title seemed to take *Halsbury* for their model while others read more like polemical articles or scholarly monographs[92]. Most titles however have not attracted this criticism.

### 3.3.2. The name

The name of the new work – "*The Laws of Scotland, Stair Memorial Encyclopaedia*" – was explained by Sir Thomas Smith in an article in 1985[93] responding to criticisms by a practitioner[94]. The *Stair Memorial Encyclopaedia* was not a new edition of the Dunedin *Encyclopaedia* but an entirely new work. Without the authority of W Green & Son a name could not be selected which might involve confusion with *Green's Encyclopaedia of Scots Law* or the Dunedin *Encyclopaedia*. The words "Stair Memorial" commemorate the tercentenary in 1981 of the publication in 1681 of the first edition of Stair's *Institutions*.

---

87  Cf S Waddams *Dimensions of Private Law, Categories and Concepts in Anglo-American Legal Reasoning* (2003) p 9.

88  Eg there are separate titles on the specific contracts (eg agency and mandate; banking; bill of exchange; carriage; caution; deposit; donation; employment; and insurance): see Annexes 1 and 2 below.

89  The apt description in *Stair Memorial Encyclopaedia* Reissue, "Constitutional Law" (2002) para 47 (Professor Neil Walker).

90  See *Stair Memorial Encyclopaedia*, vol 5 (1987) paras 338–360.

91  See *Stair Memorial Encyclopaedia*, vol 5 (1987) paras 711–719.

92  P Jackson, review (1987) 32 JLSS 409 at p 410.

93  T B Smith "The Name of the Encyclopaedia" 1985 SLT (News) 197.

94  Letter to editor by Mr A D Moffat, 1985 SLT (News) 137. The criticisms were somewhat odd namely that "laws" is unusual in describing a civilian system; that the use of the words "of Scotland" was at odds with tradition; and that the term "encyclopaedia" suggested something American and obsolescent.

### 3.3.3. The plan of arrangement

T B Smith explained the thinking of the general editors underlying the layout of the *Encyclopaedia* in articles in 1982[95] and 1985[96] and in the Introduction to vol 1 published in 1987. He disclosed that ideally the general editors would have preferred "an entirely systematic layout of the whole legal system" on the model set out in the chapter on the "Structure of Scots Law" in D M Walker's *Scottish Legal System*[97]. In making a distinction between public law and private law and the headings for the contents of private law, Walker's structure was strongly influenced by the Institutional tradition. So it is not surprising that Smith, whose *Short Commentary on the Law of Scotland* (1962) was a one-volume overview in that tradition, should have had this preference. The general editors however found the material to be "too complex" for such treatment, citing as examples of complexity the overlap of public and private law (eg in titles such as *Agriculture*) and of civil and criminal sanctions (eg in consumer and factory legislation). The impact of the regulatory state on private law was even then well documented[98] and the way in which public law regulatory enactments are entwined with private law rules was and is plain for all to see[99]. Scots lawyers had debated the taxonomic issues in connection with the devolution Bills of the 1970s. The criticisms levelled by Peter Birks at the *Stair Memorial Encyclopaedia* for abandoning the Institutional pattern in favour of alphabetical arrangement[100] nowhere mention the fact that an Institutional model was the first preference of the General Editors but was found to be impractical. Having reluctantly rejected the Institutional scheme, Smith wrote in 1987 in the Introduction to vol 1 that the General Editors had considered three other options namely[101]:

"(1) Alphabetically arranged short articles on narrowly defined topics – as is the case with *Green's Encyclopaedia* and the Dunedin edition;

(2) Alphabetically arranged longer articles on broad areas of the law;

(3) Allocation of one or more volumes to each major division of the law – the pattern adopted by the *International Encyclopedia of Comparative Law*."[102]

Earlier in 1982 he had described option (2) as "the Halsbury pattern"[103]. Later, however, Smith said that the arrangement of the new *Encyclopaedia* was "substantially influenced" by the 18th century general encyclopaedias and in particular by the

---

95   T B Smith "Planning an Encyclopaedia of the Laws of Scotland" (1982) 27 JLSS 285.
96   T B Smith "The name of the Encyclopaedia" 1985 SLT (News) 197.
97   (5th edn; 1981) pp 194, 195; see now 8th edn, 2001, ch 5.
98   See eg N E Simmonds "The changing face of private law: doctrinal categories and the regulatory state" (1982) 2 Legal Studies 257.
99   See eg J Thomson "When Homer Nodded?" in H L MacQueen (ed) *Scots Law into the 21st Century; Essays in Honour of W A Wilson* (1996) p 19.
100  P Birks "The Foundation of Legal Rationality in Scotland" in R Evans-Jones (ed) *The Civil Law Tradition in Scotland* (1995) p 81; P Birks "More Logic and Less Experience" in D L Carey Miller and R Zimmermann (eds) *The Civilian Tradition in Scotland* (1997) p 167.
101  *Stair Memorial Encyclopaedia*, vol 1 (1987) Introduction by the General Editor, p xx.
102  The *IECL* volume headings are: I National Reports; II The Legal Systems of the World/ their Comparison and Unification; III Private International Law; IV Persons and Family; V Succession; VI Property and Trust; VII Contracts in General; VIII Specific Contracts; IX Commercial Transactions and Institutions; X Restitution – Unjust Enrichment and Negotiorum Gestio; XI Torts; XII Law of Transport; XIII Business and Private Organizations; XIV Copyright and Industrial Property; XV Labour Law; XVI Civil Procedure; XVII State and Economy.
103  T B Smith "Planning an Encyclopaedia of the Laws of Scotland" (1982) 27 JLSS 285 at p 288.

*Encyclopaedia Britannica* published by "a society of gentlemen" and printed in Edinburgh in 1771[104]. It was characteristic of Smith, who believed Scots law to be a fundamental cornerstone of Scotland's historic culture and identity, to find inspiration in one of the great products of the Scottish Enlightenment. Smith observed[105]:

> "According to its title page it was published on a new plan. 'The different sciences and arts were digested into distinct treatises of systems ... The various technical terms are explained as they occur in the order of the alphabet'. The plan consists in keeping important subjects together and on the other hand facilitating reference by numerous separate articles. Systems are discussed in distinct treatises and details are explained in alphabetical order, referring to the relevant larger articles. Substituting 'divisions of the law' for 'systems' and adding a glossary and index, this basically the planned structure for the *Stair Memorial Encyclopaedia* – though 'railway timetable law' which is not readily adaptable to such treatment must also be included."

The contrast was drawn between the core institutions of private law and the rest of the civil law, dismissively characterised as "railway timetable law". This hostile attitude to regulatory law was rightly criticised as "a retreat to a shrinking enclave called 'lawyers' law'" and "a recipe for stagnation"[106]. Regulatory public law is at least as extensive as private law and growing rapidly all the time. Law outside the core institutions and regimes of public and private law has a miscellaneous character and little research has been done to establish whether a rational classification, as distinct from an alphabetical arrangement, of its content would work.

## 4. THE REISSUE OF THE *STAIR MEMORIAL ENCYCLOPAEDIA* 1997 TO 2007 (CONTINUING)

### 4.1. *The Reissue of the titles*

Butterworths, the publisher of the first issue, entered into a new contract with the Law Society of Scotland in 1994 for the publication of the Reissue of the existing titles. Unlike the agreement for the original volumes, the reissue contract provided that Butterworths (Lexis Nexis Butterworths or LNB as it became) and the General Editor are solely responsible for determining which volumes will be reissued and for the appointment of contributors. Like the original *Encyclopaedia*, copyright in the Reissue titles vests in the Law Society of Scotland to which LNB pay royalties. At present, the editorial team working on the Reissue volumes (leaving aside the updating service) is very small consisting of only three people, a managing editor and a text editor both working full time as employees of LNB and a general editor working part time as an independent contractor. The seat of the *Encyclopaedia* is a branch office of LNB which is now in London House, East London Street in central Edinburgh. The Law Society of Scotland Publications Committee has been wound up, and there is no advisory board comparable to that which advised the original general editors. The Society and LNB however maintain a cordial working relationship and liaise closely on matters of common interest as and when required.

The Reissue programme was launched in March 1999 with the publication of five titles (Advertising, Animals, Arbitration, Bankruptcy and Entertainment). At first the plan was

---

104 1985 SLT (News) 197 at p 199; *Stair Memorial Encyclopaedia*, vol 1 (1987) Introduction by the General Editor, p xx.

105 1985 SLT (News) 197 at p 198.

106 I D Willock "The Scottish legal heritage revisited" in J P Grant (ed) *Independence and Devolution* (1976) 1 at pp 9, 10.

to publish the new Reissue series of titles in bound volumes containing several titles as in the case of the reissues of *Halsbury's Laws of England* and *The Laws of South Africa*. It was, however, decided to change from the publication of volumes each containing several titles to the publication of individual titles housed in binders – an idea borrowed from *The Laws of New Zealand*. This offers a more flexible format which avoids the problems associated with volumes, chiefly that of material which had been delivered by a contributor going out of date while waiting for the remaining titles. It also allows more flexibility as to the length of titles and means that each title has its own tables and index.

The aims are to publish the equivalent of two volumes (about 1,300 pages) a year, where possible to focus on areas where there have been important or extensive developments, and to include at least one significant distinctively Scots law title each year. At the time of writing (September 2007) these aims have been largely fulfilled. Progress has been slow but steady. Of 137 original titles, 46 have been reissued. The bulk of the work falls on the contributors of the titles who are paid only a very modest honorarium and whose public spirit and dedication cannot be adequately commended.

### 4.2. *The updating and online services*

The updating service of the *Stair Memorial Encyclopaedia* – called the *Laws of Scotland Service* – was begun in 1988. The *Service* is published three times a year. The first issue of each calendar year is published as a bound volume or *Cumulative Supplement*. The subsequent two issues are cumulative loose-leaf noters-up which update the *Encyclopaedia* volumes, the *Cumulative Supplement* and the Reissue titles. The electronic version of the *Stair Memorial Encyclopaedia* has been accessible online since 2000. It constitutes the only comprehensive narrative treatment of Scots law which is currently available online covering the original volumes, the Reissue titles and the updating material. The online service facilitates thorough searching in a manner which is ordinarily much quicker than consulting books[107]. Furthermore, hypertext links enable the user to move quickly between the *Encyclopaedia* narrative and the relevant cases or legislation. Consolidated indexes of the volumes and reissued titles, tables of statutes and tables of cases are issued annually to subscribers.

## 5. SOME ISSUES FOR CONSIDERATION

### 5.1. *The problem of overlap: avoiding duplication and securing coherence*

In a review of vol 1 of the *Stair Memorial Encyclopaedia*, Lord Clyde observed: "One problem which arises in a work of the magnitude of this encyclopaedia where so many writers have contributed is that of avoiding duplication of material and securing coherence of treatment. How far such duplication is inevitable or acceptable may be a matter of opinion but examples of the problem can be found"[108]. Later he noted "the conscious overlapping of subject matter which is part of the scheme of the whole work but which still may be open to question"[109]. The problem had also afflicted the Dunedin *Encyclopaedia*[110]. It surfaced in some reviews of particular volumes of the *Stair Memorial Encyclopaedia*[111].

---

107  The online version may be consulted at www.lexisnexis.co.uk.
108  J J C (Lord Clyde), book review of vol 1, 1987 SLT (News) 286 at p 287.
109  J J C, book review of vol 6, 1989 SLT (News) 117 at p 119.
110  See eg the different treatments accorded to "the rule in *Rylands v Fletcher*" in the Dunedin *Enyclopaedia*.
111  Eg reviews by Lord Clyde in 1987 SLT (News) 357 at p 360 (vols 5 and 22); 1989 SLT (News) 75 at p 77 (vol 14); 1991 SLT (News) 214 at p 215 (vol 23); and by J T Cameron (Lord Coulsfield) (1989) 34 JLSS 285 at p 286 (vol 25).

Reviewing the last volume to be published, vol 15, which was written by 17 authors, Professor Bill McBryde remarked[112]:

> "The user of the volume cannot be sure that every overlap has been discovered, or that all the relevant views in the *Encyclopaedia* have been found. The index assists only to some extent. The pleader in court who refers to one paragraph on obligations, particularly in the section on delict may be surprised to find his or her opponent cites a different paragraph on the same point. Variety of thought is to be welcomed, but in this case there will be much cursing of editors."

This problem is almost intractable. Some of the criticism may be met by good indexing and there is now an up-to-date consolidated index for the whole of the first issue. It is said that "a [self-] contradictory law book is as unthinkable as a [self-] contradictory law"[113]. But is it so unthinkable? One only has to think of those reported judgments of the House of Lords Judicial Committee in which five Lords of Appeal in Ordinary deploy five different lines of reasoning to see how difficult it can be to attain unanimity. Repetition and discordance are to some extent inevitable. It is of the nature of law, and especially the common (ie judge-made) law, to be uncertain and open to differing interpretations. Moreover, it is sometimes unclear to what primary category of the law a particular topic belongs, especially in an uncodified legal system. Furthermore though the proposition is controversial, a topic and even a category of the law may straddle more than one legal category higher up the taxonomic hierarchy. Nuisance for example is an awkward regime of principles and rules which was given its own title (in vol 14) because – so the general editors and the author (myself) believed – it straddles both the law of delict and the law of property and could not be split between them without losing the very considerable advantages of a unified treatment[114]. The possibility of overlap in a rational system of classification was sometimes denied by the late Peter Birks[115] but is accepted by other common lawyers[116]. In any event, it is not the case that one topic can be considered only once; it may have to be treated from different angles of approach according to the subject matter. Negligence for example crops up in a host of different contexts. Overlap becomes inevitable in titles dealing with what Peter Birks called "contextual categories" such as "Advertising", "Agriculture", "Building Contracts", "Medical Law", "Recreation and Sports". It is however readily conceded that so far as practicable measures should be taken to avoid unintended or unjustified duplication.

### 5.2 The debate on the taxonomy of private law: of short systematic Institutes and long alphabet-based Encyclopaedias

#### 5.2.1. General

In England, since judges rather than academics have long dominated the common law tradition, systematic concerns were neglected until recently one of the most influential

---

112  W W McBryde, review of vol 15, (1997) 1 Edin LR 400 at p 402.

113  1981 SCOLAG Bulletin 358 (Editorial Comment).

114  It is submitted that these characteristics answer the criticisms that nuisance should have been subsumed into the delict part of the title on obligations: see the reviews of vol 15 by Lord Macfadyen, (1997) 42 JLSS 99 at p 99; and by W W McBryde (1997) 1 Edin LR 400 at p 402.

115  See eg P Birks, "Unjust Enrichment and Wrongful Enrichment" (2001) 79 Texas Law Review 1769 at p 1794: "one of the basic principles of rationality, namely that a classified answer to a question must use categories which are perfectly distinct from [one] another."

116  Eg S Waddams *Dimensions of Private Law, Categories and Concepts in Anglo-American Legal Reasoning* (2003).

English legal academics of the late twentieth century, the late Peter Birks[117], conducted a long campaign in books and articles[118] to persuade common lawyers of the importance of rational and systematic classification of English law. Birks pointed out that until recently English lawyers had had at least a basic knowledge of Justinian's *Institutes* which helped them to see the legal woods from the trees but that, because English universities were giving up the teaching of the *Institutes*, English lawyers were in danger of losing their systematic and taxonomic knowledge altogether. The debate which Birks initiated on such taxonomic topics as the structure of the law of unjust(ified) enrichment and the fusion of Law and Equity has indeed triggered greater interest in the classification of English law.

Birks pointed out that the abandonment of the forms of action in 1854 had removed the main source of stability and consistency in English law and that this was made good partly by *stare decisis* and partly by the rise of university law schools which became responsible for the legal literature which gives shape and direction to the cases. Despite this "transformation of the law library", Birks argued that "there has been a serious failure to give structure to the whole" and pointed the finger of blame at *Halsbury* and its alphabetical tradition. He remarked[119]:

> "The alphabetical *Halsbury* dominates the practitioner's research. *Halsbury* represents the old way of doing things; it continues the tradition of the abridgments, much as the form of *Justinian's* Digest, still disorderly, was continuous with the great edictal commentaries. As for our beginners, the truth is that law students are never made to think about the structure of the law as a whole. Taxonomy is neglected."

Elsewhere he wrote[120]:

> "English law has not attended to the need for systematic overview. The law used to be kept stable by the forms of action ... For convenience the actions were bound together by that most basic of all systems of classification alphabetical order. From the old abridgments to the indispensable *Halsbury*[121] the Common law has been, and remains, dependent on the alphabet."

Contrasting the position in Scotland, Birks contended "that the most important item in Scots law's inheritance on its Roman side is its capacity for orderly overview, both of the law as a whole and of the large subdivisions within it – the continents and countries, so to say, which make up their map of the legal world"[122]. He went on to warn Scots lawyers that that inheritance could be lost and pointed the finger of blame at the *Stair Memorial*

---

117  1941–2004; Professor of Civil Law at Edinburgh from 1981 to 1988 and at Oxford from 1989 to 2004.

118  Eg Introduction to *Justinian's Institutes* (Krüger text translated with an Introduction by P Birks and G McLeod) (1987); P Birks "Definition and Division: A Meditation on Institutes 3.13" in *The Classification of Obligations* (1997) p 1; see also texts cited in notes 33, 100 and 115 above. For a full bibliography of Birks's publications, see A Burrows and Lord Rodger of Earlsferry (eds) *Mapping the Law; Essays in Memory of Peter Birks* (2006) pp 641–651.

119  P Birks "More Logic and Less Experience" in D L Carey Miller and R Zimmermann (eds) *The Civilian Tradition in Scotland* (1997) 167 at p 180.

120  P Birks "The Foundation of Legal Rationality in Scotland" in R Evans-Jones (ed) *The Civil Law Tradition in Scotland* (1995) p 81.

121  *Halsbury's Laws of England*, now in the reissue programme of its fourth edition, eds Lord Hailsham of St Marylebone (1973–1997), Lord Mackay of Clashfern (1997 to date) (London 1973 continuing).

122  P Birks "The Foundation of Legal Rationality in Scotland" (note 120 above) at p 81.

*Encyclopaedia*[123] which he noted is arranged alphabetically like *Halsbury s Laws of England*. He forecast that the SME "will make the Scots law seem more and more like the English law". He did recognise that the general editors "have divided the alphabetical task into blocks some of which do reflect the institutional scheme, as for example by devoting one whole volume to the law of obligations". But for him that was not enough. He declared: "The *Stair Encyclopaedia* is set to dominate the research of Scottish practitioners and judges for years to come. Superb as some of its volumes are, it will not be a friend of the characteristic Roman superiority of the Scottish legal mind"[124]. Again "the Scots lawyers should be haunted by the ghost of James Dalrymple, in whose name, of all names, the alphabet now threatens to triumph"[125].

### 5.2.2. Why a systematic structure matters

There is not much doubt why systematic structure matters. So Johnston and Zimmermann affirm: "Clear thought and principled development of the law, as well as eradication of inconsistencies, are much assisted if clarity about the underlying structure of the law can be attained."[126] Long ago Lord Kames remarked[127]:

> "In an institute of law, or of any other science, the analyzing it into its constituent parts, and the arranging every article properly, is of supreme importance. One could not conceive, without experience, how greatly accurate distribution contributes to clear conception ... No work of man is perfect: it is good, however, to be on the mending hand; and in every new attempt, to approach nearer and nearer to perfection. To compile a body of law, the parts intimately connected and every link hanging on a former, requires the utmost effort of human genius."

A good classification helps to ensure that like cases are treated alike; to expose anomalies and inconsistencies; and to find things more easily[128]. Birks also contended that "Law which has no systematic overview [cannot] ... fulfil the duty of the law to restrain arbitrary power, whether political or judicial ... neither the alphabet nor the declining influence of the Institutional scheme can provide any assurance that, in an unusual case, the right authorities will be presented to the court"[129].

### 5.2.3. The response of the *Stair Memorial Encyclopaedia* to systematic concerns

T B Smith was aware of the disadvantages of setting out Scots law in an encyclopaedia arranged alphabetically. In 1985 a practitioner had contended that "the reduction of a corpus to a collection of laws would ... cause Viscount Stair, if he saw his memorial, to assume that Scots law had not survived and that his memorial was a Scottish edition of *Halsbury's Laws of England* which so clearly impressed the editors of the earlier Scots encyclopaedia". In response T B Smith remarked[130]:

---

123  P Birks "More Logic and Less Experience" (note 119 above) at p 174.
124  P Birks "The Foundation of Legal Rationality in Scotland" (note 120 above) at p 98.
125  P Birks "More Logic and Less Experience" (note 119 above) at p 189.
126  D Johnston and R Zimmermann (eds) *Unjustified Enrichment: Key Issues in Comparative Perspective* (2002) Introduction p 25.
127  Lord Kames *Principles of Equity* (3d edn, 1773) Introduction.
128  On the advantages flowing from good classification, see E McKendrick "Taxonomy: does it matter?" in D Johnston and R Zimmermann (eds) *Unjustified Enrichment: Key Issues in Comparative Perspective* (2002) p 627 at pp 628–644.
129  P Birks "The Foundation of Legal Rationality in Scotland" (note 120 above) at p 86.
130  1985 SLT (News) 197 at p 197.

"Had the new work had been restricted to a *corpus iuris scotorum*, Mr Moffat's argument would have cogency. However, whether the fact is welcome or not, a comprehensive work for Scottish practitioners today has to range beyond the confines of an internally related corpus of Scots law such as that with which Stair was concerned. Thanks largely to his writings, that corpus has in large measure survived and *The Laws of Scotland* is so planned that the fragmentation of such chapters of the law as obligations and property is deliberately rejected. The relationship between voluntary and delictual obligations and those arisng from unjustified enrichment will be set forth in a comprehensive context; and property will be examined in its own right and not in the interstices of conveyancing or Sale of Goods Act provisions."

Smith went on to point out that "the work has also to include consideration of categories of law unrelated to the developed corpus of Scots law" such as charities, and the "vast body of modern departmental regulations" which he (quoting Lord Cooper) said "have no better title to be recognised as part of our jurisprudence than the current issue of the railway time-table"[131].

For these reasons the main categories of Scots private law – especially property and obligations which together with the law of persons (including family law) form the main pillars of a civil code in codified legal systems – were each given their own very lengthy title within which they received a systematic and comprehensive treatment. To avoid overload, specific topics were dealt with in their own separate purpose-built titles but in such a way that the structure itself was not fragmented.

It would be invidious to specify which titles were completely successful and which were not but it is agreed on all sides that the important title on property law in vol 18 (1993) was a great success. There is no space to catalogue here the achievements of this volume[132]. For present purposes it is enough to note that the study of Scottish property law had for 150 years been fragmented culminating in separate excellent but unconnected SULI volumes on land law, corporeal moveables and servitudes and none at all on incorporeal property. Confounding the fears of the critics about the fissiparous effects of legal encyclopaedias, the title on property law incorporated all of these topics, thereby unifying the subject to an extent not seen for 170 years ie since *Baron Hume's Lectures* of 1821–1822, and by this means and the excellence of its content lifted the study of property law on to a higher plane[133].

---

131  1985 SLT (News) 197 at p 198.

132  See reviews of volume 18 by D L Carey Miller 1994 SLT (News) 347; (1994) 111 SALJ 454; D J Cusine, (1994) 38 JLSS 429; and Lord Hope of Craighead, Lord President 1996 JR 74.

133  Before vol 18, property law had been the handmaiden of conveyancing; after vol 18 the roles were very properly reversed. It was made plain that, properly understood, Scots property law was and is a closed system with a recognised list of real rights (probably a *numerus clausus*) which were, for the first time ever, comprehensively identified. Further it was reaffirmed that registration in the land registers was itself constitutive of real rights. Moreover the concept of real rights was restored to its rightful place as the cornerstone of Scottish property law. The process of undermining Scottish property law by judicial plantation of beneficial interests apparently under the influence of English Equity, is halted in its tracks if not yet entirely reversed. *Ex facie* this was not achieved in a spirit of nationalist or neo-civilian irredentism but as an antidote to incoherence and as a means of articulating the unspoken premises underlying centuries of indigenous case law.

## 6. CONCLUSION

There is no doubt that the *Stair Memorial Encyclopaedia* has accessed previously untapped legal expertise and writing talent among Scots lawyers who would not otherwise have written on Scots law. Anecdotal evidence suggests that the *Encyclopaedia* is often the first port of call for research in Scots law. Its ambition to be comprehensive is unique in Scotland, and causes it to fill many gaps in the coverage of Scots law which would otherwise never be filled. So for instance Mr James P Connolly, later the author of an admirable text on Scottish construction law, while in practice in the 1980s and 1990s, became familiar with the very extensive English legal literature on this topic[134]. Such literature is very useful but is not always a reliable guide to the Scots law. Mr Connolly was sure that there must also be "an authentic Scottish jurisprudence" in construction law but apart from two old Scottish sources[135] there was little to aid his research. He generously records that in his first year of university lecturing "an excellent piece of scholarship was published in the *Stair Memorial Encyclopaedia* on 'Building Contracts', written by Arnott and Wolffe"[136] which "launched [his] teaching and research on to a different level"[137]. It seems to me that if the *Encyclopaedia* can replicate this experience in similar areas where "an authentic Scottish jurisprudence" lies neglected, whether or not buried under English texts, it will have achieved the main aims set for it by its founders.

---

134  Eg *Emden's Construction Law*; *Hudson's Building and Engineering Contracts*; *Keating on Building Contracts*; and Walker Smith *The Standard Forms of Building Contract*.

135  A I Connell *Law Affecting Building Operations and Architects' and Builders' Contracts* (1903); A M Hamilton "Building and Engineering Contracts" in *Dunedin Encyclopaedia* (1927) vol 2.

136  See *Stair Memorial Encyclopaedia* "Building Contracts" (1994) vol 3 (J M Arnott and W J Wolffe).

137  J P Connolly *Construction Law* (1999) Preface.

# Annexe 1

## List of volumes and original titles in first issue of
## *Stair Memorial Encyclopaedia* (1987–1996)
## [(137 titles in 25 volumes)]

VOLUME 1
Accountants, Accounting and Auditing; Administrative Law*; Admiralty; Advertising*; Agency and Mandate*; Agriculture*;

VOLUME 2
Alcoholic Liquor; Animals*; Arbitration*; Armed Forces*; Associations and Clubs; Aviation*; Banking and Financial Institutions*; Bankruptcy*; Betting, Gaming and Lotteries*;

VOLUME 3
Building Contracts; Building Controls; Building Societies; Burial and Cremation; Carriage*; Cautionary Obligations and Representations as to Credit; Charities; Children and Young Persons*; Churches and Other Religious Bodies;

VOLUME 4
Civil Jurisdiction; Commercial Paper*; Companies; Competition Law*;

VOLUME 5
Compulsory Acquisition and Compensation; Constitutional Law*; Consumer Credit;

VOLUME 6
Consumer Protection*; Contempt of Court; Conveyancing*; Courts and Competency;

VOLUME 7
Criminal Law*; Crown; Customs and Excise;

VOLUME 8
Deposit; Diligence and Enforcement of Judgments; Donation; Education;

VOLUME 9
Employment*; Energy*; Entertainment*; Environment*;

VOLUME 10
European Community Law and Institutions; Evidence*; Fire Services; Firearms and Explosives*;

VOLUME 11
Fisheries; Food, Dairies and Slaughterhouses*; Forestry; Fraud; Game; General Legal Concepts; Guardianship; Harbours; Health Services*; Heraldry; Hotels and Tourism; Housing;

VOLUME 12
Human Rights in Europe*; Immigration and Extradition*; Industrial and Provident Societies; Credit Unions and Friendly Societies; Insurance; Interest; Interpretation of Statutes, Deeds and Other Instruments; Investor Protection;

VOLUME 13
Judicial and Other Remedies; Landlord and Tenant; Lawburrows; Legal Aid; Legal Profession; Libraries, Museums and Galleries; Liferent and Fee; Loan;

## VOLUME 14
Local Government*; Location; Leasing and Hire of Moveables*; Medical and Allied Professions*; Medicines, Poisons and Drugs*; Meetings*; Mental Health; Messengers-at-Arms and Sheriff Officers;
Mines and Quarries; Money and Means of Exchange; Nationality and Citizenship*; Nuisance*;

## VOLUME 15
Obligations; Parliamentary and Other Elections;

## VOLUME 16
Partnership; Passports and Other Travel Formalities; Peerages; Penal Establishments; Personal Bar; Police; Posts and Telecommunications; Precedence; Prescription and Limitation;

## VOLUME 17
Press and Broadcasting; Private International Law; Prize; Procedure (Civil)*; Procedure (Criminal)*;

## VOLUME 18
Property;

## VOLUME 19
Provisional Orders and Private Legislation; Public Corporations; Public Health; Public International Law*; Public Registers and Records*; Railways, Canals and Tramways*; Recreation and Sports; Registration of Births, Deaths and Marriages; Revenue;

## VOLUME 20
Rights in Security; Road Traffic*; Roads; Sale and Exchange (Moveable and Immoveable);

## VOLUME 21
Sea and Continental Shelf*; Shipping and Navigation*; Social Security*;

## VOLUME 22
Social Work; Sources of Law (Formal); Sources of Law (General and Historical); Legal Method and Reform; Time;

## VOLUME 23
Town and Country Planning; Trade Unions and Trade Disputes*; Tribunals and Inquiries;

## VOLUME 24
Trusts, Trustees and Judicial Factors; Udal Law; Valuation for Rating;

## VOLUME 25
Valuations; Veterinary Surgery; Water and Water Rights; Water Supply; Wills and Succession.

* Titles reissued: see Annexe 2

# Annexe 2

## List of Reissue titles as at October 2007

Administrative Law (1999)
Advertising (1999)
Agency and Mandate (2001)
Agriculture (2001)
Animals (incorporating Veterinary Surgery) (1999)
Arbitration (1998)
Armed Forces (2005)
Aviation (2003)
Banking, Money and Commercial Paper (2000)
Bankruptcy (1999)
Betting, Gaming and Lotteries (1999)
Carriage (2002)
Child and Family Law (comprising Children and Young Persons and Family Law) (2004)
Competition Law (2001)
Constitutional Law (2002)
Consumer Protection (2006)
Conveyancing (2005)
Criminal Law (2005)
Employment (2000)
Energy (2000)
Electricity (2003)
Entertainment (1999)
Environment (2007)
Evidence (2006)
Firearms and Explosives (2006)
Food Law (2003) (previously Food, Dairies and Slaughterhouses)
Health Services (2007)
Human Rights (2003)
Immigration (2003) (originally Immigration and Extradition; (Extradition to be reissued separately)
Local Government (incorporating Meetings) (1999)
Leasing and Hire of Moveables (2001)
Medical Law (2006)
Medicines, Poisons and Drugs (2000)
Nationality and Citizenship (2003)
Nuisance (2001)
Procedure (Civil) (2007)
Procedure (Criminal) (2002)
Public International Law (2007)
Public Registers and Records (2006)
Railways, Canals and Tramways (2005)
Road Traffic (2004)
Sea and Continental Shelf (2006)
Shipping and Navigation (2005)
Social Security (2000)
Trade Unions and Trade Disputes (2001).

# A SOLICITOR'S JOURNEY TO THE BENCH

## HIS HONOUR JUDGE ROBERT WINSTANLEY

When I was a child it was common for an aunt or uncle who had not seen me for some time to inquire "What do you want to be when you grow up?". I recollect that at about the age of ten I began to answer that I wanted to be an archaeologist. I am not sure why I did this: I doubt if I really knew what an archaeologist was; perhaps I was trying to be different. This was the late 1950s, still the era of the steam train, and I reckon that a survey of my contemporaries would have shown that a large proportion of them were choosing to be engine drivers. Certainly neither I nor any of my childhood friends were telling our uncles and aunts that we wanted to be a judge when we grew up. A judge would have occupied a near mystical position in our minds, one that seemed lofty and unattainable.

There came a time, however, when to become a judge was my ambition in life. My first public admission of this ambition occurred in the late 1980s, by which time, of course, I was quite grown up.

It came about in this way. I was by this time a solicitor in private practice. I was also a member of the Council of the Law Society. The staff member responsible for producing the society's in-house magazine decided that an interesting article might be produced by conducting a survey of the council members' interests and aspirations and publishing the results. I duly received my copy of the survey form and completed it to reveal my hitherto secret ambition to become a circuit judge.

The reaction to the publication of my revelation was interesting. First of all it was noteworthy that there was a reaction at all. A number of my colleagues on the council and members of staff actually sought me out and questioned me about it.

Then there was the nature of the reaction. Some of my questioners were genuinely surprised that I could harbour this ambition at all. They simply did not know that it was possible for a solicitor to become a circuit judge. They would, I am sure, have heard of Dr Beeching and have known that he had reorganised our railway system in 1963. What they seemed less aware of was that in 1970 Dr Beeching had gone on to reorganise our courts and in the course of doing so had made it possible for solicitors to become circuit judges for the first time.

Others were taken aback that I could publicly admit to such an ambition. They seemed to believe that if you were so unfortunate as to be struck with the ambition to become a judge you should clasp it tightly to your chest. It should certainly not see the light of day.

My impression was that many solicitors did not know that the bench was open to them as a possible career path. I knew the path was there. What I did not, in the late 1980s, know was how to follow that path. I felt that by "coming out" I could do a little to inform other solicitors that the path was there, and at the same time I might discover for myself how to follow it.

How had I come to nurture this ambition?

I had an enjoyable career in the law, passing my first few years in the law in very pleasant surroundings of Lincoln's Inn as an articled clerk and then solicitor with one of the oldest firms in Lincoln's Inn. In my sometimes esoteric practice there I had learnt amongst other things about settled heirlooms and the powers of a tenant for life under the Settled Land Act 1925.

I moved in the mid-1970s to the rather more prosaic surroundings of Islington. There a friend from my university days and I founded a practice which was to be my occupation for the next 20 years. The contrast with Lincoln's Inn could hardly have been greater: many of our clients were legally aided; we practised in areas of the law, such as crime and immigration, which had not featured large at the Inn. I joined the duty solicitor schemes which in those far-off days were just being established in our local magistrates' courts. This was an essential activity for any solicitor who wished to develop a criminal practice.

I had always been keen to practise as an advocate in courts and tribunals. Islington gave me more scope for this activity than Lincoln's Inn had done. My time in Lincoln's Inn had endowed me with one very useful piece of knowledge. From my duties as a writ issuer and filer of affidavits I knew my way around the labyrinthine corridors of the Royal Courts of Justice. I knew where the bear garden was and what to look for when I got there. So when I appeared before masters or the judge in chambers I was confident that I would at least find my way to the right room.

We had done some divorce work in Lincolns' Inn, so I knew how to take a nervous petitioner through her undefended divorce petition in the days when we still had to do that. You knew that judges did not mind you leading your client on her name; after all, you were not giving much away there. On the other hand there were judges who would object to you leading your client on her address. Also it was important not to refer to your client's husband as the respondent. To do so courted the response "Who are you talking about?" from an anxious and stressed female petitioner.

In Islington we acted for a large number of social landlords so I was a regular in my local county courts presenting my clients' claims for possession in the general possession lists. I became well known to the local registrars (I know they became district judges but I have not got to that time yet) and county court judges, which sometimes caused embarrassment. In one court I acted for a particular kind of landlord whose tenants for legal reasons had no security of tenure. When my case was called on in a packed court, and the registrar's opening words to the tenant were "I'm sorry, but as this is one of Mr Winstanley's cases I will have to make an order for possession against you", I at any rate felt embarrassed.

I had a lot of positive help from the bench over my years as an advocate. I was not always as careful with my court dress as I should have been. One day in a central London county court, I was the last advocate in court, waiting to make an application to the county court judge. I concluded my application, and being aware of some courtroom etiquette I waited and bowed the judge out of court. As I was packing up my books, the judge's clerk rushed back into court. He asked me not to leave as the judge wanted to speak to me. I waited, anxiously trying to identify what heinous sin I could possibly have committed. In the end I never saw the judge. The judge's clerk returned to me with a wing collar and set of pleading bands, both beautifully laundered, saying "These are a present from His Honour, and don't ever appear in his court in that state again". The judge was perfectly right: my collar and bands were in a disgusting state. In a pointed but pleasant way the judge conveyed an important message to me which I took to heart.

I received similar consideration from another judge in the same court on a different occasion. I was representing a client in a complex landlord and tenant dispute. A point came in argument where it was apparent that my client was not legally but was perhaps morally obliged to pay rent to the other party. The judge invited me to take instructions from my client. Turning to my client, I gave succinct and clear advice in four short words. Unfortunately the last of these words did not refer as politely to my opponent's lay client as it should have done. My opponent drew this to the judge's attention who very politically chose to turn a deaf ear to what had happened.

The great limitation for a solicitor advocate at this time was the inability to appear in the higher courts. I seized whatever opportunities I could, and took on a client who came to me with a criminal case from Llandudno Magistrates' Court which had already been committed to Caernarvon Crown Court. Why was I so keen to take on this criminal case at a court 150 miles away from my office? It was hardly the most attractive of commercial propositions. It was because before the coming of the railway, Caernarvon Crown Court had been more than a day's horse ride from the nearest set of barristers' chambers. In these circumstances, the chairmen of quarter sessions and recorders who tried cases at what was probably then the Quarter Sessions sitting at Caernarvon had felt driven to allow rights of audience before them to local solicitors to enable the despatch of business. These rights of audience for solicitors had survived into the late twentieth century. I took advantage of them and conducted the trial myself. Similarly, since a solicitor has always been able to appear as advocate before a court-martial for a member of the armed forces charged with a criminal offence, I had an interesting and professionally rewarding trip to Germany to appear in such a case.

I was very conscious of the campaign that the Law Society mounted from the mid-1980s onwards to achieve rights of audience in the higher courts for solicitors. I was part of it. Progress was very slow. Lady Marr's report seemed to favour some change but opposition to her recommendations forestalled any change arising from her report. The Courts and Legal Services Act 1990 seemed to herald a brave new world. For the first time there was a statutory framework under which solicitors could in theory gain rights of audience in the higher courts. However, the tortuous deliberations of the Lord Chancellor's advisory committee resulted in that statute remaining a dead letter until February 1994. In that month I was one of a group of forty or so solicitors who were the first to be allowed the right to represent their clients in the higher courts.

But I get ahead of myself. By the mid-1980s, as well as appearing for landlords in the county court possession list I was fairly regularly conducting as advocate some quite substantial trials in the county court.

In the late 1980s I received a call from the local county court which came as a surprise. On the line was the Chief Clerk. The registrar had gone down with flu and could not come in to hear the cases listed for him that day. There was a long list of applications before the registrar awaiting determination. The request which the chief clerk made to me was "Can you come to court and sit as a deputy registrar and take the registrar's list?"

As far as I am concerned, life's challenges are there to be accepted. I agreed to sit in for the registrar and heard the registrar's list that day, and soon found out that it was one thing to appear before the registrar with perhaps two or three applications of your own in the list, but quite another to hear the whole list. As a solicitor advocate you know your cases. You go to court having familiarised yourself with the facts of each case and having researched any issues of law that might arise. As a judge hearing a long list of applications you have to acquaint yourself rapidly with the facts of each case before you. You have to be prepared to help litigants, particularly those who are not represented, to put their cases effectively before you. I realised now why an encyclopaedic knowledge of county court procedure, which I did not have and the registrar always seemed to have when I was before him, could be such an asset.

This was the start of my judicial career. It was an interesting and challenging way to start, but things could not happen today as they happened to me more than 20 years ago. And I think that it is a good thing that a practitioner cannot begin his or her career as a judge in the way that I did. Some training is required which fortunately now is well provided.

More calls came in from my local county court. I was drafted in to sit as a deputy registrar on a fairly regular basis. After a while, and out of the blue, I received a letter from the Lord Chancellor's department, politely thanking me for helping out at the county court and making gentle inquiry of my qualification and suitability to sit as a deputy registrar. This inquiry was pursued by asking me to fill in a lengthy form which was in fact an application for the post of deputy registrar.

I continued to act as a deputy registrar. My sittings were arranged in a very informal way. At one county court in London there were two resident registrars. One of them used to go off for periods of four weeks at a time to sit as a recorder in the Crown Court. His brother registrar telephoned me (and presumably three other deputy registrars) whenever this happened, to request that I sit as a deputy registrar for the whole of the one of the four weeks that his colleague was away in the Crown Court. His promise (which he always kept) was that if you accepted the offer you would have exactly the same work that the absent registrar would have had that week. The sheer variety of the work made it a challenge for someone who on a day-to-day basis was still a practitioner. A day's contested ancillary relief hearing could be particularly testing.

I had the considerable pleasure of attending the first ever induction course for deputy registrars a year or so after I had started to sit. (I remember being very engagingly instructed by Ron Howe from the Southend County Court and Mike Hawthorn from the Kingston County Court. I tender my apologies to those I have not mentioned by name. All the course tutors were enthusiastic and helpful.) This course was held in the very attractive Jacobean surroundings of Madingley Hall, just outside Cambridge. It must have been one of the earliest courses organised by a body that has since featured large in my continuing education: the Judicial Studies Board (JSB). My judicial career has subsequently taken me on many more courses organised by the JSB though, to my regret, never again to the delightful surroundings of Madingley Hall.

I sat as a deputy registrar for three or four years. This experience, which had come my way by chance, turned my thoughts towards the idea of a "career" as a judge. It was not that I wanted to leave practice. I was in my early forties. I was still young (or at any rate considered that I was) and enjoying my work as a solicitor, but was beginning to think that by the time I was fifty I might be losing my enthusiasm for turning out in the middle of the night to represent someone at a police station. I decided to apply to become an assistant recorder.

Another application form had to be filled in, less onerous this time as the form was similar, if not identical, to the form I had completed to continue my deputy registrarship. An interview at the House of Lords followed, conducted by a senior civil servant from the Lord Chancellor's department. My interviewer was friendly enough, though the sight of a second official taking a shorthand note of our exchanges gave me the feeling that I needed to measure my replies very carefully.

Acceptance of my application led to my second experience of the training and continuing education provided by the JSB. In the early 1990s I attended an induction course for part-time judges who were about to start trying cases in the Crown Court. This course was held in rather less elegant surroundings than I had enjoyed before: an Electricity Board conference centre at Bricket Wood near Watford.

The training and continuing education that I have received over the years from the JSB has been absolutely excellent. The JSB reviews every course that it runs, and is always looking for ways to improve the delivery and reception of its teaching. Good though the induction course was that I attended, I am quite certain that 17 years of refinement have considerably improved the quality of these courses. In particular there has been an increasing emphasis over the years on the element of individual participation through the syndicate sessions.

What started well at Brickett Wood was to continue into the future with regular refresher courses. I started with little idea of how to put together a summing up to a jury. One of the very well achieved objects of the course was that I finished it with some guidance in my mind on the ingredients necessary to a summing up and some idea of how to structure it.

No course could ever prepare a would-be judge for all the gremlins which he or she might meet in the Crown Court. We were, however, presented with a very good selection of practical problems. The hands-on "syndicate" sessions, where judicial pupils grapple in small groups with all sorts of trial and sentencing issues, were an excellent feature of those earlier days of JSB instruction.

Another point of interest was the broad range of legal backgrounds represented by those attending. There were, as you would expect, many members of the Bar on the course who had considerable experience as practitioners in the Crown Court. They were generous in sharing their knowledge and experience, particularly in the small syndicate groups where practical problems are discussed.

I was by no means the only solicitor on the course. Amongst those attending were a partner from one of the large well-known city firms and a partner from an old established firm in Lincoln's Inn. These putative assistant recorders had no previous experience of conducting cases in the criminal courts. They had not witnessed a summing up. There were members of the Bar on the course whose experience of criminal practice was similarly limited. I remember in particular a talented and erudite silk whose very high-powered practice was substantially concerned with representing the government on applications for judicial review. She had never practised in the criminal courts.

I met all of these people from time to time on future courses or in the Crown Courts of central London as we tried cases as assistant recorders. Naturally we discussed our experiences as trial judges in criminal cases. We had all encountered and agonised about the problematic situations that arise from time to time in criminal jury trials, but everyone I spoke to felt equipped to try jury trials in the Crown Court.

I do not believe that the process of becoming a part-time judge has changed fundamentally since I went through it 17 years ago. To the extent that it has changed, to my mind, the changes that have taken place are only for the better.

Assistant recorders do not exist any more. A decision of the European Court established that their tenure was not sufficiently secure and independent of the executive. These days the initial application is to sit as a recorder.

Applications are no longer made as and when an individual feels that the time has arrived for him or her to become a part-time judge. Competitions are held when it is felt that the pool of recorders needs to be topped up. Anyone who wants to be a recorder needs to keep an eye out for the advertisement which appears in the legal and national press announcing a new competition.

Unless an applicant is a very special case, the application he or she makes is to sit as a recorder trying criminal cases in the Crown Court. Referees are required, but it is not necessary to put forward referees who can speak to the applicant's ability as a court advocate. Neither is it necessary for an applicant to have appeared as an advocate in the courts. Applicants who pass the initial screening process will be invited to attend an interview, conducted by a panel of three: a lay magistrate, a circuit judge and a civil servant. Anyone chosen to become a recorder will be asked to attend a JSB "criminal" induction course.

Before any part-time judge tries a case there is a period of "sitting in" in the Crown Court with an experienced circuit judge. These days the period of is usually two weeks, but may be reduced to one for those with experience of practising in the Crown Court. The period of "sitting in" provides valuable first-hand experience of the Crown Court for those who have never ventured there before. To sit on the bench alongside a judge and hear a summing up being delivered in an actual case helps the judicial pupil enormously. There is no substitute for witnessing the real thing. The JSB course provides the basic structure and content of a summing up, but in the courtroom, you discover that each judge has his or her individual style. An individual style is an important aid to the judge's task of communicating with the jury, which is really what summing up is all about.

The message that I would want to get across to anyone with ambitions to become a judge is that courtroom experience is not necessary. My background may have involved practice as an advocate but I have met solicitors who have sat in the Crown Court and who had had as practitioners no courtroom experience at all.

What is needed is the knowledge and ability to manage a criminal trial. The excellent training given to recorders is able to equip anyone with the basic knowledge needed to try these cases. So far as ability is concerned, the trial management skills of the judge in my view are not the same as the skills deployed by the courtroom advocate. To an extent these management skills can be acquired on the job: the system allows for that. Inevitably someone who is just beginning their career as a recorder will be given the shorter, less serious and less complex cases to try, but that is not to say that these cases will be without their problems.

Well, the great day comes; the judicial aspirant is appointed a recorder. Before the new recorder can actually try a case there is first of all the little matter of being sworn in. To me, the experience seemed something akin to a mass baptism. There were 48 of us gathered in a court room in the Royal Courts of Justice to be sworn in by Mr Justice Hidden. The running order was: first, QCs in order of seniority of appointment; second, junior Bar in order of seniority of call; and third and last, solicitors (there were two of us) in order of seniority of admission. The other solicitor being sworn in was a stipendiary magistrate who had been appointed to that position some years ago. As Mr Justice Hidden began to work his way through the 48 of us it dawned on me that I was going to be in that exposed position of being the very last to take my oaths. I grew anxious about fluffing my lines but fortunately my nerve held and I got through without mishap.

These days the ceremony for swearing in a recorder is a little different. The new recorder is sworn in at a Crown Court by the resident judge in a court room at 10 am on the day when he or she is to begin trying criminal cases. Court staff and other advocates and judges and the relatives and friends of the new recorder make sure that the occasion is well attended. There are welcoming words from the resident judge and an opportunity for a few words of reply from the recorder. To me these occasions have always seemed warm and friendly, and perhaps more importantly, more personal than they used to be.

I enjoyed my time as an assistant recorder and then recorder though at times it felt somewhat surreal to be presiding as a judge in a court where in my practice as a lawyer I did not have the right to address the court.

There was an extremely engaging and helpful person whom you telephoned at the circuit office to arrange your sittings. I want to call this person a "young lady" because this is how she came across on the telephone, but I have to confess that in those days I never actually met her. Almost always there were vacancies for a recorder to sit in the chosen period and very often a selection of courts to choose from. In this way I made my way around most of the Crown Courts of central London. It seemed to be a case of "have wig, will travel".

After about 18 months as an assistant recorder trying criminal cases only, I was offered the chance to obtain a civil "ticket" (an authorisation to try cases in the county court). Once again I received great assistance and support to prepare for this. There was a civil induction course. The hands-on teaching from experienced district and circuit judges gave a good grounding for dealing with the practical problems that can face a judge sitting in the county court. There was another period of sitting in. In this part of the training I witnessed at first hand the whole range of cases that I might soon be trying myself in the county court. The county courts of central London became then part of my itinerary as a recorder.

A part-time judge is expected to sit at least 20 days a year and no more than 50. I found the part-time sitting genuinely refreshing because it was so different in its routine from my practice as a solicitor; in a curious sort of way I found that sitting as a part-time judge was like being on holiday. I tried hard not to attend my office in the periods when I was sitting as a recorder, but realistically the pressures of practice meant that this was an objective I could not always achieve. I am well aware that most solicitors and barristers have to give attention, sometimes considerable attention, to their practice while they sit as part-time judges.

A solicitor in private practice needs sympathetic and enlightened partners to take time away from the business to sit as a part-time judge. I was fortunate in this respect. To have one partner away for four or five weeks a year sitting as a judge can cause problems between partners. I heard of one extreme case where the part-time judge was faced with giving up sitting or giving up his partnership. It is easy to understand the feelings of the partners who have no wish to sit as a recorder or district judge. Their focus is quite naturally on running a successful practice. The absence of a partner sitting as judge will seem to the other partners to contribute little to this objective.

I wonder if there is not room for a broader view than this. Many solicitors' practices earn a substantial part of their fees from litigation work. Many such firms are expanding and developing the advocacy services that they offer from their own resources. To provide an efficient and effective level of service in their advocacy and litigation work, in my view solicitors need to be able to provide timely and balanced advice to a client on the strengths and weaknesses of the client's case. It may be a personal view but I have long believed that for this kind of advice to be effective it cannot be based simply upon an assessment of the client's proof of evidence and researching legal texts. The advisor needs a feel for what a judge is likely to do, what is likely to make a judge decide a case one way rather than the other.

Barristers practise in chambers with colleagues who sit part-time at all levels of the judiciary, and moreover are much more likely than solicitors to have informal contact with judges. These features of practice as a barrister mean that barristers grow up in practice with a good idea of what makes a judge tick.

Solicitors do not have these advantages. There is, however, one sure means of getting some idea of the way judges think, the way they approach and analyse evidence and submissions on the law; that is to sit as a part-time judge, to be a judge yourself. A solicitor who sits as a part-time judge can bring enormous practical benefit to his or her practice. In advising on a dispute, a solicitor who sits as a part-time judge is likely to have a good feel for what will and what will not work, and is better placed to predict the likely outcome of the dispute.

At a much more basic level, the solicitor-recorder will in the course of sitting have come across document presentation which has not assisted understanding of a case. The solicitor-recorder will be well placed to advise on how a case should be presented to a judge so that a case does not fail because it has been obscured by poorly presented evidence.

All in all, I enjoyed the years I spent running my practice as a solicitor and sitting as a part-time judge. The variety and interest that was introduced to my professional life by sitting as a recorder sustained me in the frenetic and sometimes anxious work of running a busy inner city legal aid practice.

As I said earlier it was my settled and open ambition to become a circuit judge if I could. I had begun to take gentle soundings of judges that I met as to how you moved on to a permanent judgeship. As far as I could tell, most recorders who became full-time judges did so because someone asked them if they would like to be appointed a full-time judge. The person who did the asking and the occasion of the asking seemed to be matters of chance and circumstance. The invitation might be made over the telephone by a senior civil servant or by a senior member of the Bar or of the judiciary at some legal social function.

Quite frankly, I had little idea how to go about taking the initiative in seeking an appointment. My anxieties on this front were removed by the announcement in the mid-1990s of the first competition for those seeking appointment as a circuit judge. The competition was advertised in the legal and national press. Those who were eligible for appointment were invited to complete an application form, and after an initial sift of applications those selected for the next stage were invited for a formal interview. A successful candidate was told that subject to the usual checks, the Lord Chancellor was prepared to offer him or her an appointment as a circuit judge.

The introduction of open competition for those seeking to become a judge was in my view the major advance in the judicial appointments system of the past dozen years. Anyone running a large business who regularly needs to appoint people to an important position would surely at the very least choose from candidates who have put themselves forward, who have been seen personally in interview and who have been spoken for by a referee. One of the essential fairnesses of such a system is that solicitor and barrister applicants will be equally familiar with it.

I have heard solicitors express anxiety that they simply do not know a suitable referee to support an application for a judicial position. I believe that this anxiety is based on the misunderstanding that they need to provide a referee who can speak to their ability in court. This is wrong: as with an application for any post, the "employer" seeks an outside view, from someone with personal knowledge of the applicant, of the applicant's general standing and ability.

It is only since 1970 that it has been possible for solicitors to become circuit judges. There are about 550 circuit judges, about 60 of whom were in practice as a solicitor prior to their appointment. It has only been possible for a practising solicitor or former solicitor circuit judge to become a High Court judge since 1990. There is one High Court judge currently sitting who was first appointed a judge from the solicitors' branch of the profession. One judge drawn from the ranks of practising solicitors has so far been appointed to sit in the Court of Appeal.

I believe that the bench is all the better for the appointment of judges who practised as solicitors. An institution like the judiciary should be drawn from as broad a church as possible. The practising background of barristers and solicitors is different, but that is not to say that either is superior. What the appointment of solicitors brings to the judiciary is something different. That is the great virtue of the changes in relatively modern times which have permitted practising solicitors to become judges.

When I began to sit full time as a circuit judge I soon realised that I still had a great deal to learn. The part-time sitting and training are excellent preparation for a full-time appointment. Still, the variety and unpredictability of the trial process will always throw up new and challenging situations. Perhaps this is one of the attractions of the work.

Fortunately, there is a strong support system which helps a judge to cope with these situations. Fellow judges will spare time to help each other out, and sometimes simply being able to articulate a problem to another judge in itself helps to find an answer. Also, between them, judges have a considerable reservoir of legal and practical experience. Another judge's experience may not provide the direct answer to a question, but often it can set the questioner on the correct road.

I would like to think that over the years a judge can develop a familiarity with the fact that problems will arise in trial work from time to time and cease to be quite so fazed when difficulties do occur. A judge can come to recognise that to pause and decide on a solution which can be rationally justified is the best that can be achieved, whatever the problem might be. Sometimes it is not the solution which is most important: what may count for more is the rationalisation of the solution which the judge decides upon. This frame of mind can at least help a judge to put the last problem out of mind and get on with addressing the next.

Sometimes I am asked "What is it like to be a judge?" My short and honest response is "It's nice work if you can get it".

Many solicitors and barristers who become judges will come to the work having had some responsibility for (or comparable to) running a business. They will have had to deal with staffing problems, perhaps the difficult and unpleasant duty of dealing with an employee who is perceived not to be performing satisfactorily. All will have dealt with the equally challenging and important task of appointing a new member of their organisation. There will be VAT returns to make, tax returns to file and possibly a business overdraft to manage. Work has to be attracted to the organisation if it is to survive. A trial judge faces none of these tasks. The court staff is managed by the court manager. The court listing officer presents the judge with cases to try. After years as a busy practitioner it is a delight to able to focus on the one case that the judge is trying at any one time.

A trial judge is not burdened by a great deal of administrative responsibility. This enables the judge to function almost entirely as a lawyer. This is a considerable attraction of the job. One of my reasons for becoming a lawyer was that I was interested in the law and its disciplines. As a solicitor I was becoming more concerned with running a business than the practice of the law. Appointment as a judge took me back to my days at university where my connexion with the law had begun. At university I was trying to understand the law and apply it to factual situations. I was doing much the same thing as a judge. The difference was that as a judge the factual situations I dealt with were real human interest situations.

The task of a trial judge is to manage human conflict to a final resolution. The opposing parties in any trial may need some "umpiring" decisions along the way as the trial of whatever issue divides them proceeds. It is important to get these decisions right so that all parties have a fair trial and hopefully can feel that they have had a fair trial. What the judge really delivers at the end in a civil trial is a judgment, the reasoned decision which decides where truth and justice lies between the claims that the parties are making against each other. The evidence has to be analysed and the law applied to whatever findings of fact the judge has reached. The creation of a judgment, whether it is an ex tempore oral judgment or a reserved written judgment, is a fascinating and pleasurable intellectual exercise. On top of all this the trial judge is fortunate enough to get paid for doing this work which is so rewarding in itself.

Family cases concerning children have an additional dimension. It is not enough to decide simply where truth and justice lie. The judge in these cases has to present a judgment in a way that will minimise any feeling that there is a winner or loser. The welfare of the children which is that paramount concern of the judge will often require that one parent is not cast as a guilty party with nothing to contribute to the future of the children. The parent who is not getting all that he or she asked for must be left with a feeling of worth, must be encouraged, even if there are hard findings of fact to be made, to continue to play a part in the lives of the children.

The equivalent task for a judge in a criminal trial is the preparation and delivery of a summing up to a jury. This is a task which differs significantly from the delivery of a judgment in a civil case. A summing up is a presentation, a presentation in which the judge is trying to communicate with the 12 people who are the jury. Sometimes the legal issues are complex. If so, they must be simplified. They must be made readily understandable. This can often be accomplished by providing the jury with written directions.

A criminal trial unfolds before a jury in the order in which the prosecution and defence call their witnesses. This is not necessarily the order in which the events which are the subject matter of the trial have unfolded. The judge's task is to organise the evidence for the jury so that it tells a story or, as is often the case, two stories; the story that the prosecution want to tell and the story that the defence want to tell.

The preparation of a summing up is a creative and intellectually rewarding task. Again, I say that a judge is fortunate to be able to able to earn his living by doing this work.

The work of the circuit judge is rewarding work, work that many solicitors are capable of doing. The system provides great assistance and guidance to a lawyer who has an ambition to become a circuit judge. I would encourage any solicitor with that ambition to apply to become a recorder. The experience of sitting as a judge has enriched my professional life. I am sure it could do the same for others.

# UNDERSTANDING THE LAW: WHO NEEDS IT?

## JOSHUA ROZENBERG

Should the law be understandable to all? Or is that a counsel of perfection?

Most of us would say that our laws should be as easy as possible to understand – but there are those who argue that lay people should not even try to interpret legislation. Francis Bennion, a former Parliamentary draftsman, once suggested it might be "positively dangerous to encourage non-lawyers to think they can understand legal texts unaided by expert advice". Writing in *The Times*, he claimed that unexplained "terms of art" and references in legal texts could not be "fully understood by non-experts in law, any more that medical language can be fully understood by non-experts in medicine" (24 January 1995).

Statutory language is much clearer now than it was when Mr Bennion first turned his hand to drafting legislation in the 1950s. But anyone who based a business transaction on his own interpretation of a statute would certainly be taking something of a risk. There might, after all, be some case-law on the subject.

Like the editors of *Halsbury's Laws of England*, I explain the law to people who would rather not rely on their own interpretations of it. However, there are important differences between book editors and reporters. As a journalist, I hope that my stories will be easier for non-lawyers to understand than the pages of a legal encyclopaedia. But I accept that my reports will be less complete, and therefore less accurate.

Though *Halsbury's* can be read with profit by all who are willing to apply their minds to the task, this great encyclopaedia of the law is aimed mainly at lawyers. As a result, it uses as many words as are necessary to provide a sufficiently accurate and comprehensive account of each topic it covers. Journalists, however, must use as few words as possible to give an approximate version of the subject being reported.

This is not just because editors must squeeze a lot of stories into every newspaper or broadcast. It is because there are limits on the number of words that the reader or listener is thought to be capable of taking in. These limits may vary, of course. A book extract in one of the weekend newspaper supplements may run to 5,000 words. By contrast, the average television news report could contain 300 words or fewer. A story on radio news might use half that number – although, paradoxically, it may convey more information.

Why, though, do I say that a journalist may want to give an approximate version of the story? First, because it will be easier to understand – especially on radio or television. For example, if I were to tell you that 151,654 divorce petitions were filed in 2005 compared with 167,193 the year before, 177,223 in 2002, 162,450 in 1978 and 54,036 in 1968, you might have some difficulty in absorbing this information. But you would find it much easier to understand if I told you that latest figures show the number of people wanting to get divorced at a little over 150,000 a year; that the numbers are steadily going down from a peak of nearly 180,000 five years ago; and that the figure tripled between 1968 and 1978.

Before beginning this paragraph, you might have let your eyes stray back to the raw statistics I quoted, just to check that my reworking of the figures was accurate. You would have found this much harder to do if you were following to a live broadcast – though technology does now make it possible for us to "listen again".

The second reason why a journalist will give an approximate version of the story is that it is the essence of journalism. This is not meant to be a dig at the fabled inaccuracy of every story that you ever happen to know something about. It is simply that journalism involves leaving out some of the details, and that must inevitably provide no more than a partial account of the story. How could it be otherwise if one has to précis a 50-page judgment in three or four paragraphs?

But summarising a decision is the easy part. These days, you sometimes have to try to rein in the story like an unruly horse and stop it running away from you. Otherwise there is a risk that an inaccurate version of the story will gain ground and overtake the truth.

The first reason for this is that some lawyers are not as objective as they might be when explaining a court ruling to the press. At an early stage in my career as the BBC's legal correspondent, I heard one evening that the coroner's jury at an inquest about which I knew little had just returned a verdict of unlawful killing on a group of victims who died abroad. Immediately afterwards, a solicitor for the bereaved families emerged from court to announce that, as a result, those responsible for the killings would soon face manslaughter charges.

How could this be? Though the people killed had been British, those responsible for their deaths were not. How could the alleged killers face charges in the courts of England and Wales? I knew that foreigners could be tried in Britain for crimes committed here. I knew that British citizens could be tried in the United Kingdom for murder or manslaughter committed abroad. But I did not think that a similar principle would apply to deaths taking place in a foreign country – even if the victims had been British.

Sadly, the nearest set of *Halsbury's Laws* was in another building. I rang a leading member of the criminal Bar at home. He thought my view of the law sounded right but, without his books, he could not be sure.

With time running out, I appeared live on the main evening news and told several million viewers I could not see how anyone could face prosecution. Later that evening, I caught up with the families' solicitor and asked him, somewhat anxiously, if I had been right. "Certainly", he replied. Why, then had he said otherwise? "It's what the clients wanted to hear", he replied cheerily.

Ever since then, however much pressure I may be under to provide an instant summary of a lengthy ruling, I have been wary of relying on instant claims from lawyers on one side or the other. Solicitors involved in a case are usually able to steal a march on the press because civil judgments are almost always reserved and sent to the lawyers in draft a day or two in advance. On the whole, this privilege is not abused and the judgment is generally not leaked to the media. But it means that the lawyers can be ready with a partial summary of the case while the reporters are still desperately trying to work out which side has won.

Of course, campaign groups and their lawyers would not last long if their analysis was totally false. But they would not be very effective campaigners if they did not know how to put the best gloss on a ruling. It is the job of a legal journalist to decide which comments are a helpful corrective to the reporter's ignorance and which are no more than wishful thinking.

Non-specialist reporters lack the knowledge, time and perhaps even the inclination to check the reliability of comments made by lawyers and campaigners immediately after a ruling. Lack of knowledge is understandable. Lack of time is forgivable – although it means that the first few paragraphs of news-agency reports are more likely to quote what was said by counsel at the original hearing than what was said by the court in its ruling. Much more serious, though, is the risk that reporters will run an inaccurate account of a ruling simply because it makes for a better story.

I am not suggesting that journalists regularly falsify their reports. But they may be inclined to suspend their normal healthy scepticism when faced with a story that they would dearly like to believe. Once that happens, other journalists are inevitably dragged along in its wake. If a juicy story has appeared in an evening newspaper and on a 24-hour news channel, the next day's newspapers may be unwilling to hold back – even if they are assured that the piece they have just read is unlikely to be the truth, the whole truth and nothing but the truth.

Take this story that appeared in *The Sun* on 17 May 2007:

> "A JUDGE stunned a court yesterday by admitting he did not know what a WEBSITE was. Judge Peter Openshaw brought a shuddering halt to the trial of three men accused of internet terror offences as a witness was being quizzed about an extremist web forum. He told shocked prosecutors at Woolwich Crown Court, South East London: 'The trouble is I don't understand the language. I don't really understand what a website is.' Prosecutor Mark Ellison then tried to help the judge by explaining. But confused Judge Openshaw, 59, said: "I haven't quite grasped the concepts.' Later he said he hoped a computer expert would give 'simple' evidence when called to the stand – because otherwise he would not understand it. Judge Openshaw said: 'Will you ask him to keep it simple? We've got to start from basics.'"

Since this story was based on a report from the Reuters news agency, it appeared in newspapers from Canada to Australia under such predictable headlines as "Judge tangled by web". But what actually happened?

Mr Justice Openshaw, to give him his correct title, did not deny using the words attributed to him, implausible though they sound. He did, however, complain that his remarks had been taken out of context. A statement issued on his behalf explained he was in the fifth week of a trial based largely on computer-generated evidence:

> "Trial judges always seek to ensure that everyone in court is able to follow all of the proceedings. They will regularly ask questions, not for their own benefit – but on behalf of all those following a case, in the interests of justice. In this specific case, immediately prior to the judge's comment, the prosecution counsel had referred to various internet forums with postings of comments relevant to the case. Mr Justice Openshaw was simply clarifying the evidence presented, in an easily understandable form for all those in court. Mr Justice Openshaw is entirely computer-literate and indeed has taken notes on his own computer in court for many years."

That statement – from the Judicial Communications Office – received only limited coverage. And there was even less press interest in a note handed to the judge after the trial, also released to the press. It read:

> "We, the jury, would like you to know that we are sorry for any embarrassment caused around the media coverage regarding the website comment. We were not as shocked as the media stated, and we appreciate that you were clarifying the information. Once again, we would like to thank you. Yours sincerely, the jurors in court number 1."

The tendency of newspapers to feed readers' prejudices and misconceptions is exacerbated by the recent "dumbing-down" of the daily press. A paper cannot afford to ignore a story that might appear in one of its rivals just because its correspondent considers that the story, as written, is likely to be misleading. Newspapers these days are competing for a younger audience. New readers are likely to be less well educated than their parents. Taken as a whole, this audience is seen as less concerned about abstract legal concepts, and perhaps more interested in "news you can use" – consumer stories and personal finance. In the news pages of a modern newspaper, stories about concepts and ideas have to clamour for attention a little more loudly than before.

But not all is lost. Look beyond the front pages and you will still find serious analysis of legal issues. Search more widely and you will find a wealth of material on the Internet, often provided free of charge by solicitors' firms and barristers' chambers. Some of this is even written clearly enough for non-lawyers to understand.

I am becoming increasingly convinced that the future of serious legal journalism is to be found on the Internet. At 7.00 every working morning, a company called Courtserve e-mails me a summary of all the legal stories in that day's newspapers. It is put together in the early hours by a freelance journalist – living in Spain, I believe – who scans the newspaper websites for stories of interest to lawyers. These stories were originally written for the printed media and then added to a website. But already we are seeing legal journalists writing directly for the web, posting their stories throughout the 24-hour news cycle rather than at a time to suit print distribution deadlines. Stories from these websites, aggregated either by other websites or by an expatriate journalist in some convenient time-zone, are becoming required reading for well-informed lawyers.

If newspaper coverage of legal issues is as down-market as I have made out, do we really need the media at all? Would it not be better if we trained lawyers to communicate better with the public? Surely we could simplify or codify our laws, making them accessible to all?

I do not suppose that many readers will be surprised by my views on this. To me, legal reporters and commentators are an essential part of our democratic process. Their role is to break down the inevitable barrier between the lay person and the law.

A good journalist will look for the essence of a story and explain its importance in terms that a non-specialist will understand. If the story is a court ruling, the reader will almost certainly want to know who has won. This may not, of course, be as simple as it sounds. In the law reports, judgments are printed with a "headnote" summarising the outcome. But the raw judgment, as delivered by the court, does not usually come ready-packaged in this way.

Take, for example, a typical ruling by the House of Lords, which remains our highest court at least until 2009. There is the judgment on the Law Lords' website, available to you, the reader, as early as it normally reaches me, the reporter. But the each of the five judges who sits in a normal hearing may deliver his or her own ruling. So you, the reader, must first work out how many judges have decided in favour of the appellant and how many are against. Then, you can work out whether the appeal has been successful – bearing in mind that, if more than one party was dissatisfied with the ruling below, there may be cross-appellants as well as appellants.

After that, you should be able to see which side has won. But bear in mind that the outcome of the case itself may be less important to the public than the point of law it establishes – or perhaps its relevance to another, more newsworthy, case. So the "intro" – the all-important "top line" that will hook the casual reader and persuade him or her to read on – may not be the court's decision at all.

Not all legal stories are about court rulings, of course. A campaign group may be calling for reform; the government of the day may be changing its policies; or the reporter may have been asked to explain the legal issue of the day. If the item is to appear as a news report, then the journalist's duty is to report it in a neutral, factual way. If, however, the correspondent has the luxury of writing a column, then it may be as one-sided and opinionated as the opening speech in any piece of litigation.

Here, the journalist is acting as an intermediary between the public and the law, alerting readers to developments that they might not otherwise discover and exposing the public to opinions that might otherwise not come their way.

Either way, though, the reporter has an important obligation to the public, and one that was recognised by the House of Lords Constitution Committee in a report it published in July 2007.

"We believe that the media, especially the popular tabloid press, all too often indulge in distorted and irresponsible coverage of the judiciary, treating judges as 'fair game'", peers said.

> "A responsible press should show greater restraint and desist from blaming judges for their interpretation of legislation which has been promulgated by politicians. If the media object to a judgment or sentencing decision, we suggest they focus their efforts on persuading the Government to rectify the legal and policy framework."

The Constitution Committee's comments, in its report on *Relations between the executive, the judiciary and Parliament* (HL Paper 151), seem to have been intended as a counterbalance to its criticism of the Lord Chancellor, Lord Falconer, for not springing to the judges' defence on sentencing. In June 2006, at a time when *The Sunday Times* and then *The Sun* were "naming and shaming" judges whose "unduly lenient" sentences had been increased on appeal, the Recorder of Cardiff, Judge Griffith Williams, was forced to cut a notional 18-year minimum term on a paedophile, Craig Sweeney, to less than six years because of sentencing guidelines. The press tended to play down the fact that Sweeney's sentence was one of indefinite detention; that he was unlikely to be released until some further period had elapsed; and that he would be liable to recall for re-offending. As a result, Judge Griffith Williams and the judges in general were coming under heavy media fire – stoked by the Home Secretary, John Reid, who took it upon himself to say that Sweeney's sentence, itself, was "unduly lenient".

That was on a Monday. Later in the week, I rang Lord Falconer's Department for Constitutional Affairs to see if the Lord Chancellor would be coming to the defence of the judges, only to be told by a relatively junior press officer that this was now a matter for the Lord Chief Justice. Lord Phillips of Worth Matravers had taken over as head of the judiciary some two months earlier, and it was now his job to defend the judges against public criticism.

Having left Judge Griffith Williams to swing in the wind for the best part of three days, Lord Falconer finally agreed to appear on the BBC's *Question Time* programme that Wednesday evening – although his comments were broadcast too late for Thursday's papers. Lord Falconer said "we need to be extremely careful that we don't attack the judges on these issues when it is the system". He went on: "If we attack the judges, we attack an incredibly important part of the system when it is not their fault." But the Lord Chancellor also defended Mr Reid, maintaining that the Home Secretary "did not attack the judge".

Lord Falconer's response helped calm the situation for a couple of days – until he was knocked off course by further criticism of Judge Griffith Williams from a most unlikely quarter. Speaking on *Any Questions*, Vera Baird QC MP, one of Lord Falconer's junior ministers, said "it seems to me that this judge has just got this formula wrong, so I'm critical of the judge for three reasons – one, starting too low; two, deducting too much for the guilty plea; and, three, getting the formula wrong".

Shortly afterwards, Mrs Baird was forced to apologise to Lord Falconer for her remarks. She remained in the government, and was later promoted to Solicitor-General. Meanwhile, the Attorney-General decided not to refer Sweeney's sentence to the Court of Appeal and Judge Griffith Williams was promoted to the High Court.

The Lords Constitution Committee – which took oral evidence from journalists, including myself – was highly critical of Lord Falconer, while admitting that the senior judges could have acted more quickly.

"The Sweeney case was the first big test of whether the new relationship between the Lord Chancellor and the judiciary was working properly and it is clear that there was a systemic failure", peers said.

"Ensuring that ministers do not impugn individual judges, and restraining and reprimanding those who do, is one of the most important duties of the Lord Chancellor. In this case, Lord Falconer did not fulfil this duty in a satisfactory manner. The senior judiciary could also have acted more quickly to head off the inflammatory and unfair press coverage which followed the sentencing decision."

In the committee's view –

"the key to harmonious relations between the judiciary and the executive is ensuring that ministers do not violate the independence of the judiciary in the first place. To this end, we recommend that when the Ministerial Code is next revised the Prime Minister should insert strongly worded guidelines setting out the principles governing public comment by ministers on individual judges."

The Lords committee also considered the way in which Tony Blair's government had set up the Ministry of Justice. This episode, too, brings the media's role into sharp focus.

The first we knew that responsibility for prisons was to be moved from the Home Office to what was then called the Department for Constitutional Affairs was in late January 2007, when *The Sunday Telegraph* was briefed by "sources close to the Home Secretary". As if by magic, the Lord Chancellor immediately popped up on television to confirm the story. That was not just the first the press and public knew of the plans; it was also the first the Lord Chief Justice had heard of it. Early the following month, the judiciary raised important concerns with the Lord Chancellor about resources and sentencing. But nearly another month was to pass before senior judges were invited to join a working party chaired by Lord Falconer's Permanent Secretary whose terms of reference prohibited any discussion of their main concerns.

Judges being judges, they went along with this rather shabby treatment. True, a week before the government made its formal announcement they protested that they had not been consulted. And, true, the Lord Chief Justice issued a brief but strongly-worded response when the announcement was made. But that was all.

I wrote a column in *The Daily Telegraph*, taking the government's side. But I had very little to go on. The following week, Lord Falconer gave evidence to the Commons Constitutional Affairs Committee. It was clear from the questions he was asked that the judges must have written to the committee, arguing against the proposals. But neither the judges nor the committee was prepared to release the judges' written comments to the press. Fortunately, I managed to get hold of the documents and published their comments over a series of two or three pieces.

Were the judges annoyed at the leak? On the contrary, they were delighted. They had some powerful arguments, they wanted them circulated, they expected the Commons committee to publish their evidence sooner or later and they thanked me for the coverage. Even so, they were not prepared to let me know how their negotiations with the government were getting on. Either they didn't trust me, or they felt it was wrong to brief me – I hope the latter.

Since the judges were unwilling to go public with their concerns, the issue failed to capture the public's imagination and Lord Falconer was successful in setting up his Ministry of Justice in May 2007 – a couple of months before he was succeeded by Jack Straw. Senior judges were thwarted in their attempts to obtain what they saw as the necessary safeguards to protect judicial independence. They were left with no control over their own staff or budget, vulnerable to any increase in prison spending. Having failed to obtain the independent review they sought, the judges pinned their hopes on doing a deal with the new Justice Secretary and Lord Chancellor, Jack Straw.

For the Constitution Committee, this was all too reminiscent of events four years earlier when Tony Blair attempted to abolish the post of Lord Chancellor. "We are disappointed that the Government seem to have learnt little or nothing from the debacle surrounding the constitutional reforms initiated in 2003", peers said.

> "The creation of the Ministry of Justice clearly has important implications for the judiciary. The new dispensation created by the Constitutional Reform Act 2005 and the Concordat [between the Government and the judiciary] requires the Government to treat the judiciary as partners, not merely as subjects of change. By omitting to consult the judiciary at a sufficiently early stage, by drawing the parameters of the negotiations too tightly and by proceeding with the creation of the new ministry before important aspects had been resolved, the Government failed to do this."

This is true enough, but sometimes the judges seem to be their own worst enemies. As a commentator, I do my best to explain their rulings, however difficult they may be to understand. The Lords committee explored in some detail whether the judges would get a better press if they beefed up the Judicial Communications Office, currently staffed by experienced and well-regarded press officers who, however, are not required to have legal qualifications. Peers suggested the judges could take on a legally-qualified spokesman, such as a retired judge, who could explain judicial decisions – though not attempt to justify them. "Whilst judges should never be asked to justify their decisions outside the courtroom, it is desirable for them to communicate with the public and the media on appropriate issues", the committee said. However, its members seemed disturbed to find that I and my colleagues speak regularly to judges on an unattributable basis. Demonstrating a certain level of naiveté, they believed this mirrored the "spin culture" of Westminster and Whitehall and said they were "strongly of the opinion that, whatever the media pressure, judges should not give off-the-record briefings". If only they knew.

Ultimately, though, the public will be no better informed than the reporters themselves. What if they find the door to the courtroom barred?

A week before Lord Falconer lost his job as Lord Chancellor in June 2007, he published a consultation paper called "Openness in family courts – a new approach". In the best traditions of *Yes, Minister*, the government's new approach to openness was, predictably, to have less of it. Far from providing more access to press and public, the government proposed that those courts currently open to reporters – the family proceedings courts, run by magistrates – should normally be closed. Reporters would not be allowed to attend any family court without permission from the judge or magistrates.

Lord Falconer did not attempt to disguise the fact that this was a complete U-turn on proposals that had been strongly supported by his deputy, Harriet Harman, less than a year earlier. "We have listened to what people said in response to our original proposals", the Lord Chancellor said. "We have carefully considered the responses. And we have changed our mind."

Family courts deal with public-law cases – where, for example, a child is taken into the care of a local authority. They also deal with private-law cases, where separated parents may fight over where a child should live and how often it should see the non-resident parent. Under the government's original proposals, the media would have had the right to attend family proceedings – although the court would have been able to exclude reporters or impose reporting restrictions where appropriate. But there was no support for this idea from children's organisations or the judges. "Generally, the media was not seen as 'a proxy for the public' or responsible for scrutinising the courts, but instead it was seen as only interested in reporting on certain types of (often high profile) case", Lord Falconer's paper said in 2007. The judges, in particular, said it was neither in the public interest, nor in the interests of the children involved in family proceedings, "that intensely private matters should be laid bare to the public at large".

Writing in *The Times*, David Pannick, QC, dismissed the consultation paper as "poorly reasoned and wrong in principle". He asked: "If there are clear restrictions on reporting any details that may identify a child or the family, why is 'the welfare of children at stake'?" In his view, there was no evidence that children had been harmed by existing rules that permitted reporters to attend family cases in the Court of Appeal or the family proceedings court. Moreover, the highest standards of justice were needed when the state was removing a child from its parent. "The spur of publicity advances that goal", wrote Mr Pannick. "Secrecy is a breeding ground for complacency and injustice. It also promotes rumour and speculation, which inevitably damage public confidence." As for the government's complaint that the media were interested only in higher profile cases, this showed a misunderstanding of the function of a free press. "It is for the media, not the Government or children's organisations, to decide which cases to attend and why" (17 July 2007).

Normally, I would agree with David Pannick. His stirring support for a free press is a delight to hear. All my instincts tell me to challenge any move that would exclude me and my fellow reporters from the courts. And yet, for once, I find myself holding back.

First, how do you distinguish between journalists who are allowed into court and members of the public who are not? Journalism is not a profession: it has no governing body that can appoint members and exclude them if they misbehave. Instead, it is no more than a trade that can be practised by anyone – and, one might say, often is. It could be suggested that the courts should be open only to those reporters on an approved list. But who is to draw up that list, and why should they have the power to exclude a lone "blogger" who wishes to publish the proceedings on his website? Of course, someone who does not work for a reputable news organisation would have little incentive to observe restrictions on identifying the parties to a family dispute. But that, by itself, would surely not be grounds for excluding someone with no record of law-breaking.

Ultimately, the courts would decide – as presumably they must on the rare occasions when reporters cover family proceedings courts. But would family judges really start behaving differently if there was a journalist in court? Will reporters really turn up if a case is not a particularly sensational one? I very much doubt it. Far fewer cases in the courts are covered by reporters these days – even from the news agencies. Fewer still of their reports are carried in the mainstream newspapers.

If cases are to go unreported by legal journalists or unexplained by legal commentators, it is all the more important for the law to be understandable. Of course we must not satisfy accuracy for popular appeal. Other things being equal, though, the law should be plain and open to all. Better still, we should have clear laws backed up by even clearer explanations and commentaries.

# THE CENTENARY OF THE PUBLICATION OF "THE LAWS OF ENGLAND" EDITED BY LORD HALSBURY

## AN ADDRESS BY ANDREW HOLROYD[1]
## 27TH SEPTEMBER 2007

I am absolutely delighted to have this opportunity to address such a distinguished audience.

On behalf of everyone at the Law Society of England and Wales, let me begin by congratulating *Halsbury's*. To produce volume after volume of *The Laws of England* for a century is a truly remarkable achievement, and a testament to the hard work and dedication of everyone involved over those 100 years.

Like many of you, I am sure, I first discovered *Halsbury's* almost as soon as I began my career. I was told it was the first port of call to find out something I did not know. But as I was quick to find out that it was equally – if not more – invaluable to find out something I should have known. So part of Lord Halsbury's legacy is not just helping generations of solicitors do their jobs – but helping generations to keep their jobs too!

Delivering speeches and speaking at events like this is always a pleasure, but I must confess that preparing for them can, sometimes, be a less enjoyable process. Not so, however, for tonight. The present and the future are often best viewed through the prism of the past, and it has been fascinating to look back over the last 100 years.

In 1907 the most significant legal development was on the 27 February: the opening of the current Old Bailey building – the scene of so many infamous criminal trials. The Britain of 1907 was of course very different from today. A world power, but a more divided nation; economically, socially and politically. Edward VII was King and probably the least well known occupant of number 10 of the twentieth century, Sir Henry Campbell-Bannerman, was Prime Minister.

I am told there were 56 different Public and General Acts of Parliament in 1907! Some would probably raise a few eyebrows today. The Deceased Wife's Sister's Marriage Act, for instance, declared that – and you need to listen carefully here:

> "it shall not be lawful for a man to marry the sister of his divorced wife, or his wife by whom he has been divorced, during the lifetime of such wife."

I have not gone as far as to check Hansard but I am pretty confident it was not an issue the Law Society lobbied heavily on!

Not all the legislation, however, is so unfamiliar. The Probation of Offenders Act 1907 serves as a salient reminder that the challenges that lie at the heart of the criminal justice system today are not quite as new as some "red tops" might have us believe.

It is also only when you see the original copies of the Acts of Parliament from the turn of the last century that you see just how concise they were compared with today. There really is no more striking a reminder of the sheer volume of legislation churned out by the Houses of Parliament today. The question is of course how many of the thousands of new offences created now are truly effective, beyond the political posturing and point scoring?

Away from politics and Parliament, 1907 also saw Rudyard Kipling win the Nobel Prize for Literature, and across the pond a future star of the silver screen – one Marion

---

1 President of the Law Society of England and Wales.

Robert Morrison – was born. To begin with Marion majored in pre-law at University before changing career paths and changing names – to John Wayne – where he so often *was* the law.

Had he stuck with his studies Marion would have graduated in the States in around 1932 – and it is from that year, 1932, that happened to be the furthest back I could find preliminary solicitors' exam papers for England and Wales.

Aside from being the perfect test for any budding Greek, Latin, Spanish or German translators, basic geography was seen as critical to being a good solicitor – and who could quibble with that? Take this for example:

> "From a detailed description of the physical features of the Scandinavian
> Peninsula show the similarity and dissimilarity existing between Norway and
> Sweden. Name chief mountains, rivers and lakes."

Any takers? But it is the English composition section that is my personal favourite. Students had several choices:

> "God made the country, man made the town but the devil made the suburbs"

> "Write a correspondence between two exceedingly polite gentlemen, each of
> whom is convinced that the other is trying to swindle him."

> "Write a ghost story which need not be original."

Scary stuff indeed! Surely there is no more appropriate definition of a jack of all trades than someone who specialises in Norwegian fjords, correspondence between exceedingly polite gentlemen and writing unoriginal ghost stories – with a little law on the side too!

The solicitors of the 1930s were generalists in the truest sense of the word. What a contrast with 2007 where solicitors specialise in ever more esoteric areas of the law: from working on the regulation of energy markets to setting up school academies; from sports law to hedge funds; and from working in-house to being a solicitor advocate.

But while what we do and how we do it has changed dramatically over the past two decades, what about our values? Some people say they are just as important today as they ever were. I profoundly disagree, because I say they are more important today than ever: more important because the more diverse our work, and the more profit and business drive our work, the more important our principles become.

Just consider our new solicitors' Code of Conduct. It does not matter if your client is a CEO or is receiving legal aid, those core values and duties: of upholding the rules of law and the administration of justice, integrity, independence; of acting in the best interest of the client; of providing a good standard of service; and of not behaving in a way that is likely to diminish the trust the public places in you or the profession – are of fundamental importance to everything that we do.

They also not only distinguish us from the increasing band of unqualified legal pretenders, but help bind every branch of the profession. Whatever the future of legal services, I hope it is a future where our shared values remain sacrosanct.

Now it is a quintessentially British thing not to boast, but I do think we should not be afraid to celebrate the profession – and its contribution to both the economy and wider society.

That is why I would like to take this opportunity to conspicuously plug the Law Society's Excellence Awards 2007, to be hosted by the BBC's Jeremy Vine! Deadlines for entries may have closed but as we are looking back at the history of the profession I do think one award – that for *Social Responsibility* – has particular relevance this evening.

In some ways our profession is only just beginning to catch up with other sectors, where it has been the norm to have a polished CSR (Corporate Social Responsibility) programme for some time. But while the term may seem like relatively new, business-speak to some, it is in fact something in which our profession has a great heritage.

It is also something that again underlines the yawning gap between the public perception of our profession – an almost Dickensian view of an industry whose one great principle is to make money for itself – and the reality: solicitors and barristers quietly undertaking hours of *pro bono* work, and getting involved with and helping their communities.

We at the Law Society will be doing our bit to promote the wealth and breadth of *pro bono* work during Pro Bono Week in November. But CSR is about far more than just *pro bono*. It is about treating staff well, about taking equality and diversity seriously, and about having a proper respect for our environment and green issues. That is why it is something the Law Society is going to play an increasing role in promoting and leading within the profession, and something I am very passionate about.

Looking ahead, in many ways I believe the next decade will herald greater change in the profession than the last ten decades combined. Some, sadly, do not look positive, such as the extreme financial pressures on legal aid. But it is not all doom and gloom.

The Legal Services Bill will usher in changes that will open up door after door for solicitors – from working closer with other types of lawyer and other professionals, to offering a far broader range of services through new business structures.

Globalisation too is changing the profession irrevocably. I recently found myself reading Thomas L Friedman's book *The World is Flat* which is an enlightening American perspective on the effects of Globalisation. In it he quotes an African proverb.

"Every morning in Africa a gazelle wakes up. It knows it must run faster than the fastest lion or it will be killed.

Every morning in Africa a lion wakes up. It knows it must run faster than the slowest gazelle or it will starve.

It doesn't matter whether you are a gazelle or a lion, when the sun comes up you had better start running."

Both China and India have the potential to become leading players on the global stage, as technology and instant communication level out the world. The message that we had better keep running and stay competitive is one we need to hear. So while the opportunities for solicitors – from globalisation to the Legal Services Bill – may never have been greater, in order to take full advantage we must be alert and ready. We must be participants not spectators.

The role of the Law Society is therefore critical. It is our responsibility to ensure that every solicitor is fully informed of how the profession is changing and how it will affect them. But we cannot inform them if we do not communicate with them. And we cannot communicate with them if we do not reflect them.

That is why we are taking steps to mirror the profession like never before. I am excited about the launch of our new Junior and International Lawyers Divisions in the Autumn, both of which will help reflect today's younger, more international profession, and both of which illustrate our new, more targeted and more focused approach to communications.

Just as globalisation is transforming legal services, the technological revolution – most notably advances in IT – is transforming our profession. It is hard to keep up! Laptops are giving way to palmtops; i-pods to i-phones; and I read in an edition of the Gazette only last month that lawyers could be amongst the first to embrace the "e-book" – in essence electronic paper.

Exciting, but it is the client that will be the greatest driver of change. Today we no longer have a monopoly on information. The largest bookshelf in the world is the Internet and it has given unprecedented access to information at the touch of the button.

This raises a challenge. Many of our clients now come to us well aware of what the law is and how it works, so over time our role will have to change to reflect their new demands. In this world where information is increasingly free and easy to access I am sure information providers, including *Halsbury's*, will be faced with similar challenges: how to continue to evolve; how to continue to produce a product that solicitors need; how to stay ahead of the game.

The Law Society Library is one of our greatest assets and the library team has been working in partnership with LexisNexis to develop an interactive online service which exploits the depth of information and expertise held in Chancery Lane. With this and other improvements in technology, the benefits of being part of a broad legal community can be reaped by practitioners around the country, and they in turn can develop their practices to improve their businesses and the services they offer.

*Halsbury's* has been so successful because like all great successes, if it did not exist someone would have had to invent it. With English law so important on the international stage and with London such an important jurisdiction of choice will there be an increased international demand for information services? Will the ever more specialised legal services market create a demand for more bespoke services? *Halsbury's* services perhaps?

Lord Halsbury and the then Managing Director of Butterworths, Stanley Shaw Bond, declared their guide would be "the greatest work on English law ever published". Rarely are grand ambitions so exhaustively and comprehensively fulfilled and I am sure that if *Halsbury's* continues to be nimble and innovative this institution of legal publishing will endure and endure.

So on that note, let me congratulate everyone at *Halsbury's* once again, and here's to another 100 years of success.

# THE CENTENARY OF THE PUBLICATION OF "THE LAWS OF ENGLAND" EDITED BY LORD HALSBURY

## AN ADDRESS BY GEOFFREY VOS QC[1]
## 27TH SEPTEMBER 2007

I am honoured and delighted to have been asked to address this momentous centenary event. For every lawyer of every generation since 1907, Lord Halsbury's Laws of England has been an invaluable resource. It has been a work that has been a reference of both first and last resort. As we used to have been allowed to say, *Halsbury* has been the lawyer's *tabula in naufragio* or "table in a storm".

I want to consider this evening the development in the use of legal research materials over the 100 years that *Halsbury* has been available. Of course, I cannot speak with any authority about what happened in 1907, but I can speculate that the lawyer's tools changed little between 1907 and the time when I began to study law in 1973.

When I started at the Bar in my present Chancery chambers in Lincoln's Inn in 1979, things were much as they had been for many years. Members of Chambers were provided with a telephone on their desk, but it was on one of those PABX systems connected to an old fashioned telephone with a circular dial. It was not regarded as quite normal for barristers to talk to solicitors on the telephone – and it was certainly frowned upon if written instructions had not been provided first. The Chambers' typist would type opinions from manuscript drafts on foolscap paper, and amendments to that typing – for junior members at least – would often take days rather than hours. In short, the pace of professional practice was in a different time warp from that to which we have now become accustomed.

The quality of advice depended largely on the quality of the available library. This was one reason why so many specialist barristers practised in London, because access to the libraries of the Inns of Court was so crucial. No Chambers could have all the necessary materials to allow specialist barristers to advise on recherché topics concerning settlements, easements, drains, profits à prendre, clubs and societies, and so many more.

This was why *Halsbury's Laws* became such an instant success when it appeared in 1907. It substituted for an entire law library, at least so long as one wanted a reliable version of the law on any subject, without wishing to extend the boundaries of legal knowledge or insight too far. That is not a criticism. "The Laws of England" set out to be a "complete statement of the Laws of England", not a code, nor an encyclopaedia. One finds that the authors of individual sections are allowed to express an opinion on a topic of a difficulty or controversy, so as to ensure that the reader knows where there are areas that require further research.

Since the 1970s, however, the accelerated development of information technology and methods of instant communication have revolutionised both legal research and the way in which lawyers do business.

First came the introduction of the fax machine. Many of you may remember the rolls of specially oily paper that stuck together and made it impossible to collate a fax longer than ten pages. The change from telex was indeed a revolution. Telex machines were only

---

1 Chairman of the Bar Council of England and Wales

available to a limited audience and required specialist users. Fax machines began quickly to appear in every solicitor's office where a telephone line was installed.

The first noticeable change occasioned by the fax was the speed with which lawyers were required to react either to their client's requests for advice or guidance, or (perhaps more importantly) to their opponents' litigation and transactional machinations. There was no longer the luxury of taking days to answer a letter – and no longer the ability to assume that any letter took three days to arrive, and five over a weekend. The pace of business life was hotting up, and lawyers were no exception.

Some of you may also recall how the fax first affected law reporting. Remember that, up to the days of the fax machine, law reports appeared only in the "Times" newspaper or in well regulated series of reports that made unchallengeable editorial decisions about what cases were fit to be reported where. At about the same time as the fax, Butterworths introduced Lexis with clumsy red terminals and complex passwords to find transcripts of cases that they had discovered rejected by the traditional reports. Other "unreported" cases died *in limine*, forgotten and irrelevant. Counsel and even litigants in person could, with difficulty, obtain access to the Supreme Court Library to obtain dusty transcripts of such long forgotten decisions, but the advocate who cited them did so with foreboding, knowing that no self-respecting Court of Appeal would pay great attention to a case that the Law Reporters had decided to omit from their then slim volumes.

Then came the faxed law reports providing summaries of numerous decisions that had been delivered the previous day. There was no time for these new age law reporters to consider whether the case had decided anything at all, yet alone whether it had decided anything important. In many cases, these embryonic Internet reporters did not have access to a transcript of the entire decision before the faxed report hit the wires: "*report and be damned*" was their motto. And they changed legal research, and our entire profession at a stroke. There was no turning the clock back. Changes have simply accelerated. Eventually we had e-mailed reports and huge legal data bases. But all the power of the Supreme Court Rules Committee cannot prevent Counsel finding huge numbers of irrelevant "unreported" cases through massive Internet search engines available worldwide from every Court in the common law world and beyond. We have information overload writ large. And that information overload affects judges, counsel and solicitors equally. It is simply not possible to say that a case is irrelevant until you have read it. That means that judges cannot safely prevent the citation of authority, however much they make counsel certify its importance.

The overload of cases is, as I have said, not only from within our own jurisdiction. Every jurisdiction, however small, publishes its decisions (normally all of them without selection) on the Internet. And we refer to these decisions from all corners of the globe, including particularly the Commonwealth, transmitted to us instantly over the Internet, first in summary form, followed almost instantly by full transcripts and digests.

This creates a hollow ring to the part of Viscount Simonds' 1952 preface to the third edition of *Halsbury's Laws* when he said:

> "... but it was brought home to me how far we have travelled from the days of darkest Africa when I read this extract from a report of the Durban office of the publishers: [so many] Sets sold in five towns on the shores of Lake Victoria ... and the same story can be told of every corner of the continents where the British flag is flown."

The days when we exported a few copies of *Halsbury's Laws* to the African, Asian and Australasian continents, and thought that we had provided legal enlightenment, are indeed long gone.

The sad counterpoint to my quotation from Viscount Simonds about exporting a few volumes to Africa is that legal texts are now so expensive that the Bar Council spends much time trying to collect second hand and outdated volumes to send to African lawyers and law firms.

We need now to consider how these dramatic changes have affected the job of the text book writer. For, of course, *Halsbury* is, in reality, a text book: a peculiarly complete text book, but a text book nonetheless.

Well, it is worth starting this part of my address by considering the intervals in which Halsbury has produced its new editions.

The 1st edition began its publication in 1907 and the final volume was completed in 1917, shortly before the end of the 1st World War.

The 2nd edition began its publication in 1931, just 24 years after the inauguration of *Halsbury's Laws*, and the 3rd edition was commenced 21 years later in 1952.

It will be recalled that all these editions were in bound form with supplements published from time to time.

The 4th edition, still in bound form, began publication in 1973, and I am now informed that the 5th edition will begin publication next year. But the 5th edition will be a seamless continuation of the 4th edition, with a few changes in organisation and style. The 5th edition, like the fourth, will remain in bound form, continually updating volumes as they become out of date.

Alongside *Halsbury's* 4th edition, the revolution has taken place. Text books have moved from bound volumes to loose leaf volumes, and thence to the Internet, with continual updating. This allows the authors to revise their considered view of the law with every decision that is published or is made available on line, however immaterial or insignificant that case may be.

These developments call into question the value of many of the text books that those of us engaged regularly in serious legal research are wont to use. Some are so regularly updated by reference to decisions that would probably best be forgotten rather than reported, as to make them useless.

This creates an interesting position. The great text books do not need updating every day, every week, every month or even every year. That is because they provide an insight into the state of the law and its development, which does not require repeated revision. In all but the most quickly developing areas of law, there are only a few important decisions every decade, and they need careful reflection and consideration before anything very useful can be written about them. This process takes place by the production of academic articles adopting extreme positions, rebutting them, and then reaching an accord or a received position. It is that position that, in all but the most unusual circumstances, finds its way into the great text books and into *Halsbury's Laws*.

If proof were needed that important decisions are irregular, one can remember the very few cases in generations past that were ever discovered later and published as notes in future editions of the Law Reports, because they had been overlooked.

So what then does the future hold? Lawyers need tools to ensure that they understand the basic premises of the law. Only dedicated legal researchers arguing cases at the zenith of learning require every possible decision and article relayed to them.

In the future, the great text book publishers will recognise these distinctions. They will know that there remains a difference between seminal cases and cases that decide nothing, and they will provide ways in which users of their works can distinguish between differing grades of legal materials.

*Halsbury's Laws* may well have made the right decision to produce an imperceptible transition between their 4th and 5th editions, and to continue to publish the volumes in bound form. In making a complete statement of the law, the publishers should not be deluded into thinking that that statement needs alteration at every whim of every published report. The truly insightful textbook remains valuable for years without update. Spencer

Bower's books on estoppel provide a classic example. *Halsbury's Laws* can do the same, provided it sticks to its roots, and attempts to continue to state the law.

But how do we lawyers manage to cope with the new state of things? How do we know when we should chase every last decision that has been published from any jurisdiction, and when not? The answer is that we need to revise our thinking on legal education. We need to be trained, when we are taught to use legal materials, so that we can easily discern what is concerned with legal principle and what is not. We need to learn how to distinguish useless reported decisions from useful ones, and we need to be sure that we do not cite cases simply because they are recent or because "they are there". *Halsbury's Laws* can help with this task, as can the publishers of legal materials generally. Methods need to be devised on the Internet to help lawyers, hard-pressed by their clients, to distinguish between new material that needs attention and new material that can be safely disregarded unread.

The most important thing a lawyer can learn is how the law works. Almost everything, even some questions of statutory construction, can be divined from a proper understanding of the basic principles. It is these basics, derived as they are from few cases, that the real text books need to tackle. Legal researchers can then find all the new decisions they want from the Internet to satisfy themselves that they have done their jobs. But if they understand the principles of the area of law in which they practise, they will be doing their clients a far greater service, and will not often need to make those unsatisfying trawls through legions of cases that turn out all too often to have been decided on their facts.

Halsbury's challenge for the twenty-first century is to make sure that it continues to state the basic principles of law with the clarity and insight that it has done for the last 100 years. It must also be at the forefront of devising the methods, of which I have spoken, to assist lawyers to find out easily and quickly what new developments can be safely ignored. If the publishers match up to these tasks, many copies of *Halsbury's Laws of England* will still be used at home and overseas, and lawyers will truly be able to describe it as the greatest and most complete legal textbook of all time.

# APPENDIX 1
## CONTRIBUTORS AND CONSULTANTS TO HALSBURY'S LAWS

**First Edition**

R B D Acland

Charles Edward Allan

Berthold Alder

Lord Alverstone

Judge Amphlett

Sir Robert Anderson

W F A Archibald

E H Tindal Atkinson

Charles L Attenborough

Judge Austin

Sir Horace E Avory

H T Baker

J H Balfour Browne

W E Ball

F C A Barrett-Lennard

Dunbar Plunkett Barton

Judge Baugh-Allen

F T Villiers Bayly

W F Beddoes

Sir William Bell

Arthur Anderson Bethune

W A Bewes

Henry C A Bingley

Harold B Bompas

George Albert Bonner

J H Boome

Sir Albert Bosanquet

E Bowen-Rowlands

G Spencer Bower

William Bowstead

G W Brabant

Sir Edward W Brabrook

G A Hariom Branson

F E Bray

Sir Reginald More Bray

Sir Gainsford Bruce

F R Bush

P T Carden

Cecil T Carr

Sir Edward Carson

T H Carson

George Cave

C H Chadwick

John Chadwick

Kenneth E Chalmers

Sir Mackenzie Dalzell Chalmers

Edward J M Chaplin

G W Chapman

Herbert Chitty

T Willes Chitty

C L Chute

O L Leigh Clare

J W Clark

E Percival Clarke

Edward Clarke

Sidney Wrangel Clarke

J K F Cleave

H Clover

Arthur Cohen

B A Cohen

E A Cohen

Herman Cohen

S O Henn Collins

H A de Colyar

R G Nicholson Combe

Alan C Comerford

A Cooper-Key

E Knowles Corrie

J S Cotton

Montague H Crackanthorpe

Norman Craig

Thomas Cuthbertson

C Tindale Davis

J Norman Daynes

Sir Henry Bargrave Deane

Bertrand W Devas

Kenelm E Digby

Henry William Disney

H E Duke

W H Dumsday

Sir Charles Swinfen Eady

J Bromley Eames
C Johston Edwards
Montague R Emanuel
William Ernst-Browning
Frank Evans
Sir Harry Trelawney Eve
C J W Farwell
Sir George Farwell
J V Vesey Fitzgerald
Urquhart A Forbes
L T Ford
Sir Edward Fry
Cecil B Gedge
H Geen
E L Gibbon
Henry Martley Giveen
Alexander Glen
Randolph Glen
Sir Francis Gore
Eric Gore-Browne
Sir Henry J L Graham
Alexander Grant
H B D Grazebrook
A J H Green
W A Greene
Hubert F F Greenland
Earnest Greenwood
Harry Greenwood
H C Gutteridge
Maurice L Gwyer
Viscount Haldane of Cloan
H B Hans Hamilton
W F Hamilton
Harold Hardy
E R Hardy Ivamy
David Harrison
W English Harrison
Cuthbert Headlam
H S Q Henriques
N Arthur Heywood
G R Hill
A A Hudson
Herbert Hull
W E Hume-Williams
Cecil A Hunt

Sir Robert Hunter
Thomas Hynes
A R Ingpen
T A Ingram
Sir Rufus Daniel Isaacs
F Washington Kingdon
C M Knowles
S F Jackson
Charles Fuhr Jemmett
Austin Fleeming Jenkin
A H Jessel
G M Edwardes Jones
Alfred Bray Kempe
G H B Kenrick
Walter C A Ker
Humphrey H King
C M Knowles
E M Konstam
E Thornton H Lawes
A Clive Lawrence
A H Lionel Leach
John M Lightwood
J H Lindsay
W A Lindsay
J Brooke Little
Charles Frederick Lloyd
M B Lloyd
Sir Frederick Low
R A McCall
Sir John Macdonell
M Muir Mackenzie
William Mackenzie
A Romer Macklin
Alexander Macmorran
Sir Malcolm Martin Macnaghten
R P Mahaffy
John W Mansfield
James Robert Vernam Marchant
E W Martelli
Arnold Stuart Massey
C J Mathew
T Henry Maxwell
Richard Edmund Meridith
Lord Mersey of Toxteth
Harold G Meyer

R Mortimer Montgomery

H Stuart Moore

T W Morgan

Samuel Moses

R G Nicholson

H L Ormsby

W W Otter-Barry

Sir John R Paget

Wyatt Paine

C J Parton

Frederick William Pearson

J G Pease

Robert Peel

A F Peterson

Coleman Phillipson

Sidney Lovell Phipson

Sir William Pickford

Sydney E Pocock

E M Pollock

W Haldane Porter

Arthur Powell

F R Y Radcliffe

R Leigh Ramsbotham

J F P Rawlinson

William Rayden

J H Redman

Herbert Reed

D D Reid

R L Reiss

Richard Ringwood

D D Robertson

George Stuart Robertson

H G Robertson

Percy Tindal Robertson

W A Robertson

E C Robinson

R C Romer

Edward Stanley Roscoe

R E Ross

Judge Ruegg

Victor Russell

Sir Albert de Rutzen

Walter C Ryde

S A Sampson

E T Sandars

P E Sandlands

A E Sansom

Walter S Scott

W L Seligman

A Towers Settle

Enry Gordon Shee

Sir Horatio Hale Shephard

Sir John Simon

Philip Vernon Smith

A W Soward

J F R Stainer

Henry Stephen

Vice-Chancellor Stewart-Smith

J I Stirling

Sir Henry Sutton

Charles J Tarring

A R Taylour

Herbert L Tebbs

H Terrell

B H Thomson

Linton T Thorpe

G E Timins

Viscount Tiverton

A F Topham

T H Tristram

Sir Arthur Underhill

Joseph Walton

E R Watson

T Lonsdale Webster

R Henslowe Wellington

A W Baker Welford

Benjamin Whitehead

C Willoughby Williams

T Cyprian Williams

Sir Roland Vaughan Williams

W Addington Willis

Judge Woodfall

R Alderson Wright

## Second Edition

Sir Edward Acton

E E Addis

Lord Amulree

Judge Archer

H Royston Askew

Lord Atkin

Sir Horace Edmund Avory

Sir Henry J F Badeley

S J Bailey

T MacDonald Baker

W Valentine Ball

C P Best

Wyndham Bewes

Norman Birkett

L K A Block

Sir Archibald Bodkin

Sir George Albert Bonner

John H Boraston

David Bowen

A W Bowyer

William Bowstead

Guy N W Boyes

Sir George Arthur Harwin Branson

G F L Bridgman

Herbert M Broughton

Denys B Buckley

Peter Bucknill

B G Burnett-Hall

Roland Burrows

T R Fitzwalter Butler

G F M Campion

Kenneth Carpmael

Lord Carson

Herbert Chitty

Sir Percival Clarke

Archibald W Cockburn

Sir Lionel Leonard Cohen

Sanford D Cole

C A Collingwood

S O Henn Collins

C John Colombos

R G Nicholson Combe

Alan C Comerford

R P Croom-Johnson

H R Darlington

David Davies

W Arthian Davies

J Norman Daynes

Kenneth Diplock

T D D Divine

Gerald Dodson

Sir Oscar F Dowson

Judge M N Drucquer

J T Edgerley

Sir Geoffrey Ellis

Sir Harry Trelawney Eve

Alexander Fachiri

W Fairley

Harry Farrar

Sir Christopher John Wickens Farwell

Maurice Fitzgerald

Viscount Finlay

Arthur H Forbes

Peter Foster

Vernon R M Gattie

W H Gattie

James A W Gibson

F Kirk Glazebrook

H Glyn-Jones

Sir Rayner Goddard

E A Godson

Robert A Gordon

Rollo F Graham-Campbell

Alexander Grant

G M Green

Sir Arthur Greer

Maurice Gwyer

Viscount Hailsham

Earl of Halsbury

W A Hammerton

Sir William Hansell

Lord Hanworth

Harold Parkinson Harker

Sir Anthony Hawke

Frank Hesketh

Lord Hewart

Philip R Higgins

Judge Hildesley

Sir George Malcolm Hillbery

Quintin Hogg

Sir William Holdsworth

H L Holman

P J Hornby

A A Hudson

Hubert Hull
Sir Travers Humphreys
Sir Thomas W H Inskip
Ralph Instone
K Greer Jackson
J C Jackson
W Eric Jackson
F E Skone James
A Berriedale Keith
Lord Kilbracken
E Gibbs Kimber
George F Kingham
F C Lambert
Sir George Phillip Langton
F W Lascelles
William Latey
Sir Geoffrey Lawrence
F H Lawson
John M Lightwood
Sir Arthur F C Coryndon Luxmoore
Sir Malcolm Martin Macaghten
Sir Henry Alfred McCardie
Judge McCleary
Sir Lynden Macassey
Kenneth W Mackinnon
Mervyn MacKinnon
Lord Macmillan
Kenneth M MacMorran
Ewen MacPherson
R P Mahaffy
R E Manningham-Buller
Theobald Mathew
Eric F M Maxwell
Lawrence Mead
Sir Frank Boyd Merriman
Lord Merrivale
Harold G Meyer
Gerald E Millis
R Moelwyn-Hughes
R M Montgomery
H Stuart Moore
Morris Morgan
H Fletcher Moulton
R L Overbury
Sir Cecil Owen

Joseph Owner
Sir John Rahere Paget
H Alleyn Palmer
Sir Herbert du Parcq
Judge Peel
V M C Pennington
A A Pereira
James A Petrie
G Godfrey Phillips
R W Poyster
H M Pratt
G Proby
W Bentley Purchase
R P Fraser Roberts
Trevor Roberts
Sir George Stuart Robertson
C D C Robinson
R A Robinson
Lord A Adair Roche
T G Roche
Alma Roper
R E Ross
Michael Rowe
Lord Sankey
Charles E Scholefield
Sir Claud Schuster
Sir Leslie Scott
Sir John Houldsworth Shaw
H J Simmons
P R Simner
Philip Skottowe
S H Granville Smith
Percy Freeman Smith
G D Squibb
Charles Stevenson
Sir John Stewart-Wallace
N F Stodgon
J B Stonebridge
H F R Sturge
Ralph Sutton
Sir Rigby Phillip Watson Swift
T G Talbot
Bruce Thomas
R A Thomas
G H Main Thompson

Laurence Tillard
Lawrence Tooth
A M Romer Topham
Alfred Frank Topham
Clive G Tottenham
Sydney G Turner
Sir Arthur Underhill
H B Vaisey
W H Waddams
Raymond Walton
A W Baker Welford
M M Wheeler
H W Wightwick
Herbert Williams
R E Lomax Vaughan Williams
W J Williams
Harold Willis
H Gordon Wilmer
R M Wilson
Sir Gerald Woods Wollaston
C Wood-Hill
Sir Raymond W Woods
Lord Wright

## Third Edition

F A Amies
H E Amos
Ralph J B Anderson
Marcus Andwyl-Davies
G F Aronson
Roy Ashton
P V Baker
C T Bailhache
A J Balcombe
R E Ball
N D Banks
Sir George Barnett
G B T Barr
Anthony R Barrowclough
A J Bateson
George Beattie
P Ingress Bell
Betram B Benas
B A Bicknell

J B H Billam
T A Blanco White
Brian H Bliss
John H Boratson
W W Boulton
Randolph Boxall
Leslie Boyd
Guy N Boyes
N Bridges-Adams
G F L Bridgman
Peter Bristow
D Bruce-Jones
B T Buckle
Peter T Bucknill
B G Burnett-Hall
C M Cahn
Kenneth Carpmael
Stephen Chapman
B L Charles
Lord Chorley
Harold Christie
Edward Clarke
Bryan Clauson
Lord Cohen
R A H Collinge
Sir Charles Collingwood
James Comyn
J F Coplestone-Boughley
C B Crabbe
T R Crawford
Sir Reginald Powell Croom-Johnson
Felix E Crowder
James Cunliffe
W D Curnock
P C M Curtis-Bennett
Sir Harold Danckwerts
Gerald Darling
J B Davidson
Arthian Davies
H J Davies
Sir Herbert Edmund Davies
B Russell Davis
J Norman Daynes
Sir Kenneth Diplock
Sir Gerald Dodson

John F Donaldson
Peter Dow
F Maurice Drake
Maurice N Drucquer
J T Edgerley
J M M Edwards
Quentin Edwards
James H S Elliot
John H Ellison
Peter Elman
Sir Francis Enever
Sir Arthur Evans
David M Trustram Eve
R Marven Everett
Sir Raymond Evershed
P N S Farrell
N Fawcett
Charles Fay
E S Fay
Sir Edward Fellowes
T G Field-Fisher
Ian Fife
H A P Fisher
H Fletcher Moulton
David Foster
Hazel M Fox
J D Fox
James Fox-Andrews
Michael Franks
Roger Frisby
Brian Galpin
Basil Garland
C E Garland
Vernon R M Gattie
Sir Frederick Gentle
Sir Hildreth Glyn-Jones
Lord Goddard
W H Goodhart
V M R Goodman
J E Gower
H R Green
R C L Gregory
R E Grindle
S Paterson Grounds
F G Guttman

Viscount Hailsham
H G Hanbury
A J Harriss
W O Hart
Peter Harvey
Elizabeth Havers
P A Hayward
Desmond Heap
Frank Hesketh
T C Hetherington
H W Hewitt
J B Hewson
E N Hickson
Sir Malcolm Hilbery
J R Brayley Hodgetts
J B Hodgson
Sir Travers Humphreys
I Hutchinson
David C Jackson
Joseph Jackson
W Eric Jackson
Basil James
F E Skone James
Raymond Jennings
J K T Jones
P E Jones
J F Josling
Sir Seymour Karminski
I M S Keely
D P Kerrigan
Lord Kilmuir
D G Knight
Sir Francis Lascelles
John Latey
W Russell Lawrence
F H Lawson
John Leonard
J F Lever
R G Lloyd
T N Lockyer
Oliver Lodge
Mervyn Longhurst
Sir Thomas Lund
J Roy V McAulay
R L McEwen

P A O McGrath
Kenneth C McGuffie
Hugh F MacMaster
Kenneth M Macmorran
Sir William McNair
Anthony Machine
S W Magnus
John Main
Harold Marnham
E J T Matthews
Spencer G Maurice
E F M Maxwell
John W Mayo
R E Megarry
Maurice Megrah
Lord Merriman
P J Millett
Helenus Milmo
Ewen E S Montagu
John Montgomerie
E Garth Moore
D M Morris
C L Morrow
E G R Moses
Hubert S P Moses
H Fletcher Moulton
M J Mustill
Sir Albert Napier
Lord Nathan
Brian Neill
B T Neill
G D Nokes
Martin Nourse
E G Nugee
Oliver Nugent
C Bruce Orr
P G Osborn
Richard O'Sullivan
Sir Hubert Parker
Harold Parrish
Sir Henry Wynn Parry
Sir Colin Hargreaves Pearson
Gerald J Ponsonby
Dennis Pugh
W B Purchase

G C Raffety
M E Reed
J P Ricks
K J S Ritchie
James Rochford
R B Roper
J H L Royle
Anita Ryan
Henry Salt
J R C Samuel-Gibbon
D Gidley Scott
Charles E Scholefield
Christopher N Shawcross
J D Shebbearde
J E S Simon
J L Simpson
C J Slade
Sir Gerald Osborne Slade
S A de Smith
N S Spendlow
J L Spiller
G D Squibb
P Stanley
Leslie F Stemp
A L G Stewart-Richardson
N F Stodgon
Olive M Stone
R F Stone
N Storr
J H G Sunnucks
Ralph Sutton
John C Taylor
A E Telling
Sefton D Temkin
S W Templeman
Michael Thomas
Dennis Thompson
P B Topham
Harold Horsfall Turner
Sydney G Turner
Gerald Ritchie Upjohn
Sir Harry Bevir Vaisey
Neville D Vandyk
G H C Vaughan
Charles W Venning

Sir Godfrey Russell Vick
E P Wallis-Jones
Raymond Walton
C Roy Waterer
Noel Waterer
Sir Robert Bernard Waterer
J D Waters
J Watson-Baker
M M Wells
James W Wellwood
G S A Wheatcroft
Charles Whitby
Bernard White
C Montgomery White
T A Blanco White
James Whiteside
Sir Maurice Whittome
Peter E Whitworth
David Widdicombe
W S Wigglesworth
Richard Orme Wilberforce
W J Williams
Harold Willis
A C C Willway
D J Willson
J P Wilson
Roy Wilson
W Granville Wingate
A S Wisdom
H W Wollaston
D C M Yardley

## Fourth Edition/Reissue
James Abrahams
John N Adams
Stephen Agar
Helen Ainsley
Alun Alesbury
F A Amies
Robert Argles
Richard Arnold
Edward Ash
T Michael Ashe
Christopher Ashford

Michael Astbury
Jonathan Auburn
Jill Aussant
Nicholas Bacon
N H Bagot
Edward Bailey
S K Bailey
Dawn Baker
J H Baker
R J Baker
Sir George Gillespie Baker
A J Balcombe
R E Ball
Nicholas Bamforth
Janice C Barber
Ian S P Barker
Sir Richard Barlas
Francis Barlow
D M W Barnes
Charles Barton
Graham Battersby
Tony Baumgartner
H J Baxter
Janet Bazley
Judith Beale
D R Beamish
Stuart Bell
Robin Bellis
Michael Beloff
Elizabeth Bennett
G Adam Bennett
Francis A R Bennion
Sir Franklin Berman
Michael Best
Emily Beswick
Ranjit Bhose
Geoffrey Bindman
Diane Birch
Michael Birks
T H P Bishop
Alastair Black
Jack Black
John Blackburn
Robert Blackburn
Commodore Jeffery Blackett

Mark Blackett-Ord

Carole Blackshaw

Michael Blair

T A Blanco White

Brian Bliss

L J Blom-Cooper

M B Bloor

Guy T K Boney

Charles Bonney

Margaret Booth

W W Boulton

Charles Bourne

David Bowles

J L Bowron

Leslie Boyd

Keith Brading

Anthony W Bradley

Richard J Bragg

E B H Bragiel

Nicolas Bratza

Graeme D A Brebner

John W Bridge

Adrian Briggs

James Brightwell

Sandra Bristoll

Henry Brooke

Pauline C Brown

Lord Browne-Wilkinson

Rosanna Bryant

J Graeme Bryson

R A Buckley

M J C Burgess

David Burles

Andrew Burns

Sir Stanley Burnton

Rupert Bursell

Hannah Burton

J D K Burton

James A F Buxton

Richard Buxton

Andrew H Caldecott

Duncan Calow

Judge Advocate Paul Camp

Emily C Campbell

Oliver Campbell

JP Canlin

Frances G Canning

Richard Card

DMM Carey

G P Carney

Sir Robert Carnwath

A P Carr

Gillian Carrington

Monica Carss-Frisk

Ian R Cartwright

Stuart Catchpole

John Cavanagh

Richard Cave

Eian Caws

C F Chamberlain

D R Chambers

Alexander Chandler

Catherine Churchard

David N Clarke

Giles Clarke

Wayne Clarke

Robert Clay

G B Claydon

Richard Clayton

David Clifton

G F Cloak

George Close

Stephen Cobb

Susan Cochrane

Tia Cockrell

F H Coffell

Edward Cole

J G Collier

John Stuart Collyer

Elizabeth Cooke

Philip Coppel

Judge J Corcoran

Frederick Corfield

Heather Cornwell-Kelly

Lynne Counsell

Stephen Cretney

Michael Crystal

George Cubie

T Peter E Curry

Rebecca Curtis

P C M Curtis-Bennett
Terence Charles Daintith
Tobias Davey
H J Davies
Sarah-Jane Davies
Sir Michael Davies
Suzanne Davies
F H Dean
Charles Debattista
Lord Denning
H Andrew C Densham
Barry Denyer-Green
Paul MJ Dickens
Deborah Dinan-Hayward
David Donaldson
R P A Douglas
Richard Drabble
James Driscoll
Michael Driscoll
Jeremy Duffy
Anthony Dugdale
Monica Duncan
Vivienne Eden
J T Edgerley
David Edwards
Michael Ellis
Morag Ellis
J H Ellison
Rt Hon Lord Elwyn-Jones
Francis Ferris
T G Field-Fisher
Ian Fife
Nadine Finch
James Findlay
Sally Finn
John Finnis
Michael Fitton
Susanna Fitzgerald
David H Fletcher
David Flint
Erica Foggin
Timothy G Ford
David Forsdick
Ian Foster
D J Fountaine

J D Fox
Nicola Fox
Laurie Fransman
Christopher French
John Furber
M P Furmston
Caroline Furze
Brian Galpin
Leslie Gane
Alan Gardner
J F Garner
Edward Garnier
Jonathan Gaunt
J R Gaunt
Charles Geekie
A D G George
Charles George
Tony George
Nigel Giffin
G F Gloak
Richard Glover
Richard Goldberg
Ronald Goldberg
Sir Irving Golding
Brian Golds
Roy Goode
KF Goodfellow
Lord Goodhart
William Goodhart
Richard Gordon
Laurence W Gormley
Sir Irvine Goulding
J E Gower
Joanna Goyder
David Graham
Ian Grange-Bennett
J Donald Gray
D Grazebrook
Paul Greatorex
Phil Greatrex
Andrew Green
Patrick Green
Richard Green
J G R Griggs
Sam Grodzinski

Richard W Ground

Helen Guest

Michael Gunn

Nigel Hague

Lord Hailsham of St Marylebone

A Hall-Brown

Robert Wallace Ham

Judge Susan Hamilton

Stephen Hammett

Nicholas Hancox

David Hands

Sarah Hanniford

Brenda M Hannigan

Ruth Hanson

Mark Hapgood

Evan Harding

Joseph Harper

Brian Harris

Bryan Harris

David R Harris

G Charles W Harris

Neville Harris

Stephanie Harrison

M L T Harvey

Peter Harvey

Leonard WN Hawkes

A J Hawkins

David J Hayton

Sir Desmond Heap

Andrew Henderson

Sir Peter Henderson

Claire Heppenstall

Adam Heppinstall

B A Hepple

Wendy Herring

Edmund Heward

E J D Hill

Julian Hill

Lexa Hilliard

Judge Hines

Michael Hirst

John Hobson

Brian Hogan

Brenda Hoggett

Charles Holbech

Brian A Holland

Kathryn L Holly

Susan Holmes

A T Hoolahan

C E S Horsford

M N Howard

William Howarth

Martin Howe

G C Howell

Anthony Hudson

A H Hudson

M D Huebner

A D Hughes

Richard Humphreys

Neville March Hunnings

J Martin Hunter

Muir Hunter

Robert Hunter

Peter Hurst

R K F Hutchings

Oliver Hyams

Charles Hyde

Penelope Hyde-Smith

Roderick I'Anson Banks

Richard Inglis

Cecilia Ivimy

David Iwi

Joseph Jackson

Paul Jackson

Simon Jackson

Sir Jack I H Jacob

Sir Robin Jacob

Brian W James

Jennifer James

Sir Arthur James

Thomas Jefferies

Terence Jenner

C R Jessel

Natasha Joffe

Jeremy Johnson

Nigel Johnson

P M Johnston

Gareth Jones

Stephen Jones

Peter Jorro

Stephen Jourdan
Jonathan Karas
Ian Karsten
Christopher Katkowski
Phillippa Kaufmann
John Kavanagh
William Kee
Mark Kellet
William B Kennair
F D Kennedy
Gerald Kidner
Richard Kidner
Raymond Kidwell
Hilary J King
I E King
Lesley King
Lord Kingsland
Andrew Kinnier
K M Kirby
Lynne Knapman
Samantha Knights
John Knott
Bryony Knowles
Peter Knowles
C F Kolbert
Philip Kolvin
Gregory Krikorian
Jane Kron
Camilla Lamont
Alan Langmaid
Brian Langstaff
D Lasok
K P E Lasok
D S Laughton
Nicholas Lavender
Sir John Laws
Stephen Laws
Sir Neil Lawson
Robert Lawson
F H Lawson
Sir Frederick Lawton
George A M Leggatt
Richard Leiper
J A Leonard
H John Leslie

Catherine Lester
Katya Lester
Lord Lester of Herne Hill
Graham L Lewinstein
Adam Lewis
Christopher Lewsley
Peter M Liell
Nathalie Lieven
John Livesey
Humphrey Lloyd
Ian J Lloyd
Timothy Lloyd
Campaspe Lloyd-Jacob
Clare Lockhart
Andrew R Lockhart-Mirams
Lord Lowry
Peter Lucas
Mark Lucraft
J Roy V McAulay
Jane McCafferty
R H McCall
David McClean
J D McClean
Patrick J McClean
Denis L McDonnell
Patricia Mary McDonnell
Michael McGarvey
Edmond McGovern
Bryan McGuire
W R McKay
Hugh McKay
Ewan McKendrick
A J MacKersie
Alan MacLean
Ian McLean
Iain MacLennan
John K MacLeod
E Anthony Machin
Jeannie Mackie
John Male
Jonathan Mance
Colin Manchester
Michael Mark
Charles Marquand
Andrew Martin

| | |
|---|---|
| Elizabeth De Montlaur Martin | Michael Nolan |
| J N Martin | Sir Peter North |
| Peter Martin | P M North |
| James Martin-Jenkins | Hon Sir Martin Nourse |
| Sir Anthony Mason | E G Nugee |
| Paul Matthews | Hugh O'Donovan |
| Spencer G Maurice | J A O'Keefe |
| Susannah Meadway | Donald R O'May |
| Peter Meehan | J O'Meara |
| Lindsay Megarry | Dov Ohrenstein |
| Maurice Megrah | Dawn Oliver |
| Franklin Meisel | A D M Oulton |
| Robert Merkin | Tim Owen |
| Louise Merrett | Alison Padfield |
| Richard Millett | Hugo Page |
| T P Millett | Sir Peter Pain |
| E R Mills | Nicholas Paines |
| Sir Alan Mocatta | Anthony Painter |
| Jonathan Moffett | David Palmer |
| Patrick Moloney | Norman Palmer |
| Stephen Monkcom | Robert Palmer |
| David Morgan | David Pannick |
| Derek Morgan | Rodger Parker |
| Marilynne Morgan | Rosalind A Parkin |
| J G Morgan-Owen | Harold Parrish |
| P J Morrish | Michael P Parroy |
| P H Morgan | C Parry |
| Simon Morgans | James Holroyd Pearce |
| John Morris | Linda Pearce |
| Timothy Morshead | Ian Pennicott |
| Gregor L H Moss | Sir John Pennycuick |
| Joanne R Moss | Bryn Perrins |
| Tim Mould | Philip Perrins |
| James Munby | Ingrid Persuad |
| A E Munir | Philip H Pettit |
| John Murdoch | Arthur Phillips |
| S D Musson | Jeremy Phillips |
| David Napley | Hubert Picarda |
| Sir Brian Neill | Maggy Pigott |
| William J W Neville | Benjamin Pilling |
| George Newman | Eleanor D Pinfold |
| J D Newton | Anne Pinks |
| Paul Nicholls | Rachel Platts |
| Nicholas Nicol | Richard Plender |
| Paul H Niekirk | Emily Pocock |

Prashant Popat

D C  Potter

William Poulton

Alison Powell

Jeffrey Price

Richard Price

Anya Proops

Christopher Prout

D B Pugh

Leslie M Pugh

J D Prytherch

Michael J M Quinlan

Mike Radford

G C Raffety

David M Raggatt

Simon PN Rainey

Nicholas Randall

J Rayner James

Hamilton Reade

Ruth Redmond-Cooper

Nicholas Reville

Deok-Joo Rhee

Valerie W Rice-Pyle

Jennifer Richards

H J Richardson

R B Richardson

Toby Riley-Smith

D Rippengal

Adam Robb

H G Roberts

Alice Robinson

Stephen Rock

Christopher P Rodgers

Michael Rollason

Guy R G  Roots

Dinah Rose

Dennis Rosenthal

Saul Rotherstein

Judith Rowe

Peter Rowe

Hugh Rutherford

FR Ryder

Basil E V  Sabine

Pushpinder Saini

Severine Saintier

H B Sales

Philip Sales

Richard Salter

John E A Samuels

Claire Sandbrook

Oliver Sanders

John B Saunders

Richard Sayer

Richard Scannell

Austen Science

Gideon Scott-Holland

Anthony Scrivener

Duran Seddon

J J G Sharpe

Thomas Sharpe

A M N Shaw

G W Shaw

Geoffrey Shaw

Mark Shaw

Sir Sebag Shaw

Malcolm Sheehan

Richard Sheldon

Avrom Sherr

John W  Shock

Lord Silsoe

Frances Silverman

Julia Simmonds

D F Sim

Ingrid Simler

Bernard Sims

B J Sims

I C Sinclair

John R Slater

Gordon Slynn

Charlotte Smith

Colin Smith

Iain A D Smith

Ian Smith

I T Smith

R G A Smith

S A De Smith

Tom Smith

GD Squibb

Angela Sydenham

Francis G Snyder

Andrew Sparke
S B Spence
Clive Stanbrook
J O Stansfield
Sir David Stephens
Nicola Sterry
W R Stewart Smith
Karen Steyn
N F Stogdon
Julie Stone
Timothy Straker
Harry Street
Richard H B Sturt
Colin Stutt
J H G Sunnucks
Michael Supperstone
William Swadling
Jonathan Swift
Angela Sydenham
Lloyd Tamlyn
James Tayler
George Taylor
P W E Taylor
Arthur Telling
Sir Sydney Templeman
Gareth Thomas
HM Thomas
Neil C Thomas
Roger Thomas
Andrew Thompson
Mark P Thompson
Andrew Thornhill
Anthony Thornton
R I Threlfall
John Tiley
Christopher Tite
Gregory J Tolhurst
Adam Tolley
Felicity Toube
R N Trounson
R H Tudway
Michael G Tugendhat
Charles E L Turnbull
Adrian J Turner
Jonathan Turner

Michael Turner
E L G Tyler
Mark Tyler
John A Usher
J A Vallance White
Neville Vandyk
David Vaughan
HDS Venables
Mary Vitoria
Carol Wadsworth-Jones
John Waite
Robert Wakefield
I N Walden
Paul Walker
Richard Wallington
Anthony Walton
Sir Raymond Walton
Tim Ward
Owen Warnock
Rupert Warren
Malcolm Waters
Michael Waterworth
J A C Watherston
Susan Watkin
Geraint Webb
Frances Webber
Aswini Weereratne
James W Wellwood
Paschal Welsh
Christopher West
J D Westlake
Sally Weston
Marina Wheeler
Sir Michael Wheeler-Booth
Richard Whish
C B E White
Jeremy White
G L Whiteside
J Whiteside
Frank C Widdowson
Lord Widgery
Stephen Wildblood
Alan Williams
Anne Williams
D G T Williams

June Williams
Peter R Williams
Terry Williams
Adrian Williamson
Alan Willingdale
Claire Wills-Goldingham
Alec Wilson
H F W Wilson
James Wilson
Tom Winsor

Derek Wood
Jeremy Woolf
H W Wollaston
Daniel Worsley
Caroline Wright
D C M Yardley
Andrew Young
Brian Youngman
G J Zellick
Isabella Zornova

# APPENDIX 2
# PUBLISHING AND EDITORIAL TEAMS OF
# HALSBURY'S LAWS

**First Edition**

Charles Edward Allan
Hugh H L Bellot
Arthur Anderson Bethune
Harold B Bompas
Alfred Bucknill
Kenneth E Chalmers
Edward J M Chaplin
T Willes Chitty
Sidney W Clarke
H Clover
F Hardinge Dalston
Henry William Disney
Montague R Emanuel
Cecil B Gedge
Hubert F F Greenland
Harry Greenwood
A E Gathorne Hardy
Gerard R Hill
G M Edwardes Jones
Austin Fleeming Jenkin
Humphrey H King
Charles Frederick Lloyd
John W Mansfield
James Robert Vernam Marchant
H Fletcher Moulton
W W Otter-Barry
R Leigh Ramsbotham
D D Robertson
G Stuart Robertson
W A Robertson
E C Robinson
R E Ross
Aubrey J Spencer
H A Steward
J Felix Waley
A W Baker Welford
W Addington Willis
James Wylie

**Second Edition**

John Burke
Roland Burrows
S G G Edgar
M I Mail
Harold G Meyer
Harold Parrish
Charles W Venning

**Third Edition**

C C Banwell
J T Edgerley
L G Jory
F G Kearney
M I Mail
Judith J Mitchell
Joy G Orr
J W Pitts
David W Smart
K T Watson
Ian Young

**Fourth Edition/Reissue**

Kirstine Adams
Mark Arena
Judith Atkins
Sulina Bangaroo
Jennifer Bantin
C C Banwell
Wendy Barker
G P Bartholomew
Joanna Bateman
Zoe Beach
Deborah Bennet
Tamasin Berry Hart
Natalie Blackmun/Vamos
Sarah Blair
Alan Blanchard
Judith Body
Gillian Bolden
Paula Bouwer

Richard Bowater
James Bowman
Kay Boyes
Sian Brennan
Paul Brown
Sarah Brown
Caroline Bryant
Phyllis Buck
Bobby Burke
R D Butcher
Clare Byrne/Blanchard
Simon Cadde
Philippa Caddick
Catherine Calley
Margaret Cherry
Tanja Clarke
Victoria Clarke
David Connolly
Martin Cook
Christopher Costigan
Amanda Court
Rebecca Courtman
Barney Cowin
Amanda Crawford
John Crookes
Tamsin Cundy
Margaret Cunningham
G R N Cusworth
Hilary Davies
Richard Dey
Kim Dolan
Carol Doherty
Hazel Donaldson
J T Edgerley
Richard Elliott
William England
Elizabeth Ereaut
Michael Evans
Sally-Ann Evans
Frances Field
Max Findlay
Shirley Fisher
Luisa Fox
J Bray Freeman
Susan Gale

Noreen Gibbons
Karen Gibbs
Richard Gibson
Vanessa Goodson
Jane Goodwin
Thomas Gorham
B T Goudie
Vivienne Goulburn
Teresa Grant
Sumra Green
R E L Greaves
Jessica Greenaway
Helen Halvey
Elaine Hardwidge
Paul Hardy
Ilona Harris
R N G Harrison
David Hay
Elizabeth Heathfield
Wendy Herring
Simon Hetherington
A R Hewitt
Jessica Hill
Martin Hill
Gillian Hirst
Robert Histon
Gordon Hobbs
Kirsten Hobkirk
Caroline Holmes-Kaushesh
Clare Hornsby
Sarah Hornsby
Susan Hoyland
Peter Hutchesson
Peter Hyland
Elisabeth Ingham
Jan Jastrzebski
Madeleine Jones
Neil Jones
Jane Kavanagh
Susan Kellas
Neil Kennerley
Sharon Kirby
Jenni Laycock
Wendy Leiataua
Dan Leissner

Melvina Lisk

Tom MacDonald

Hina Malak

Jennifer Manwaring

Carol Marsh

William Marshall

Claire Masson

Gillian Mather

David McArdle

Philippa McCarthy

Ciara McEwen

Sarah McGuire

Sinéad Moloney

R Peter Moore

Alison Morley

Kenneth Mugford

Julianne Mulholland

Terence Munyard

Angus Murray

Andrea Naylor

Jean Neal

Lorna Newton

Paul H Niekirk

Michael Noone

Judith O'Brien

A P O'Dowd

Roseleen O'Toole

Victoria Ogier

Nicola Palmer/Burdon

Kate Pamphilon

Karen Panaghiston

Stephen L Parkinson

Stephen Partridge

Margaret Pavey

Frances Pemberton

Silvia Perrini

Katie Piper

John Pitman

Mary Rose Plummer

Gouri Preece

Heather Probert

Amanda Proctor

Ian Pye

Anne Radford

S G Rae

Sophie Raphael

Fiona Rawlinson

Geraint Rees

Lisa Renkin

Robert J M  Rice

Zigurds Richters

David Roberts

Hilary Roberts

Melanie Robertson

Mark Rogers

Jane Ruddick

Sarah Ryan

Deborah Saunders

Christoph Schliack

Gordon H Scott

Matthew Seex

Sheila Sellars

Jane Semple

Justine Senior

David W  Smart

Matthew Smith

Peter Smith

Lynne Smithard

Robert Spicer

Wendy Spilling

Susan Starbuck

Vera Steele

W A  Steiner

Heon Stevenson

Peter Stickland

Nicholas Storey

D L  Summers

J H G Sunnucks

Louise Taylor

J M Tipson

Mary W Treacher

Celia Trenton

Andrew Turner

Giovanni Vallera

Patrick Vollmer

Karen Wain/Bayley

Aislinn Walshe

F M Walter

Brook Watson

Lesley Whitbourn

David Whitcombe
Jonathan White
Claire Wilford
Anne Wilkinson
Felicity Williams
Amanda Willis
Daniel Wright
A D  Yonge
Kathryn Young